ELEMENTAL GELADE

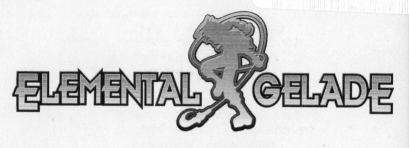

Volume 9

by
Mayumi Azuma

TOKYOPOP®

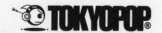

HAMBURG // LONDON // LOS ANGELES // TOKYO

ELEMENTAL GELADE

Story So Far

FOLLOWING A ROUTINE RAID, SKY PIRATE COUD VAN GIRUET DISCOVERS A MOST UNUSUAL BOUNTY--A BEAUTIFUL GIRL IN A BOX NAMED REN, WHO SAYS SHE NEEDS TO GO TO A PLACE CALLED EDEL GARDEN. BUT BEFORE COUD CAN MAKE SENSE OF IT ALL, A GROUP NAMED ARC AILE ARRIVES, STATING THAT THE GIRL IS IN FACT AN EDEL RAID (A LIVING WEAPON WHO REACTS WITH A HUMAN TO BECOME A FIGHTING MACHINE) AND THAT THEY WISH TO BUY HER. A BATTLE BREAKS OUT, DURING THE COURSE OF WHICH REN BONDS WITH COUD, BECOMING HIS WEAPON DURING THE FIGHT. REN IS SO TOUCHED BY COUD'S RESOLVE TO HELP HER THAT SHE DECIDES TO BECOME HIS PERSONAL EDEL RAID.

WITH THE HELP OF CISQUA (LEADER OF THE ARC AILE TEAM), ROWEN (HER SECOND IN COMMAND) AND HIS EDEL RAID KUEA, COUD AND REN SET OUT FOR EDEL GARDEN. BUT THE ROAD THERE IS A TREACHEROUS ONE, IN WHICH THEY FIND THEMSELVES PROTECTING REN FROM BLACK-MARKET EDEL RAID DEALERS, AS WELL AS EDEL RAID BOUNTY HUNTERS. LACK OF MONEY FORCES THEM TO STOP AT THE BETTING GROUND MILLIARD TREY, WHERE THEY HELP TO FREE AN ENSLAVED FIGHTER NAMED RASATI AND HER ADOPTED EDEL RAID SISTER, LILIA.

AS THEY TRAVEL IN THE ROPEWAY CAR THEY ARE ATTACKED BY VIRO'S BOSS, GLAUDIAS. VIRO THEN REVEALS THAT HER TRUE PURPOSE IS TO KILL COUD AND TAKE REN. (IT IS ALSO REVEALED THAT VIRO IS A TERM FOR MAN-MADE EDEL RAIDS, CREATED BY IMPLANTING ARTIFICIAL GELADES INTO HUMAN WOMEN). THEIR SALIVA IS LIKE POISON TO REAL EDEL RAIDS (VIRO SECRETLY POISONED REN BY LICKING HER GELADE STONE).

ROWEN TRIES TO CONVINCE VIRO THAT SHE CAN LIVE A LIFE OTHER THAN THAT OF A WEAPON, BUT SHE REFUSES TO LISTEN--AND HE HAS NO OTHER CHOICE BUT TO DEFEAT HER. GLAUDIAS, SEEING THAT HIS PLANS AREN'T GOING AS SMOOTHLY AS HE'D HOPED, DECIDES IT'S TIME TO RETREAT...BUT BEFORE HE LEAVES, HE DESTROYS VIRO'S GELADE, AND SHE DIES IN ROWEN'S ARMS.

ROWEN IS TAKEN TO THE DOCTOR IN THE NEARBY MOUNTAIN TOWN FOR SOME MEDICAL ATTENTION. ONCE HE'S RECOVERED, THE GANG HEADS OFF FOR EDEL GARDEN AGAIN AND SOON FIND THEMSELVES IN A BRAND NEW TOWN...

Contents

Re-No: 37

Cofful Vijyu Amibitious Palanquin—Centipretal Road

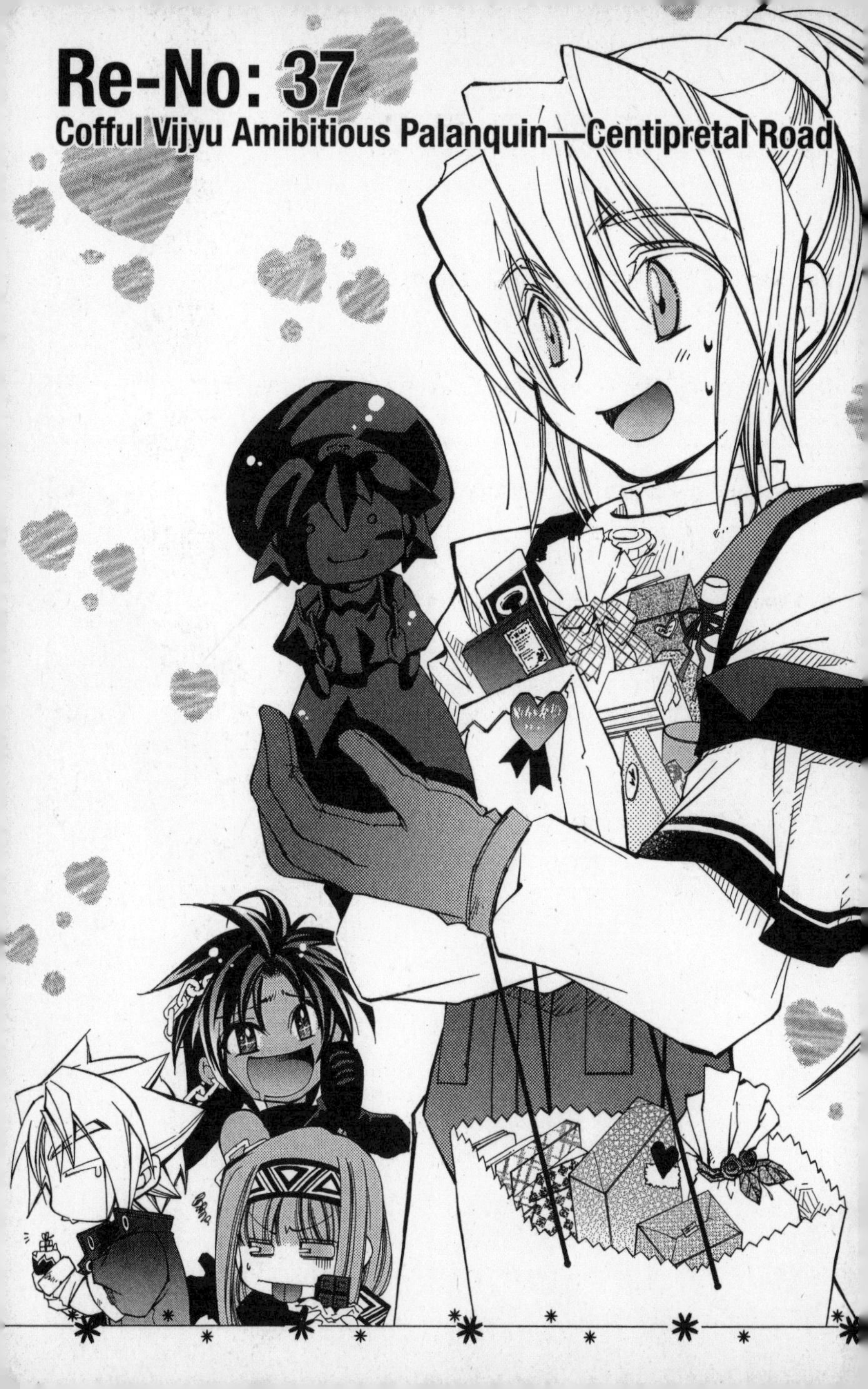

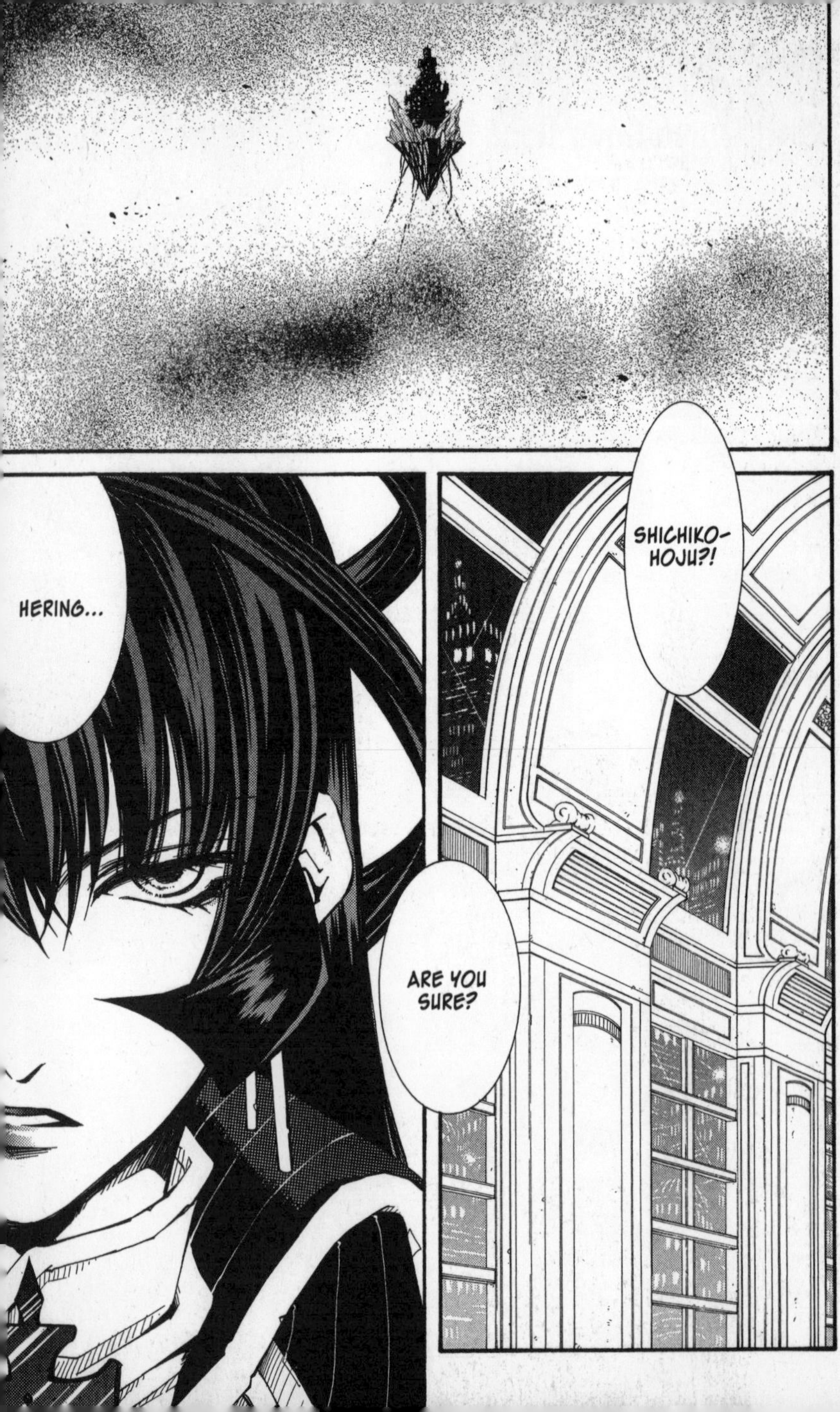
SHICHIKO-HOJU?!
ARE YOU SURE?
HERING...

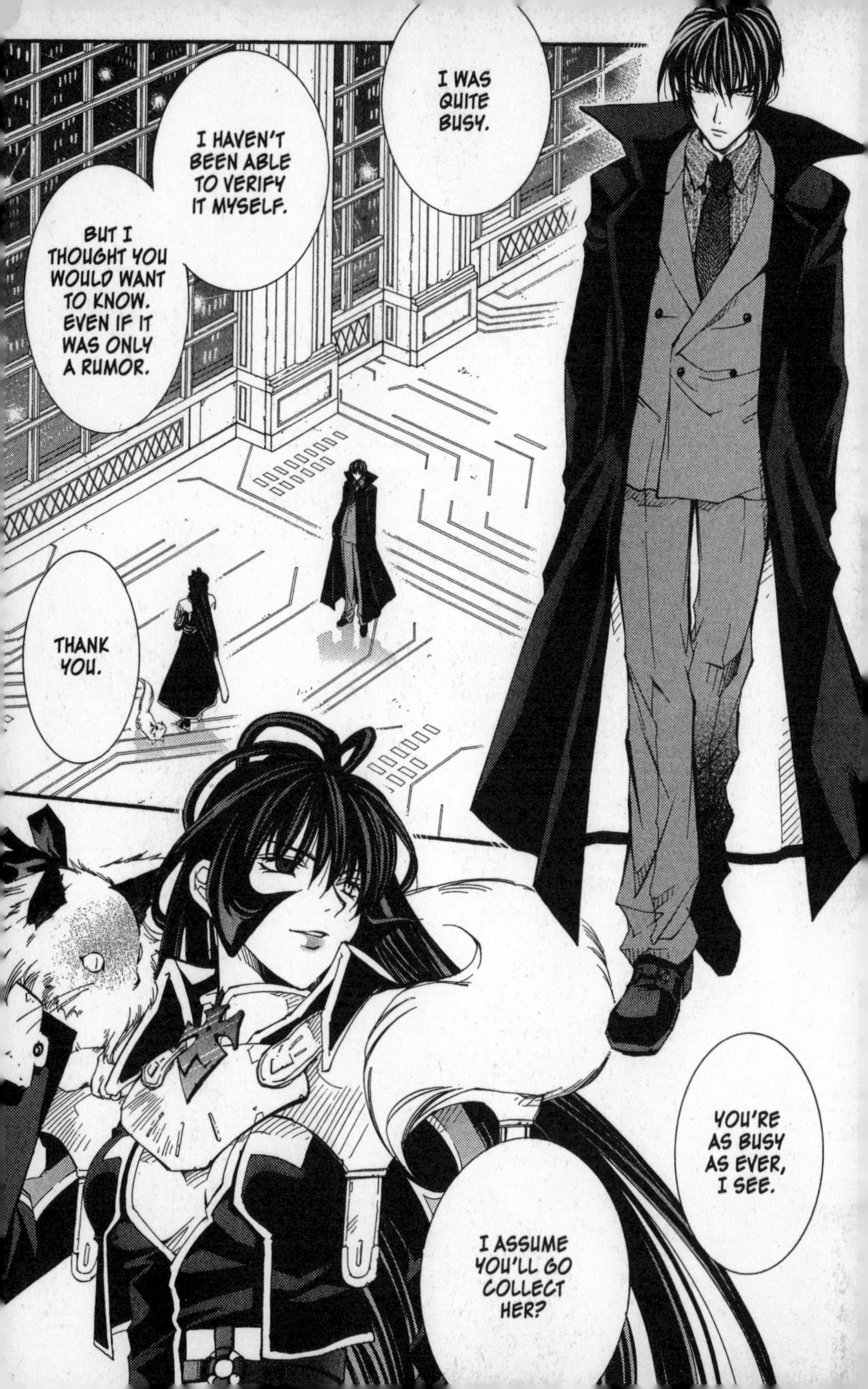
I WAS QUITE BUSY.
I HAVEN'T BEEN ABLE TO VERIFY IT MYSELF.
BUT I THOUGHT YOU WOULD WANT TO KNOW. EVEN IF IT WAS ONLY A RUMOR.
THANK YOU.
YOU'RE AS BUSY AS EVER, I SEE.
I ASSUME YOU'LL GO COLLECT HER?

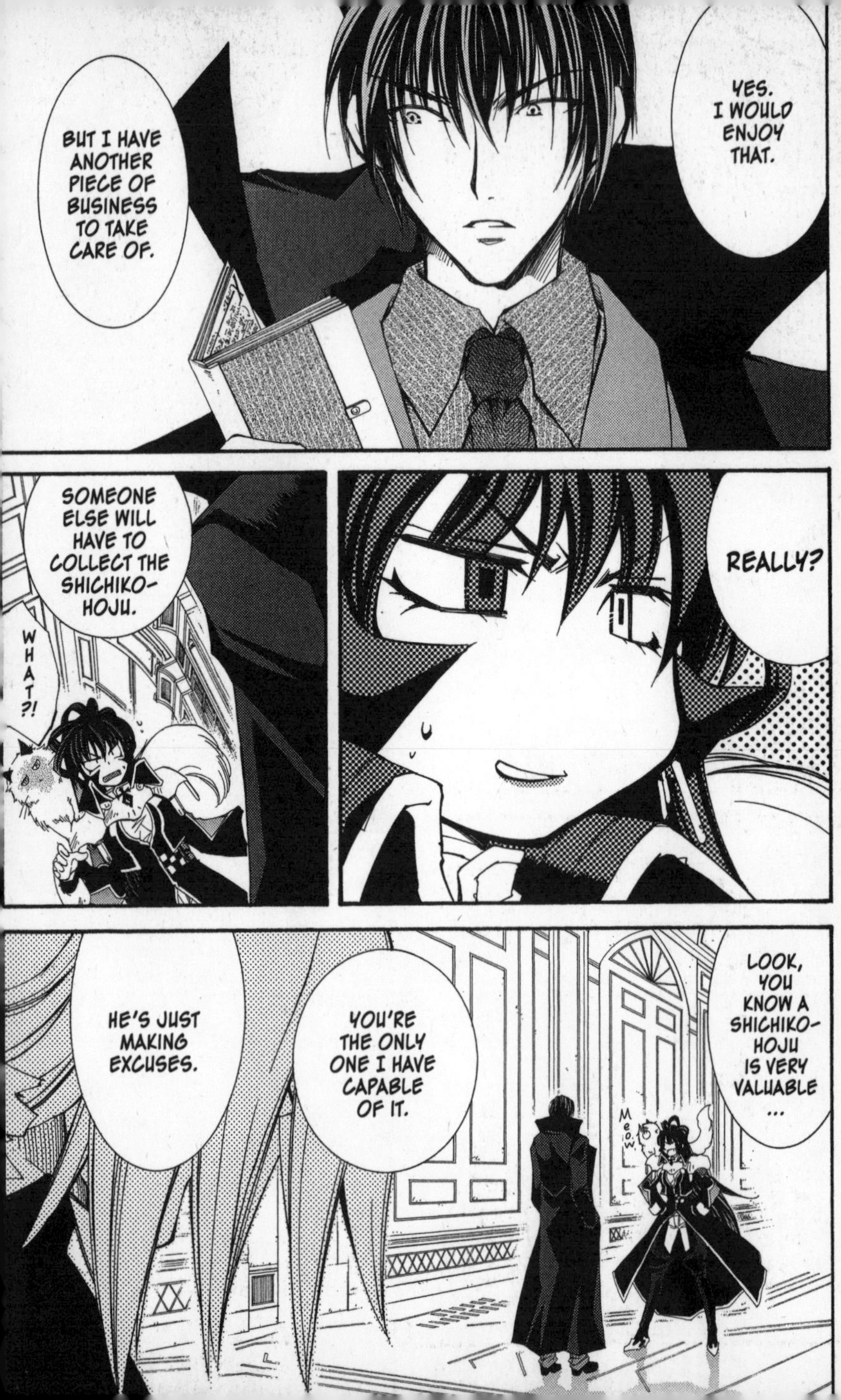
YES. I WOULD ENJOY THAT.
BUT I HAVE ANOTHER PIECE OF BUSINESS TO TAKE CARE OF.
REALLY?
SOMEONE ELSE WILL HAVE TO COLLECT THE SHICHIKO-HOJU.
WHAT?!
LOOK, YOU KNOW A SHICHIKO-HOJU IS VERY VALUABLE ...
Meow.
YOU'RE THE ONLY ONE I HAVE CAPABLE OF IT.
HE'S JUST MAKING EXCUSES.

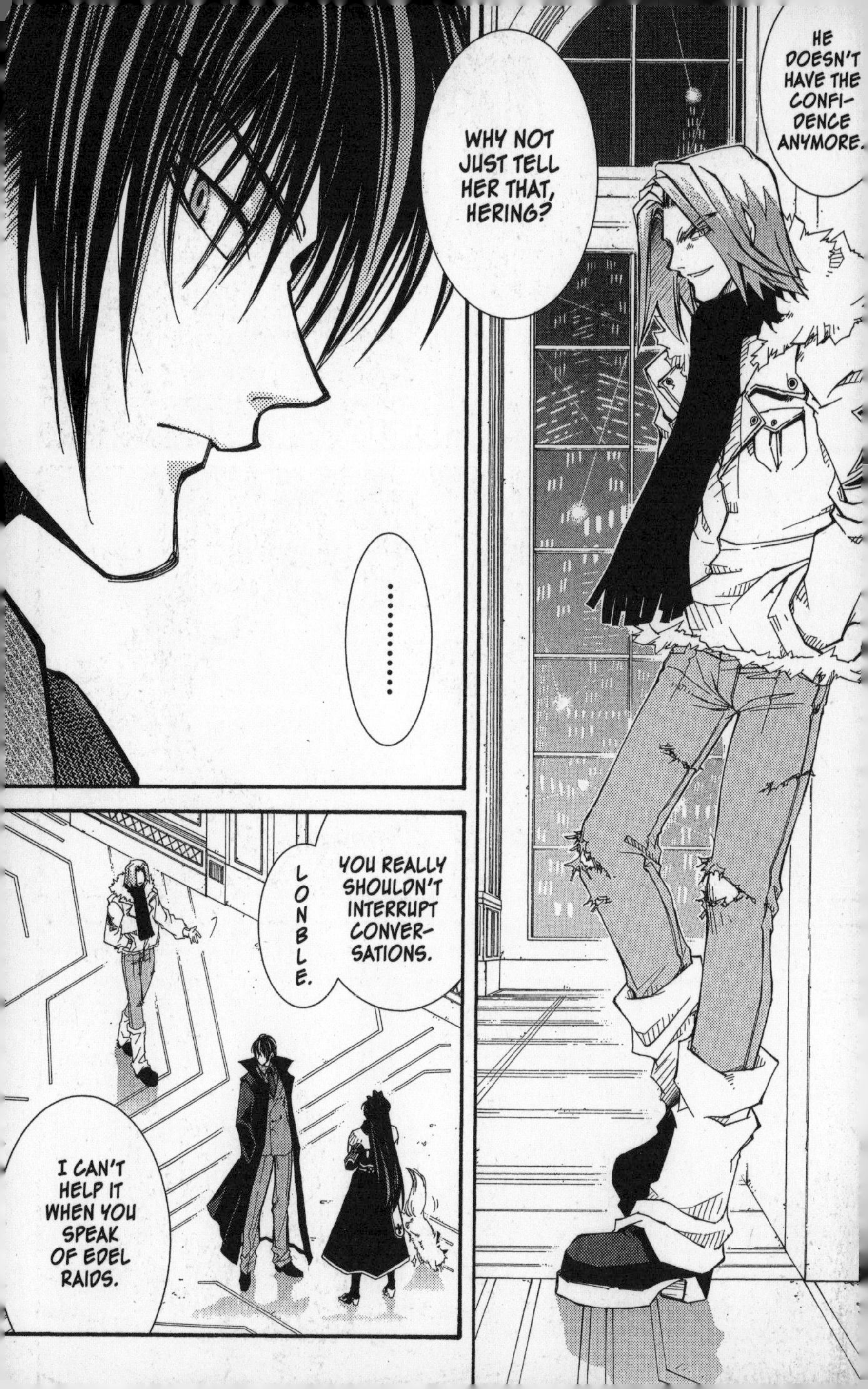
HE DOESN'T HAVE THE CONFIDENCE ANYMORE.
WHY NOT JUST TELL HER THAT, HERING?
....
YOU REALLY SHOULDN'T INTERRUPT CONVERSATIONS. LONBLE.
I CAN'T HELP IT WHEN YOU SPEAK OF EDEL RAIDS.

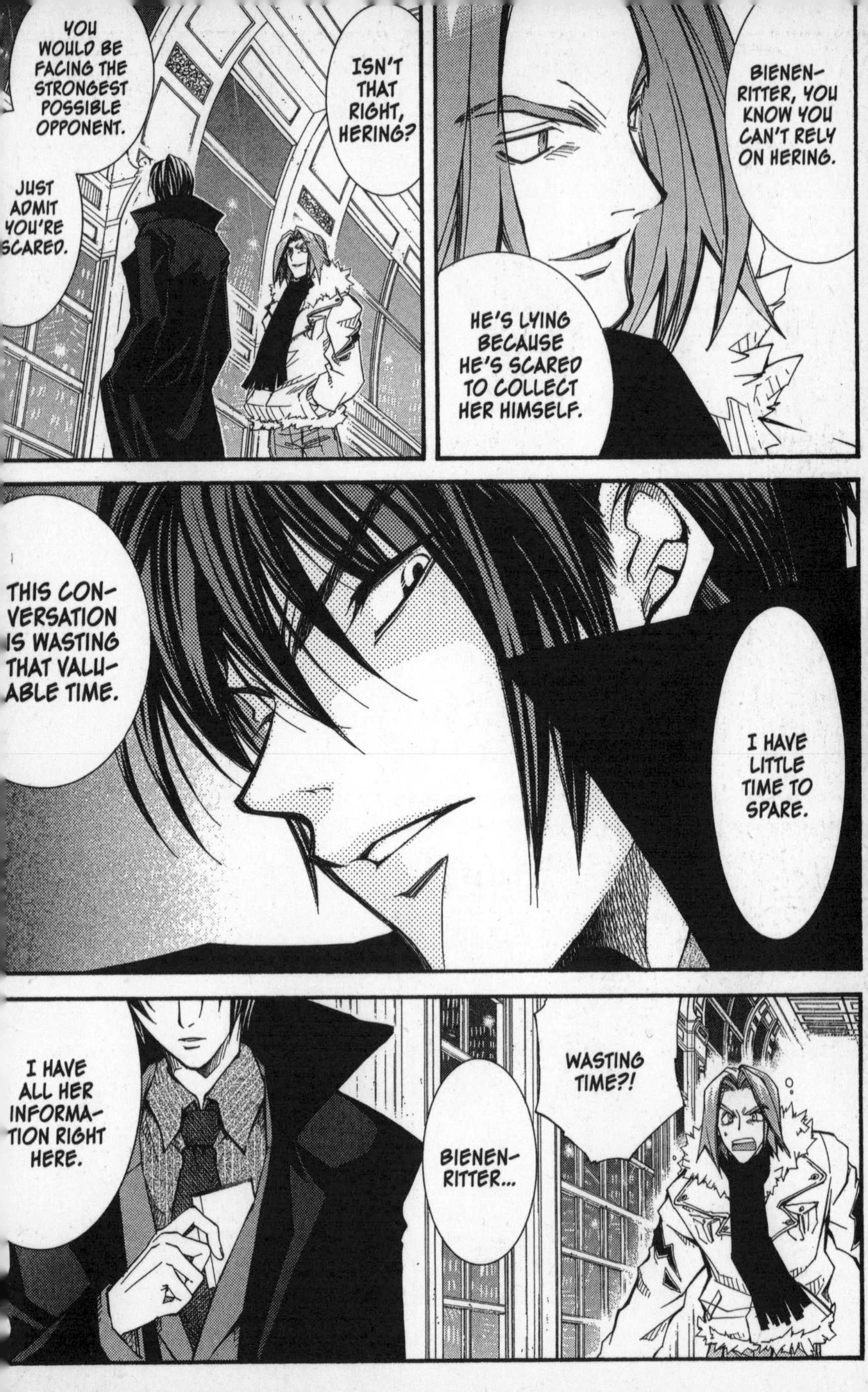
BIENEN-RITTER, YOU KNOW YOU CAN'T RELY ON HERING.
HE'S LYING BECAUSE HE'S SCARED TO COLLECT HER HIMSELF.
ISN'T THAT RIGHT, HERING?
YOU WOULD BE FACING THE STRONGEST POSSIBLE OPPONENT.
JUST ADMIT YOU'RE SCARED.
I HAVE LITTLE TIME TO SPARE.
THIS CONVERSATION IS WASTING THAT VALUABLE TIME.
WASTING TIME?!
BIENEN-RITTER...
I HAVE ALL HER INFORMATION RIGHT HERE.

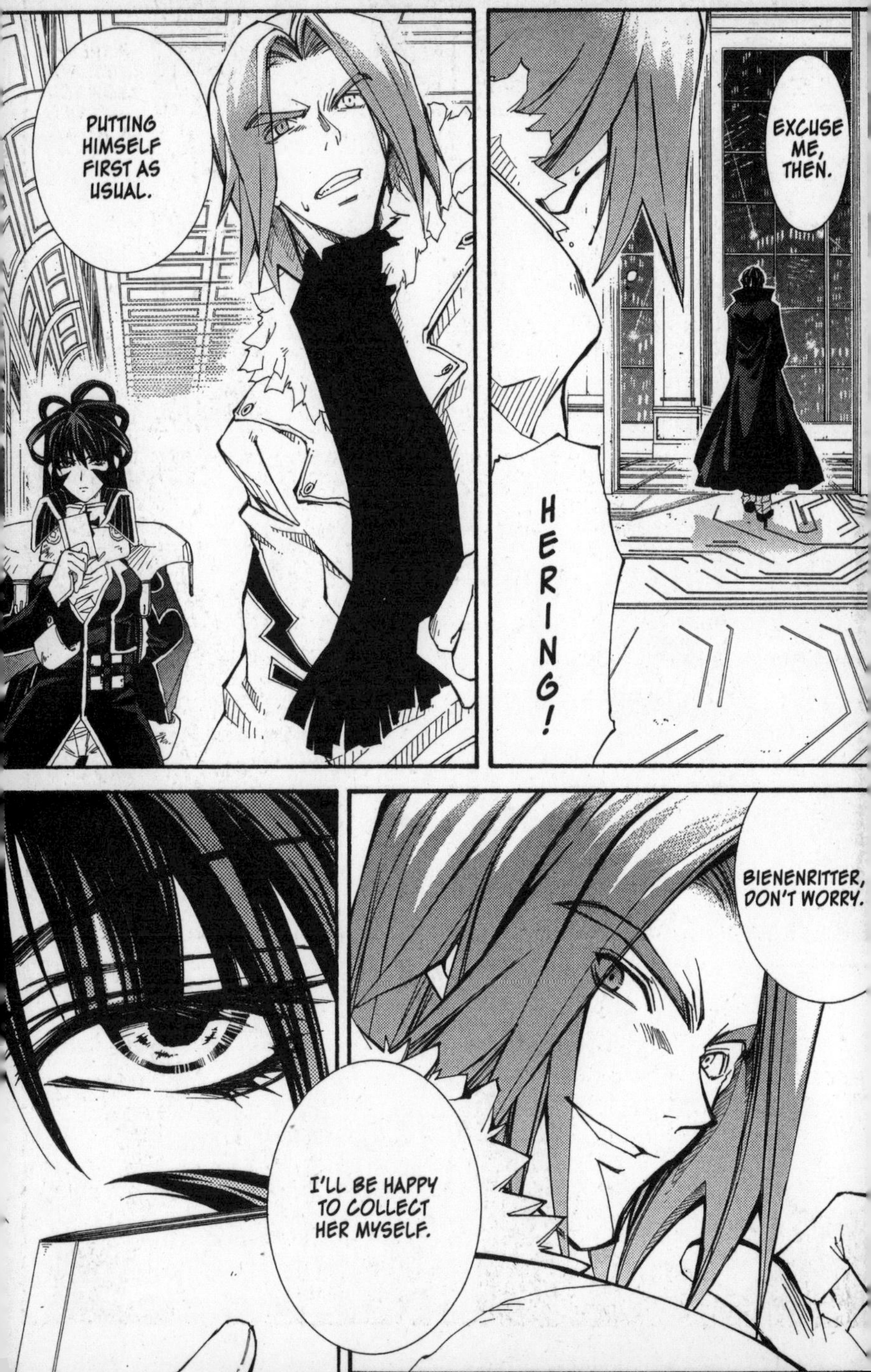
EXCUSE ME, THEN.
HERING!
PUTTING HIMSELF FIRST AS USUAL.
BIENENRITTER, DON'T WORRY.
I'LL BE HAPPY TO COLLECT HER MYSELF.

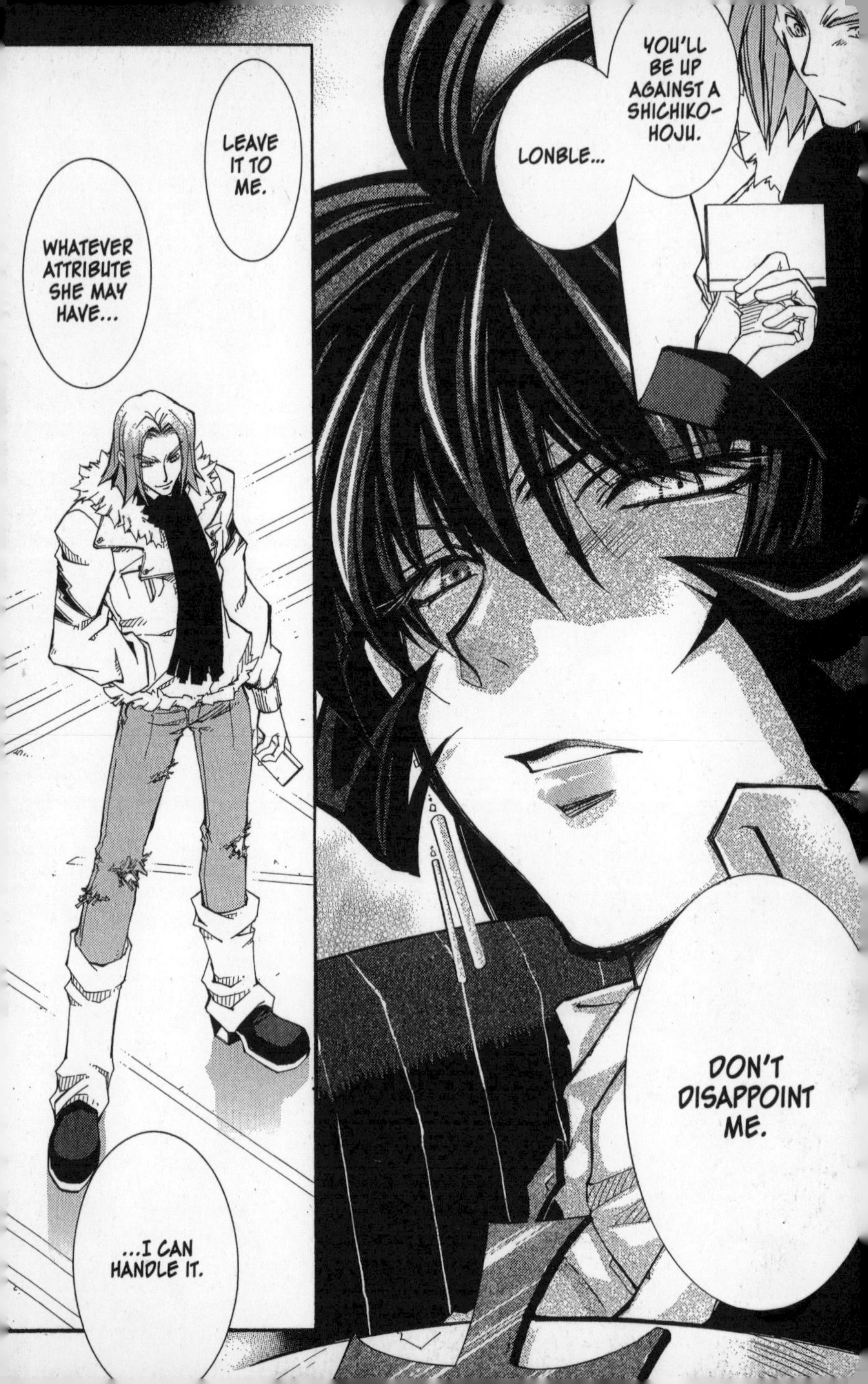
YOU'LL BE UP AGAINST A SHICHIKO-HOJU.
LONBLE...
DON'T DISAPPOINT ME.
LEAVE IT TO ME.
WHATEVER ATTRIBUTE SHE MAY HAVE...
...I CAN HANDLE IT.

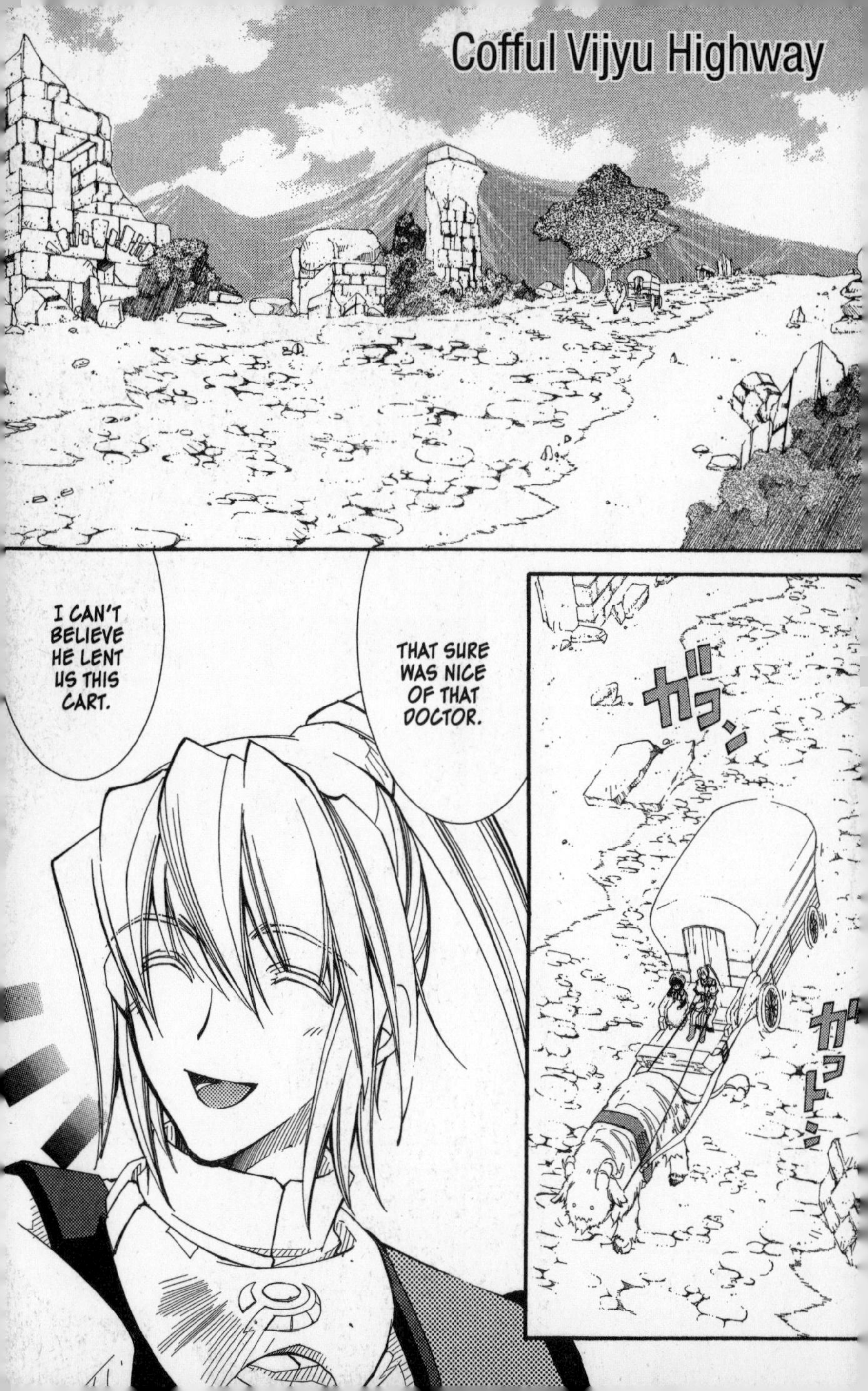
Cofful Vijyu Highway
THAT SURE WAS NICE OF THAT DOCTOR.
I CAN'T BELIEVE HE LENT US THIS CART.

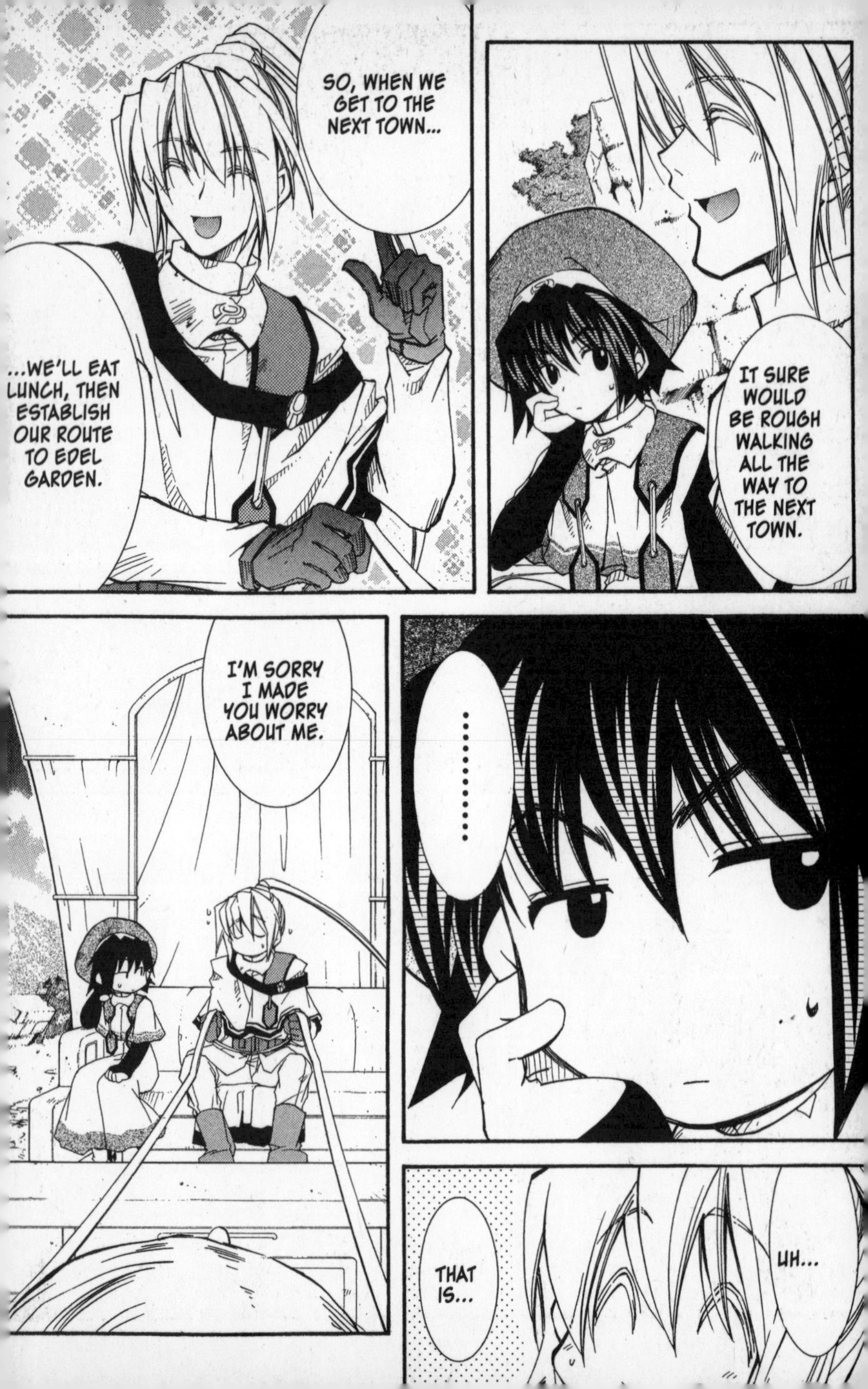
IT SURE WOULD BE ROUGH WALKING ALL THE WAY TO THE NEXT TOWN.
SO, WHEN WE GET TO THE NEXT TOWN...
...WE'LL EAT LUNCH, THEN ESTABLISH OUR ROUTE TO EDEL GARDEN.
....
UH...
THAT IS...
I'M SORRY I MADE YOU WORRY ABOUT ME.

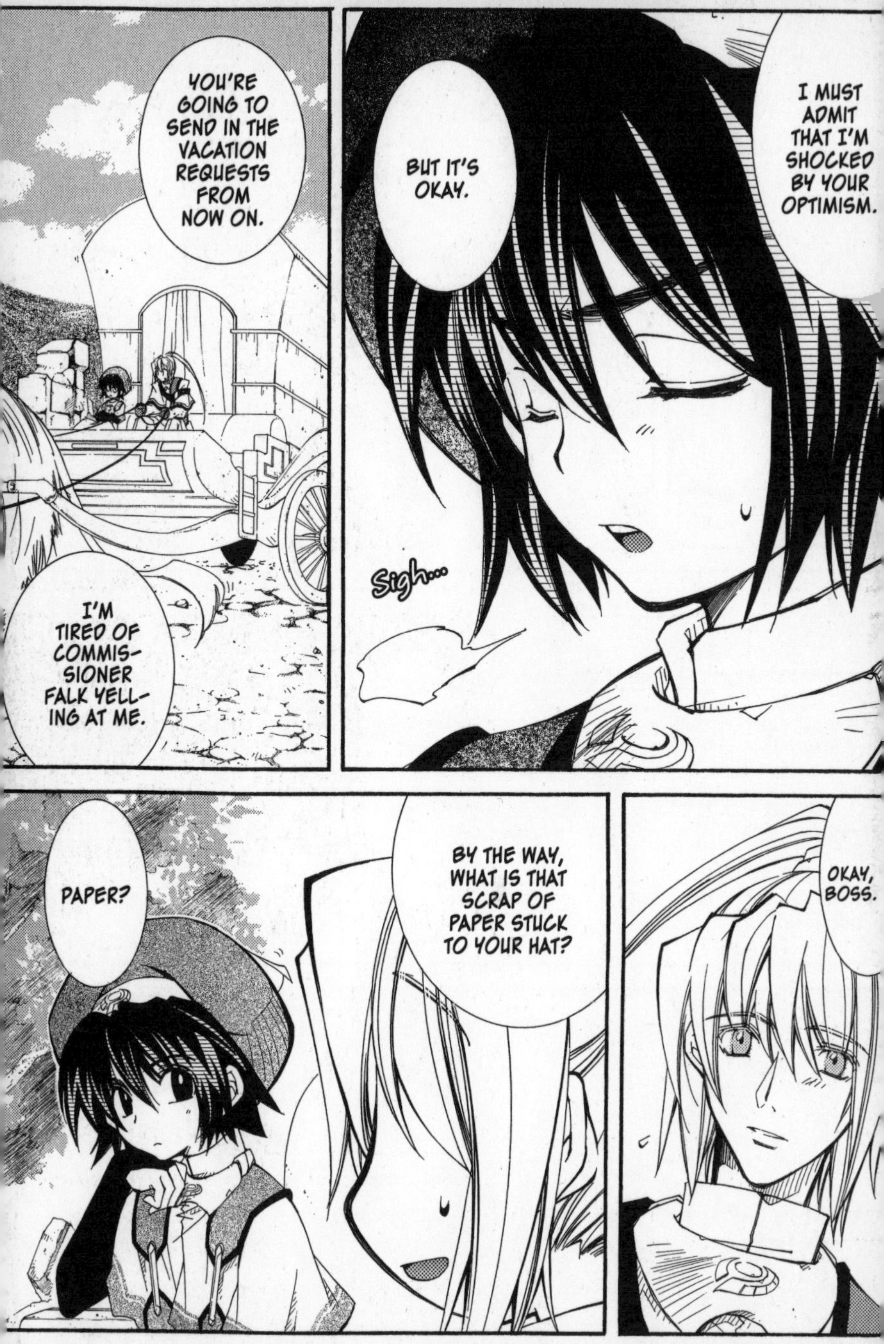

I MUST ADMIT THAT I'M SHOCKED BY YOUR OPTIMISM.
BUT IT'S OKAY.
Sigh...
YOU'RE GOING TO SEND IN THE VACATION REQUESTS FROM NOW ON.
I'M TIRED OF COMMIS-SIONER FALK YELL-ING AT ME.
OKAY, BOSS.
BY THE WAY, WHAT IS THAT SCRAP OF PAPER STUCK TO YOUR HAT?
PAPER?

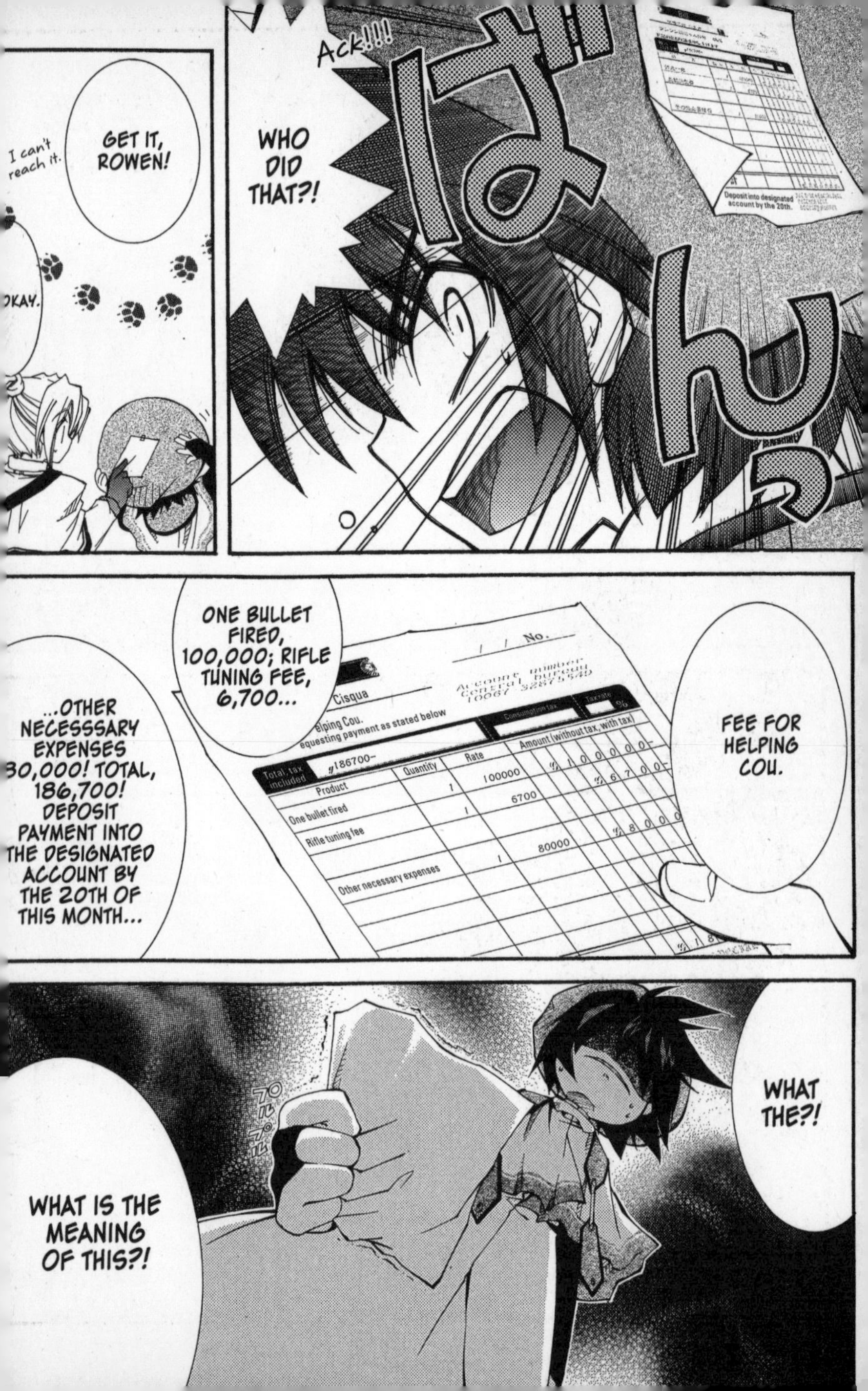
Ack!!!
WHO DID THAT?!
Deposit into designated account by the 20th.
GET IT, ROWEN!
I can't reach it.
OKAY.
FEE FOR HELPING COU.
ONE BULLET FIRED, 100,000; RIFLE TUNING FEE, 6,700...
No.
Account number Central bureau 10067 32875549
Cisqua
Consumption tax
Tax rate
%
elping Cou.
equesting payment as stated below
Amount (without tax, with tax)
Total, tax included
¥186700-
Product
Quantity
Rate
One bullet fired
1
100000
Rifle tuning fee
1
6700
Other necessary expenses
1
80000
...OTHER NECESSSARY EXPENSES 30,000! TOTAL, 186,700! DEPOSIT PAYMENT INTO THE DESIGNATED ACCOUNT BY THE 20TH OF THIS MONTH...
WHAT THE?!
WHAT IS THE MEANING OF THIS?!

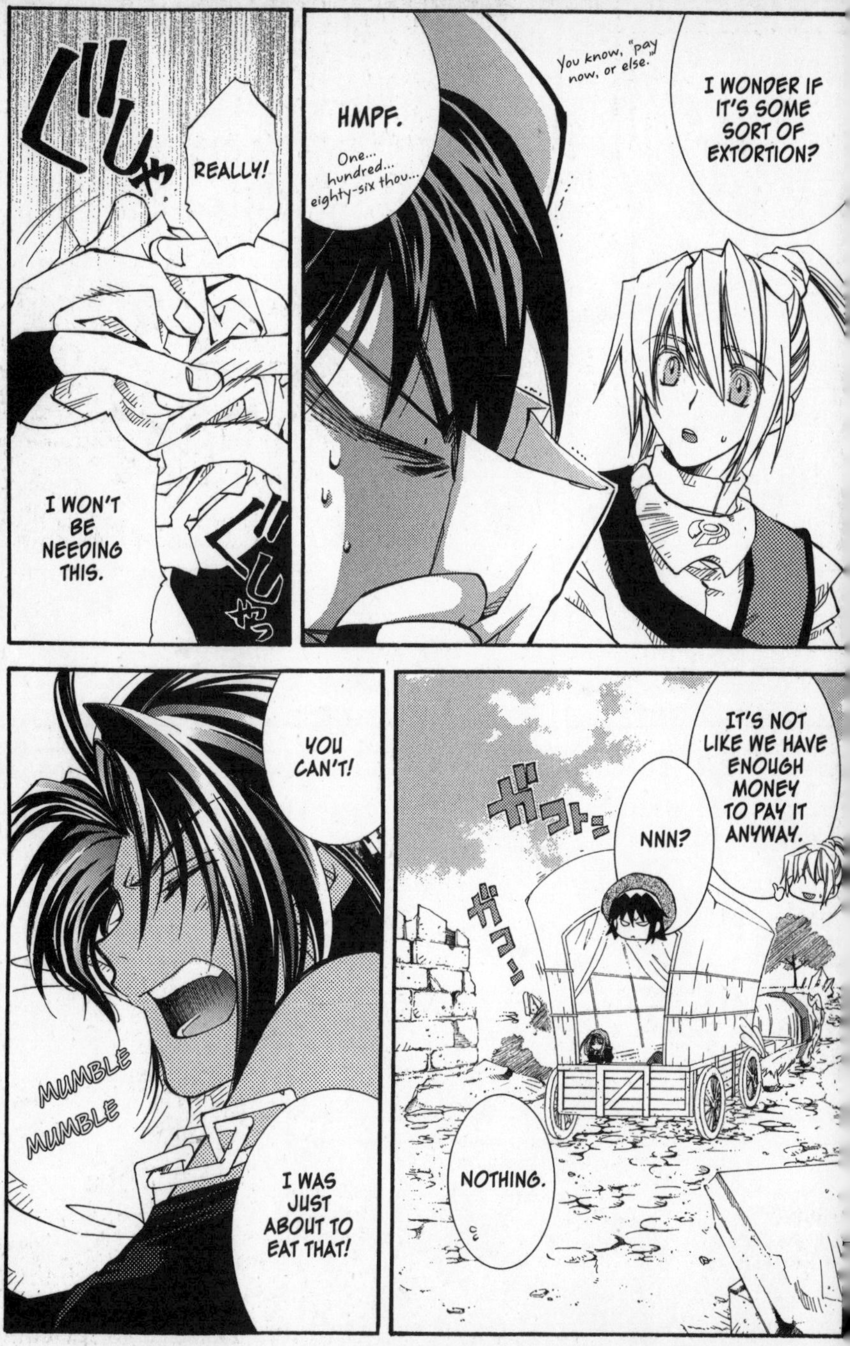
I WONDER IF IT'S SOME SORT OF EXTORTION?
You know, "pay now, or else."
HMPF.
One... hundred... eighty-six thou...
くしゃ
REALLY!
I WON'T BE NEEDING THIS.
くしゃっ
IT'S NOT LIKE WE HAVE ENOUGH MONEY TO PAY IT ANYWAY.
NNN?
NOTHING.
YOU CAN'T!
MUMBLE MUMBLE
I WAS JUST ABOUT TO EAT THAT!

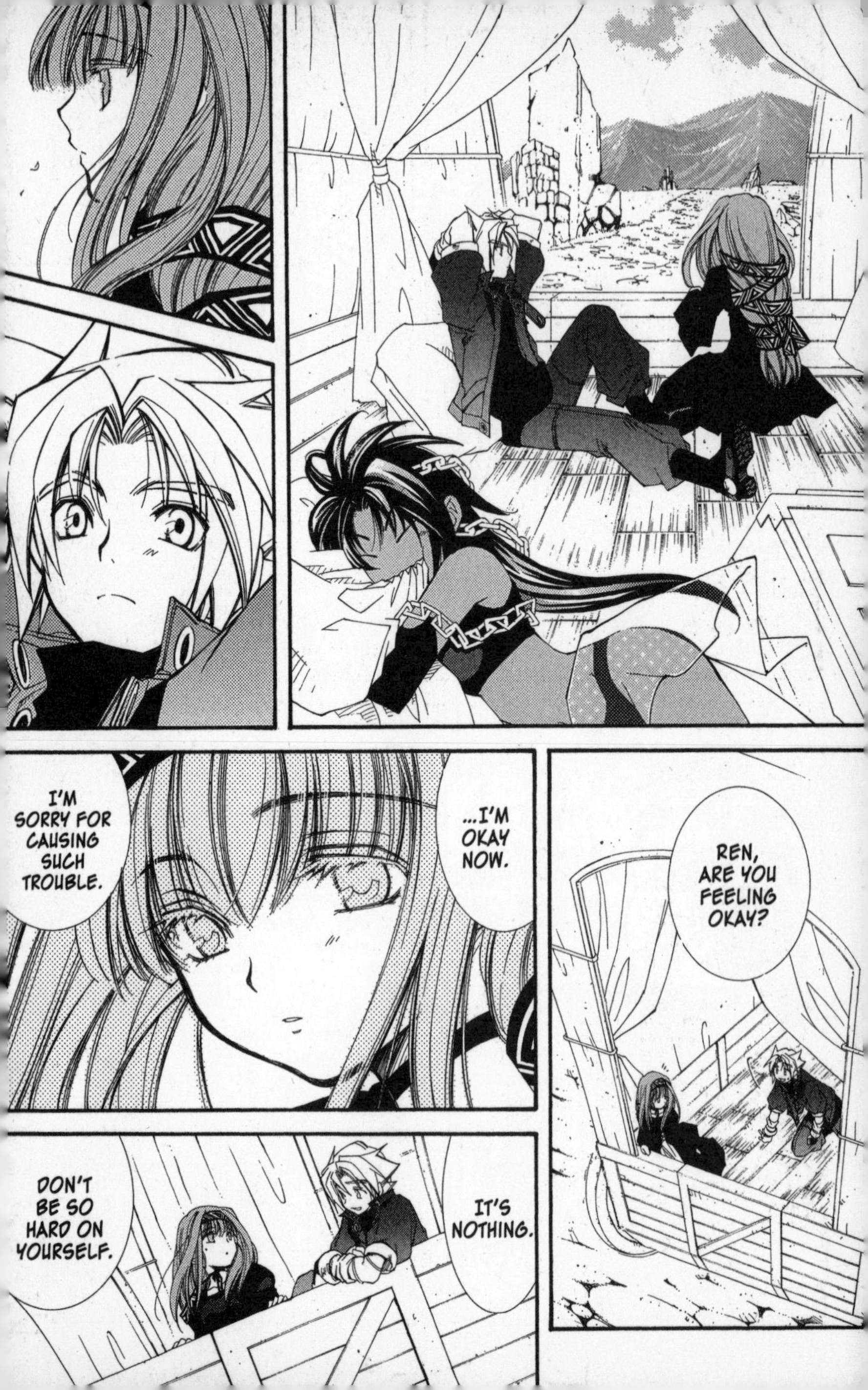
REN, ARE YOU FEELING OKAY?
...I'M OKAY NOW.
I'M SORRY FOR CAUSING SUCH TROUBLE.
IT'S NOTHING.
DON'T BE SO HARD ON YOURSELF.

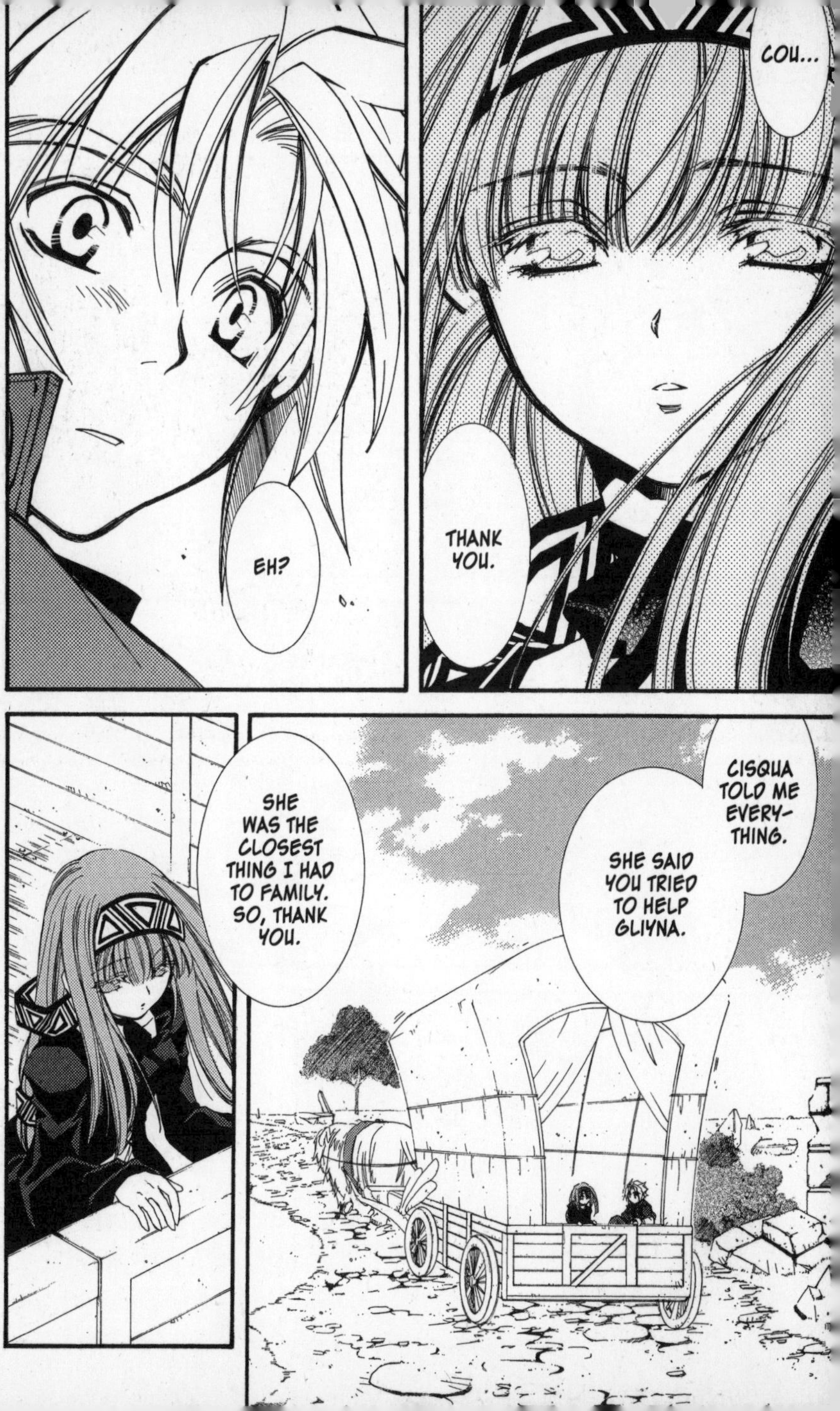
COU...
THANK YOU.
EH?
CISQUA TOLD ME EVERY-THING.
SHE SAID YOU TRIED TO HELP GLIYNA.
SHE WAS THE CLOSEST THING I HAD TO FAMILY. SO, THANK YOU.

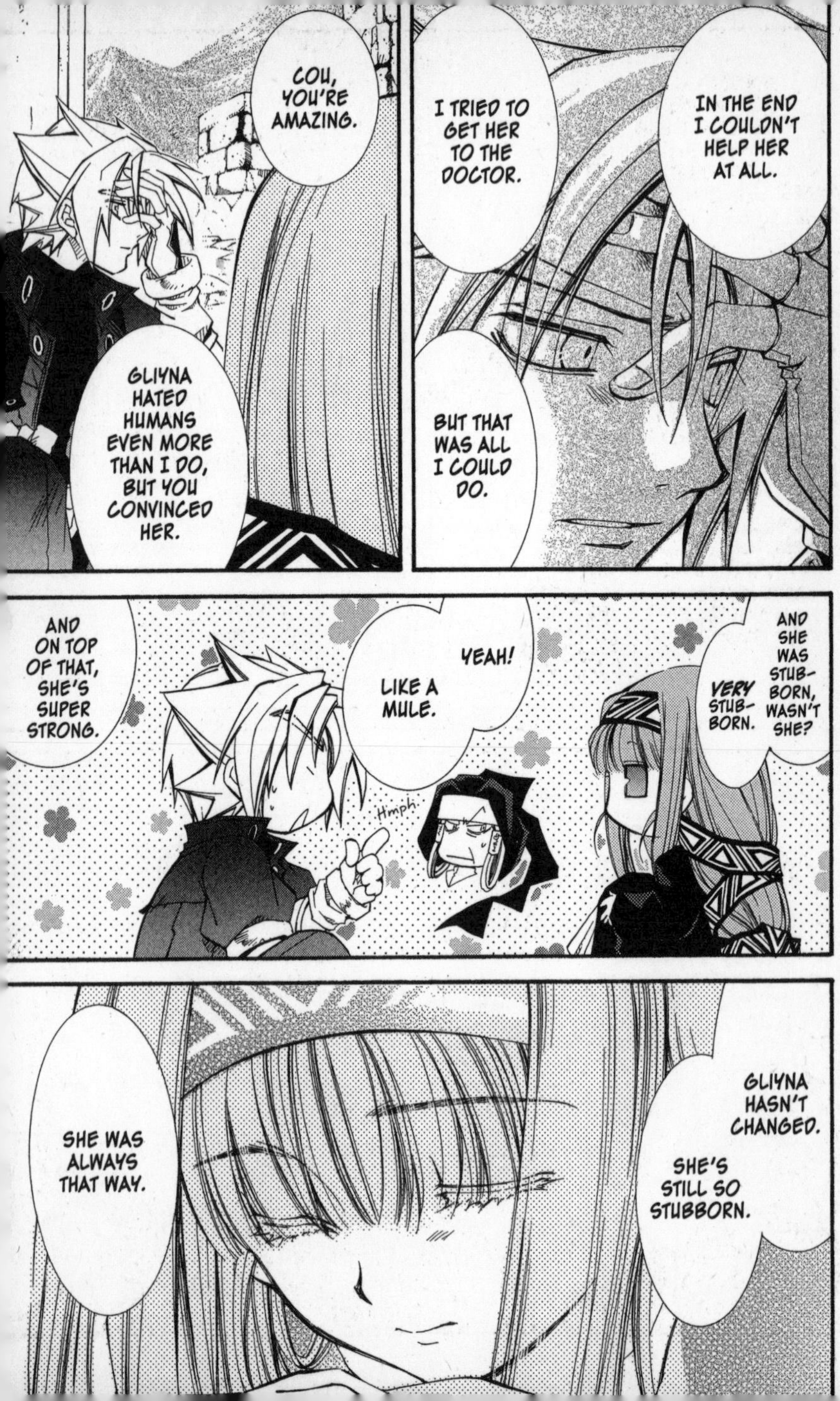
IN THE END I COULDN'T HELP HER AT ALL.
I TRIED TO GET HER TO THE DOCTOR.
BUT THAT WAS ALL I COULD DO.
COU, YOU'RE AMAZING.
GLIYNA HATED HUMANS EVEN MORE THAN I DO, BUT YOU CONVINCED HER.
AND SHE WAS STUBBORN, WASN'T SHE?
VERY STUBBORN.
YEAH!
LIKE A MULE.
Hmph.
AND ON TOP OF THAT, SHE'S SUPER STRONG.
GLIYNA HASN'T CHANGED.
SHE'S STILL SO STUBBORN.
SHE WAS ALWAYS THAT WAY.

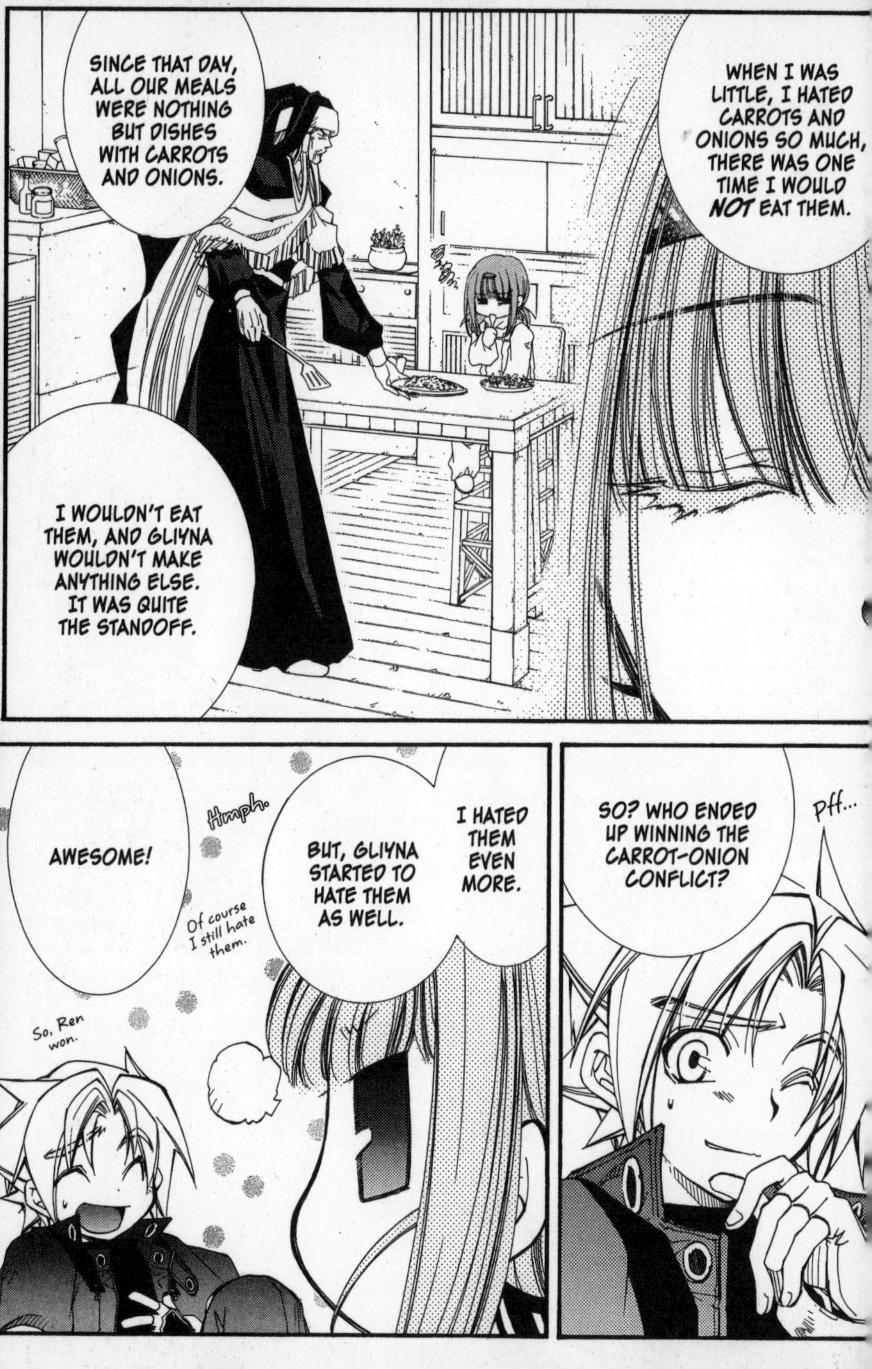
WHEN I WAS LITTLE, I HATED CARROTS AND ONIONS SO MUCH, THERE WAS ONE TIME I WOULD **NOT** EAT THEM.
SINCE THAT DAY, ALL OUR MEALS WERE NOTHING BUT DISHES WITH CARROTS AND ONIONS.
I WOULDN'T EAT THEM, AND GLIYNA WOULDN'T MAKE ANYTHING ELSE. IT WAS QUITE THE STANDOFF.
Pff...
SO? WHO ENDED UP WINNING THE CARROT-ONION CONFLICT?
I HATED THEM EVEN MORE.
BUT, GLIYNA STARTED TO HATE THEM AS WELL.
Hmph.
AWESOME!
Of course I still hate them.
So, Ren won.

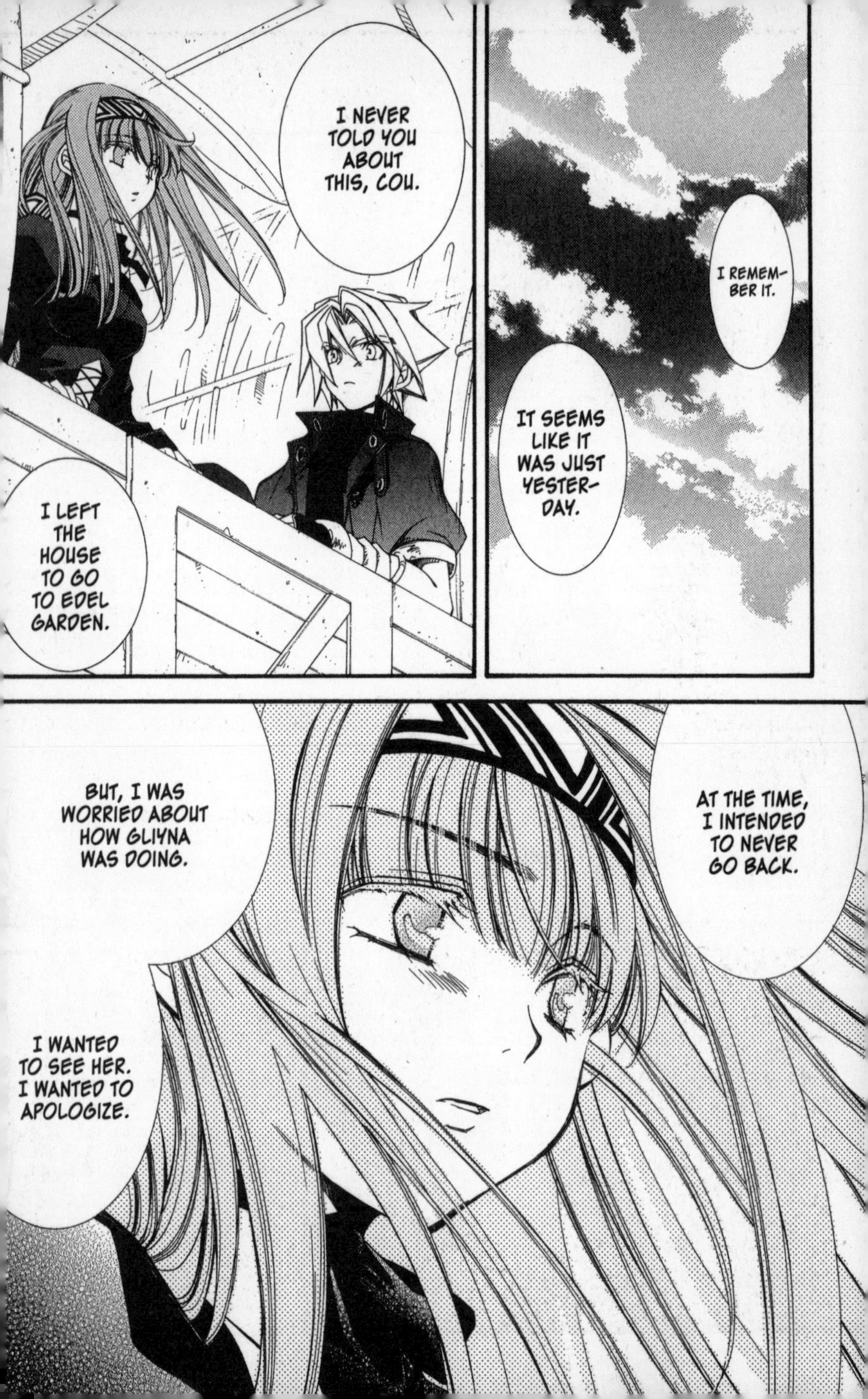
I REMEMBER IT.
IT SEEMS LIKE IT WAS JUST YESTERDAY.
I NEVER TOLD YOU ABOUT THIS, COU.
I LEFT THE HOUSE TO GO TO EDEL GARDEN.
AT THE TIME, I INTENDED TO NEVER GO BACK.
BUT, I WAS WORRIED ABOUT HOW GLIYNA WAS DOING.
I WANTED TO SEE HER. I WANTED TO APOLOGIZE.

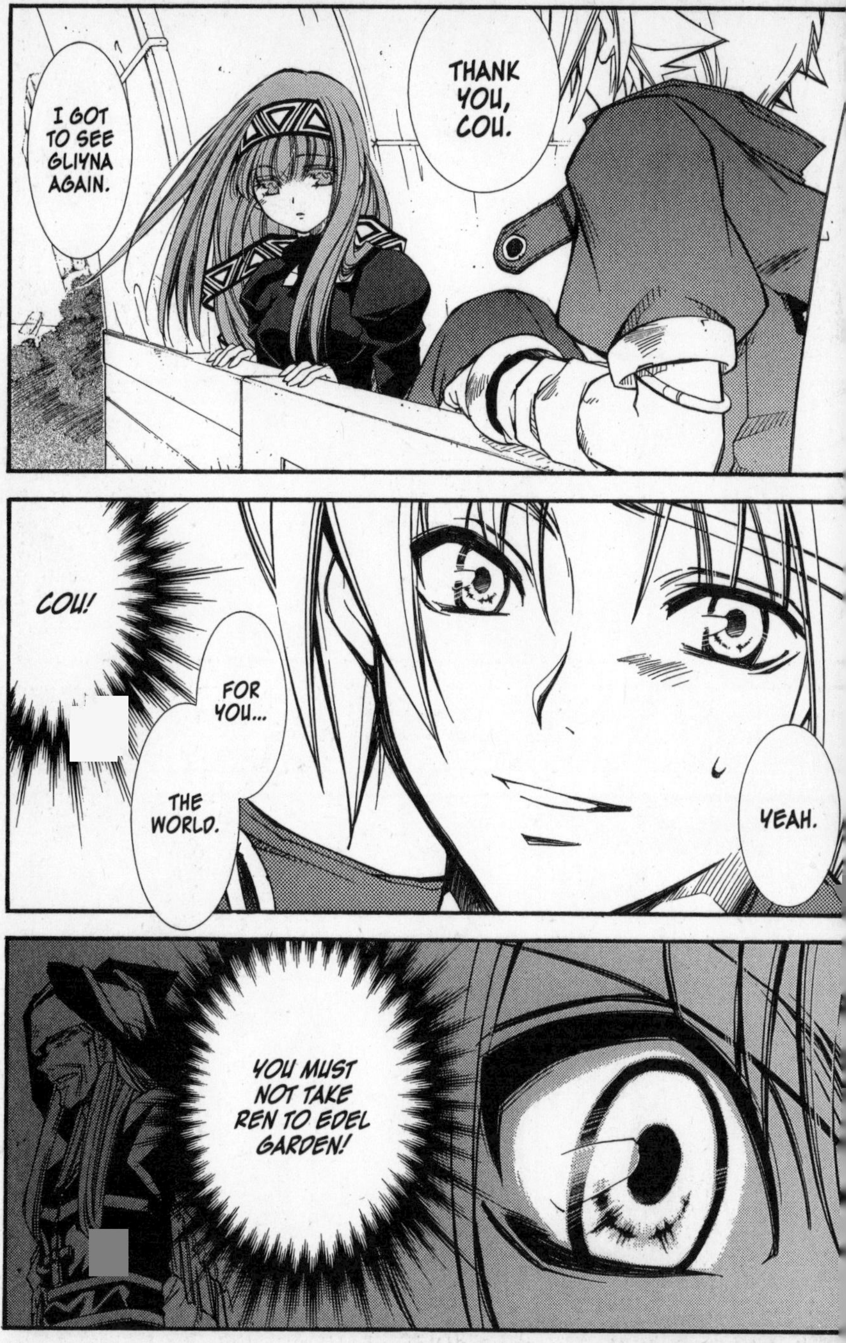
THANK YOU, COU.
I GOT TO SEE GLIYNA AGAIN.
YEAH.
FOR YOU...
THE WORLD.
COU!
YOU MUST NOT TAKE REN TO EDEL GARDEN!

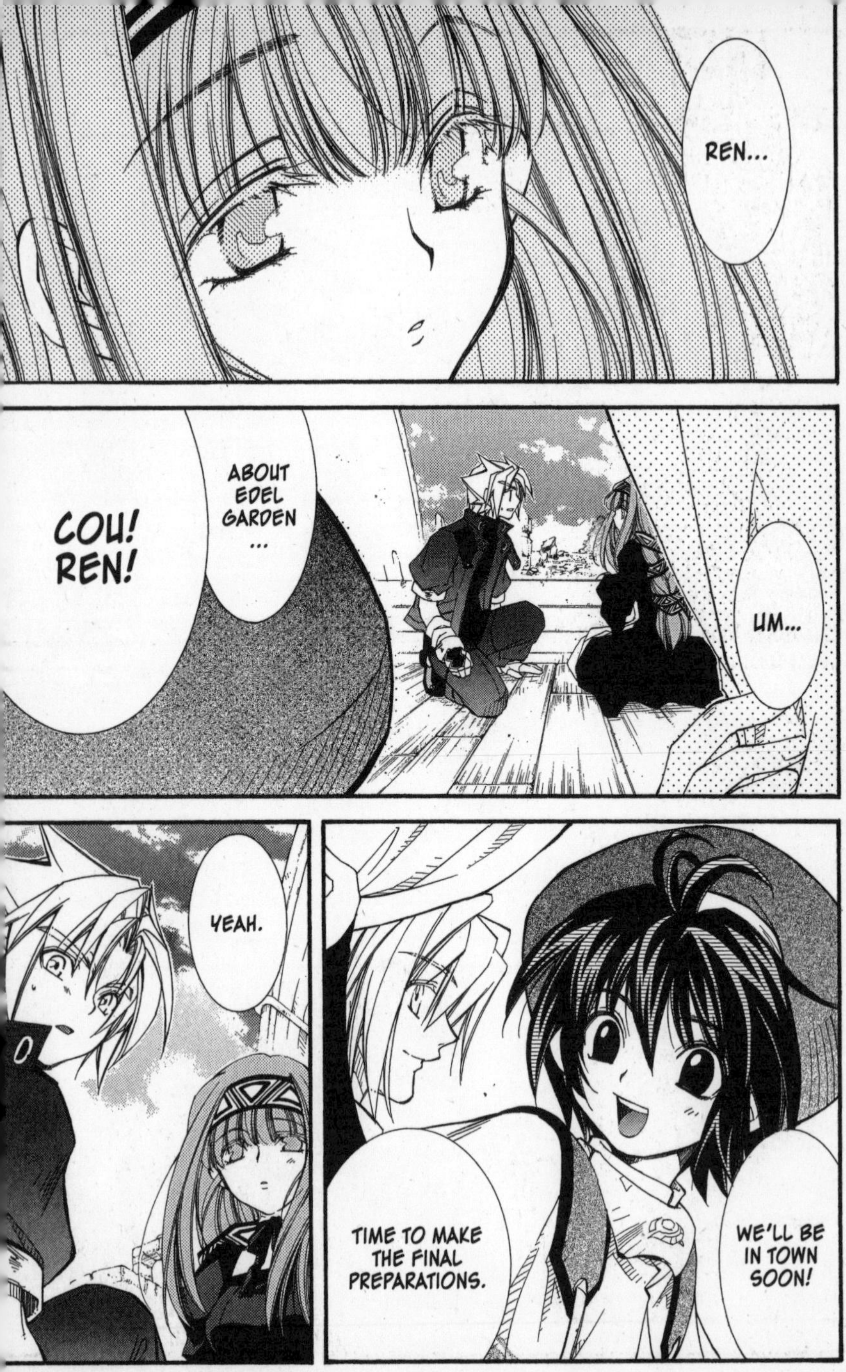
REN...
UM...
ABOUT EDEL GARDEN ...
COU! REN!
WE'LL BE IN TOWN SOON!
TIME TO MAKE THE FINAL PREPARATIONS.
YEAH.

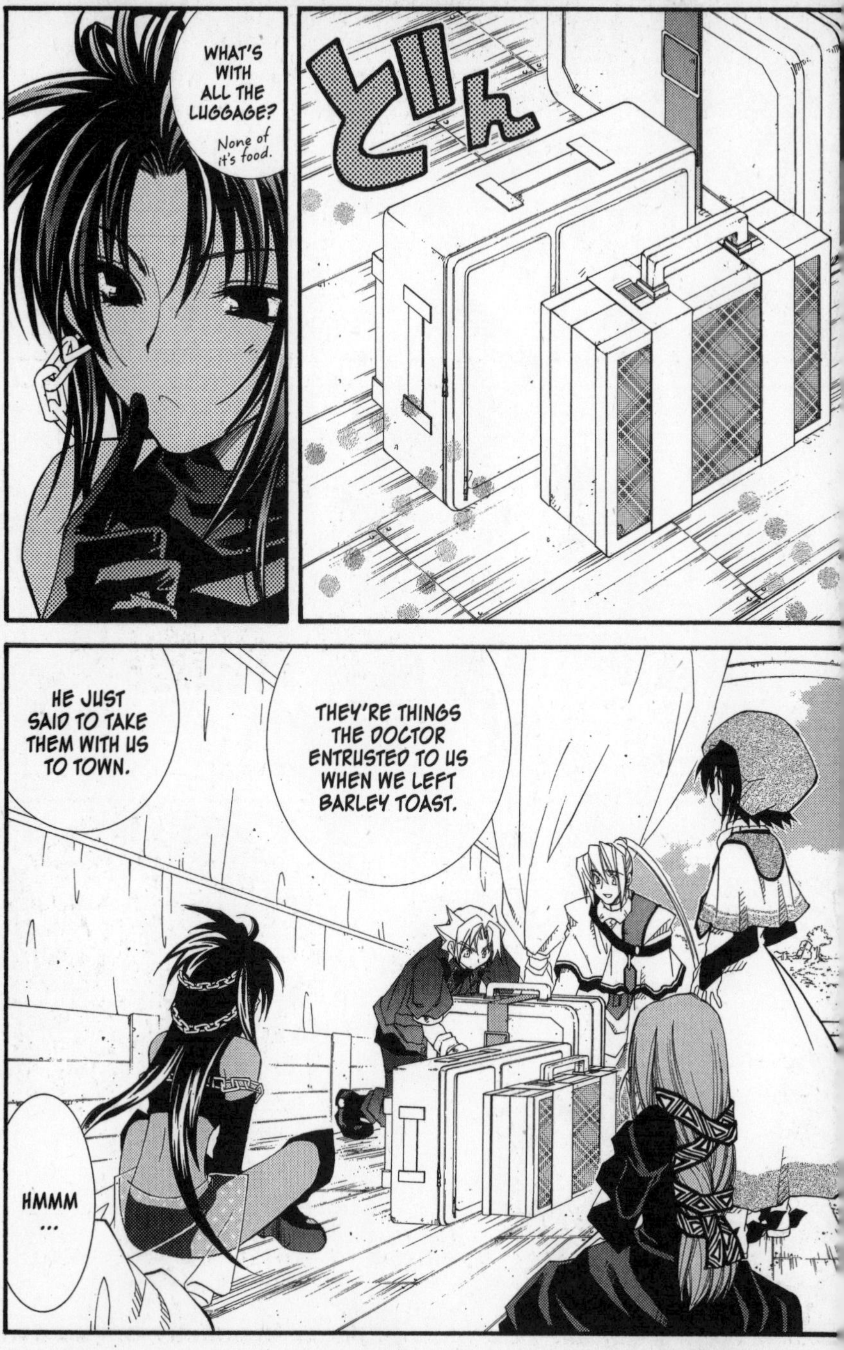
どん
WHAT'S WITH ALL THE LUGGAGE?
None of it's food.
THEY'RE THINGS THE DOCTOR ENTRUSTED TO US WHEN WE LEFT BARLEY TOAST.
HE JUST SAID TO TAKE THEM WITH US TO TOWN.
HMMM ...

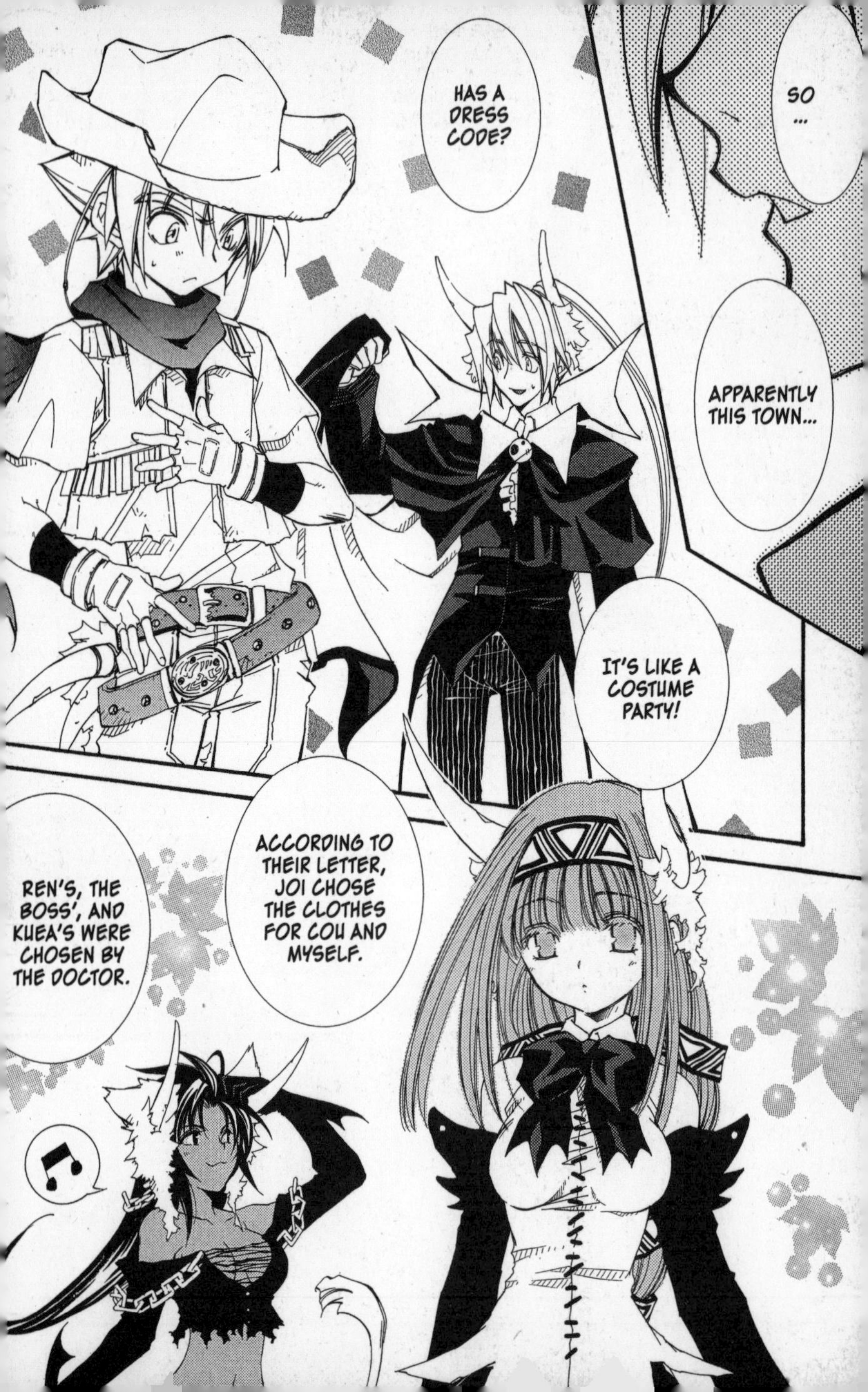
SO ...
APPARENTLY THIS TOWN...
HAS A DRESS CODE?
IT'S LIKE A COSTUME PARTY!
ACCORDING TO THEIR LETTER, JOI CHOSE THE CLOTHES FOR COU AND MYSELF.
REN'S, THE BOSS', AND KUEA'S WERE CHOSEN BY THE DOCTOR.
♪

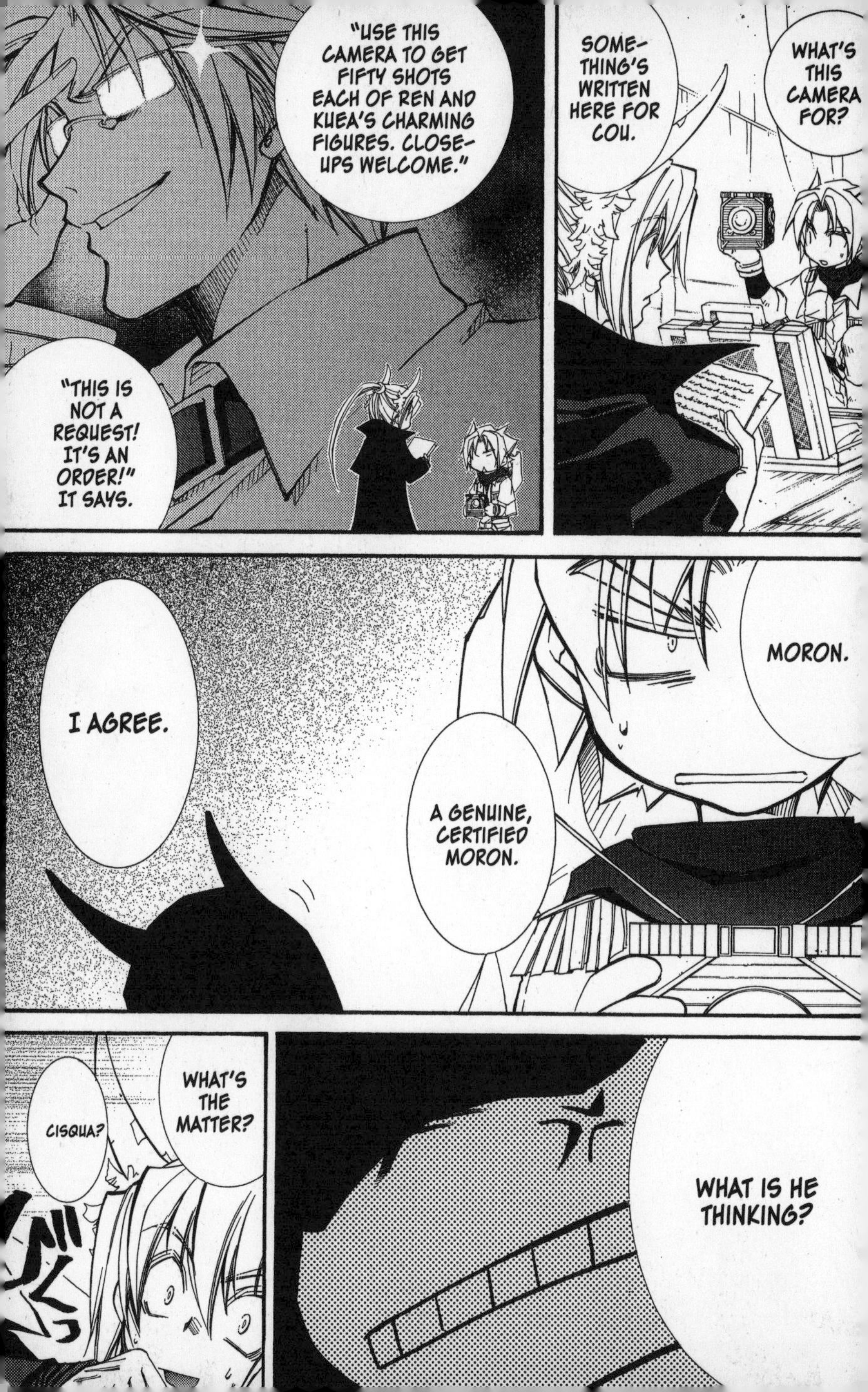
WHAT'S THIS CAMERA FOR?
SOME-THING'S WRITTEN HERE FOR COU.
"USE THIS CAMERA TO GET FIFTY SHOTS EACH OF REN AND KUEA'S CHARMING FIGURES. CLOSE-UPS WELCOME."
"THIS IS NOT A REQUEST! IT'S AN ORDER!" IT SAYS.
MORON.
A GENUINE, CERTIFIED MORON.
I AGREE.
WHAT IS HE THINKING?
WHAT'S THE MATTER?
CISQUA?

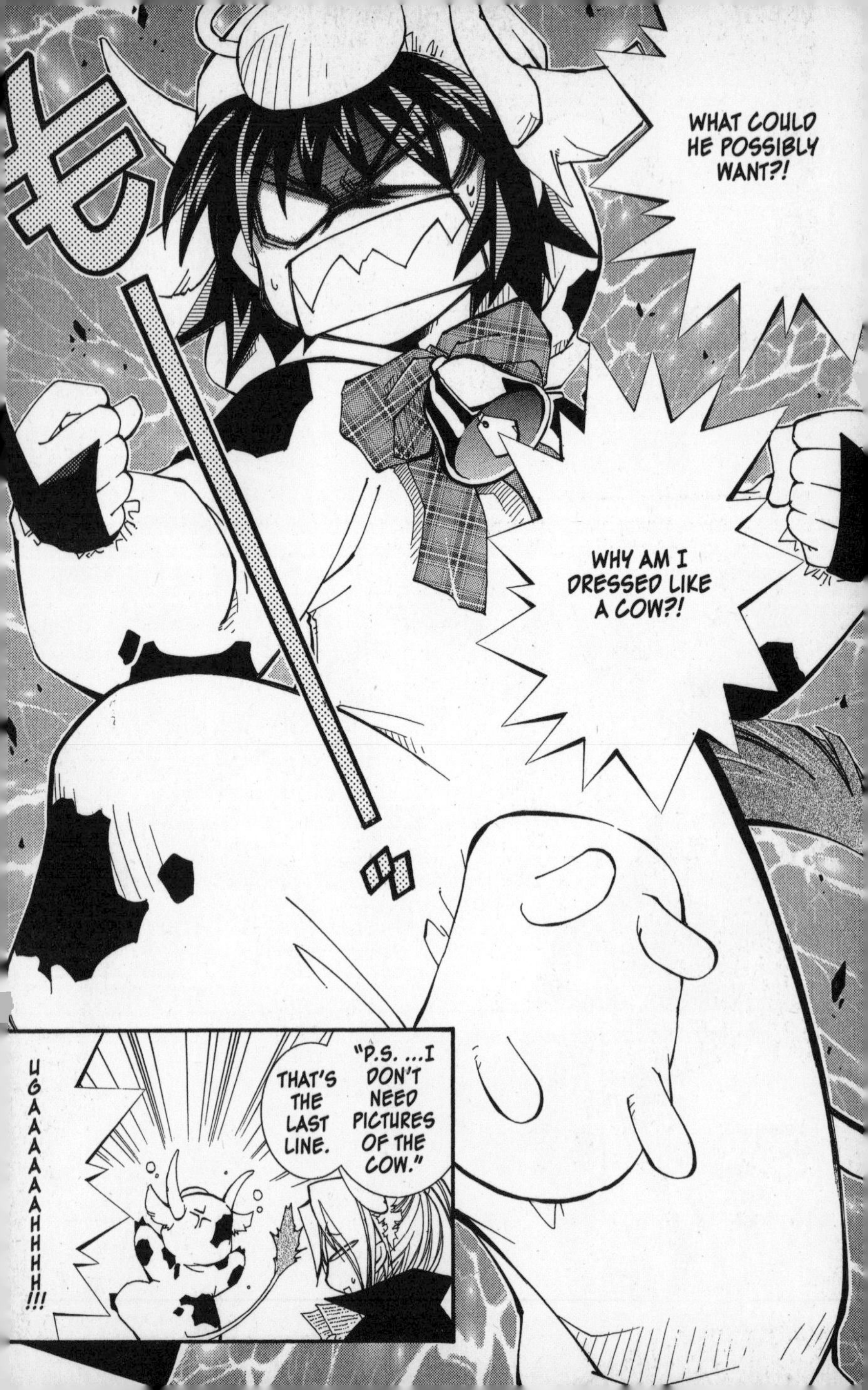
WHAT COULD HE POSSIBLY WANT?!
も
WHY AM I DRESSED LIKE A COW?!
"P.S. ...I DON'T NEED PICTURES OF THE COW."
THAT'S THE LAST LINE.
UGAAAAAAAHHHH!!!

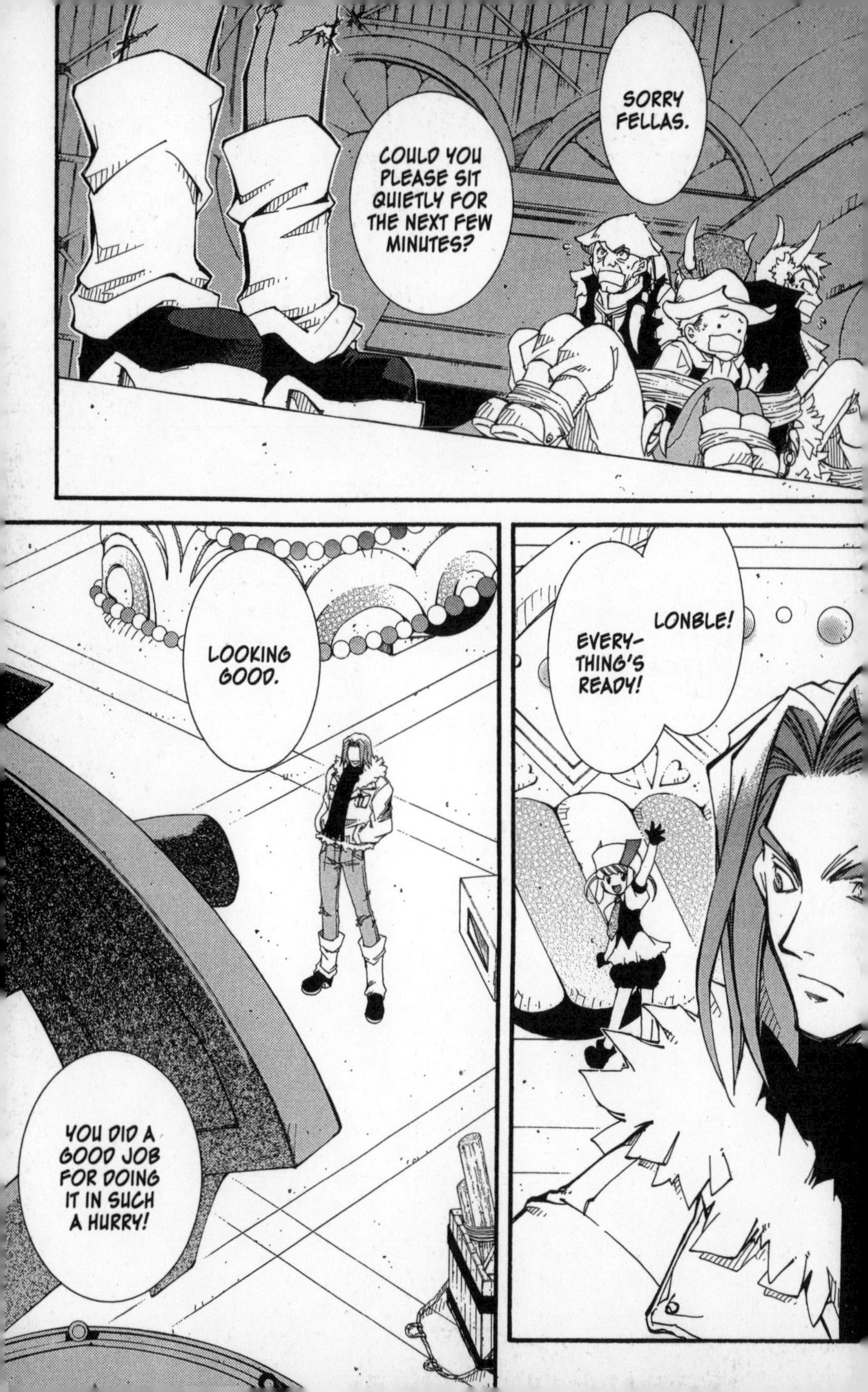
SORRY FELLAS.
COULD YOU PLEASE SIT QUIETLY FOR THE NEXT FEW MINUTES?
LONBLE! EVERY-THING'S READY!
LOOKING GOOD.
YOU DID A GOOD JOB FOR DOING IT IN SUCH A HURRY!

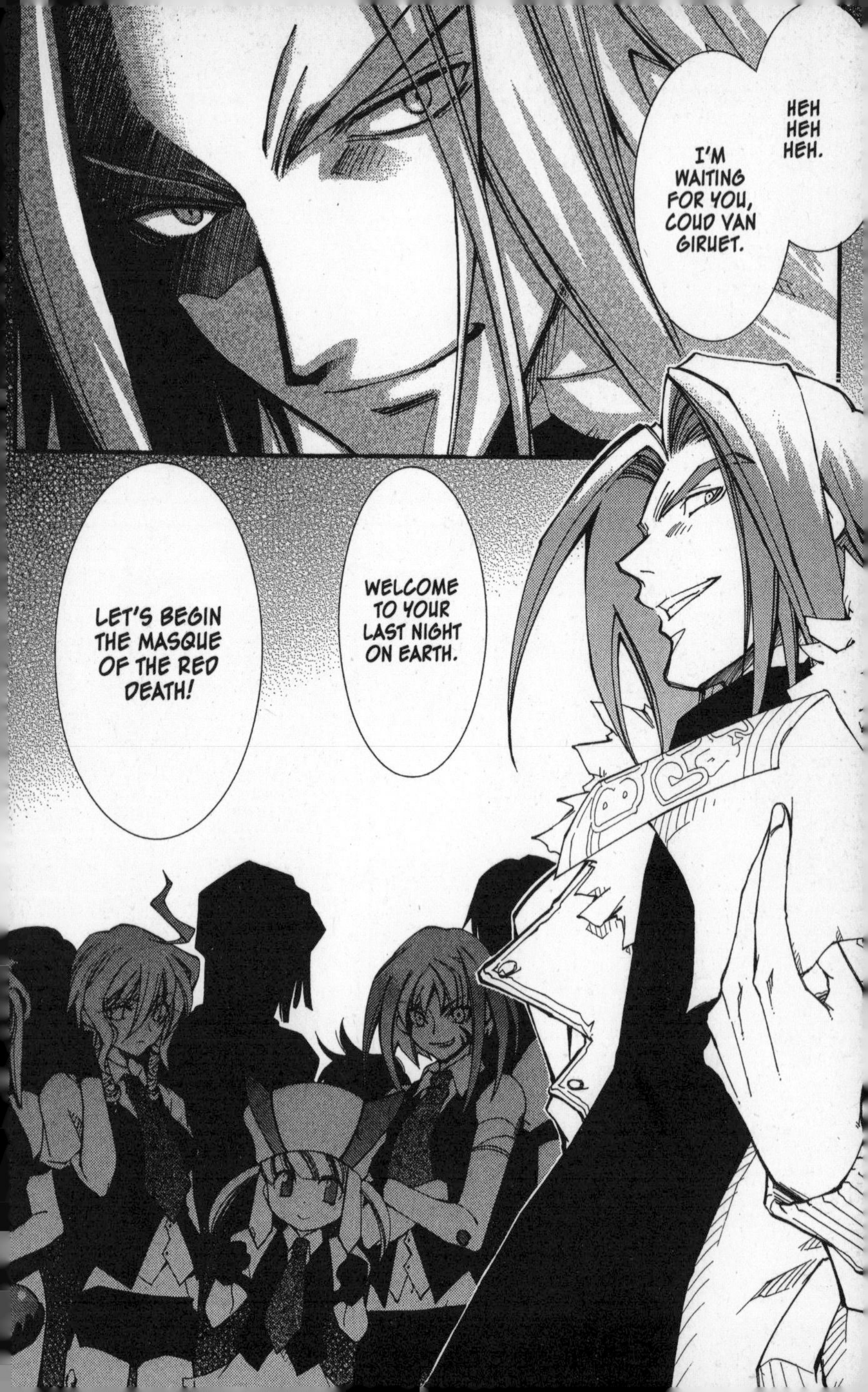
HEH HEH HEH.
I'M WAITING FOR YOU, COUD VAN GIRUET.
WELCOME TO YOUR LAST NIGHT ON EARTH.
LET'S BEGIN THE MASQUE OF THE RED DEATH!

Re-No: 38

Toro Fest—The Curtain Rises on a Long Ominous Night

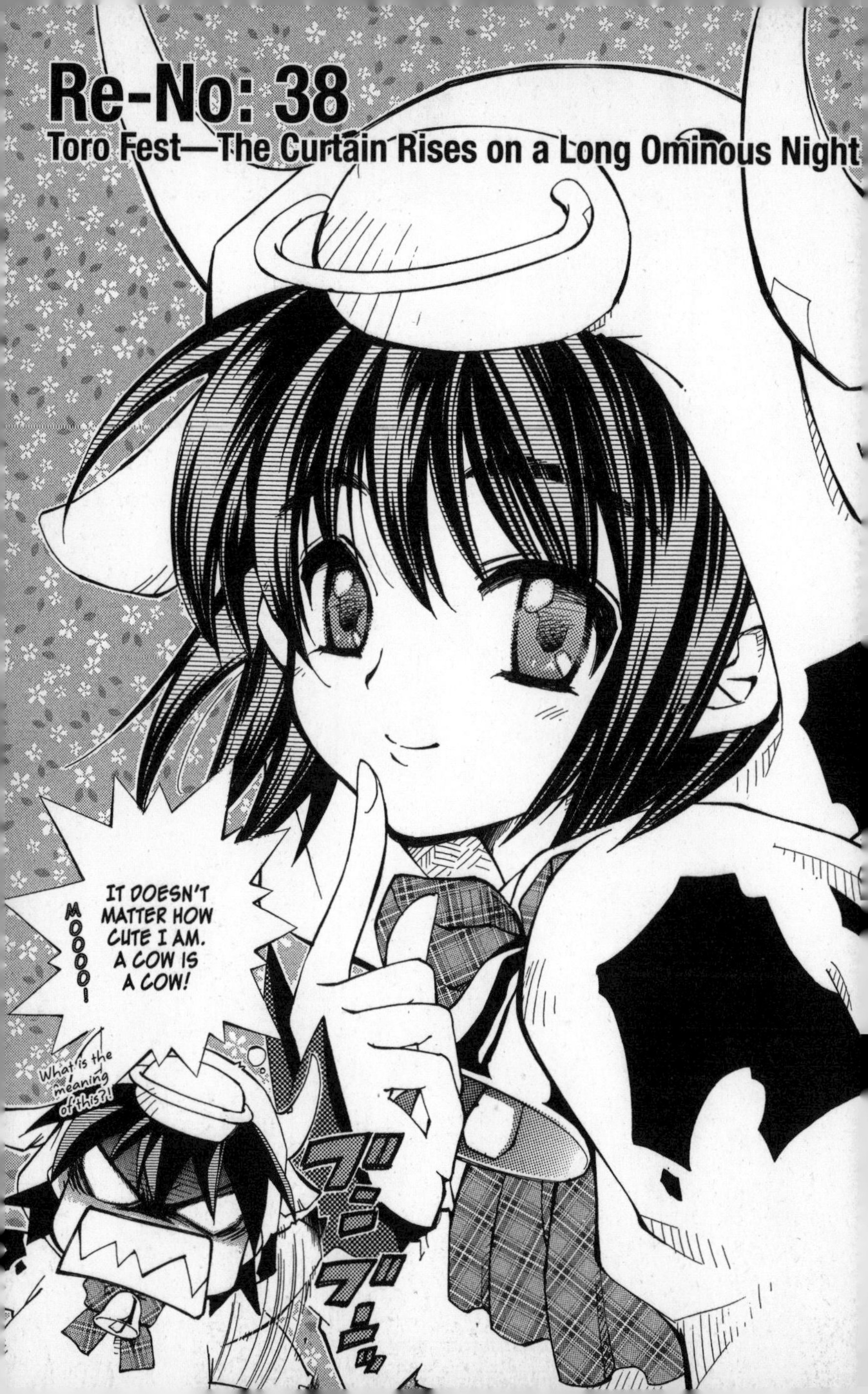
IT DOESN'T MATTER HOW CUTE I AM. A COW IS A COW!
MOOOOO!
What is the meaning of this?!

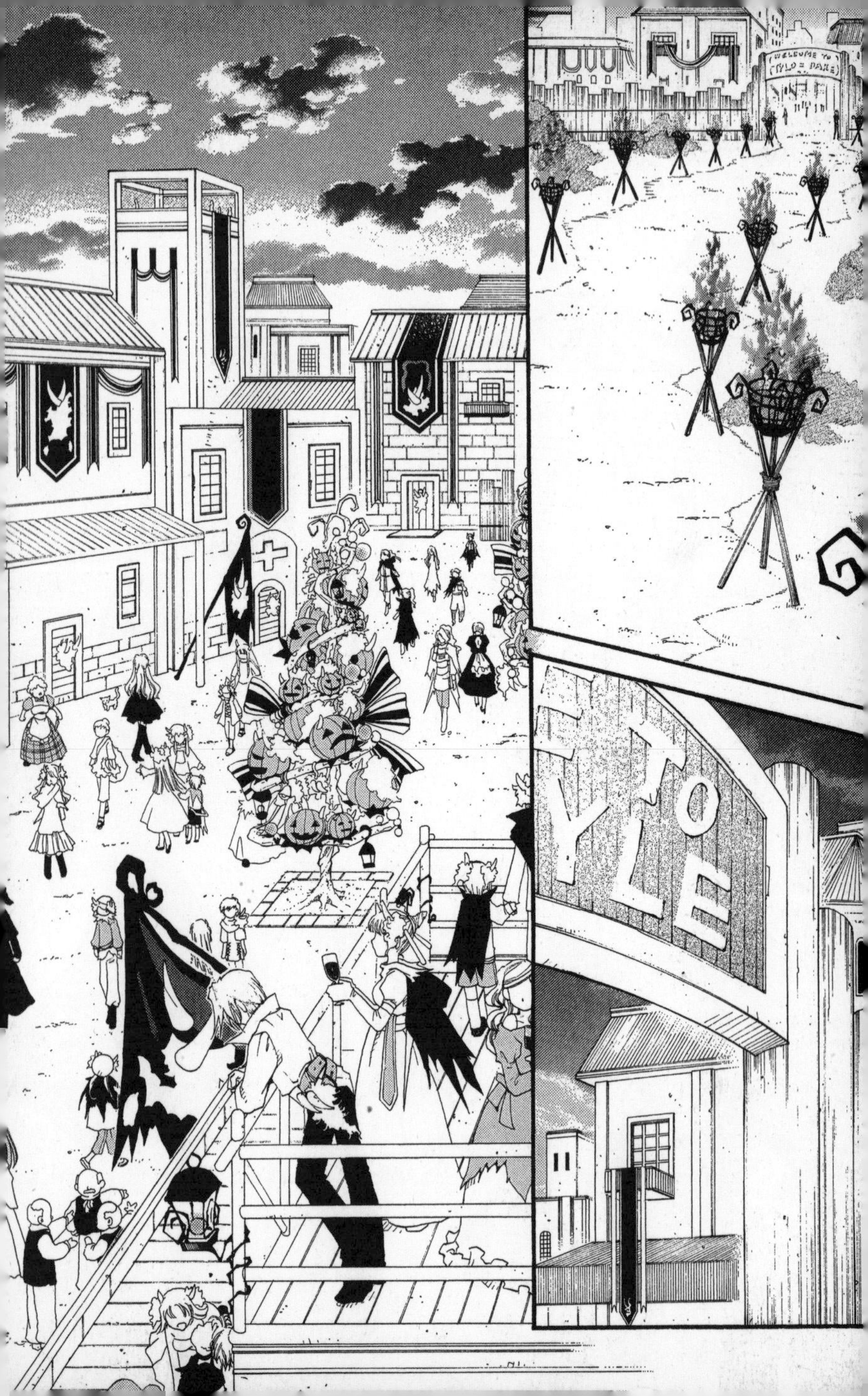

WELCOME TO
TYLO = PARK
TO
YLE

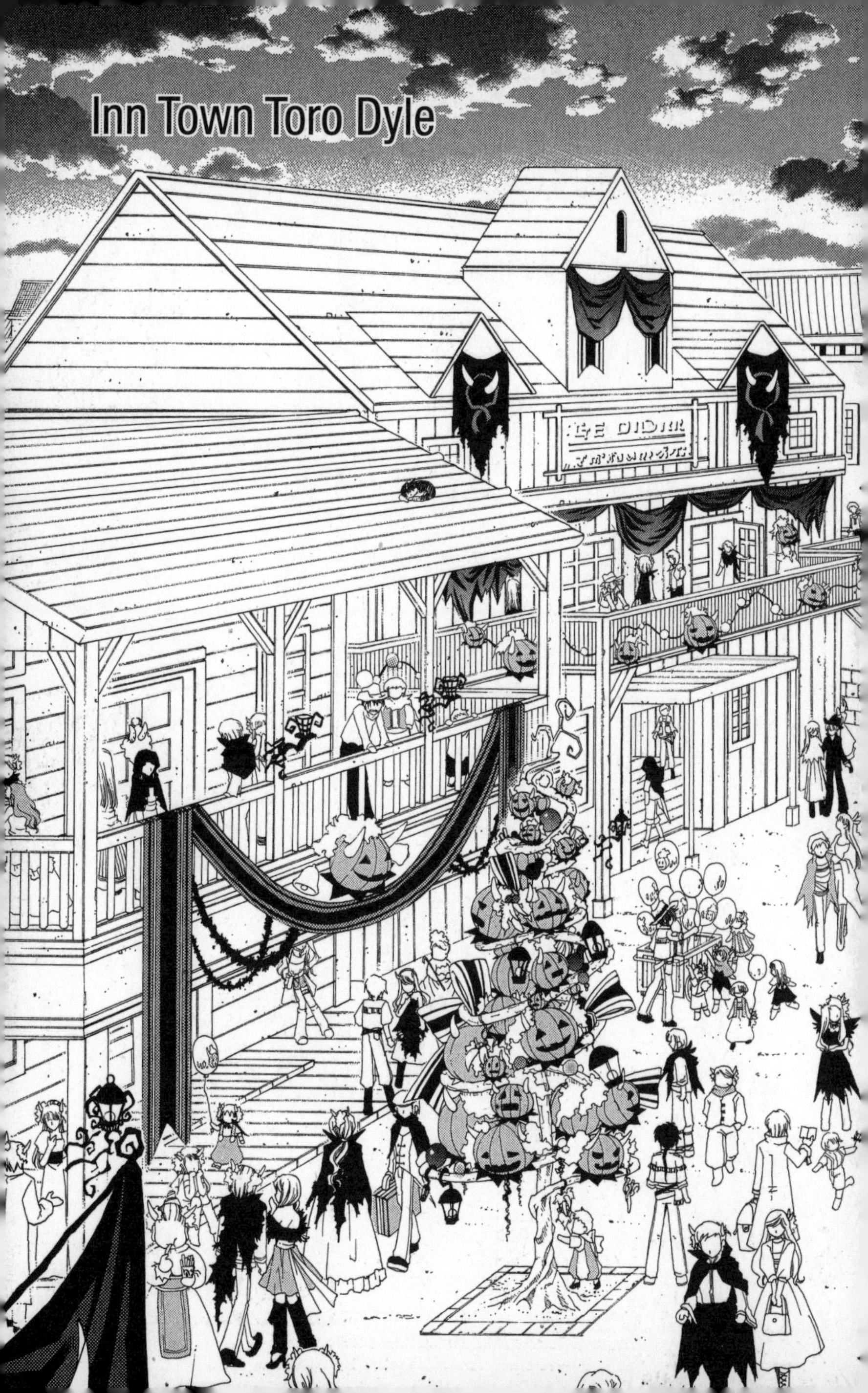
Inn Town Toro Dyle

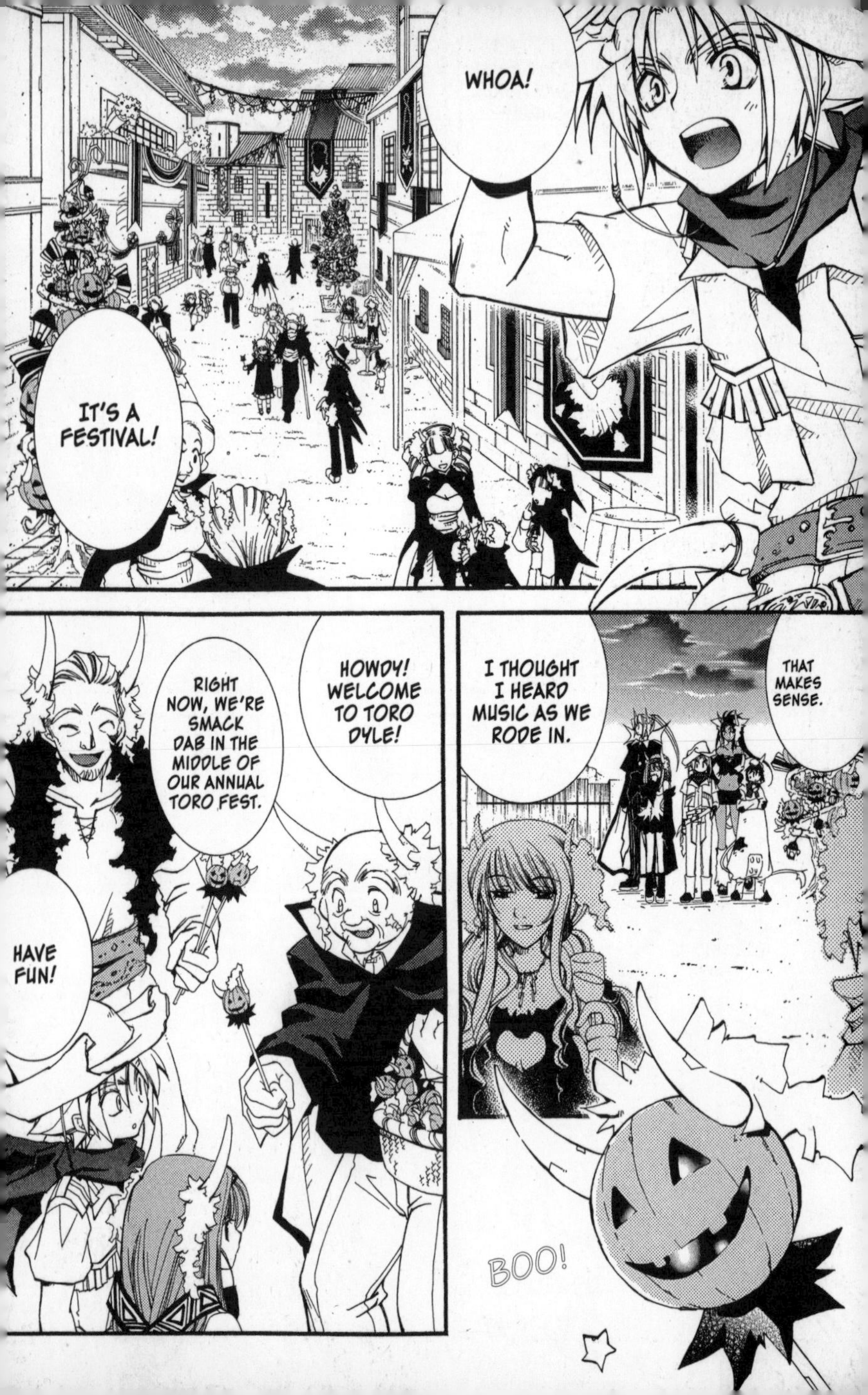
WHOA!
IT'S A FESTIVAL!
THAT MAKES SENSE.
I THOUGHT I HEARD MUSIC AS WE RODE IN.
BOO!
HOWDY! WELCOME TO TORO DYLE!
RIGHT NOW, WE'RE SMACK DAB IN THE MIDDLE OF OUR ANNUAL TORO FEST.
HAVE FUN!

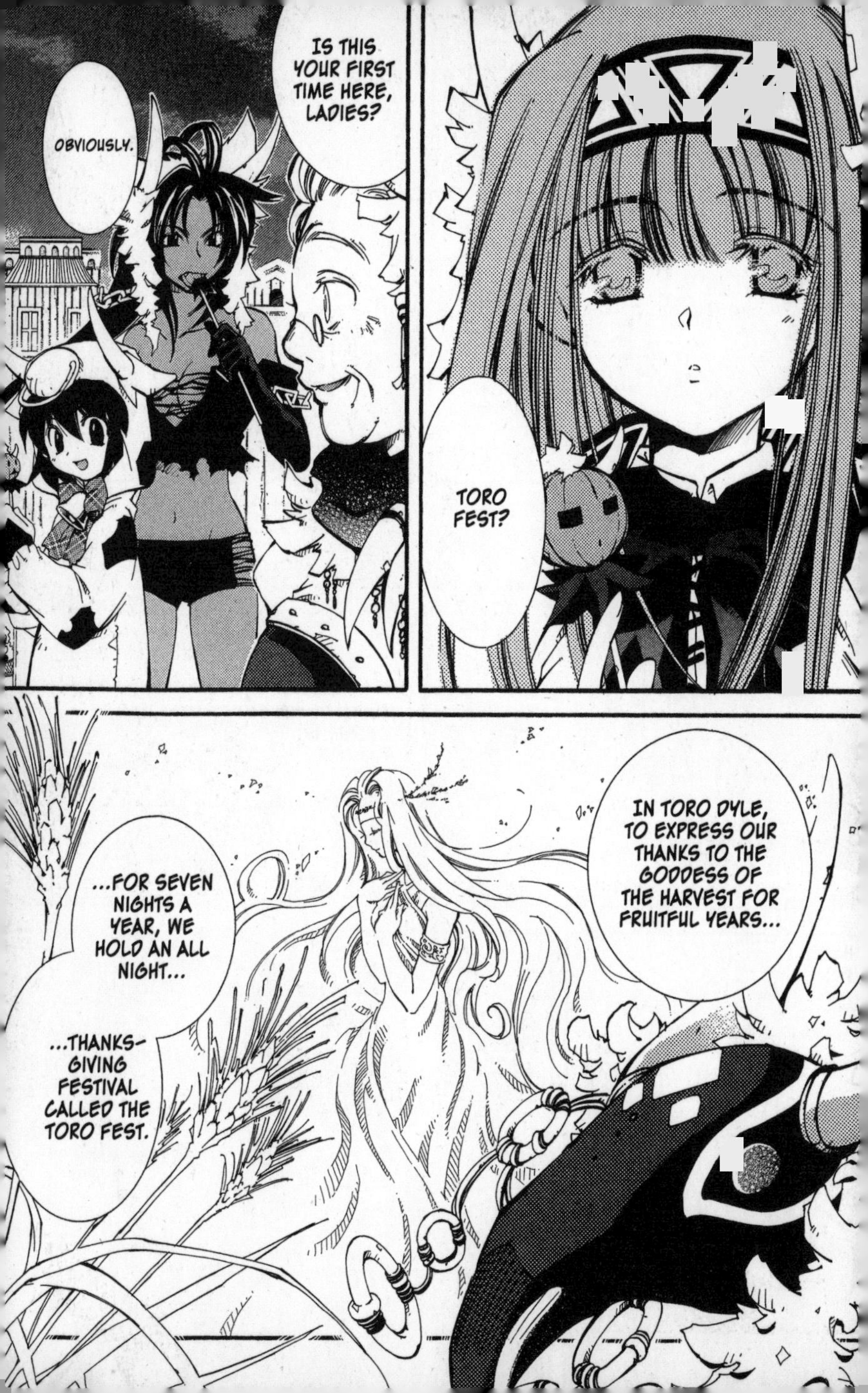
TORO FEST?
IS THIS YOUR FIRST TIME HERE, LADIES?
OBVIOUSLY.
IN TORO DYLE, TO EXPRESS OUR THANKS TO THE GODDESS OF THE HARVEST FOR FRUITFUL YEARS...
...FOR SEVEN NIGHTS A YEAR, WE HOLD AN ALL NIGHT...
...THANKS-GIVING FESTIVAL CALLED THE TORO FEST.

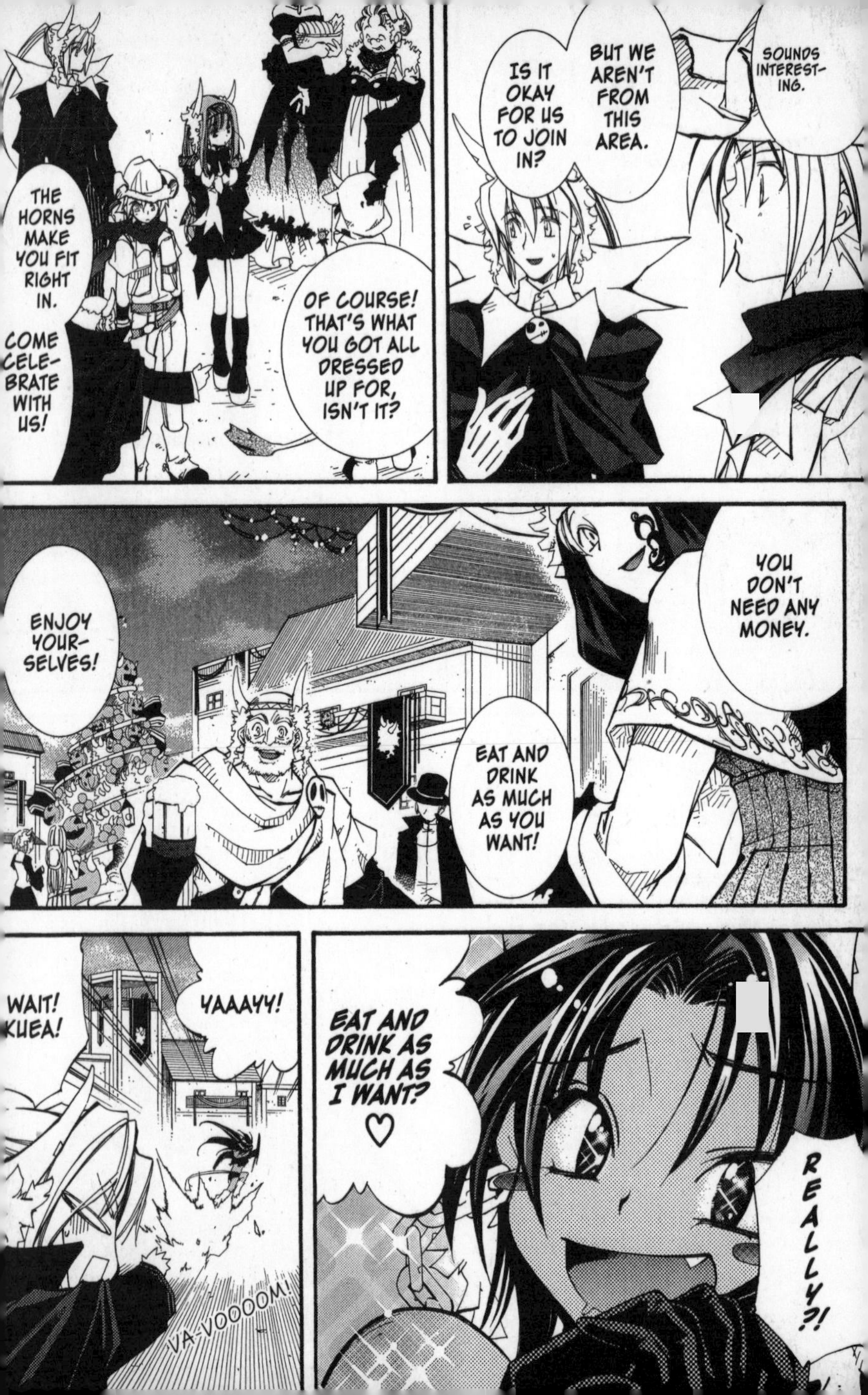
SOUNDS INTERESTING.
BUT WE AREN'T FROM THIS AREA.
IS IT OKAY FOR US TO JOIN IN?
OF COURSE! THAT'S WHAT YOU GOT ALL DRESSED UP FOR, ISN'T IT?
THE HORNS MAKE YOU FIT RIGHT IN.
COME CELEBRATE WITH US!
YOU DON'T NEED ANY MONEY.
EAT AND DRINK AS MUCH AS YOU WANT!
ENJOY YOURSELVES!
REALLY?!
EAT AND DRINK AS MUCH AS I WANT? ♡
YAAAYY!
WAIT! KUEA!
VA-VOOOOM!

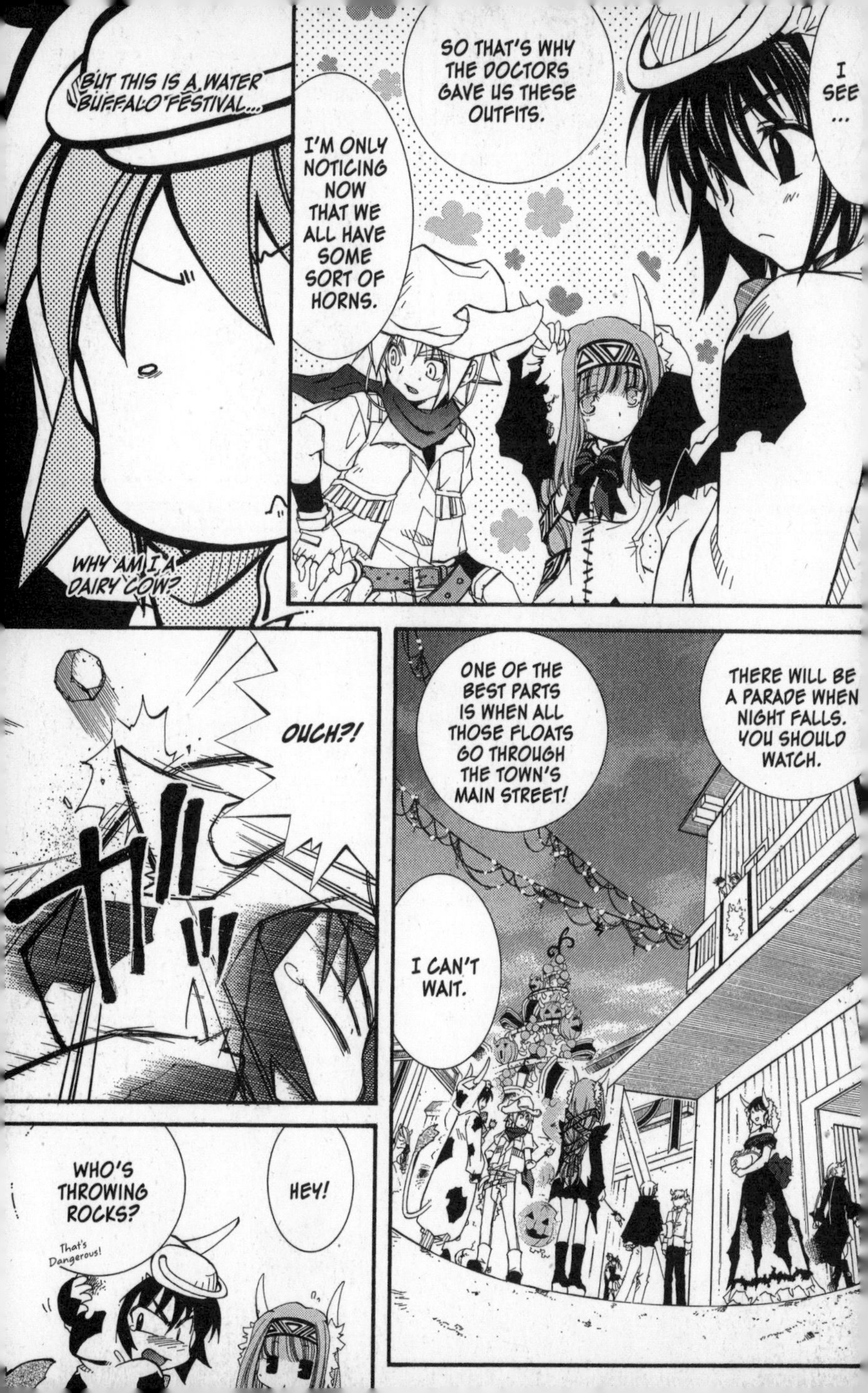
I SEE...
SO THAT'S WHY THE DOCTORS GAVE US THESE OUTFITS.
I'M ONLY NOTICING NOW THAT WE ALL HAVE SOME SORT OF HORNS.
BUT THIS IS A WATER BUFFALO FESTIVAL...
WHY AM I A DAIRY COW?
THERE WILL BE A PARADE WHEN NIGHT FALLS. YOU SHOULD WATCH.
ONE OF THE BEST PARTS IS WHEN ALL THOSE FLOATS GO THROUGH THE TOWN'S MAIN STREET!
I CAN'T WAIT.
OUCH?!
HEY!
WHO'S THROWING ROCKS?
That's Dangerous!

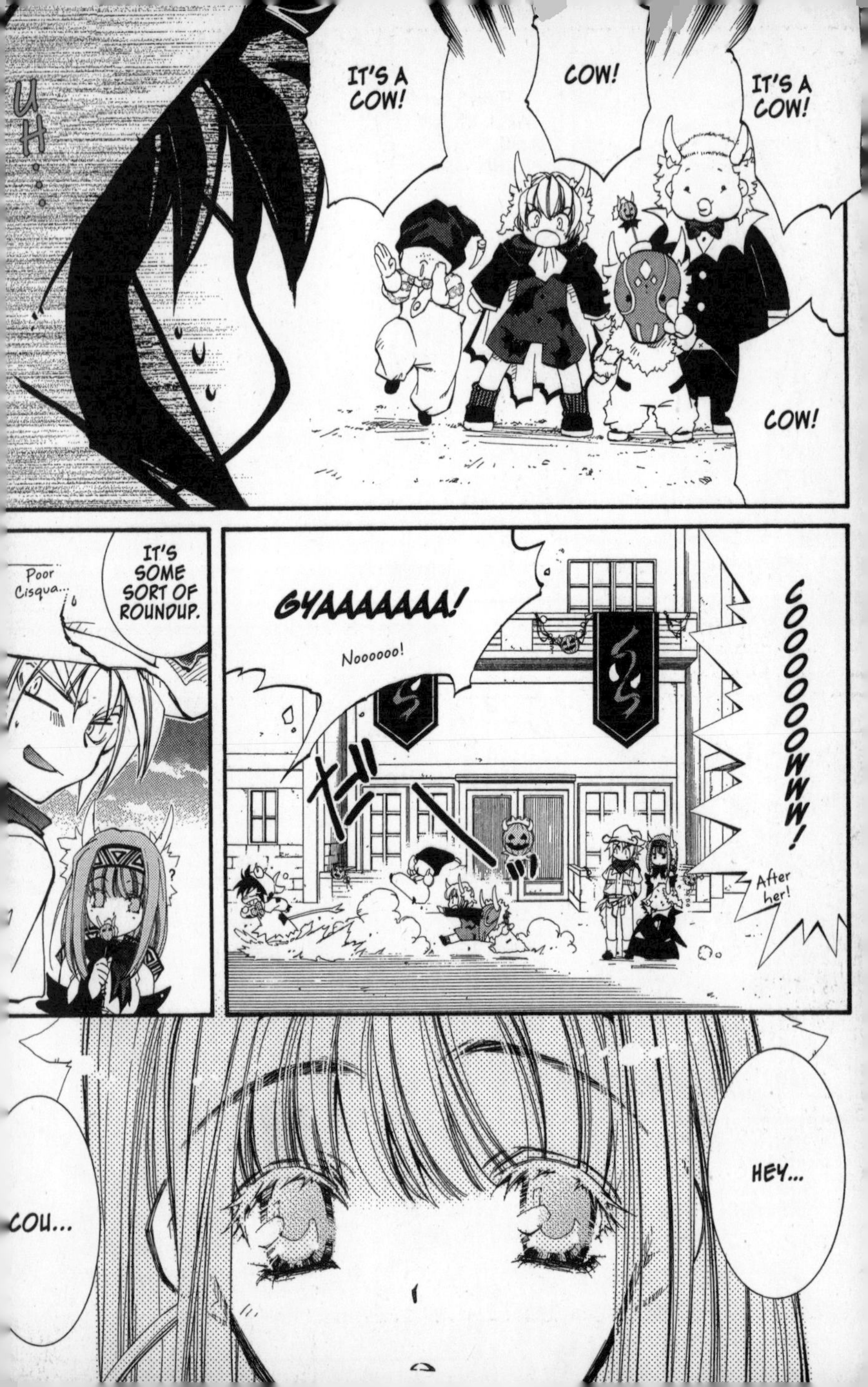
IT'S A COW!
COW!
IT'S A COW!
COW!
UH...
COOOOOOOWWW!
After her!
GYAAAAAAA!
Noooooo!
IT'S SOME SORT OF ROUNDUP.
Poor Cisqua...
HEY...
COU...

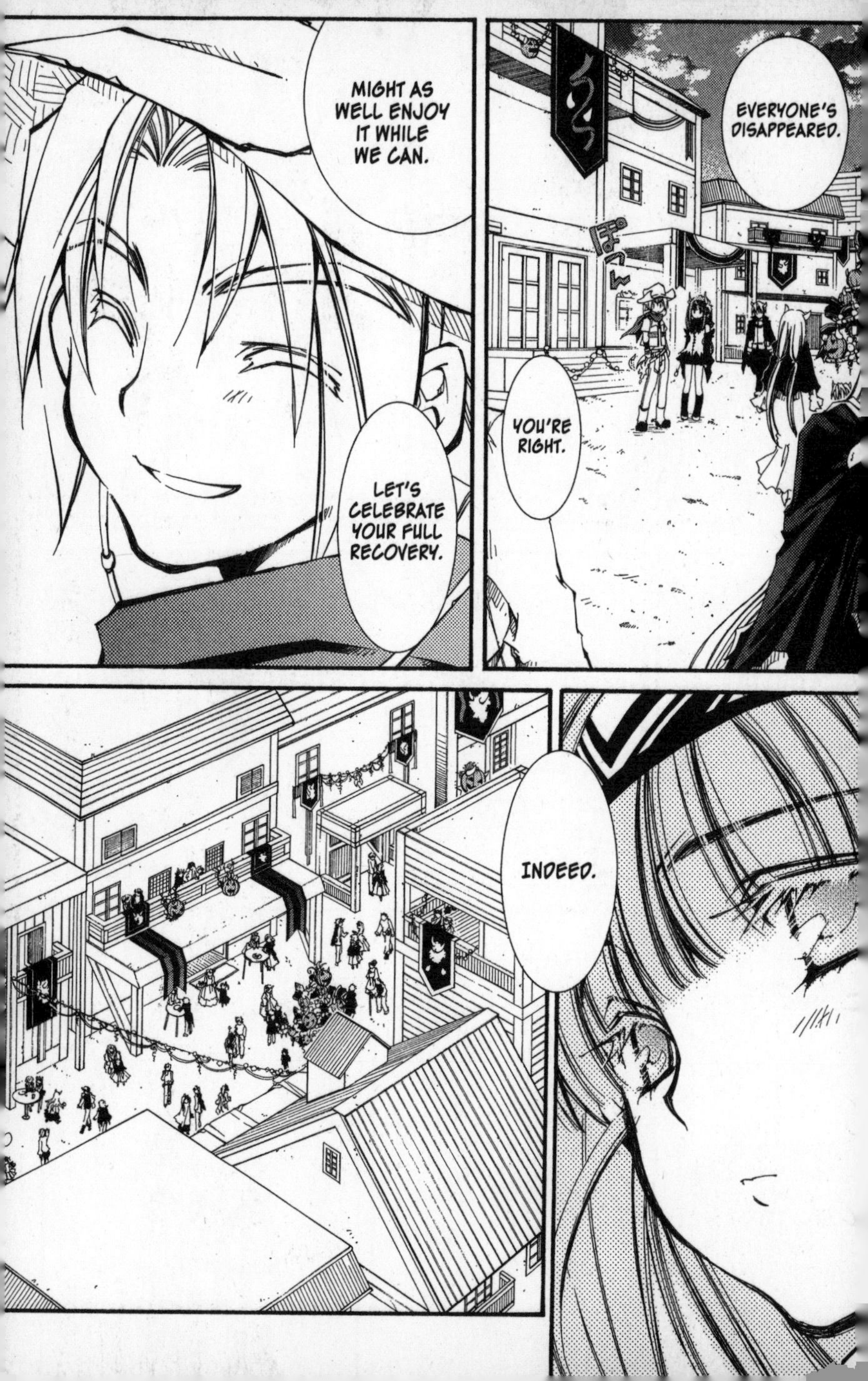
EVERYONE'S DISAPPEARED.
YOU'RE RIGHT.
MIGHT AS WELL ENJOY IT WHILE WE CAN.
LET'S CELEBRATE YOUR FULL RECOVERY.
INDEED.

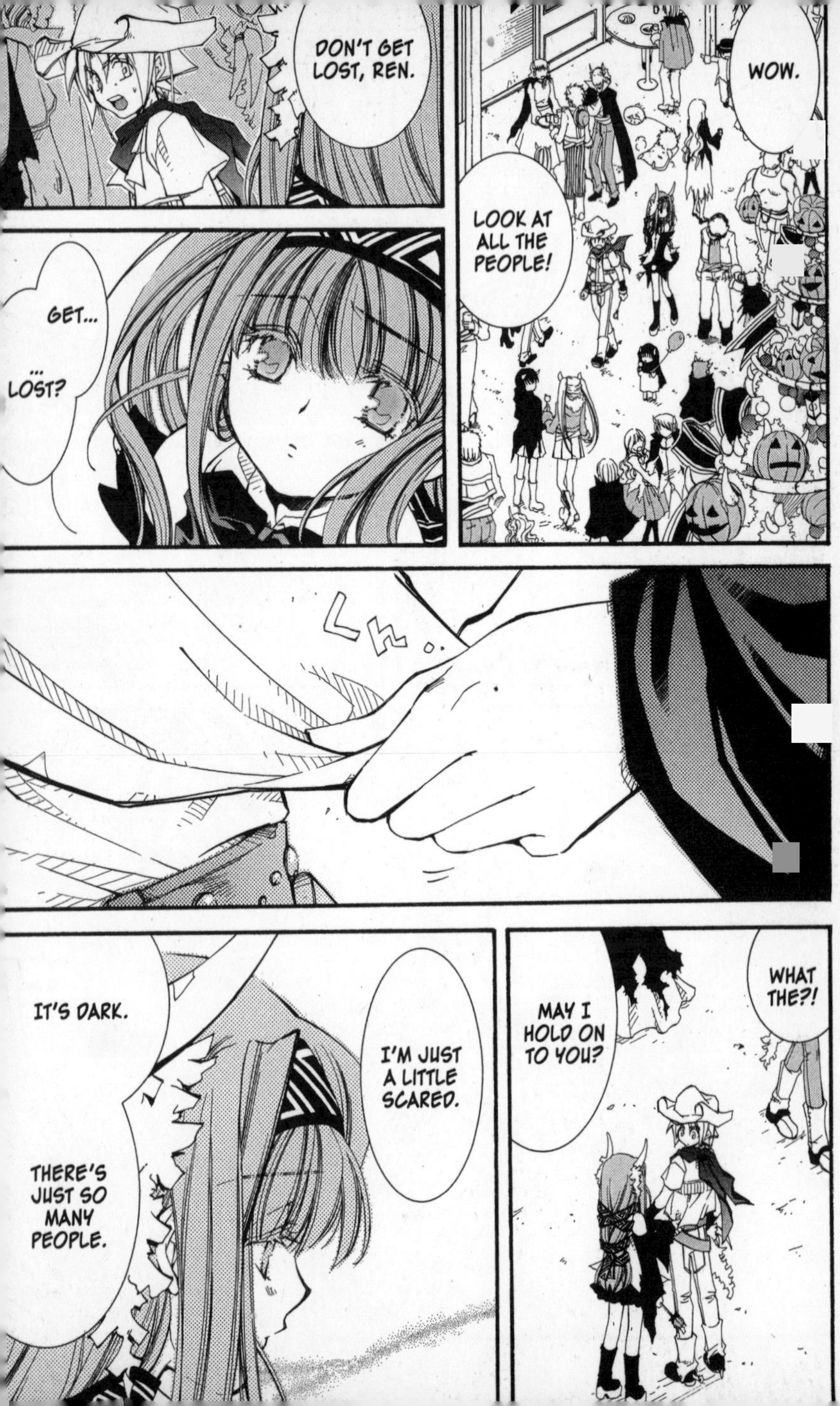
WOW.
LOOK AT ALL THE PEOPLE!
DON'T GET LOST, REN.
GET...
...LOST?
WHAT THE?!
MAY I HOLD ON TO YOU?
I'M JUST A LITTLE SCARED.
IT'S DARK.
THERE'S JUST SO MANY PEOPLE.

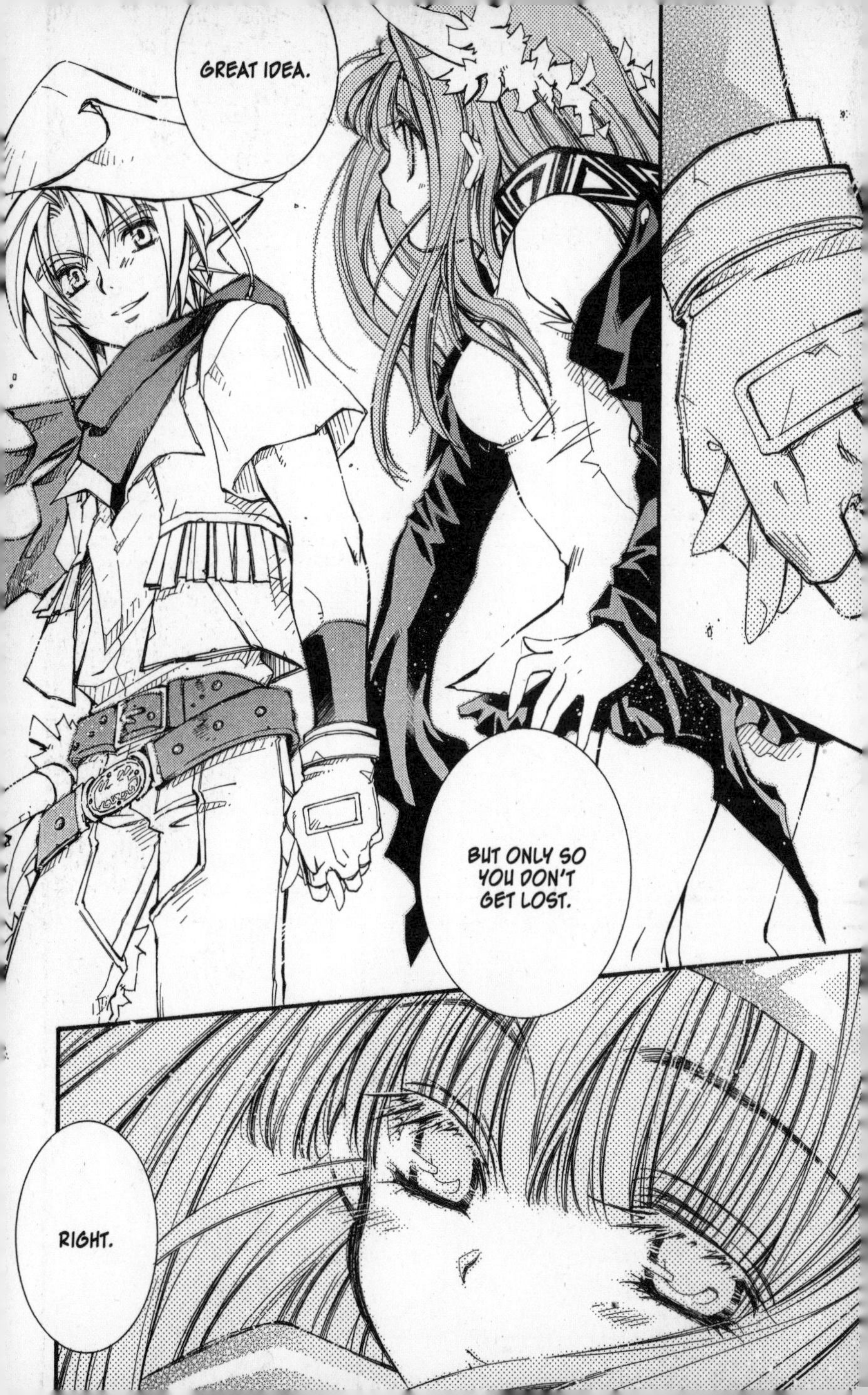
GREAT IDEA.
BUT ONLY SO YOU DON'T GET LOST.
RIGHT.

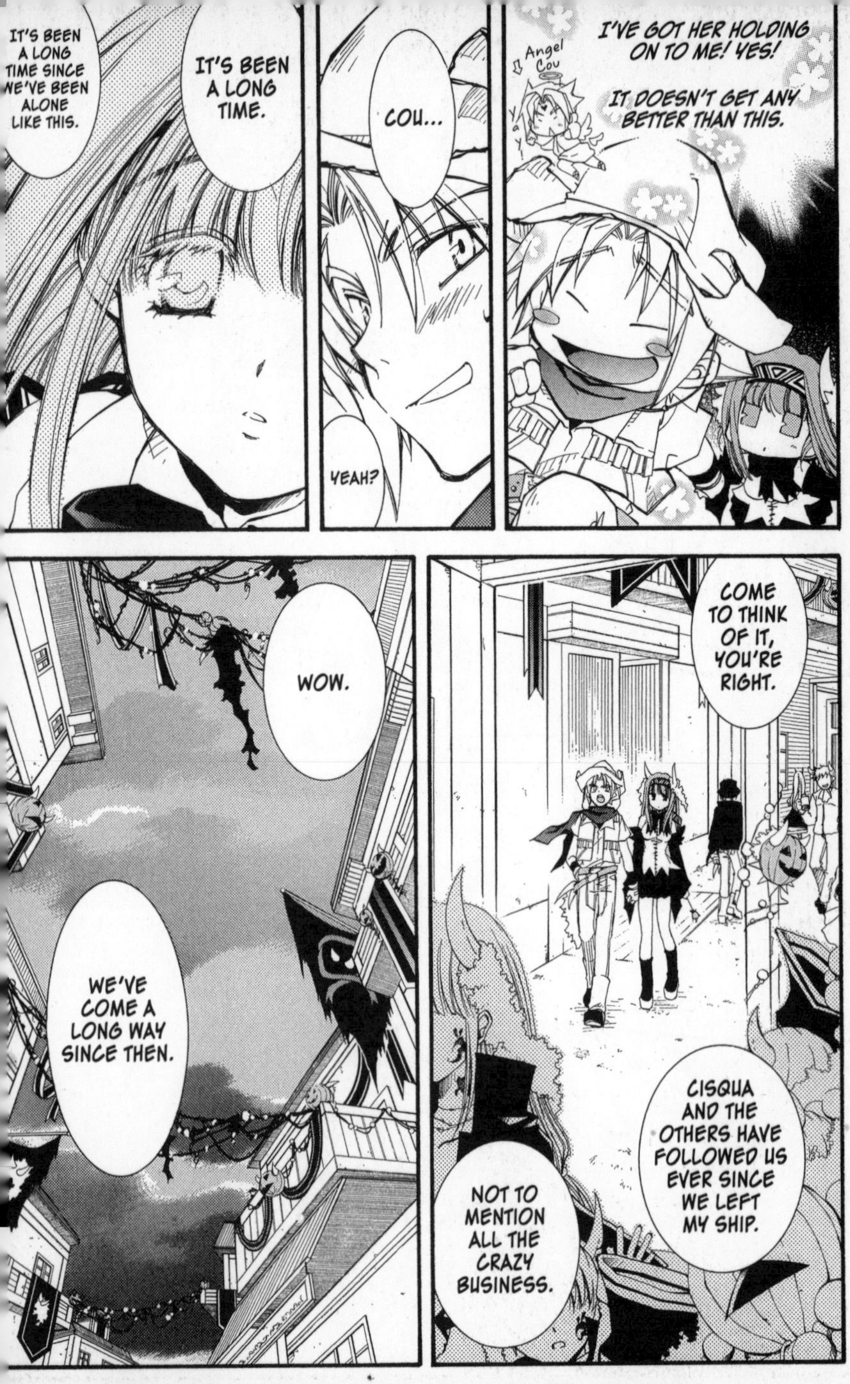
I'VE GOT HER HOLDING ON TO ME! YES!
IT DOESN'T GET ANY BETTER THAN THIS.
Angel Cou
Yay!
COU...
YEAH?
IT'S BEEN A LONG TIME.
IT'S BEEN A LONG TIME SINCE WE'VE BEEN ALONE LIKE THIS.
COME TO THINK OF IT, YOU'RE RIGHT.
CISQUA AND THE OTHERS HAVE FOLLOWED US EVER SINCE WE LEFT MY SHIP.
NOT TO MENTION ALL THE CRAZY BUSINESS.
WOW.
WE'VE COME A LONG WAY SINCE THEN.

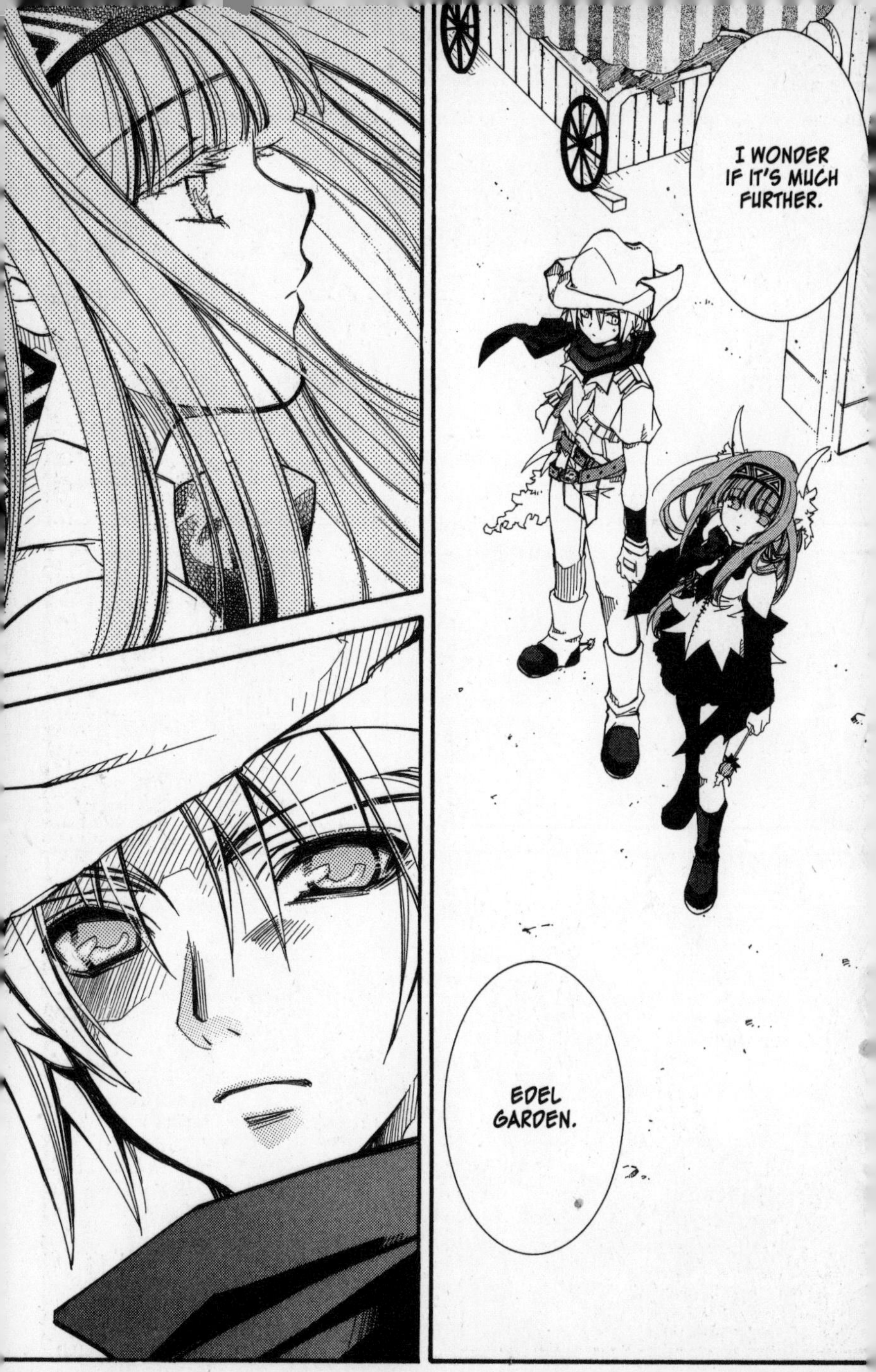
I WONDER IF IT'S MUCH FURTHER.
EDEL GARDEN.

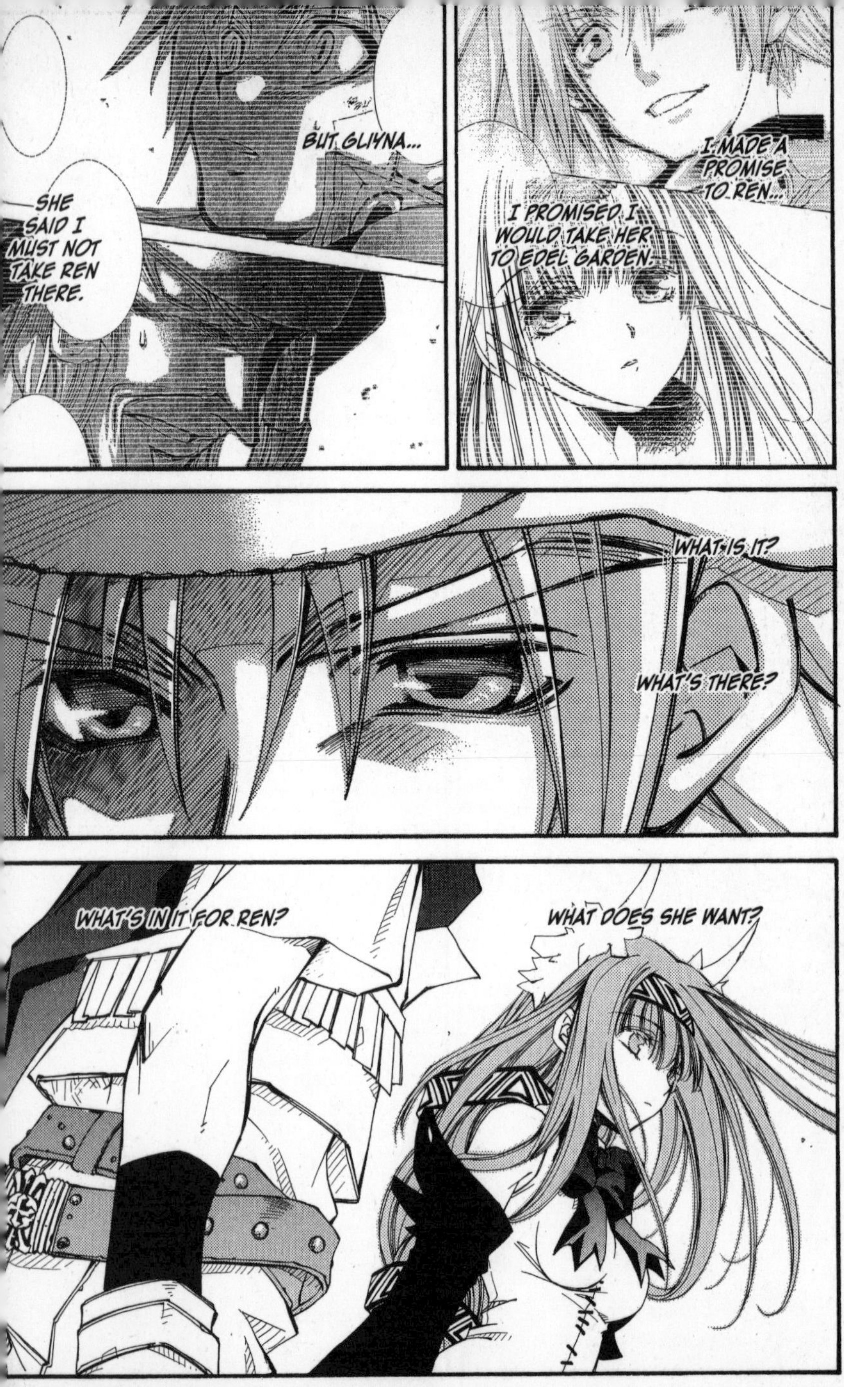
I MADE A PROMISE TO REN...
I PROMISED I WOULD TAKE HER TO EDEL GARDEN.
BUT GLIYNA...
SHE SAID I MUST NOT TAKE REN THERE.
WHAT IS IT?
WHAT'S THERE?
WHAT DOES SHE WANT?
WHAT'S IN IT FOR REN?

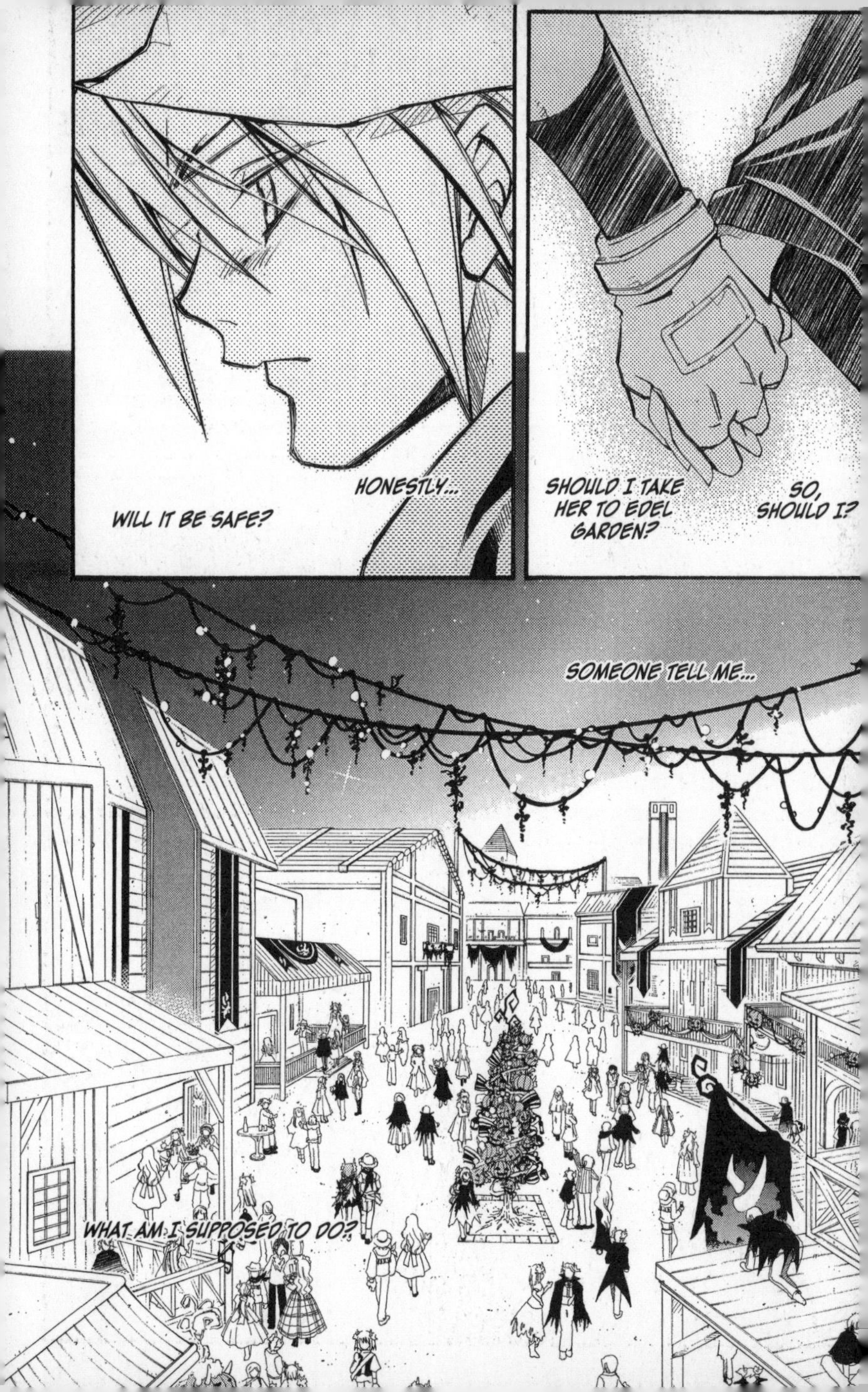
SO, SHOULD I?
SHOULD I TAKE HER TO EDEL GARDEN?
HONESTLY...
WILL IT BE SAFE?
SOMEONE TELL ME...
WHAT AM I SUPPOSED TO DO?

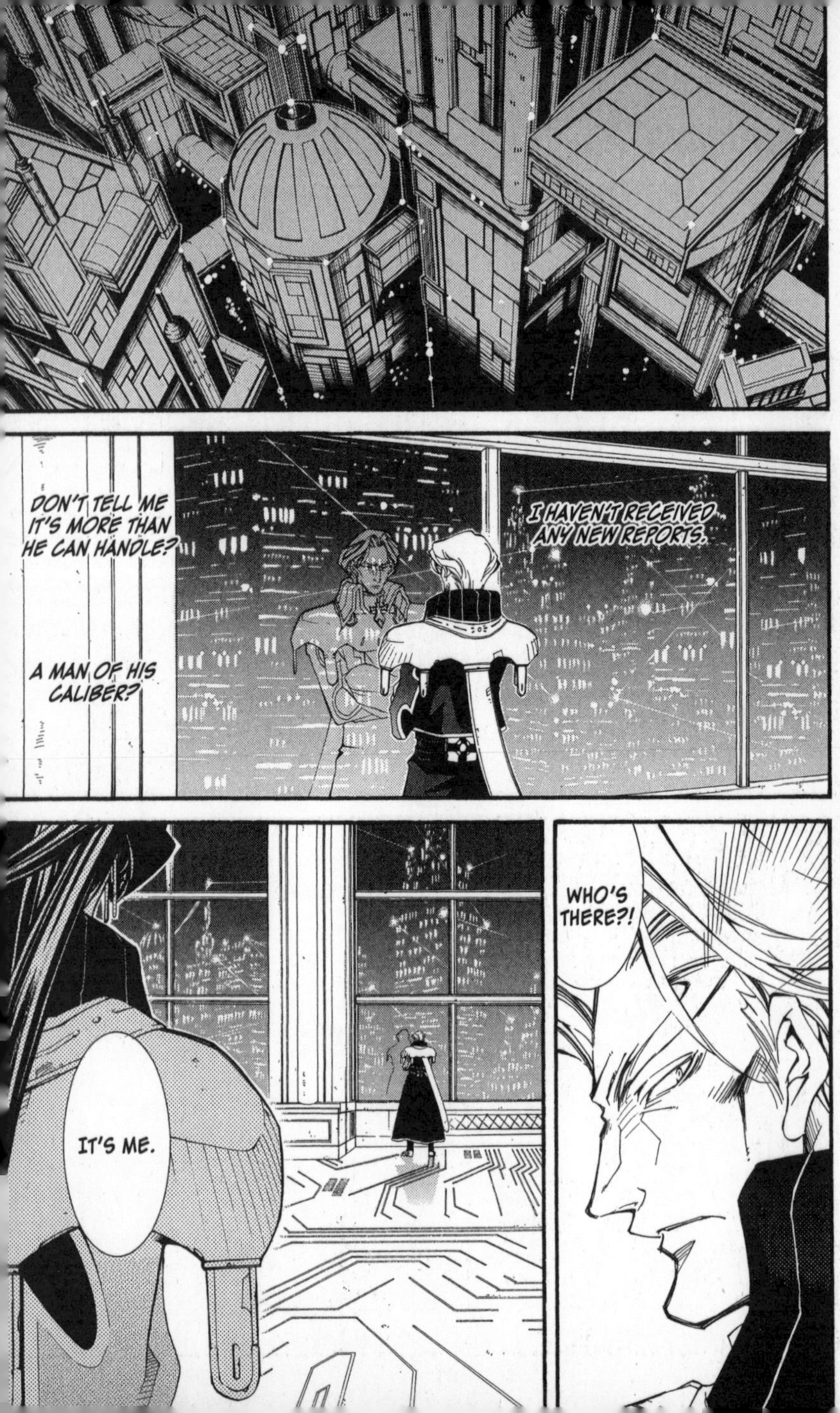
I HAVEN'T RECEIVED ANY NEW REPORTS.
DON'T TELL ME IT'S MORE THAN HE CAN HANDLE?
A MAN OF HIS CALIBER?
WHO'S THERE?!
IT'S ME.

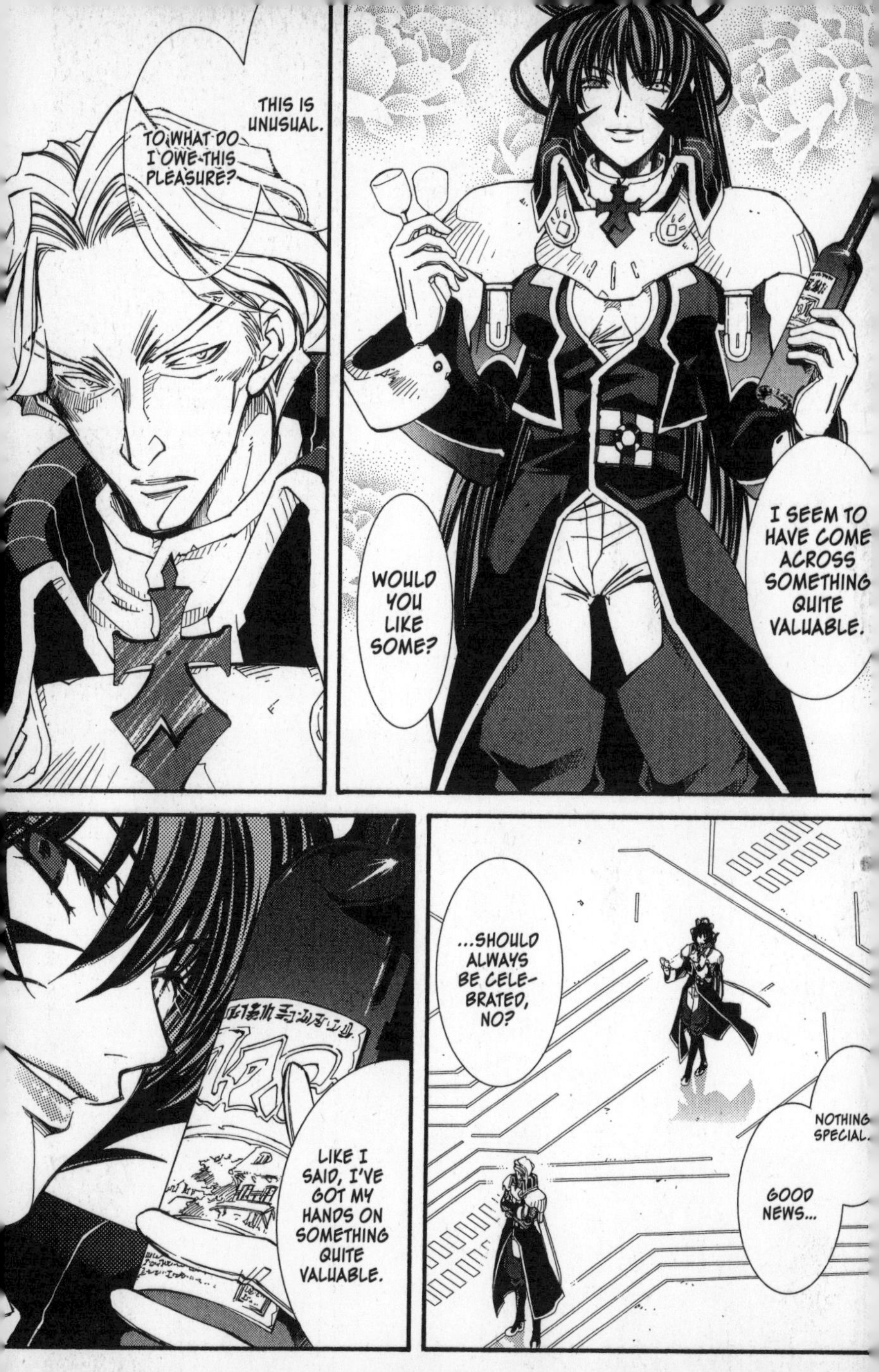
I SEEM TO HAVE COME ACROSS SOMETHING QUITE VALUABLE.
WOULD YOU LIKE SOME?
THIS IS UNUSUAL.
TO WHAT DO I OWE THIS PLEASURE?
NOTHING SPECIAL.
GOOD NEWS...
...SHOULD ALWAYS BE CELE-BRATED, NO?
LIKE I SAID, I'VE GOT MY HANDS ON SOMETHING QUITE VALUABLE.

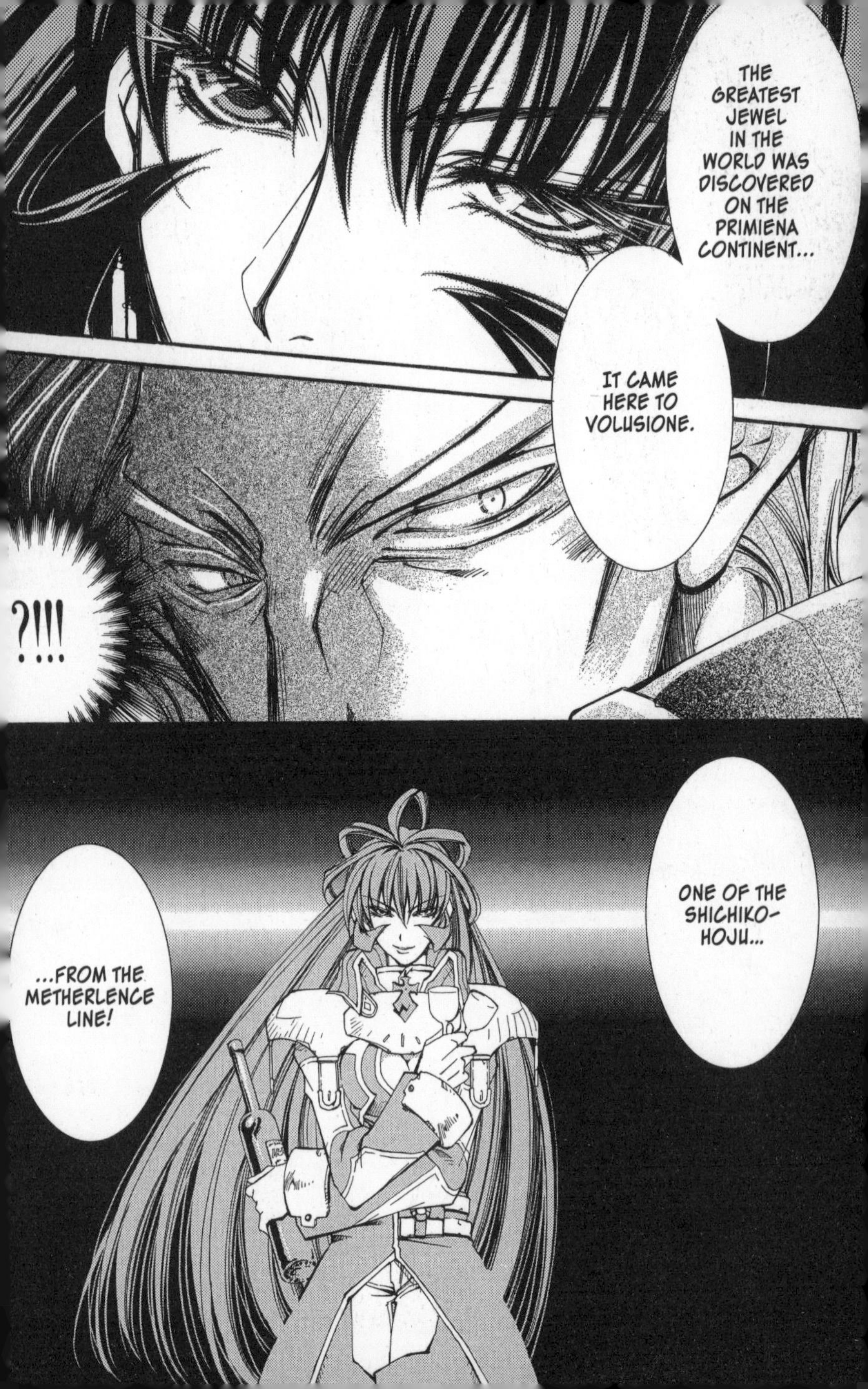
THE GREATEST JEWEL IN THE WORLD WAS DISCOVERED ON THE PRIMIENA CONTINENT...
IT CAME HERE TO VOLUSIONE.
?!!!
ONE OF THE SHICHIKO-HOJU...
...FROM THE METHERLENCE LINE!

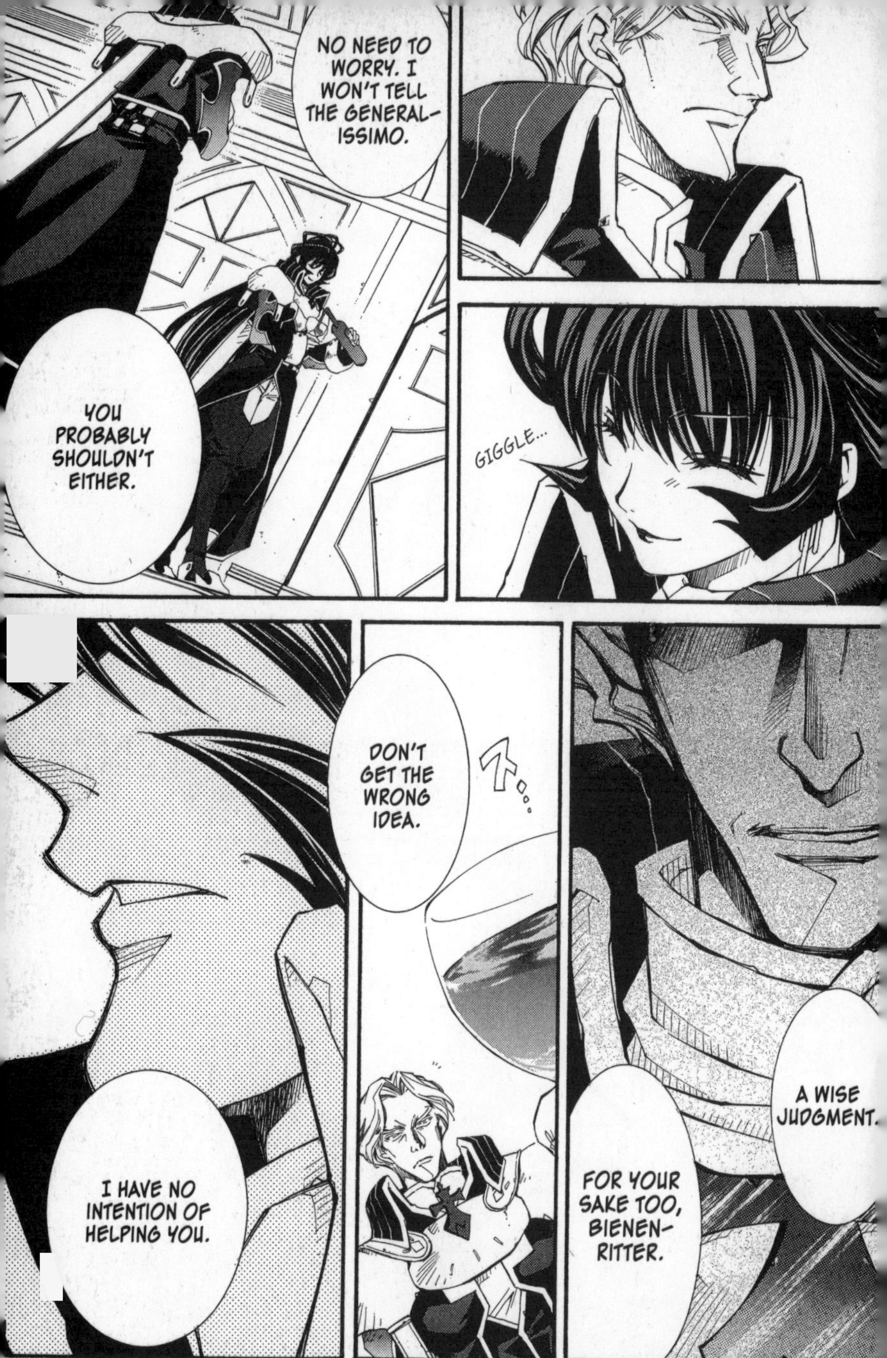
GIGGLE...
NO NEED TO WORRY. I WON'T TELL THE GENERAL-ISSIMO.
YOU PROBABLY SHOULDN'T EITHER.
A WISE JUDGMENT.
FOR YOUR SAKE TOO, BIENEN-RITTER.
DON'T GET THE WRONG IDEA.
I HAVE NO INTENTION OF HELPING YOU.

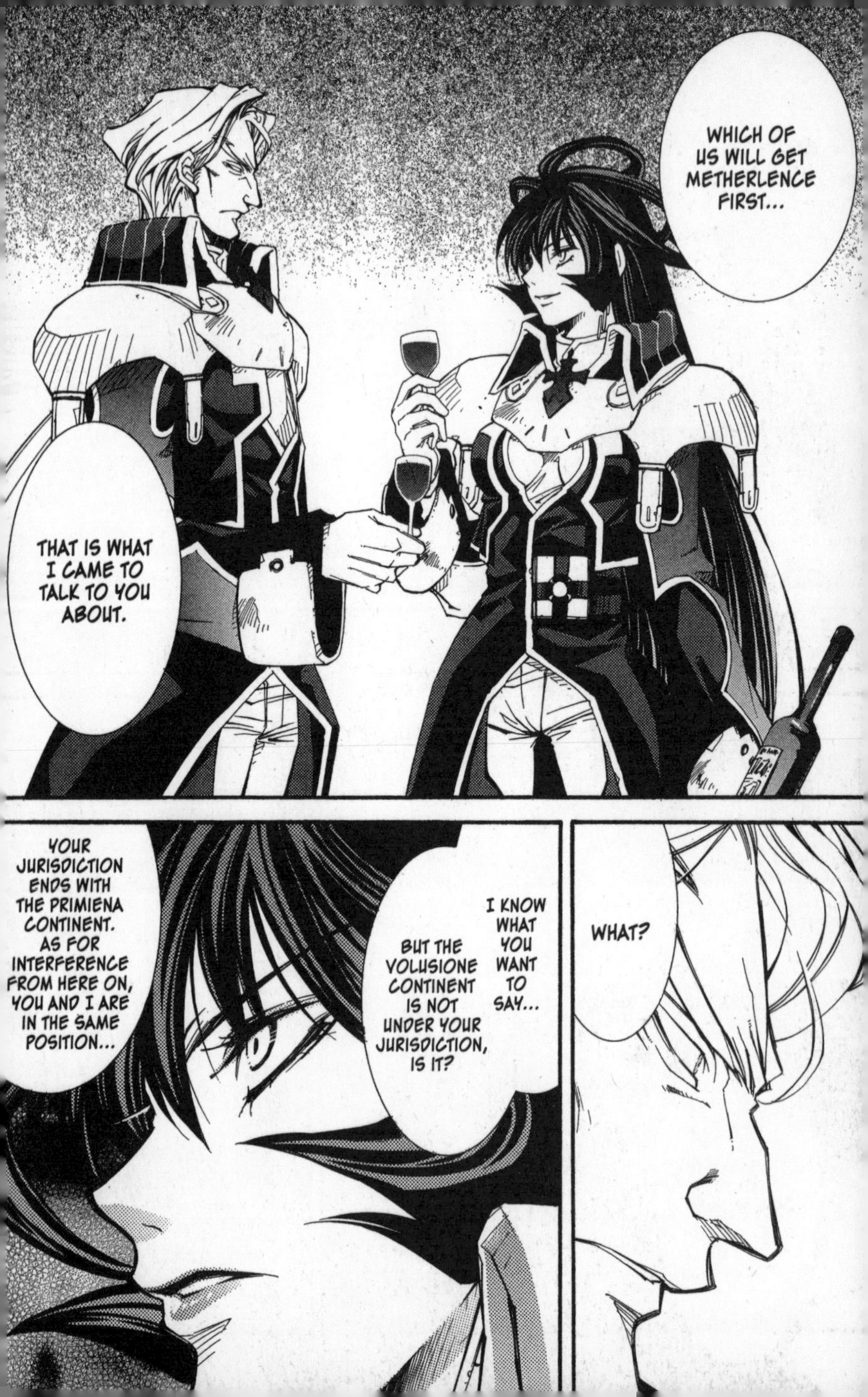
WHICH OF US WILL GET METHERLENCE FIRST...
THAT IS WHAT I CAME TO TALK TO YOU ABOUT.
WHAT?
I KNOW WHAT YOU WANT TO SAY...
BUT THE VOLUSIONE CONTINENT IS NOT UNDER YOUR JURISDICTION, IS IT?
YOUR JURISDICTION ENDS WITH THE PRIMIENA CONTINENT. AS FOR INTERFERENCE FROM HERE ON, YOU AND I ARE IN THE SAME POSITION...

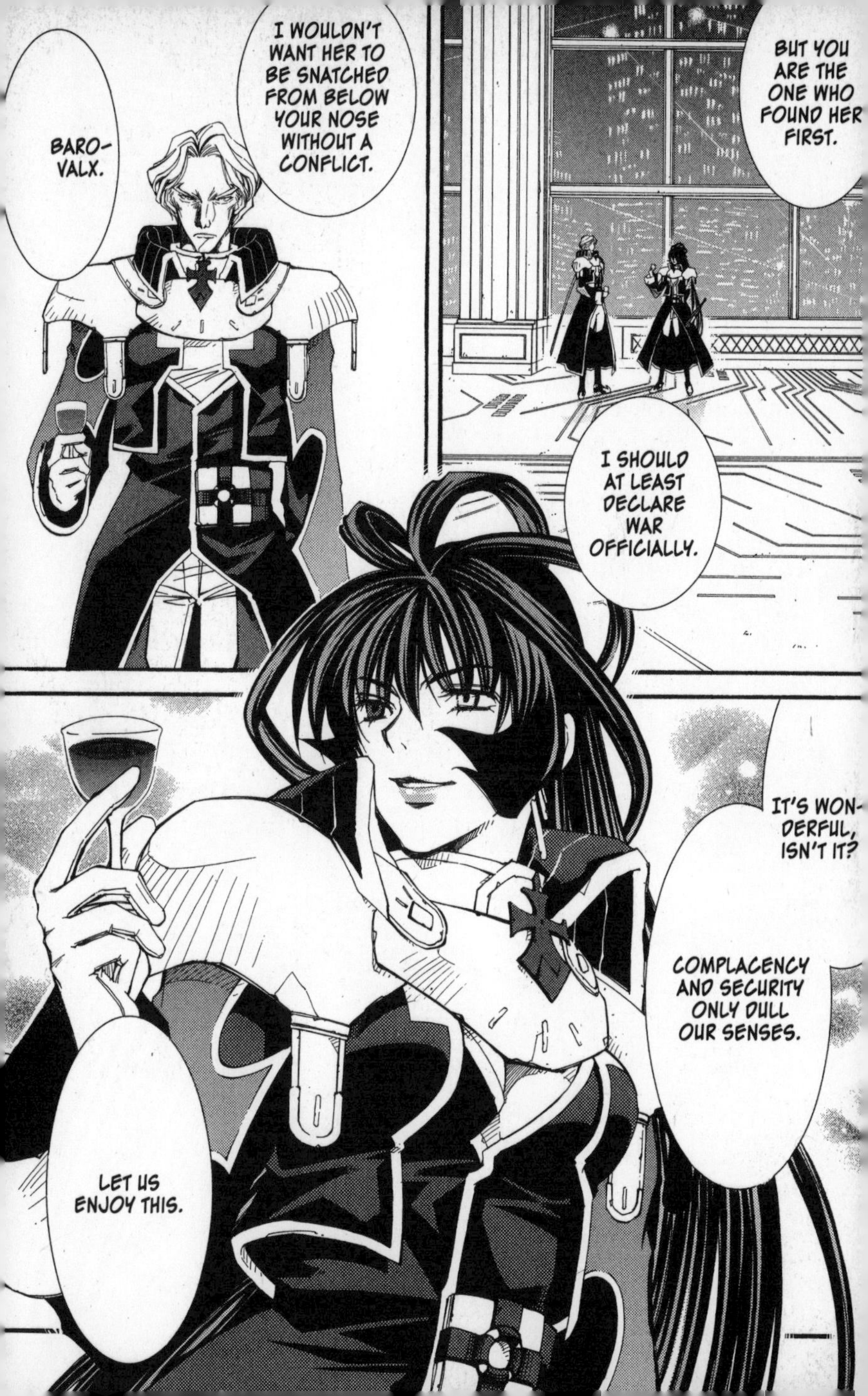
BUT YOU ARE THE ONE WHO FOUND HER FIRST.
I SHOULD AT LEAST DECLARE WAR OFFICIALLY.
I WOULDN'T WANT HER TO BE SNATCHED FROM BELOW YOUR NOSE WITHOUT A CONFLICT.
BARO-VALX.
IT'S WON-DERFUL, ISN'T IT?
COMPLACENCY AND SECURITY ONLY DULL OUR SENSES.
LET US ENJOY THIS.

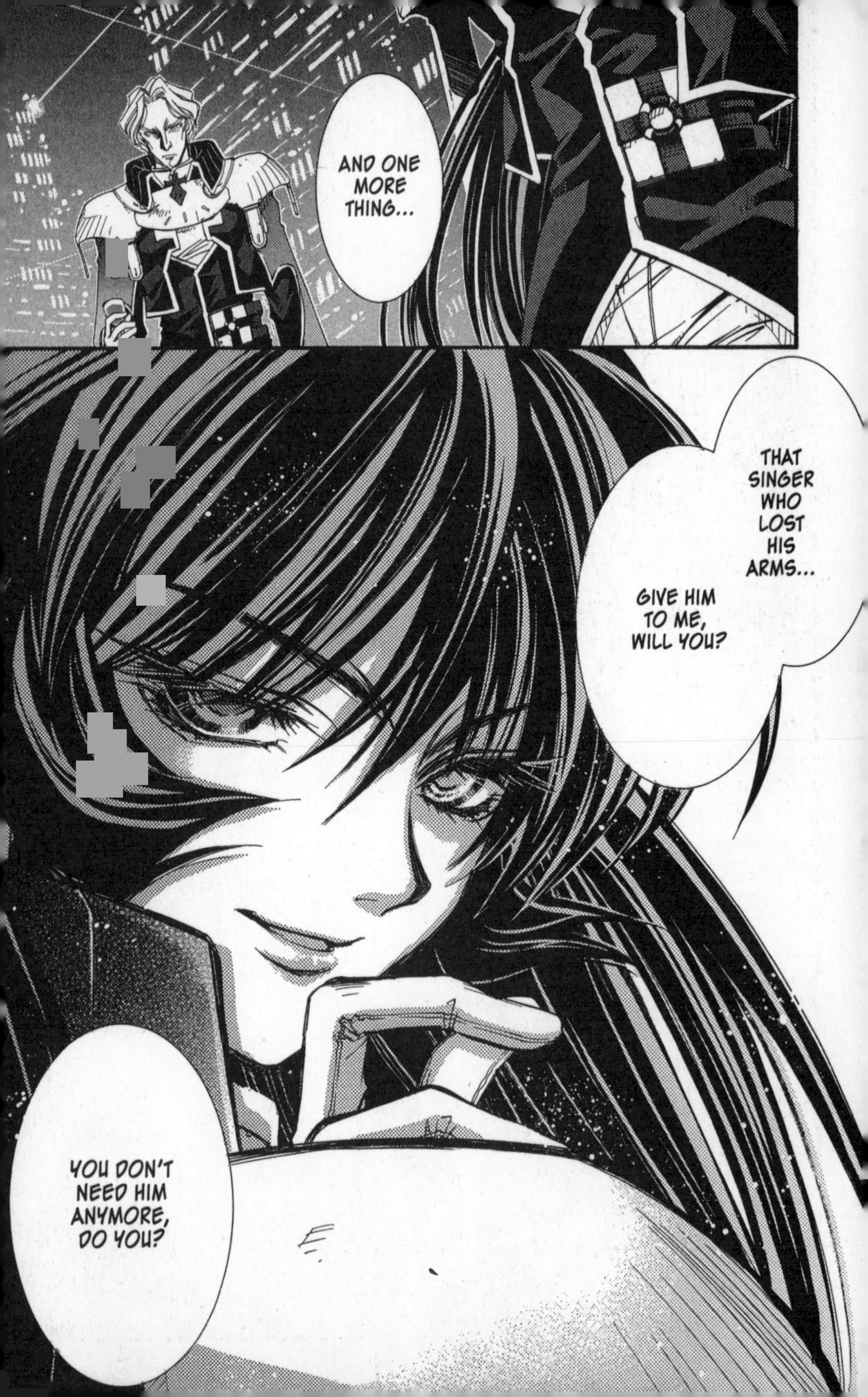
AND ONE MORE THING...
THAT SINGER WHO LOST HIS ARMS...
GIVE HIM TO ME, WILL YOU?
YOU DON'T NEED HIM ANYMORE, DO YOU?

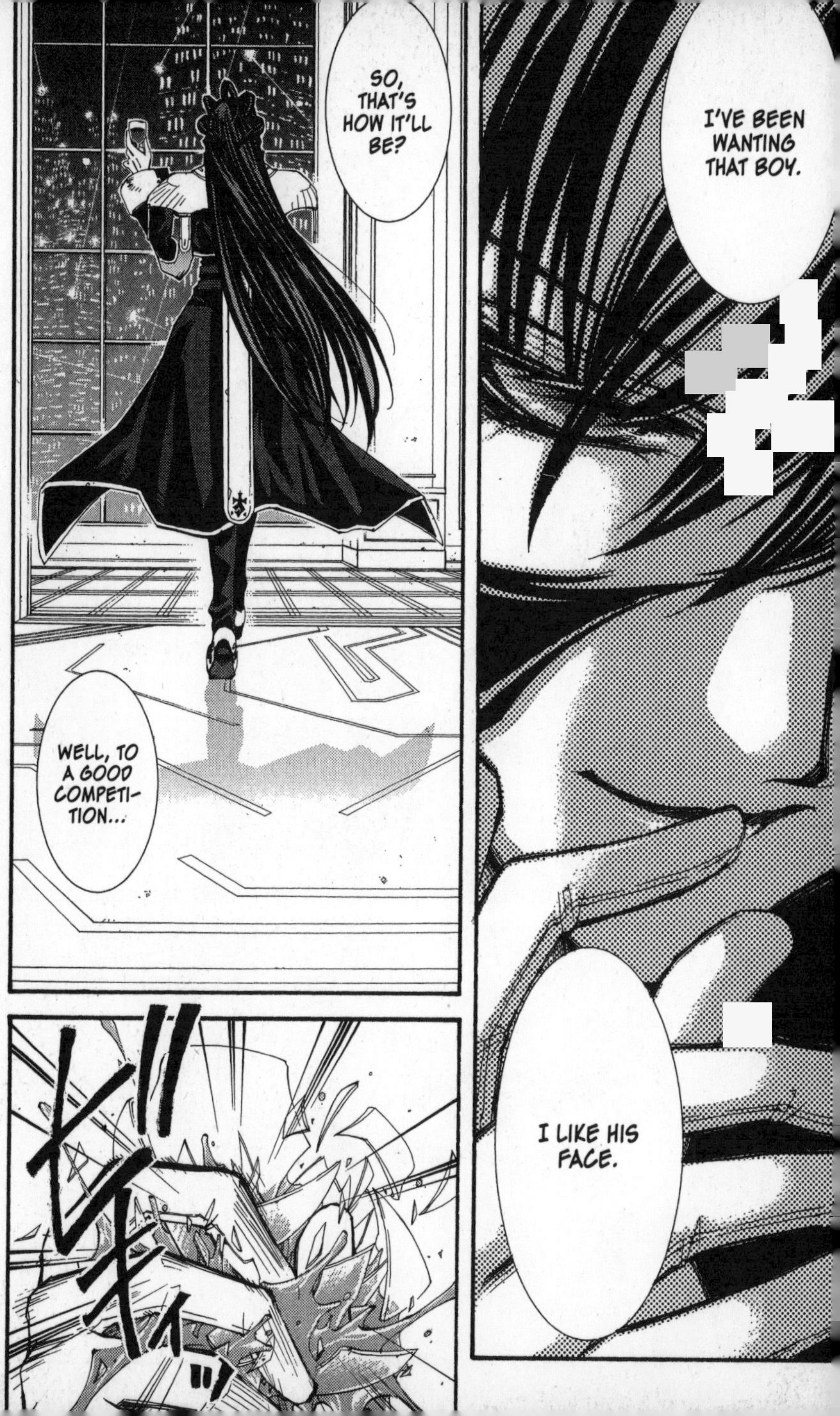
I'VE BEEN WANTING THAT BOY.
I LIKE HIS FACE.
SO, THAT'S HOW IT'LL BE?
WELL, TO A GOOD COMPETITION...

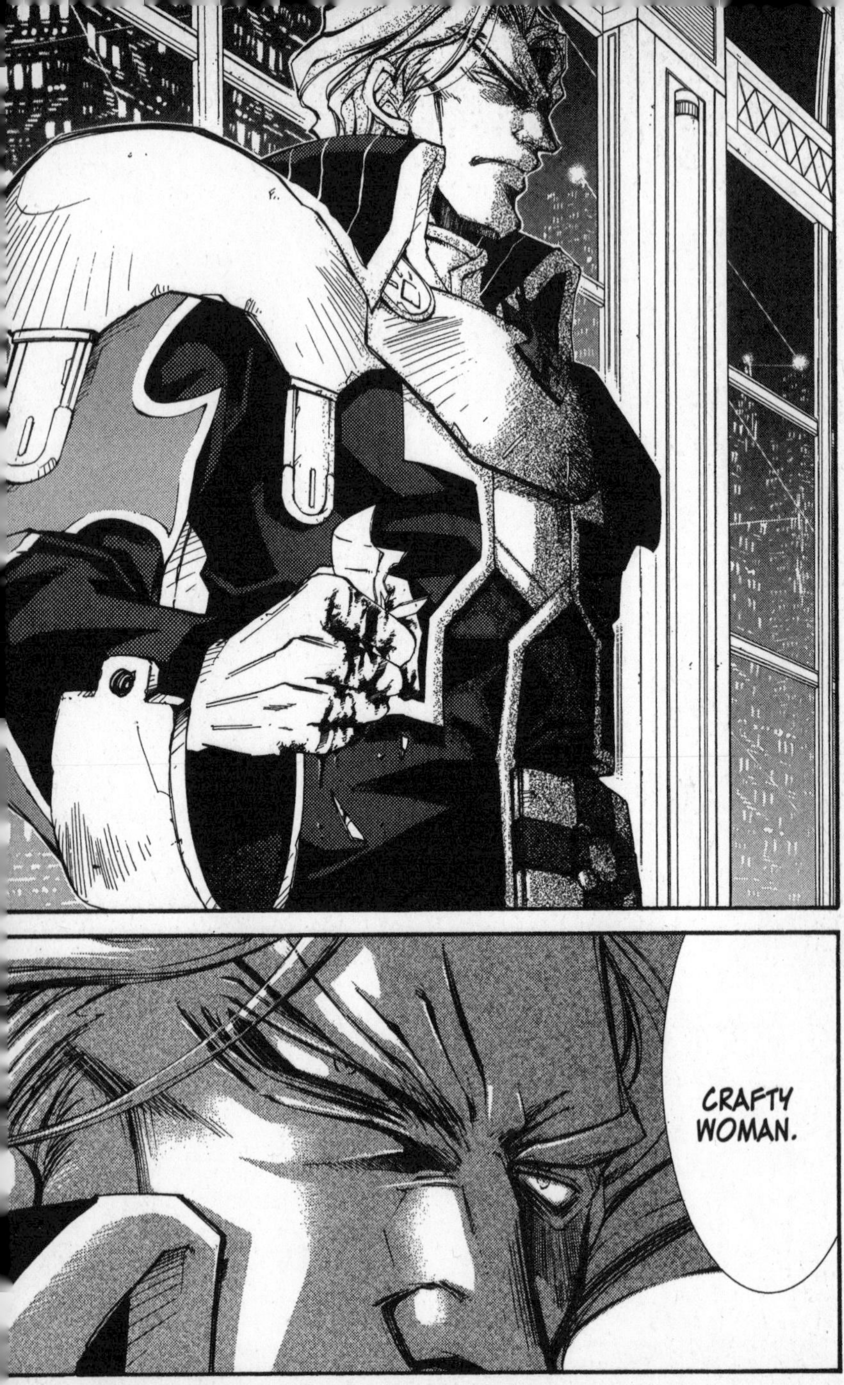
CRAFTY WOMAN.

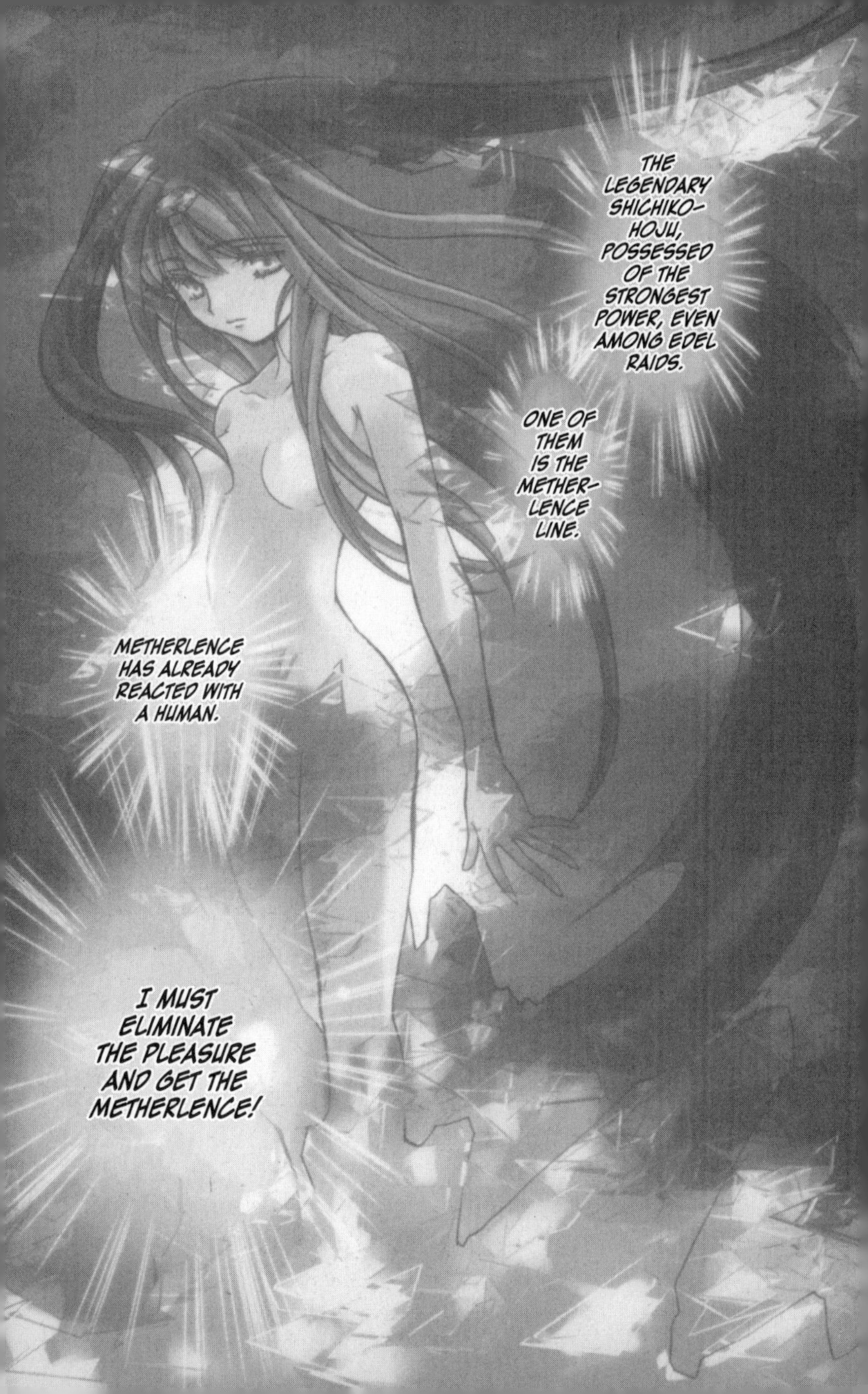
THE LEGENDARY SHICHIKO-HOJU, POSSESSED OF THE STRONGEST POWER, EVEN AMONG EDEL RAIDS.
ONE OF THEM IS THE METHER-LENCE LINE.
METHERLENCE HAS ALREADY REACTED WITH A HUMAN.
I MUST ELIMINATE THE PLEASURE AND GET THE METHERLENCE!

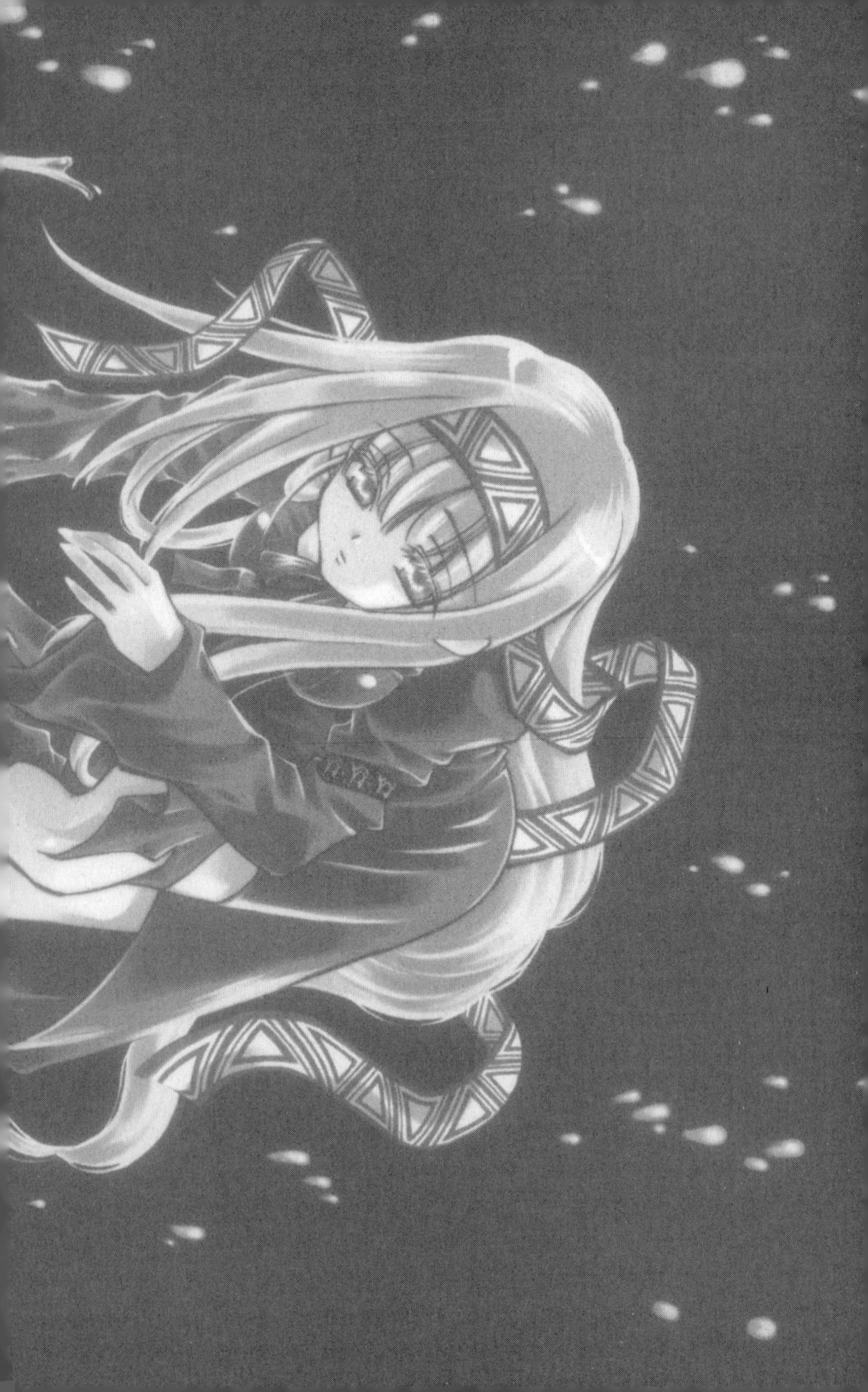

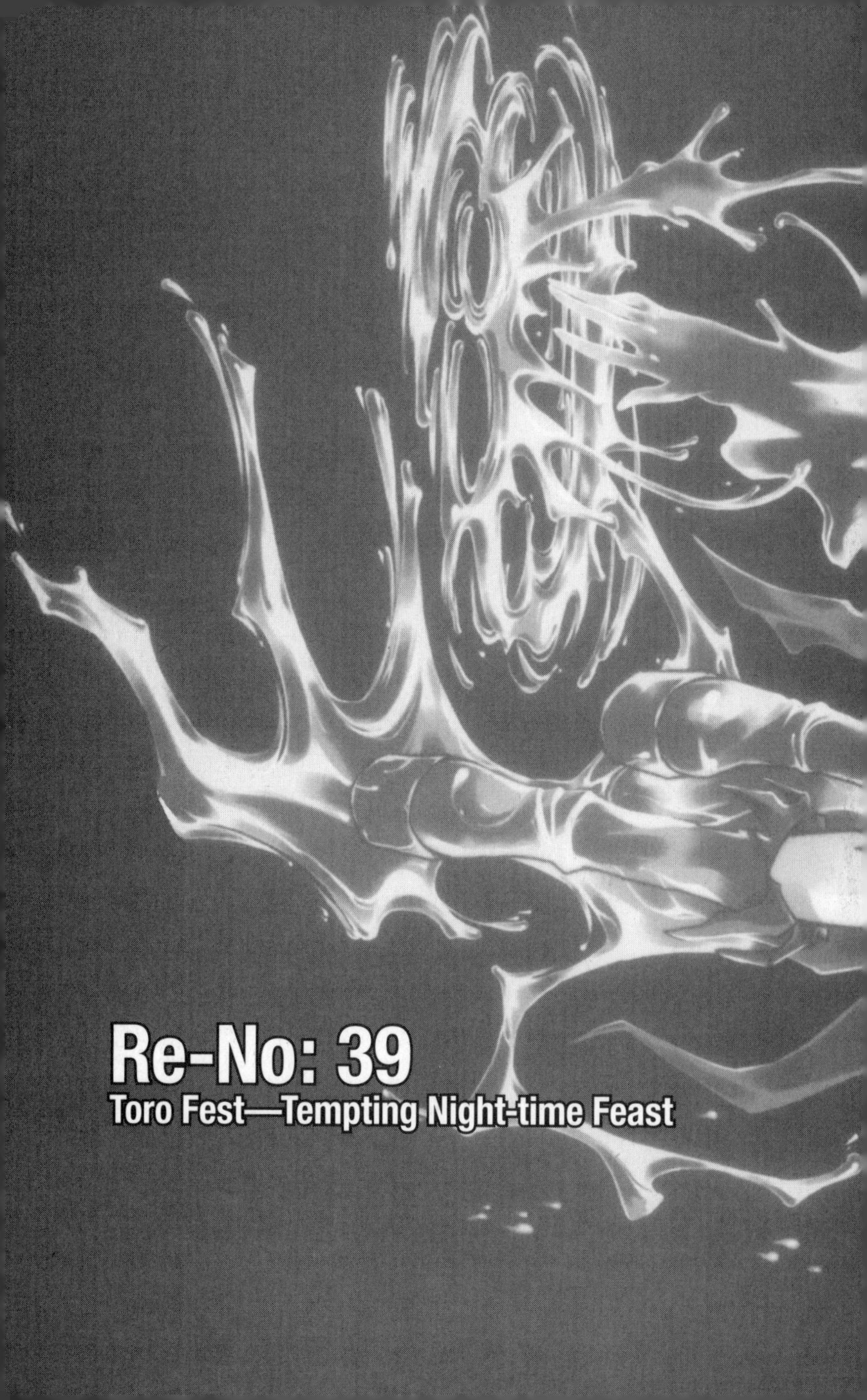

Re-No: 39

Toro Fest—Tempting Night-time Feast

ELEMENTAL GELADE

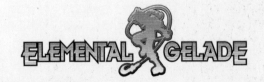

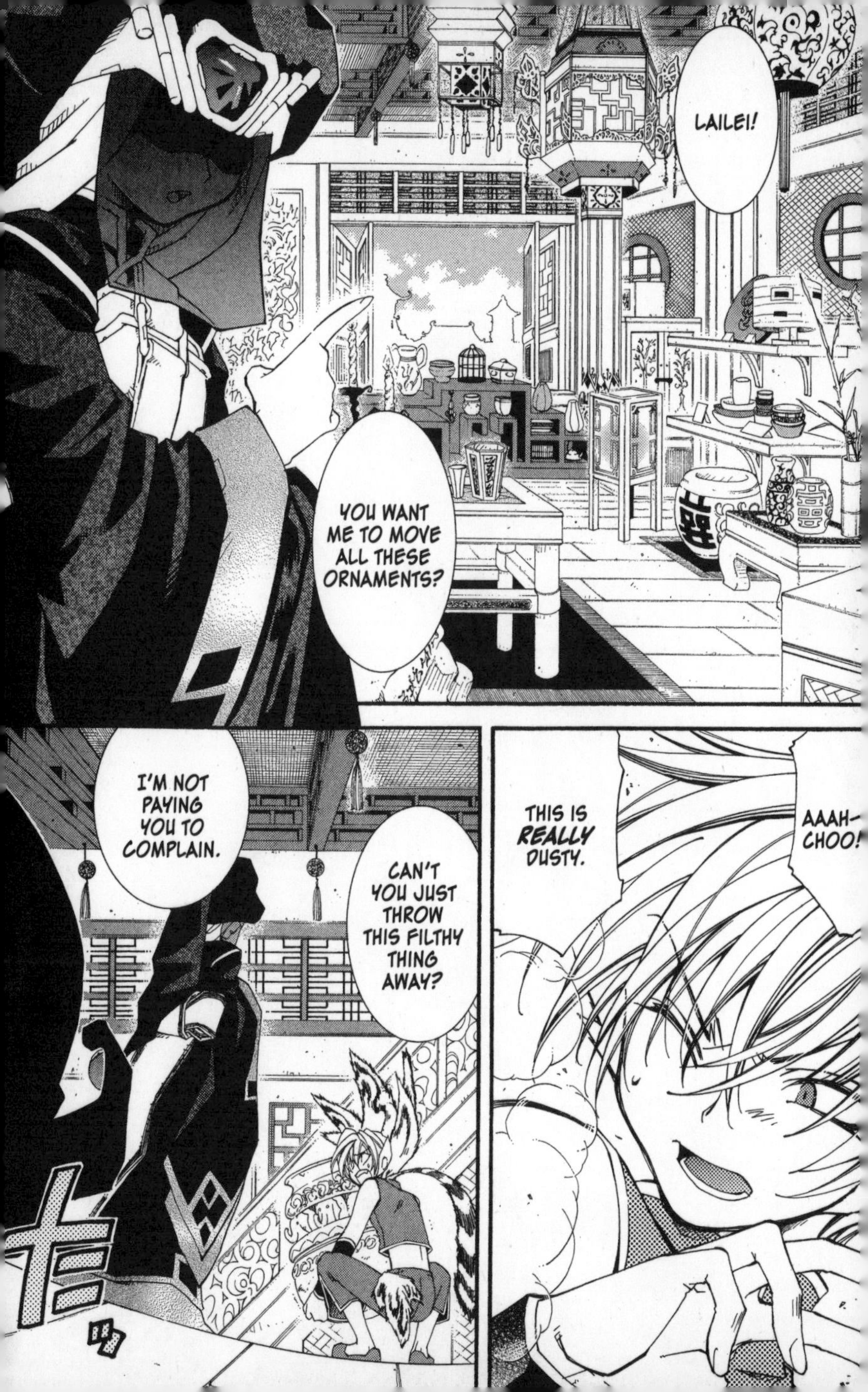
LAILEI!
YOU WANT ME TO MOVE ALL THESE ORNAMENTS?
AAAH-CHOO!
THIS IS *REALLY* DUSTY.
CAN'T YOU JUST THROW THIS FILTHY THING AWAY?
I'M NOT PAYING YOU TO COMPLAIN.

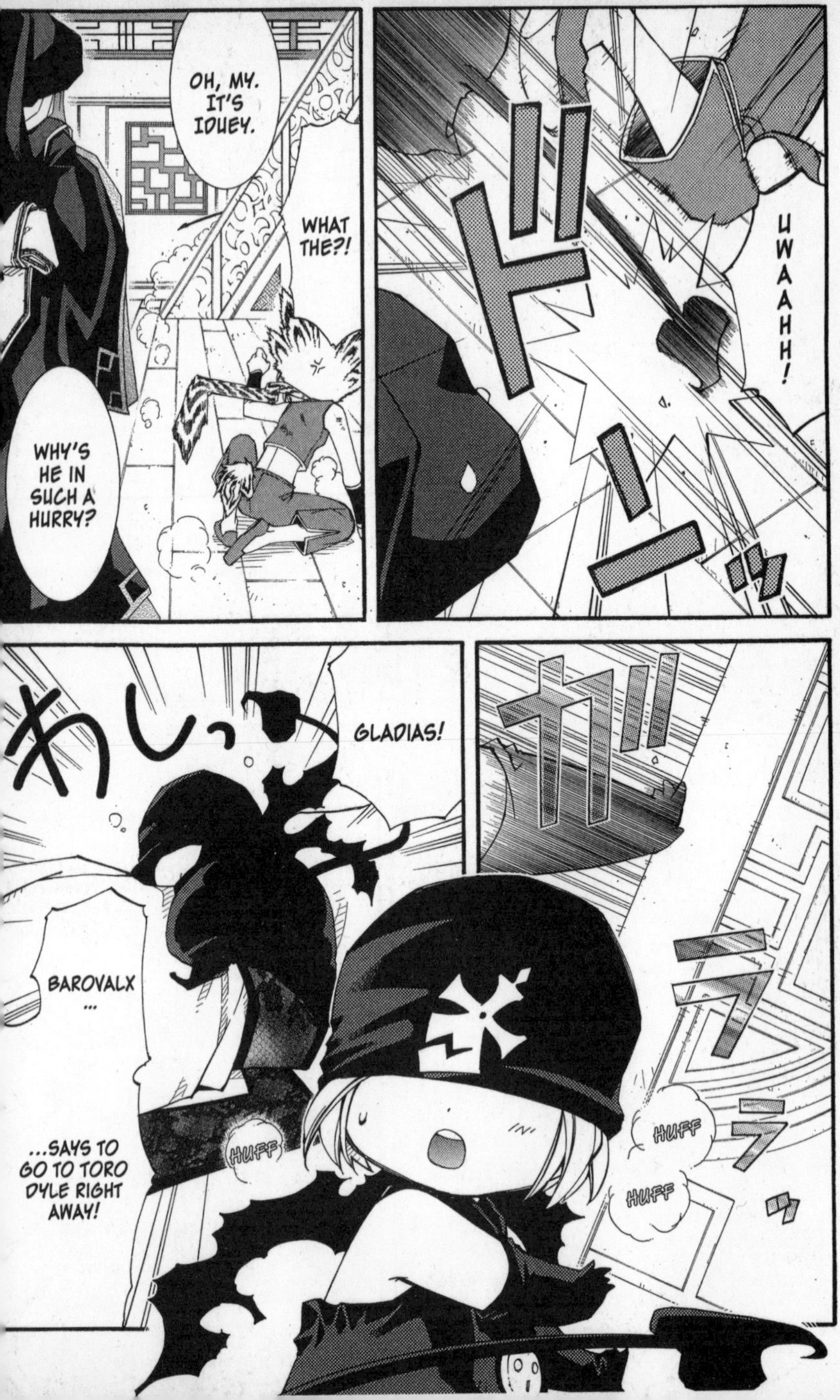
UWAAHH!
OH, MY. IT'S IDUEY.
WHAT THE?!
WHY'S HE IN SUCH A HURRY?
GLADIAS!
HUFF
HUFF
BAROVALX ...
...SAYS TO GO TO TORO DYLE RIGHT AWAY!
HUFF

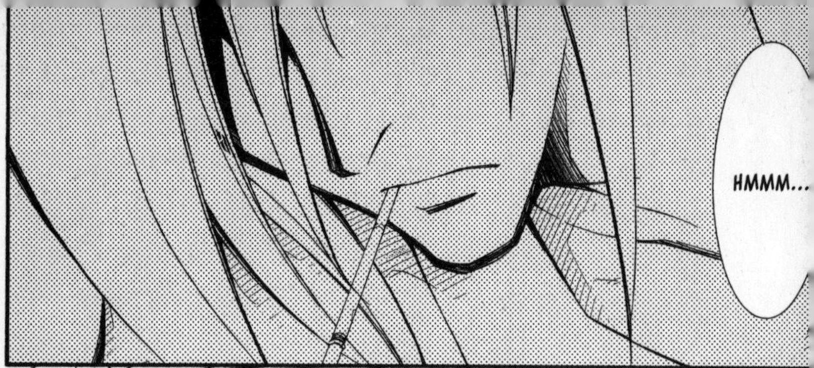
HMMM...
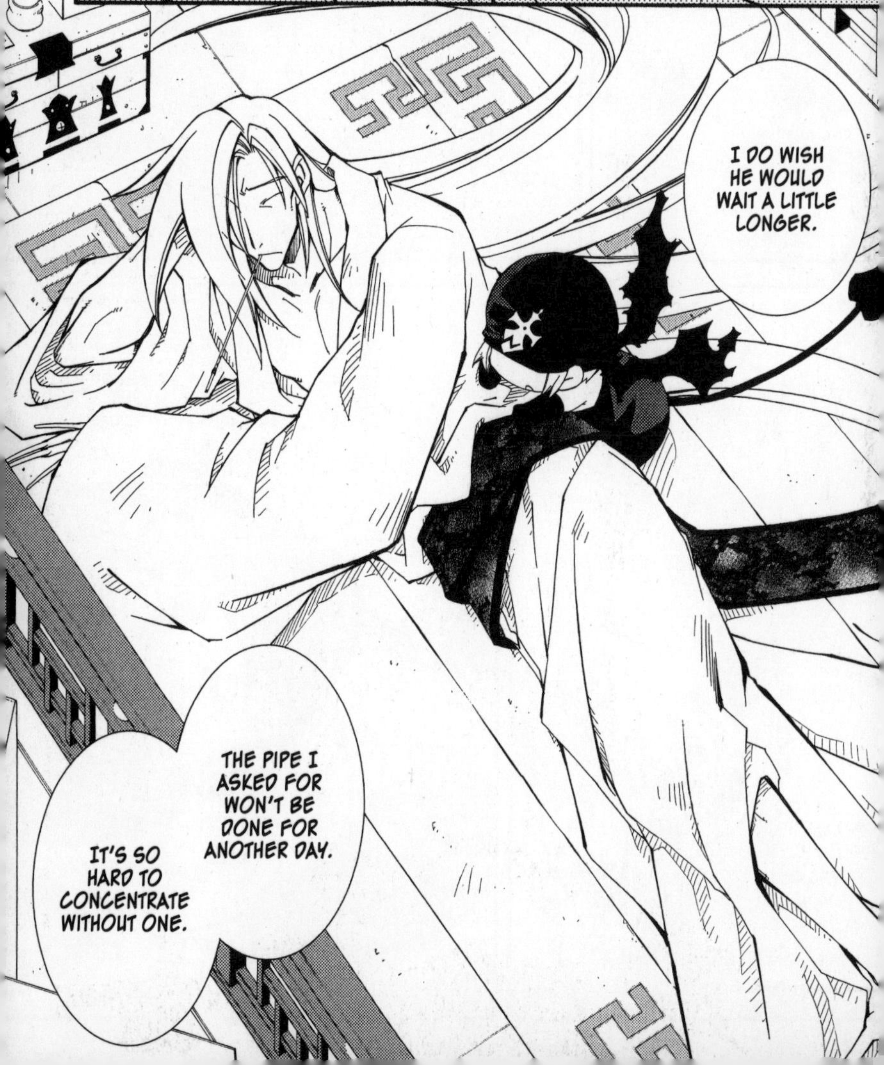
I DO WISH HE WOULD WAIT A LITTLE LONGER.
THE PIPE I ASKED FOR WON'T BE DONE FOR ANOTHER DAY.
IT'S SO HARD TO CONCENTRATE WITHOUT ONE.

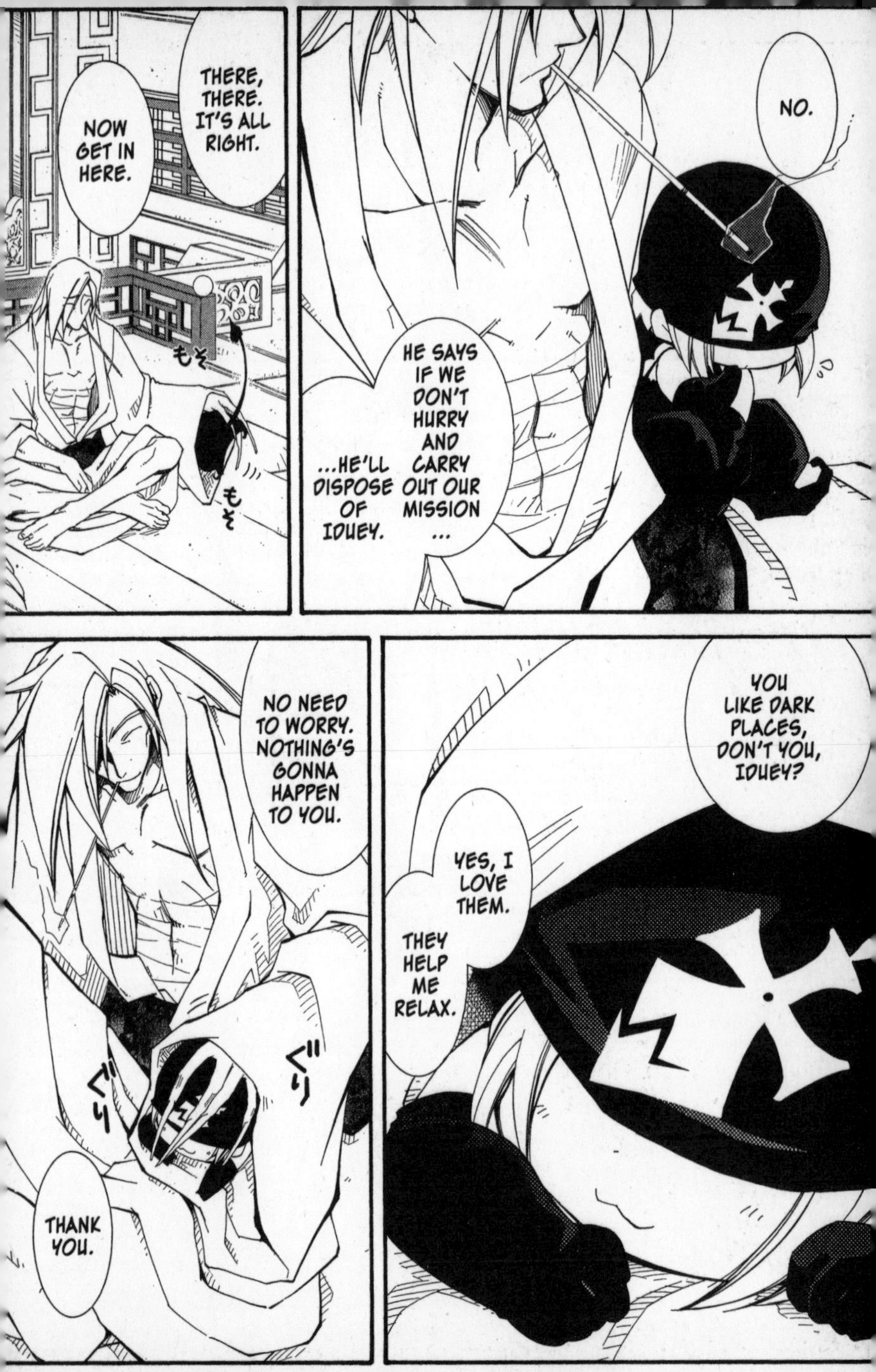
NO.
HE SAYS IF WE DON'T HURRY AND CARRY OUT OUR MISSION ...
...HE'LL DISPOSE OF IDUEY.
THERE, THERE. IT'S ALL RIGHT.
NOW GET IN HERE.
もそ
もそ
YOU LIKE DARK PLACES, DON'T YOU, IDUEY?
YES, I LOVE THEM.
THEY HELP ME RELAX.
NO NEED TO WORRY. NOTHING'S GONNA HAPPEN TO YOU.
ぐり
ぐり
THANK YOU.

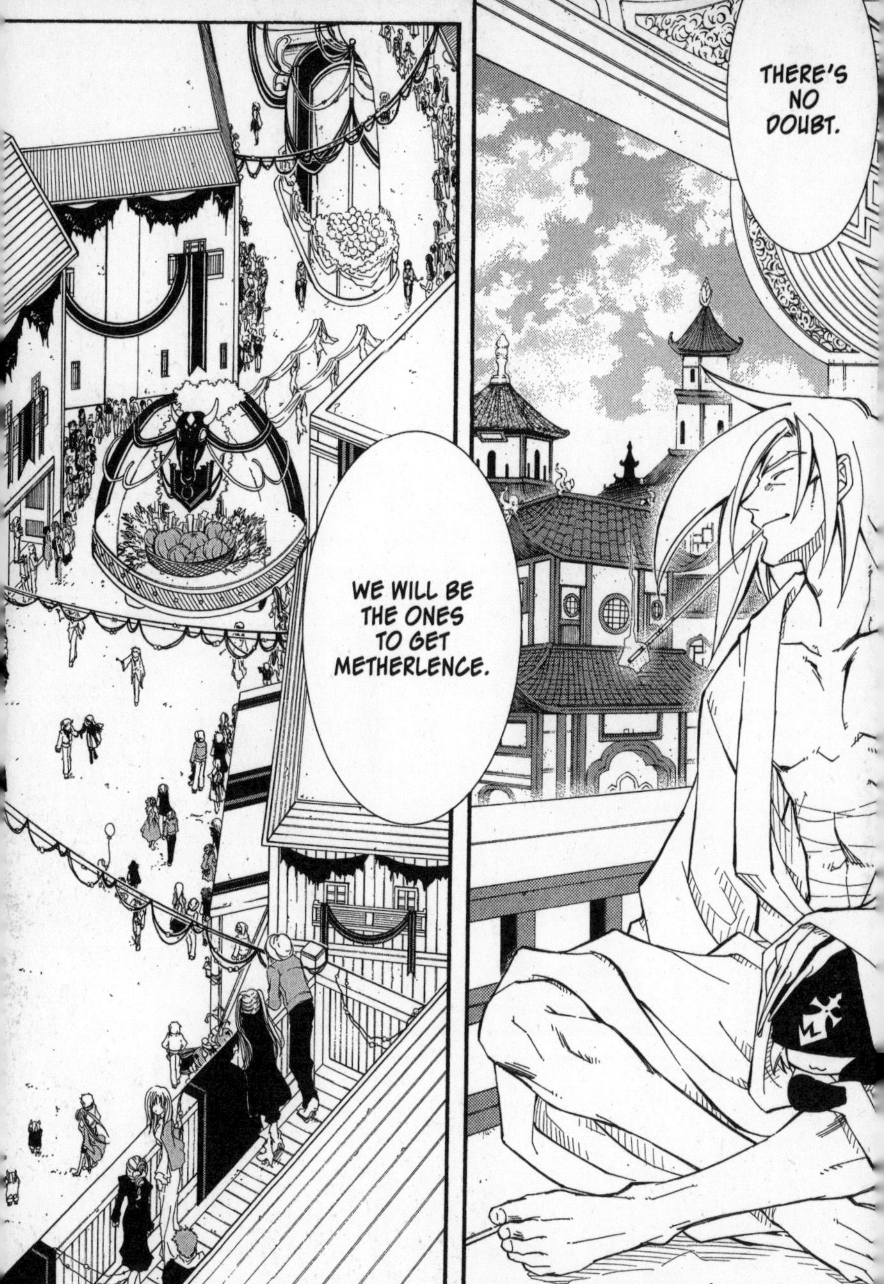
THERE'S NO DOUBT.
WE WILL BE THE ONES TO GET METHERLENCE.

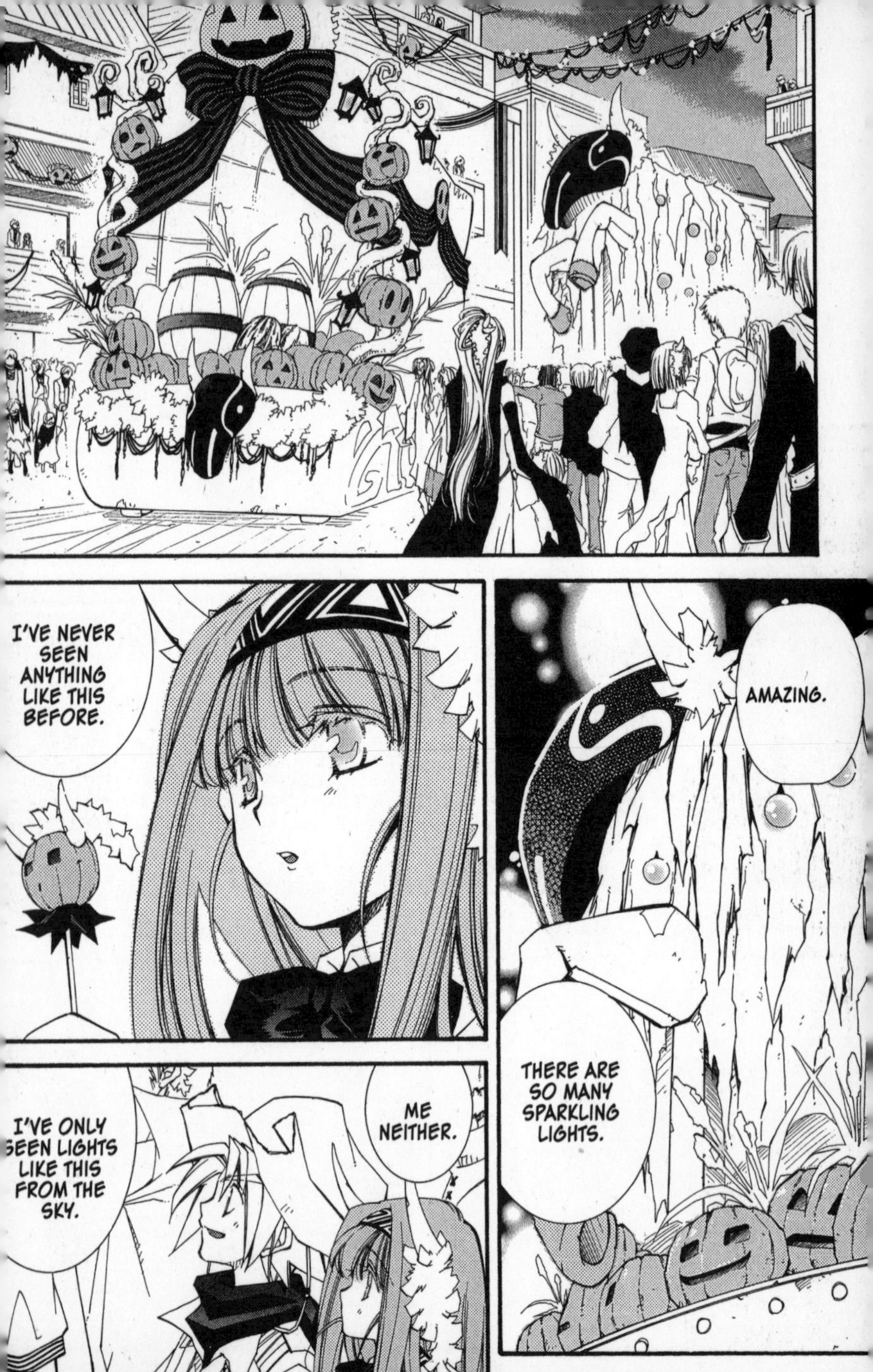
AMAZING.
THERE ARE SO MANY SPARKLING LIGHTS.
I'VE NEVER SEEN ANYTHING LIKE THIS BEFORE.
ME NEITHER.
I'VE ONLY SEEN LIGHTS LIKE THIS FROM THE SKY.

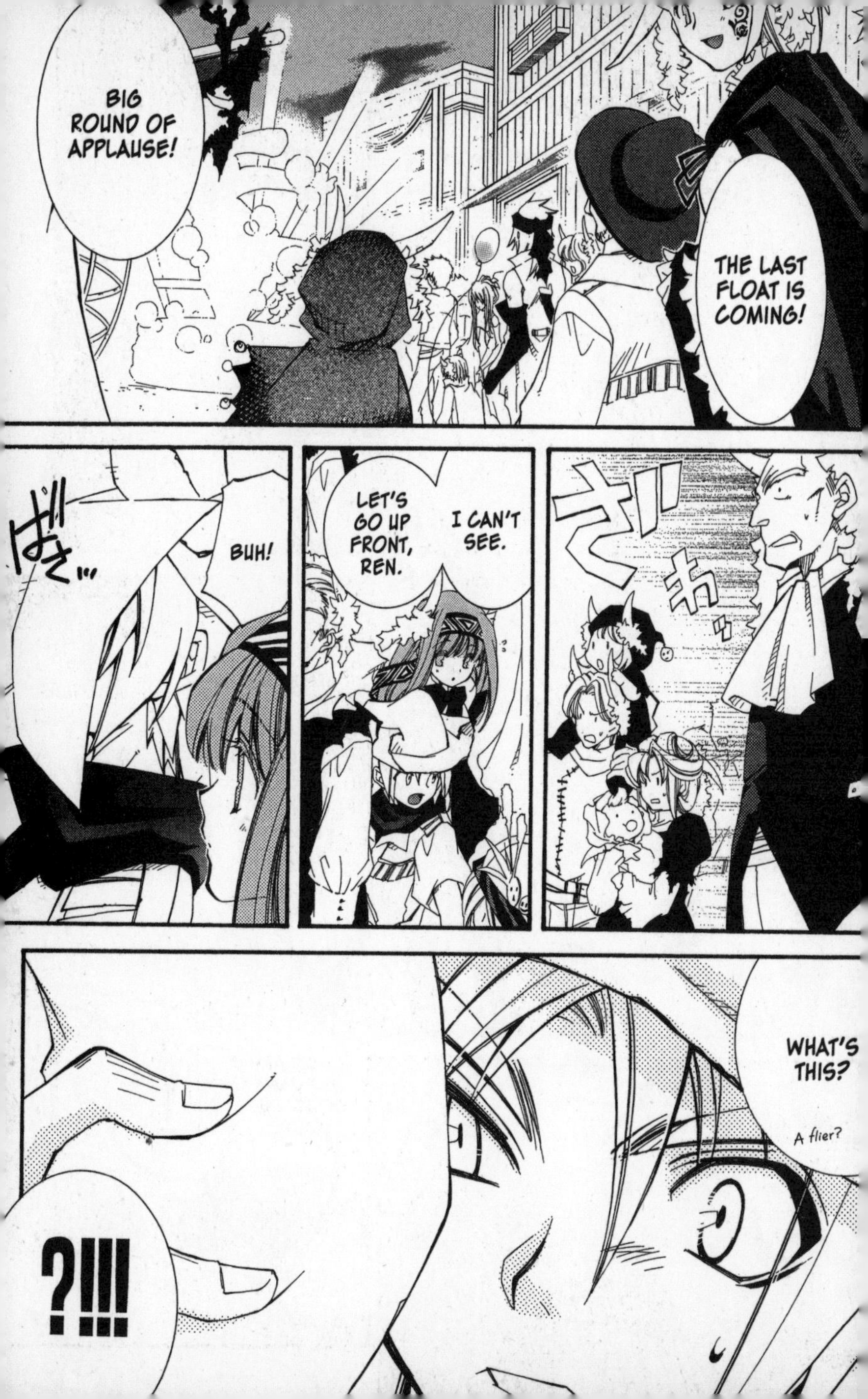
THE LAST FLOAT IS COMING!
BIG ROUND OF APPLAUSE!
I CAN'T SEE.
LET'S GO UP FRONT, REN.
BUH!
WHAT'S THIS?
A flier?
?!!!

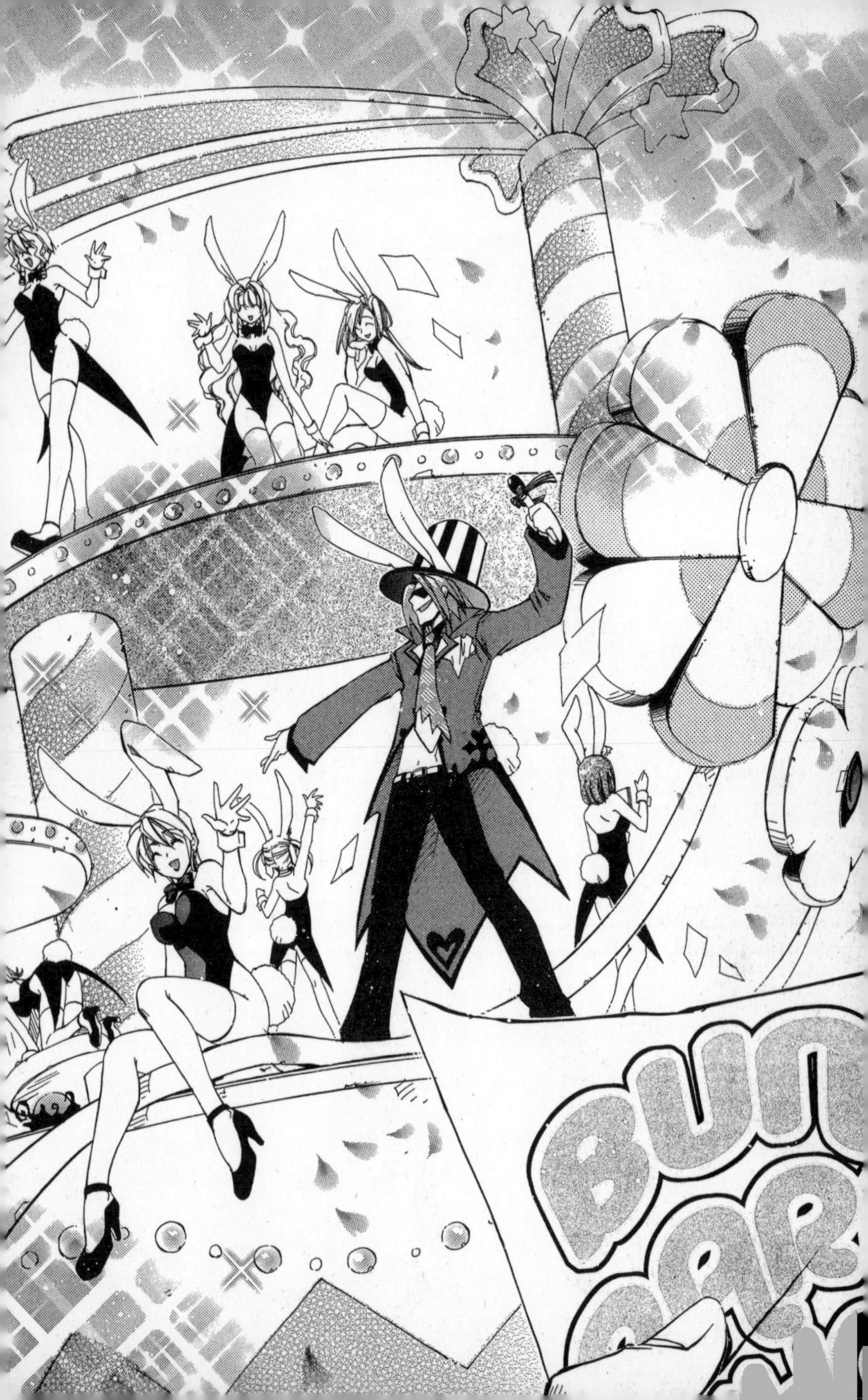

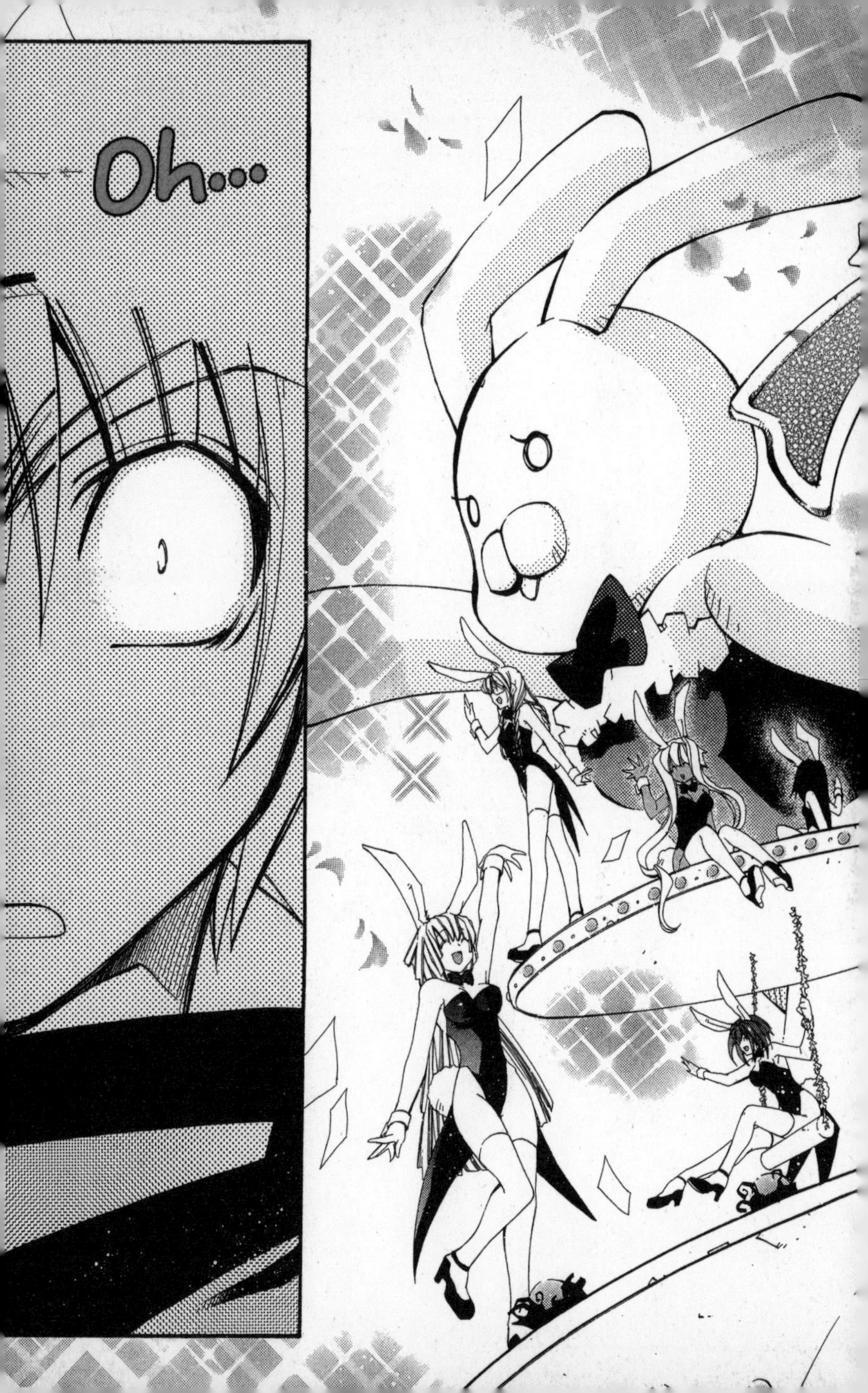
Oh...

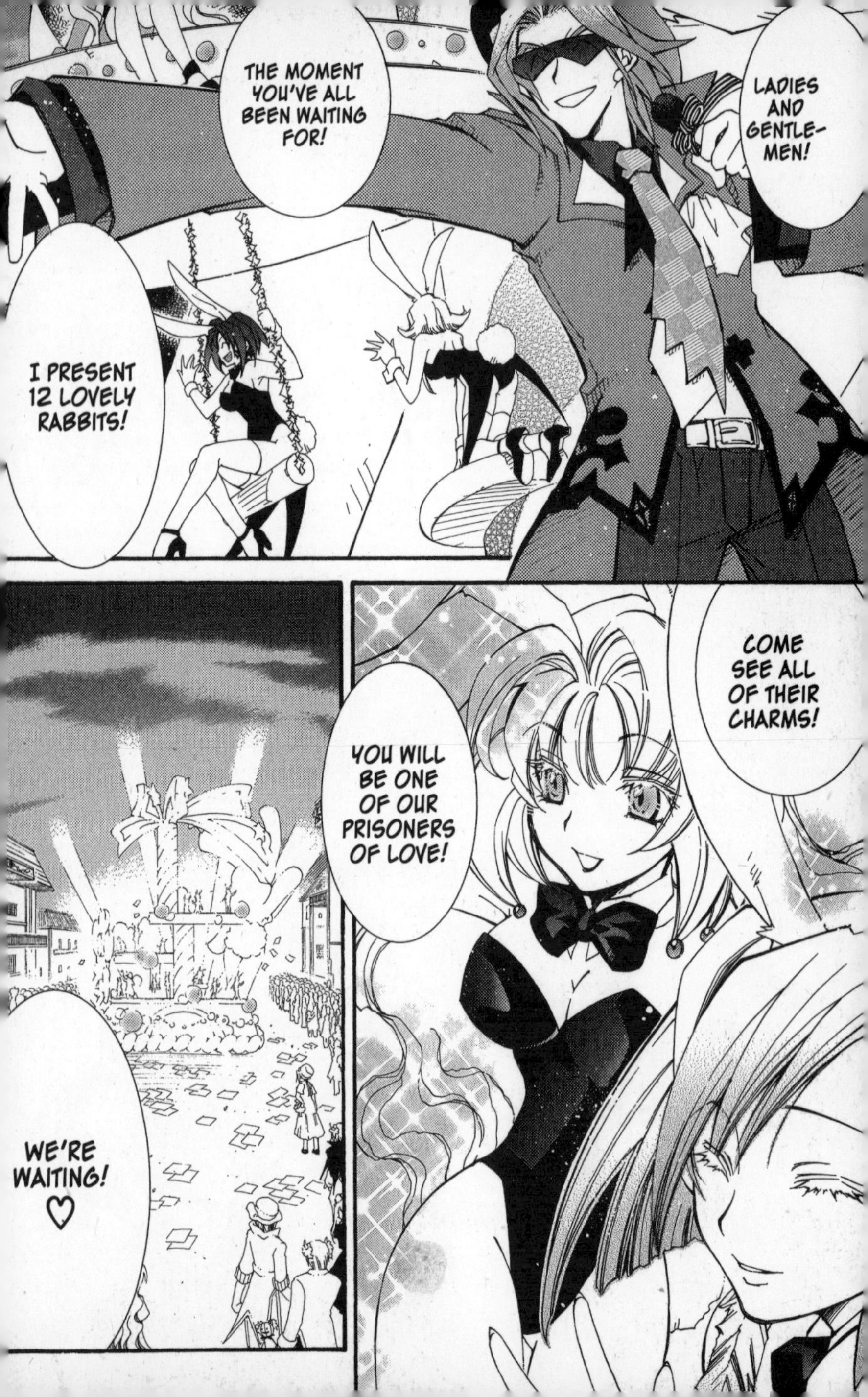
LADIES AND GENTLE-MEN!
THE MOMENT YOU'VE ALL BEEN WAITING FOR!
I PRESENT 12 LOVELY RABBITS!
COME SEE ALL OF THEIR CHARMS!
YOU WILL BE ONE OF OUR PRISONERS OF LOVE!
WE'RE WAITING! ♡

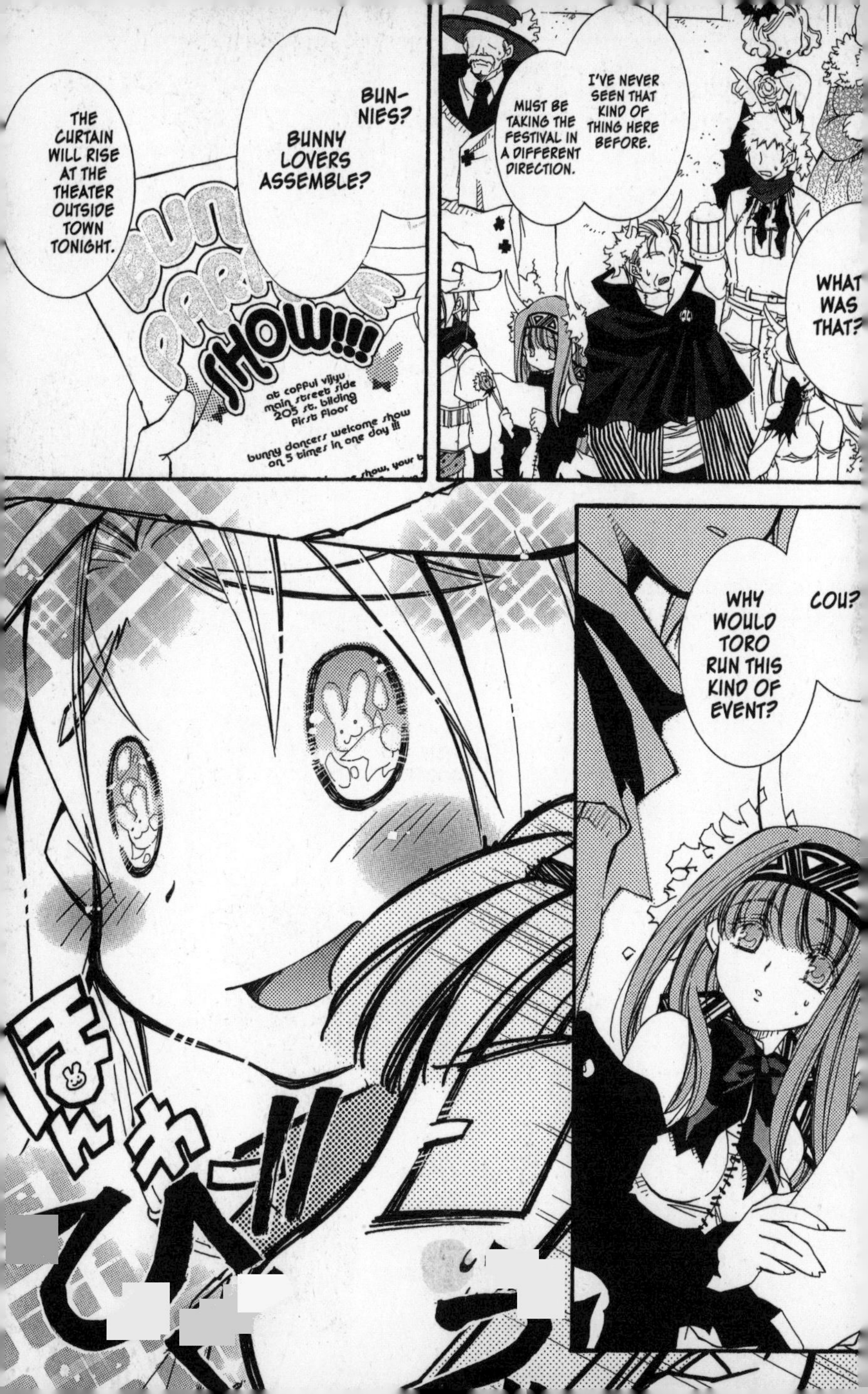
WHAT WAS THAT?
I'VE NEVER SEEN THAT KIND OF THING HERE BEFORE.
MUST BE TAKING THE FESTIVAL IN A DIFFERENT DIRECTION.
BUN-NIES?
BUNNY LOVERS ASSEMBLE?
THE CURTAIN WILL RISE AT THE THEATER OUTSIDE TOWN TONIGHT.
SHOW!!!
at cofful vijyu main street side 205 st. bilding first floor
bunny dancers welcome show on 5 times in one day !!!
COU?
WHY WOULD TORO RUN THIS KIND OF EVENT?

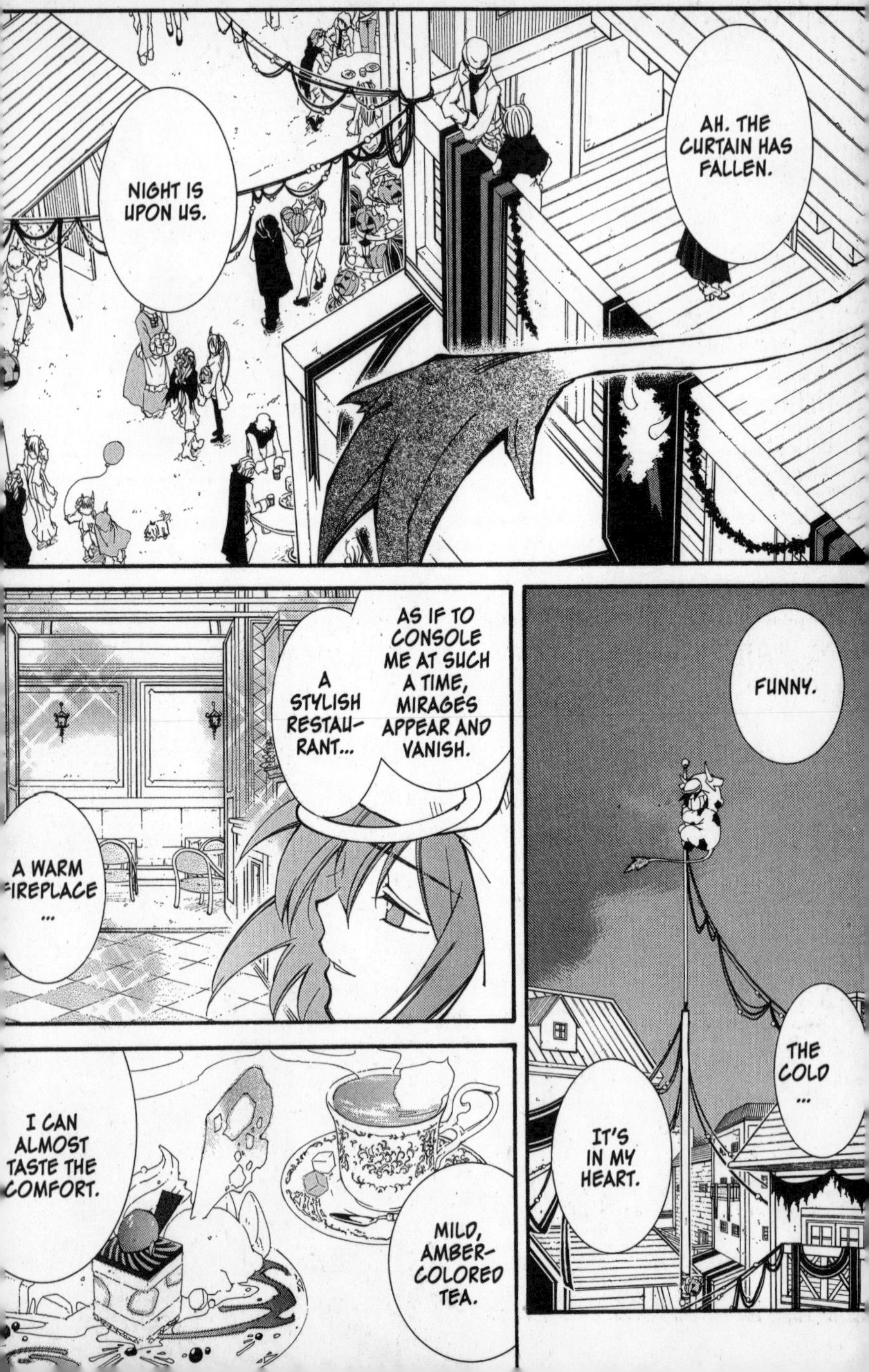
AH. THE CURTAIN HAS FALLEN.
NIGHT IS UPON US.
FUNNY.
THE COLD ...
IT'S IN MY HEART.
AS IF TO CONSOLE ME AT SUCH A TIME, MIRAGES APPEAR AND VANISH.
A STYLISH RESTAU-RANT...
A WARM FIREPLACE ...
MILD, AMBER-COLORED TEA.
I CAN ALMOST TASTE THE COMFORT.

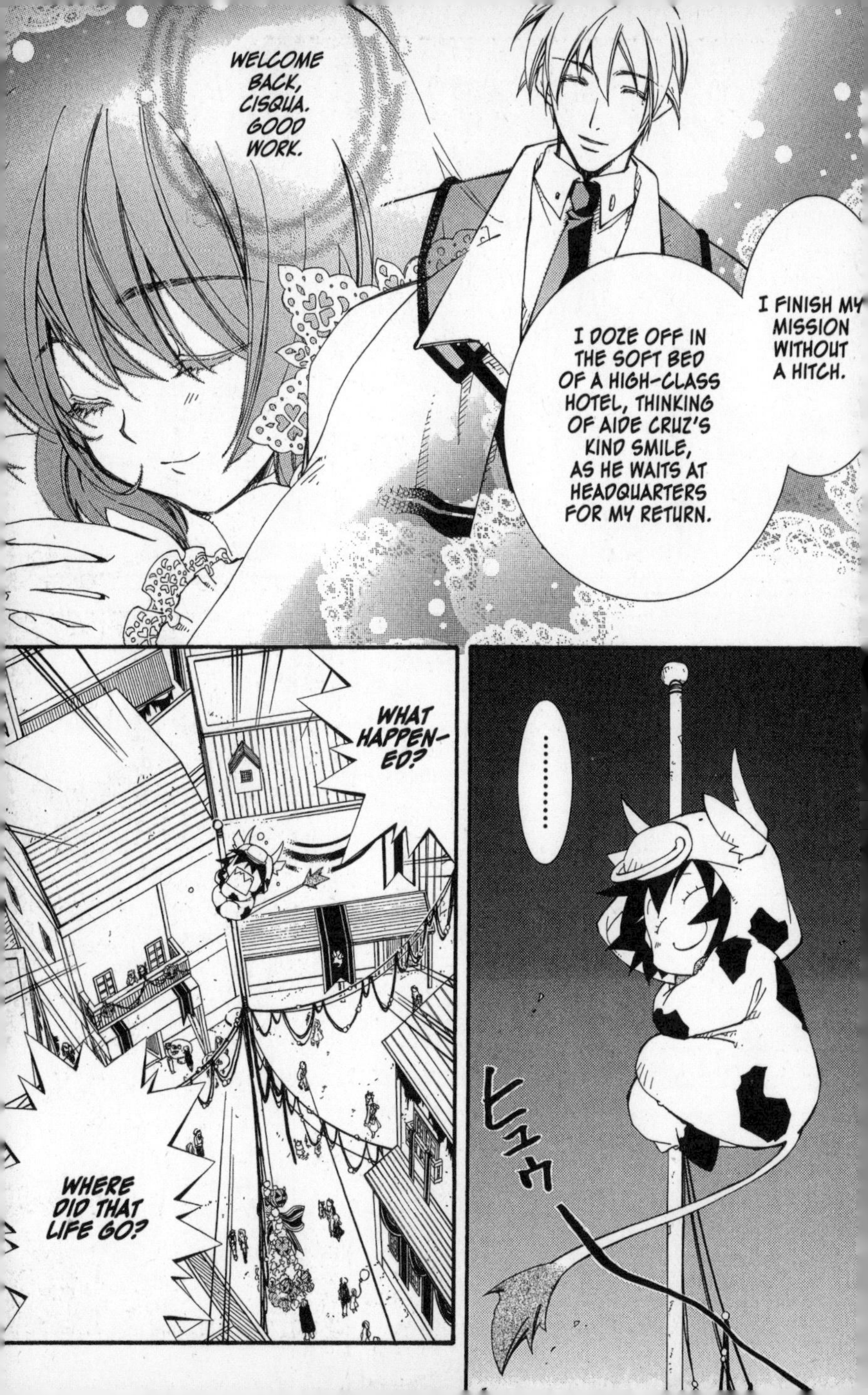
I FINISH MY MISSION WITHOUT A HITCH.
I DOZE OFF IN THE SOFT BED OF A HIGH-CLASS HOTEL, THINKING OF AIDE CRUZ'S KIND SMILE, AS HE WAITS AT HEADQUARTERS FOR MY RETURN.
WELCOME BACK, CISQUA. GOOD WORK.
....
ヒュウ
WHAT HAPPEN-ED?
WHERE DID THAT LIFE GO?

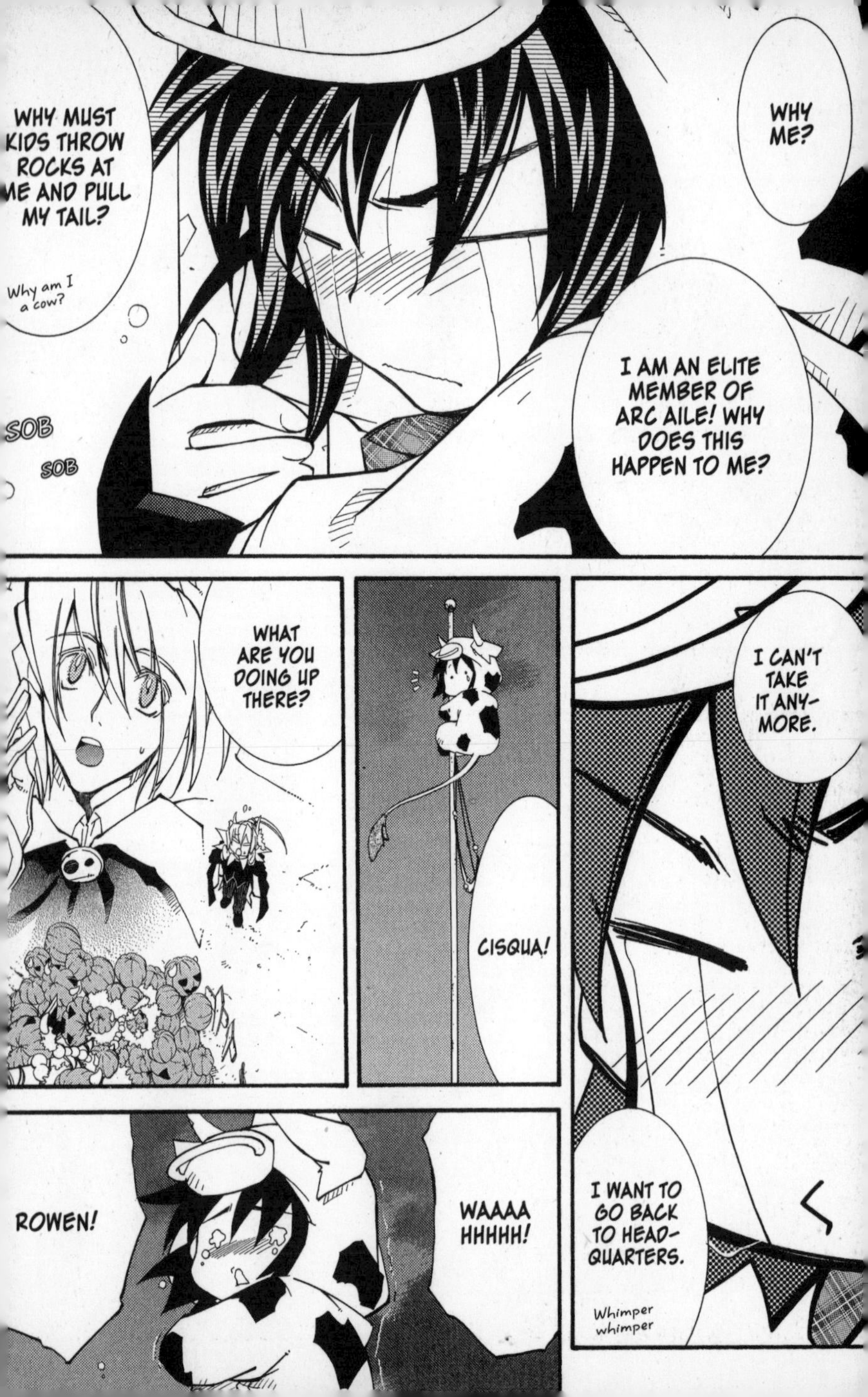
WHY ME?
I AM AN ELITE MEMBER OF ARC AILE! WHY DOES THIS HAPPEN TO ME?
WHY MUST KIDS THROW ROCKS AT ME AND PULL MY TAIL?
Why am I a cow?
SOB SOB
I CAN'T TAKE IT ANYMORE.
I WANT TO GO BACK TO HEADQUARTERS.
Whimper whimper
CISQUA!
WHAT ARE YOU DOING UP THERE?
WAAAAHHHHH!
ROWEN!

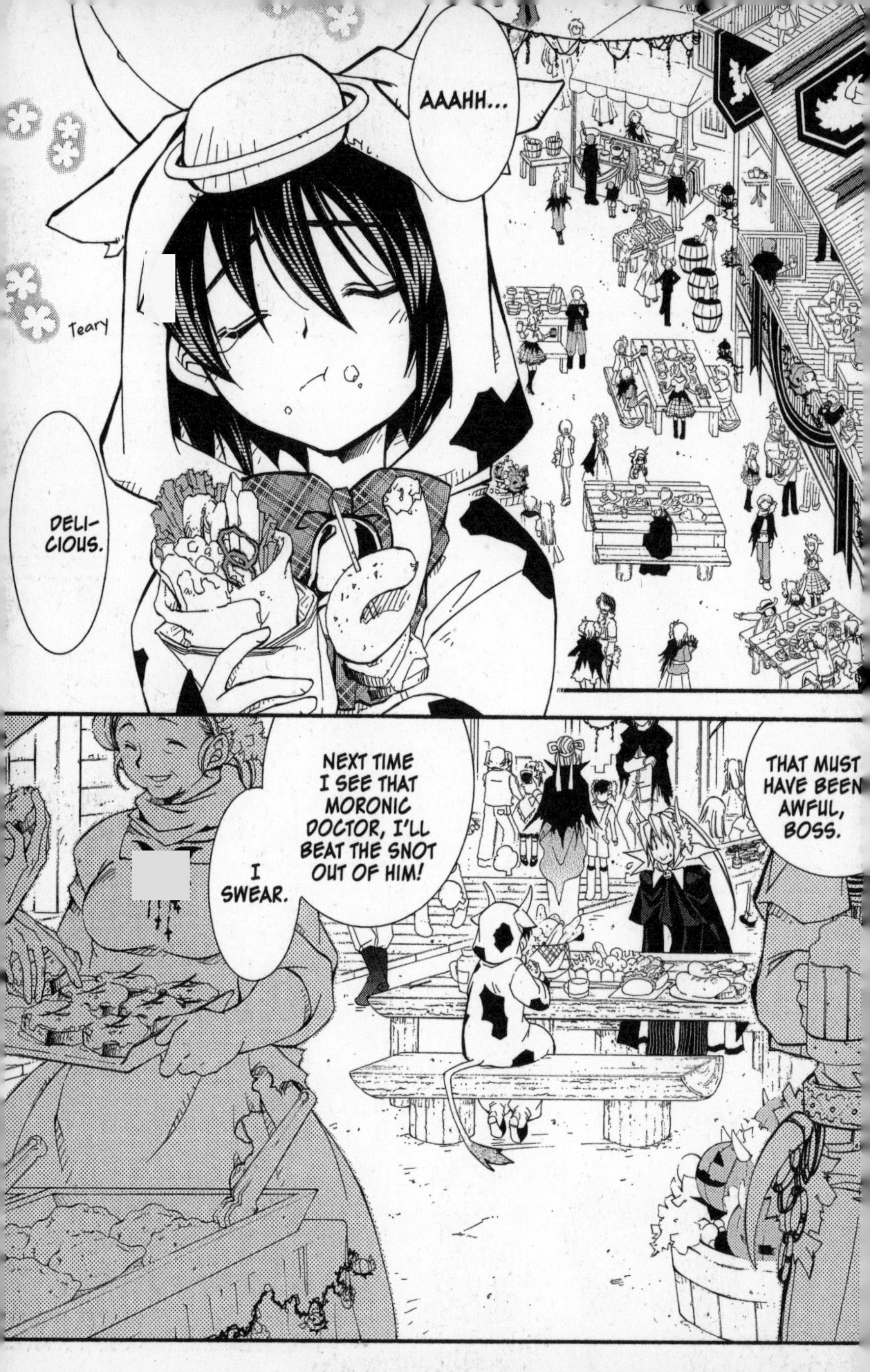
AAAHH...
Teary
DELI-CIOUS.
THAT MUST HAVE BEEN AWFUL, BOSS.
NEXT TIME I SEE THAT MORONIC DOCTOR, I'LL BEAT THE SNOT OUT OF HIM!
I SWEAR.

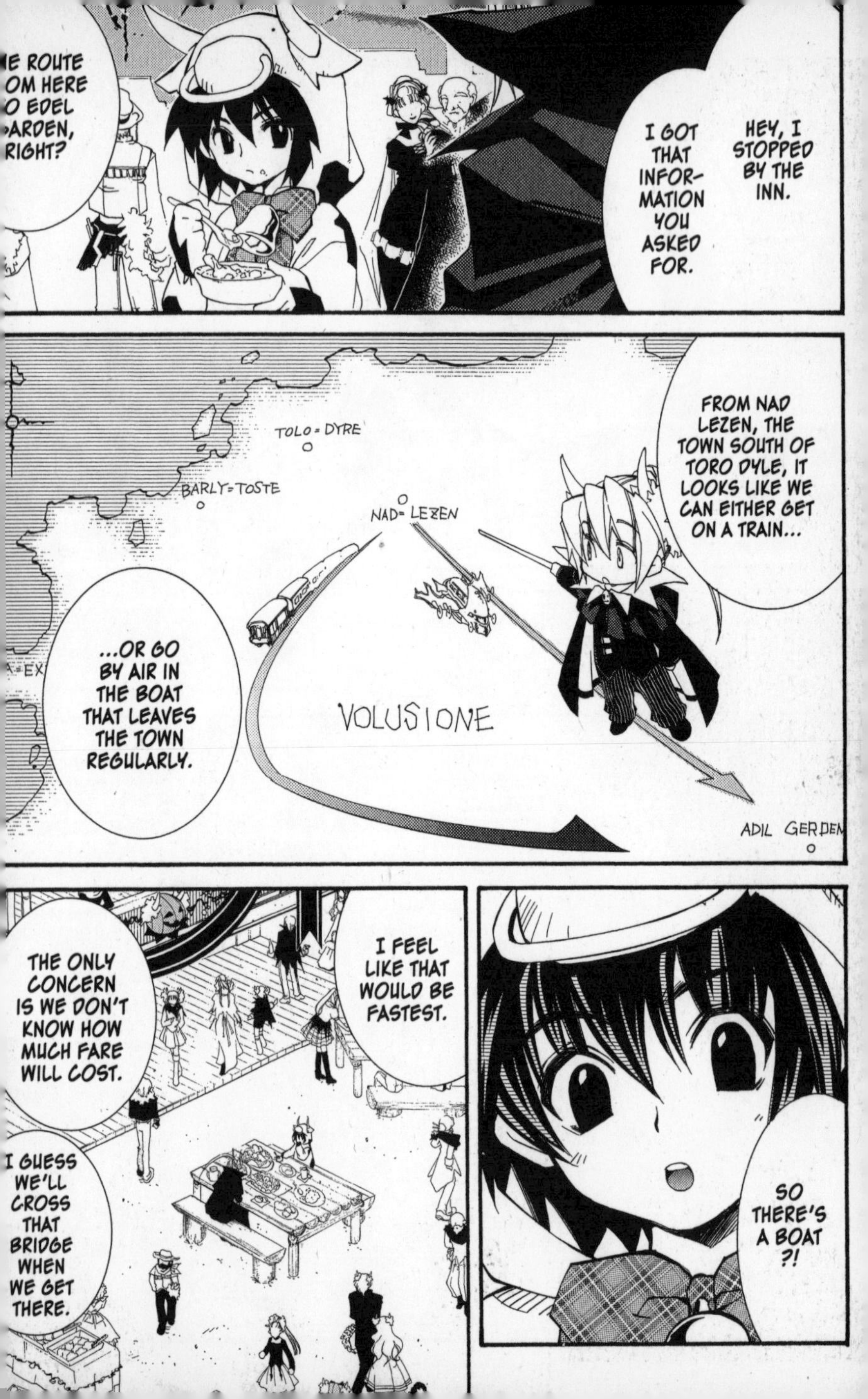
HEY, I STOPPED BY THE INN.
I GOT THAT INFORMATION YOU ASKED FOR.
E ROUTE OM HERE O EDEL ARDEN, RIGHT?
FROM NAD LEZEN, THE TOWN SOUTH OF TORO DYLE, IT LOOKS LIKE WE CAN EITHER GET ON A TRAIN...
TOLO = DYRE
BARLY=TOSTE
NAD= LEZEN
...OR GO BY AIR IN THE BOAT THAT LEAVES THE TOWN REGULARLY.
VOLUSIONE
ADIL GERDEN
SO THERE'S A BOAT ?!
I FEEL LIKE THAT WOULD BE FASTEST.
THE ONLY CONCERN IS WE DON'T KNOW HOW MUCH FARE WILL COST.
I GUESS WE'LL CROSS THAT BRIDGE WHEN WE GET THERE.

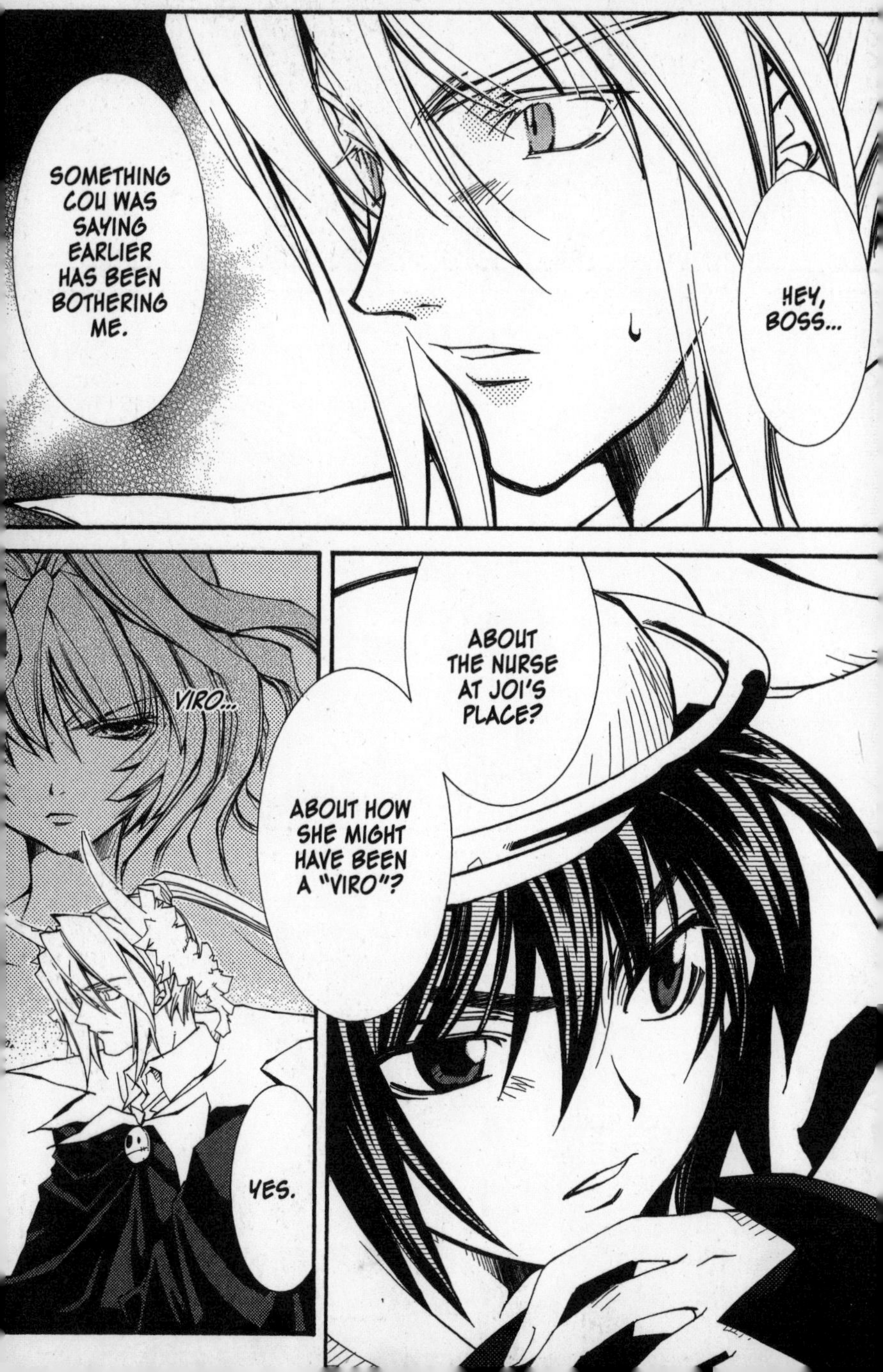
HEY, BOSS...
SOMETHING COU WAS SAYING EARLIER HAS BEEN BOTHERING ME.
ABOUT THE NURSE AT JOI'S PLACE?
ABOUT HOW SHE MIGHT HAVE BEEN A "VIRO"?
VIRO...
YES.

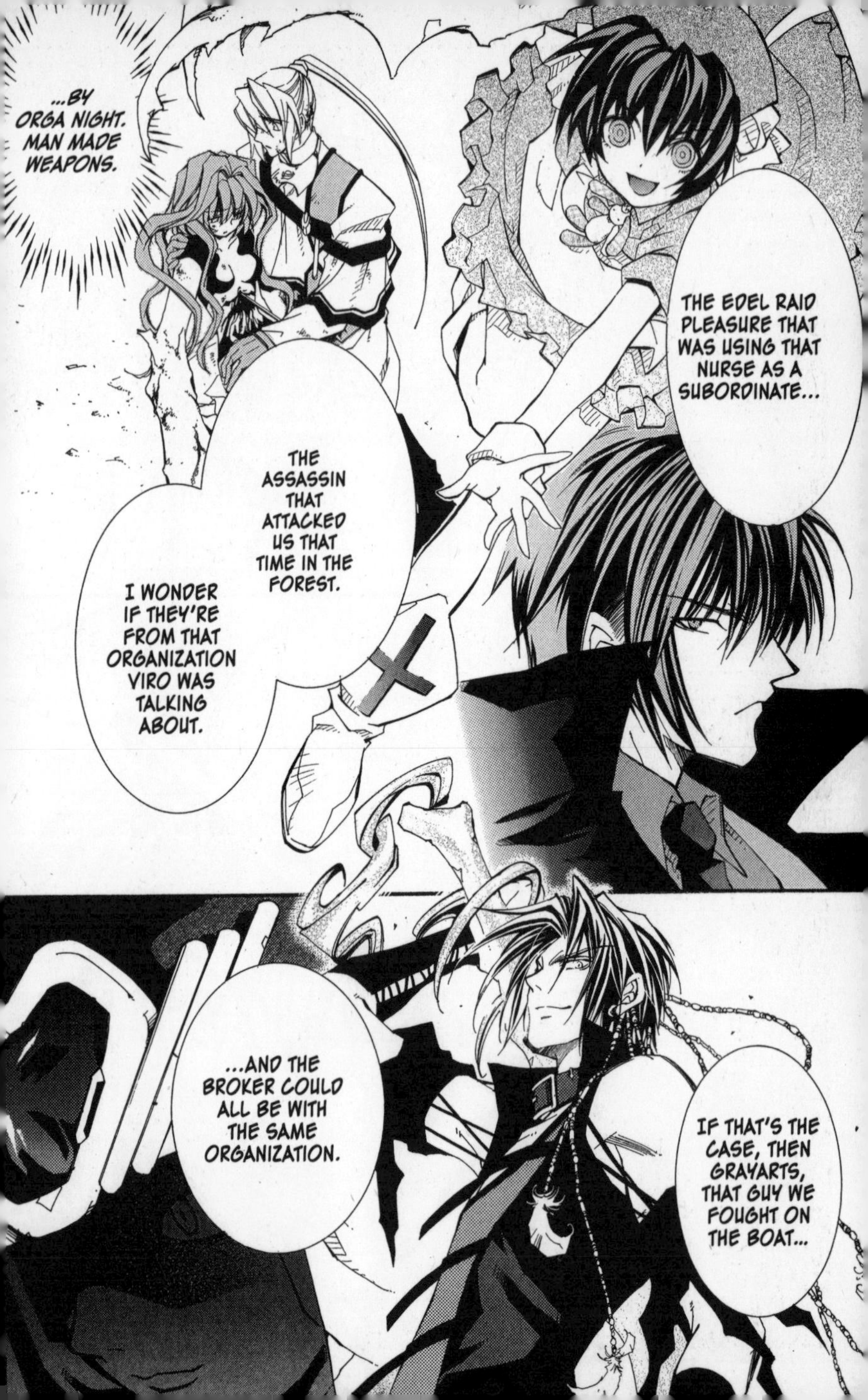
...BY ORGA NIGHT. MAN MADE WEAPONS.
THE EDEL RAID PLEASURE THAT WAS USING THAT NURSE AS A SUBORDINATE...
THE ASSASSIN THAT ATTACKED US THAT TIME IN THE FOREST.
I WONDER IF THEY'RE FROM THAT ORGANIZATION VIRO WAS TALKING ABOUT.
IF THAT'S THE CASE, THEN GRAYARTS, THAT GUY WE FOUGHT ON THE BOAT...
...AND THE BROKER COULD ALL BE WITH THE SAME ORGANIZATION.

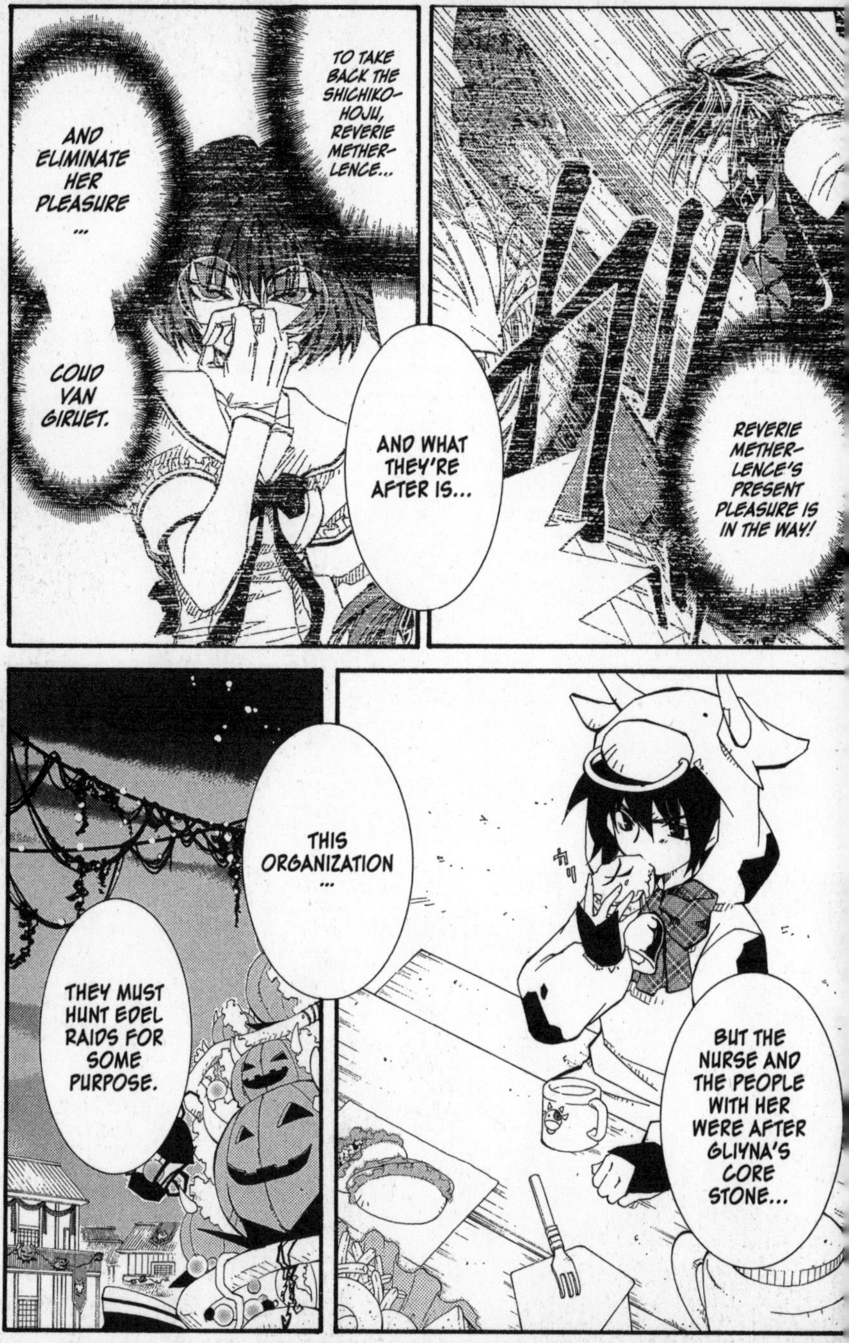
REVERIE METHER-LENCE'S PRESENT PLEASURE IS IN THE WAY!
AND WHAT THEY'RE AFTER IS...
TO TAKE BACK THE SHICHIKO-HOJU, REVERIE METHER-LENCE...
AND ELIMINATE HER PLEASURE...
COUD VAN GIRUET.
BUT THE NURSE AND THE PEOPLE WITH HER WERE AFTER GLIYNA'S CORE STONE...
THIS ORGANIZATION...
THEY MUST HUNT EDEL RAIDS FOR SOME PURPOSE.

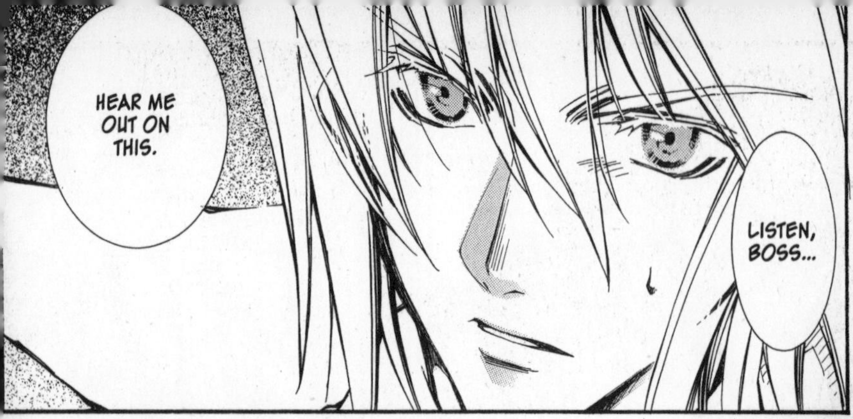
LISTEN, BOSS...
HEAR ME OUT ON THIS.
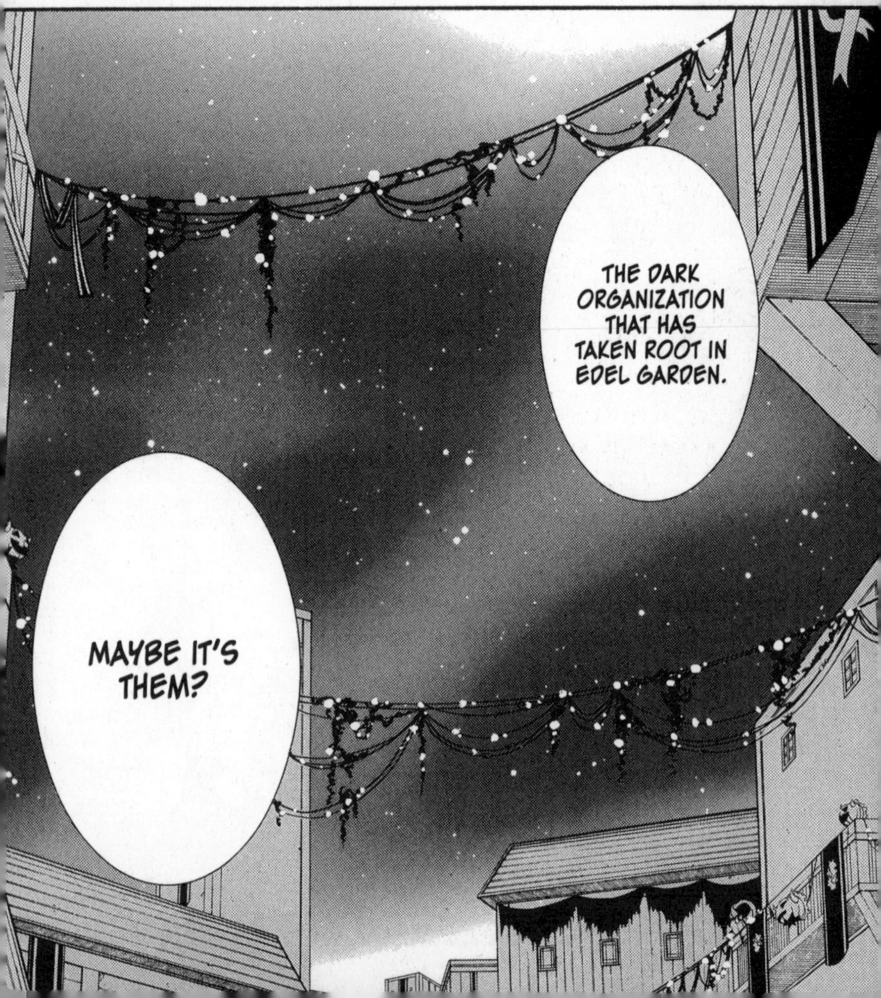
THE DARK ORGANIZATION THAT HAS TAKEN ROOT IN EDEL GARDEN.
MAYBE IT'S THEM?

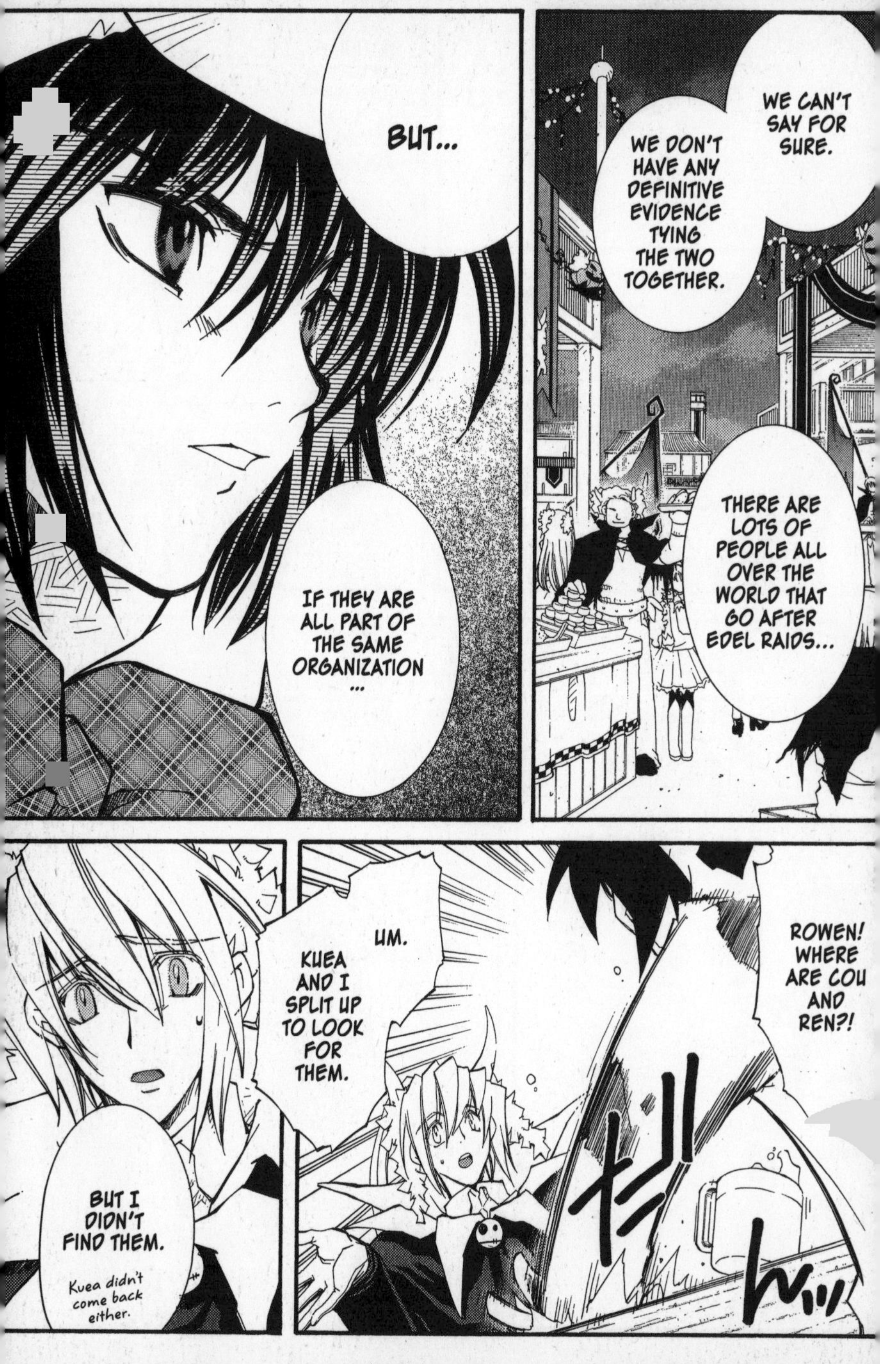
WE CAN'T SAY FOR SURE.
WE DON'T HAVE ANY DEFINITIVE EVIDENCE TYING THE TWO TOGETHER.
THERE ARE LOTS OF PEOPLE ALL OVER THE WORLD THAT GO AFTER EDEL RAIDS...
BUT...
IF THEY ARE ALL PART OF THE SAME ORGANIZATION ...
ROWEN! WHERE ARE COU AND REN?!
UM.
KUEA AND I SPLIT UP TO LOOK FOR THEM.
BUT I DIDN'T FIND THEM.
Kuea didn't come back either.

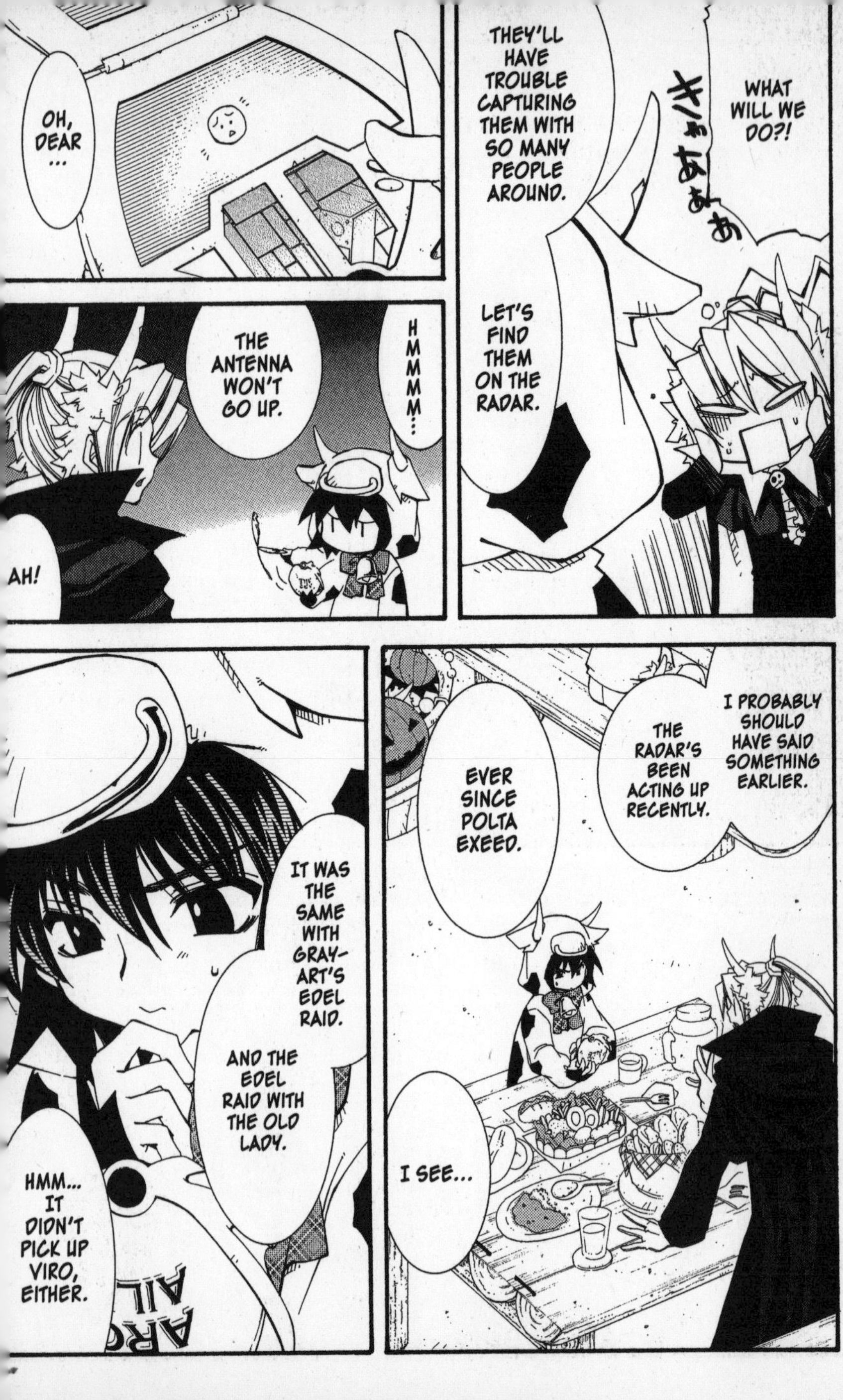
WHAT WILL WE DO?!
きゃあああ
THEY'LL HAVE TROUBLE CAPTURING THEM WITH SO MANY PEOPLE AROUND.
LET'S FIND THEM ON THE RADAR.
OH, DEAR...
HMMMM...
THE ANTENNA WON'T GO UP.
AH!
I PROBABLY SHOULD HAVE SAID SOMETHING EARLIER.
THE RADAR'S BEEN ACTING UP RECENTLY.
EVER SINCE POLTA EXEED.
I SEE...
IT WAS THE SAME WITH GRAY-ART'S EDEL RAID.
AND THE EDEL RAID WITH THE OLD LADY.
HMM... IT DIDN'T PICK UP VIRO, EITHER.

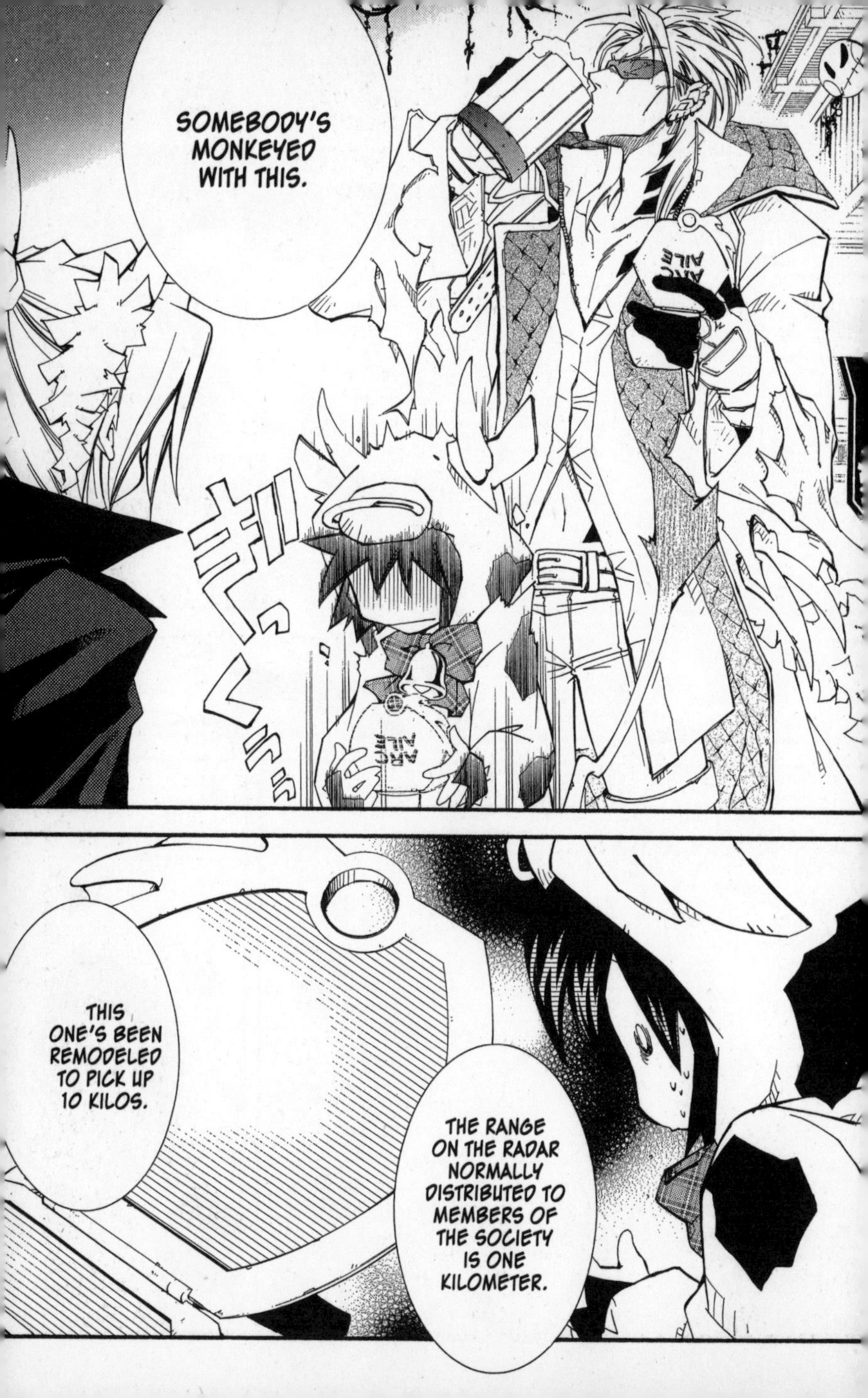

SOMEBODY'S MONKEYED WITH THIS.
THE RANGE ON THE RADAR NORMALLY DISTRIBUTED TO MEMBERS OF THE SOCIETY IS ONE KILOMETER.
THIS ONE'S BEEN REMODELED TO PICK UP 10 KILOS.

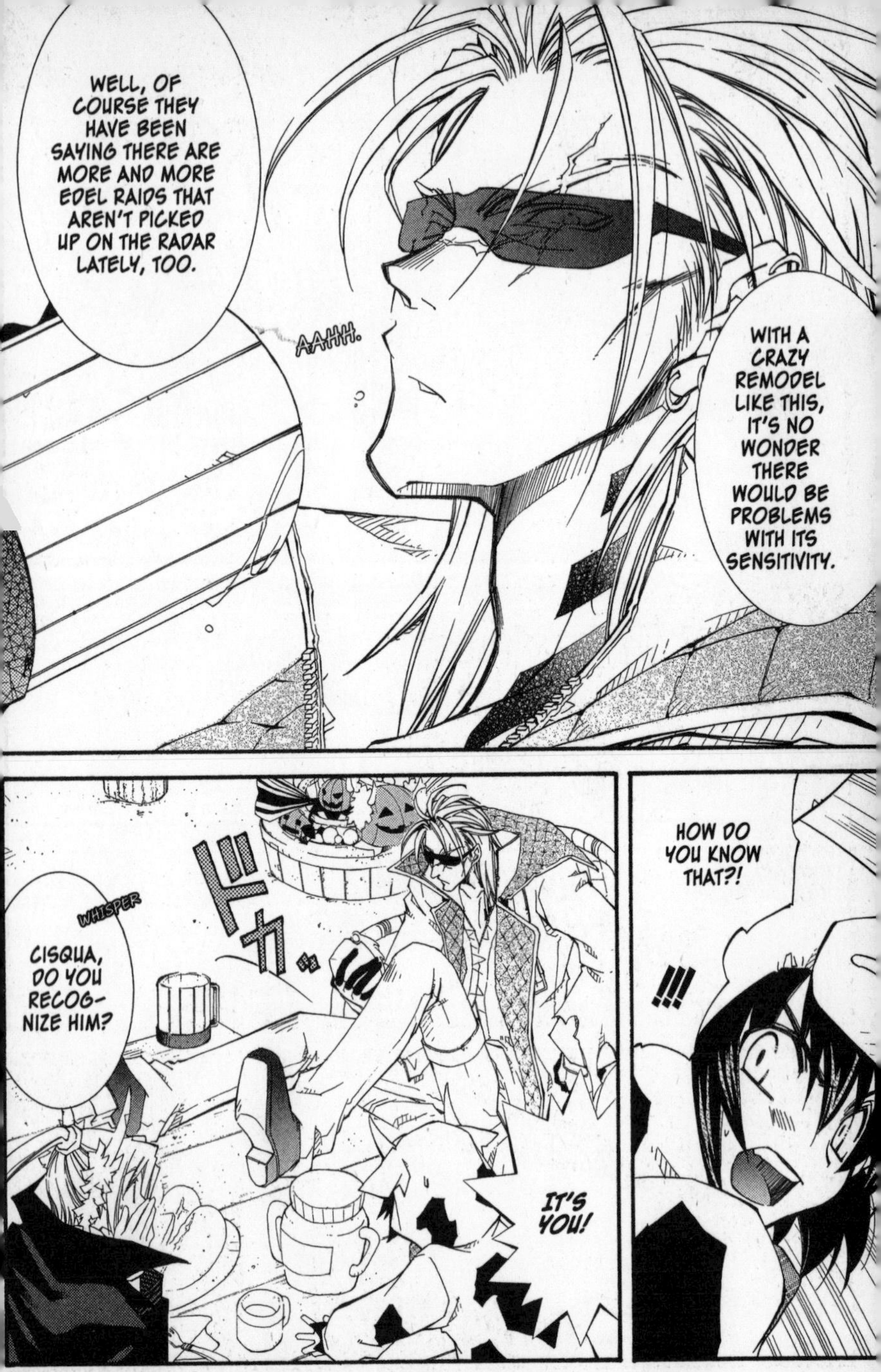
WELL, OF COURSE THEY HAVE BEEN SAYING THERE ARE MORE AND MORE EDEL RAIDS THAT AREN'T PICKED UP ON THE RADAR LATELY, TOO.
AAHH.
WITH A CRAZY REMODEL LIKE THIS, IT'S NO WONDER THERE WOULD BE PROBLEMS WITH ITS SENSITIVITY.
HOW DO YOU KNOW THAT?!
!!!
ドカ
IT'S YOU!
WHISPER
CISQUA, DO YOU RECOG-NIZE HIM?

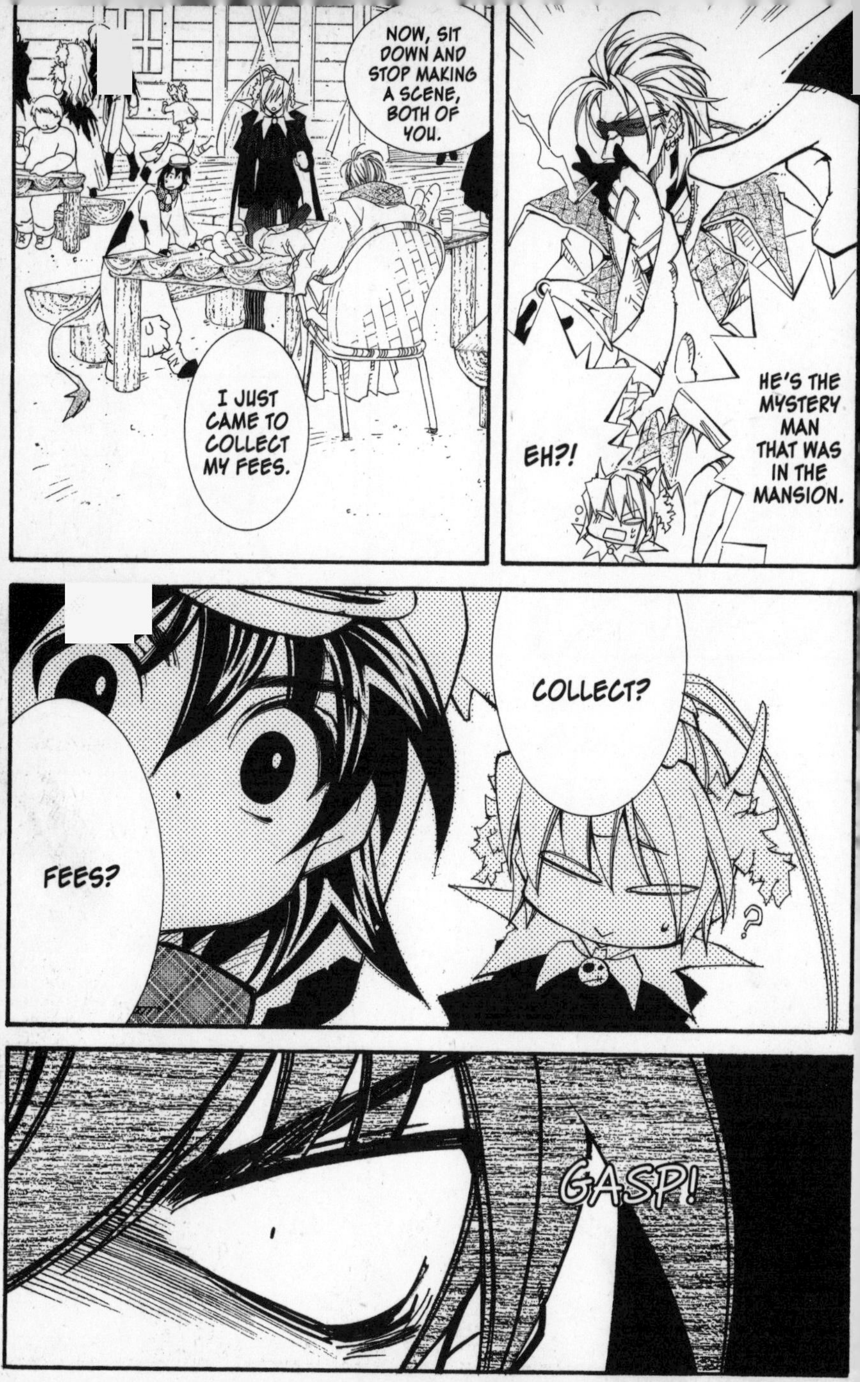
HE'S THE MYSTERY MAN THAT WAS IN THE MANSION.
EH?!
NOW, SIT DOWN AND STOP MAKING A SCENE, BOTH OF YOU.
I JUST CAME TO COLLECT MY FEES.
COLLECT?
FEES?
GASP!

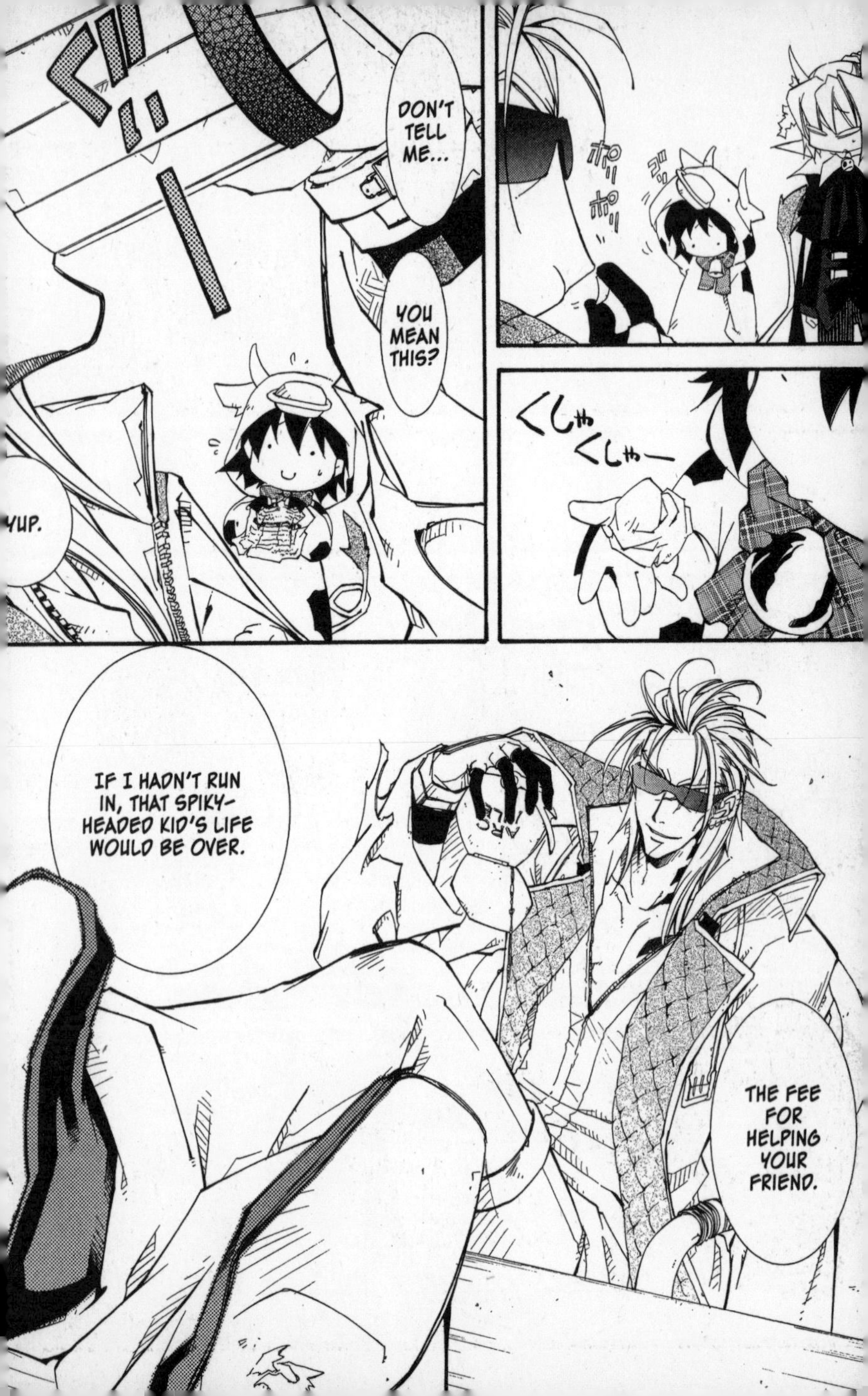
ポリ
ポリ
くしゃ
くしゃー
DON'T TELL ME...
YOU MEAN THIS?
YUP.
THE FEE FOR HELPING YOUR FRIEND.
IF I HADN'T RUN IN, THAT SPIKY-HEADED KID'S LIFE WOULD BE OVER.

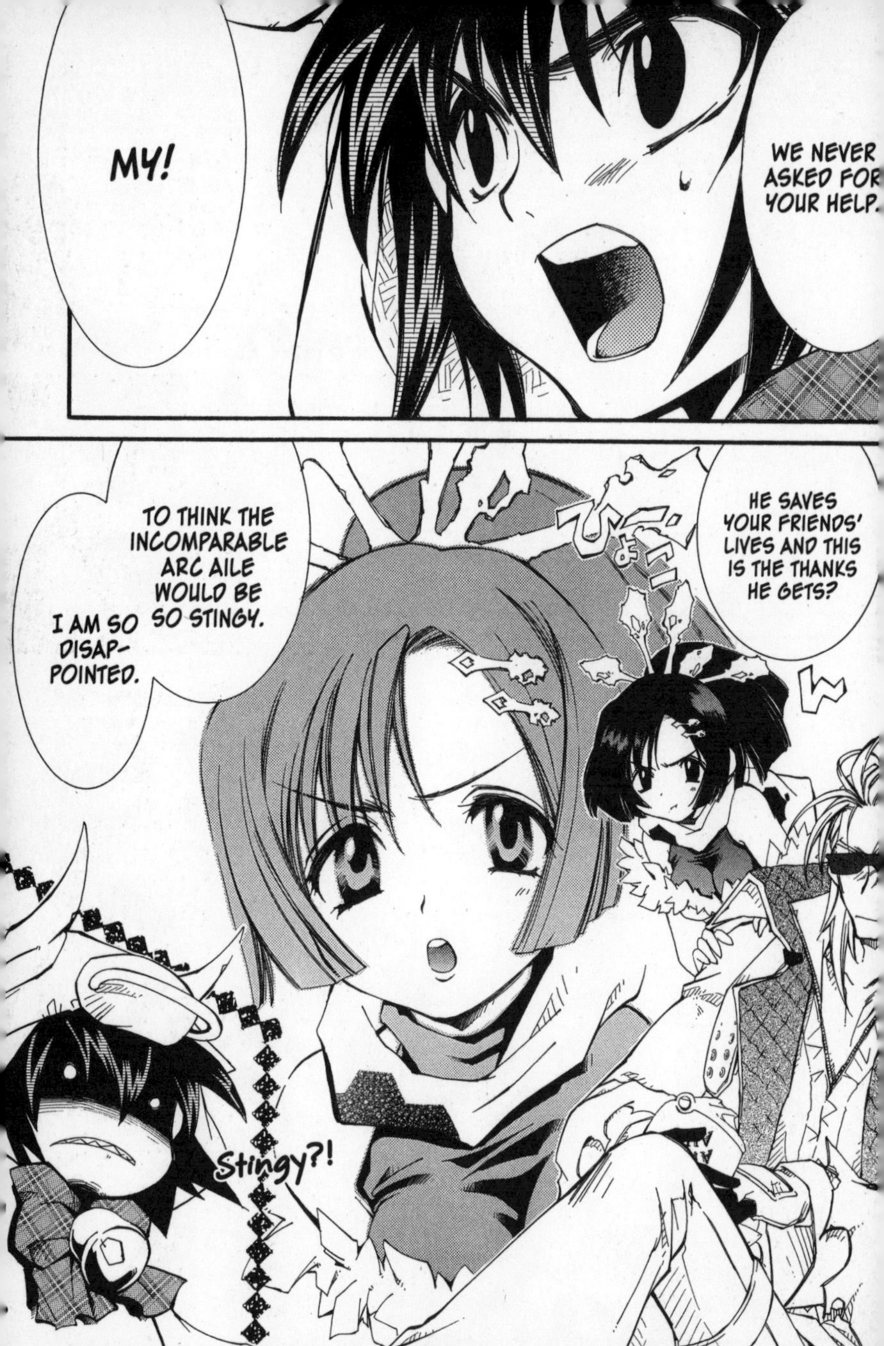
WE NEVER ASKED FOR YOUR HELP.
MY!
HE SAVES YOUR FRIENDS' LIVES AND THIS IS THE THANKS HE GETS?
TO THINK THE INCOMPARABLE ARC AILE WOULD BE SO STINGY.
I AM SO DISAP-POINTED.
Stingy?!

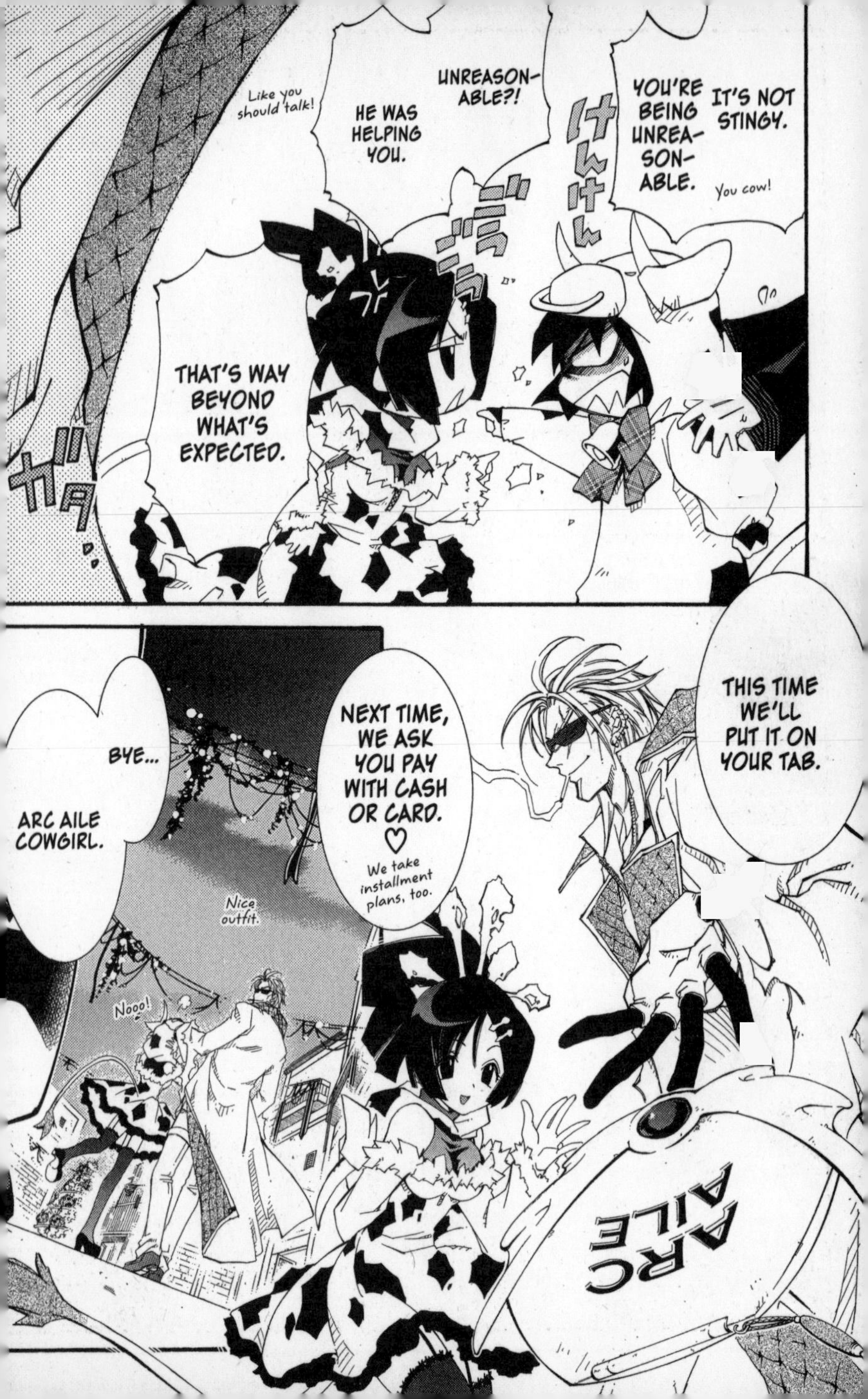
IT'S NOT STINGY.
You cow!
YOU'RE BEING UNREA-SON-ABLE.
けんけん
UNREASON-ABLE?!
HE WAS HELPING YOU.
Like you should talk!
THAT'S WAY BEYOND WHAT'S EXPECTED.
THIS TIME WE'LL PUT IT ON YOUR TAB.
NEXT TIME, WE ASK YOU PAY WITH CASH OR CARD. ♡
We take installment plans, too.
BYE...
ARC AILE COWGIRL.
Nice outfit.
Nooo!
ARC AILE

BOSS...

MAYBE IT'S A NEW KIND OF SCAM.

I'LL DEAL WITH COU LATER.

STILL, ILLEGAL REMODELING...

If the Commissioner finds out...

IT'S NOT LIKE THAT!

I JUST TWEAKED THE SENSITIVITY A LITTLE.

OH MY!

!!!

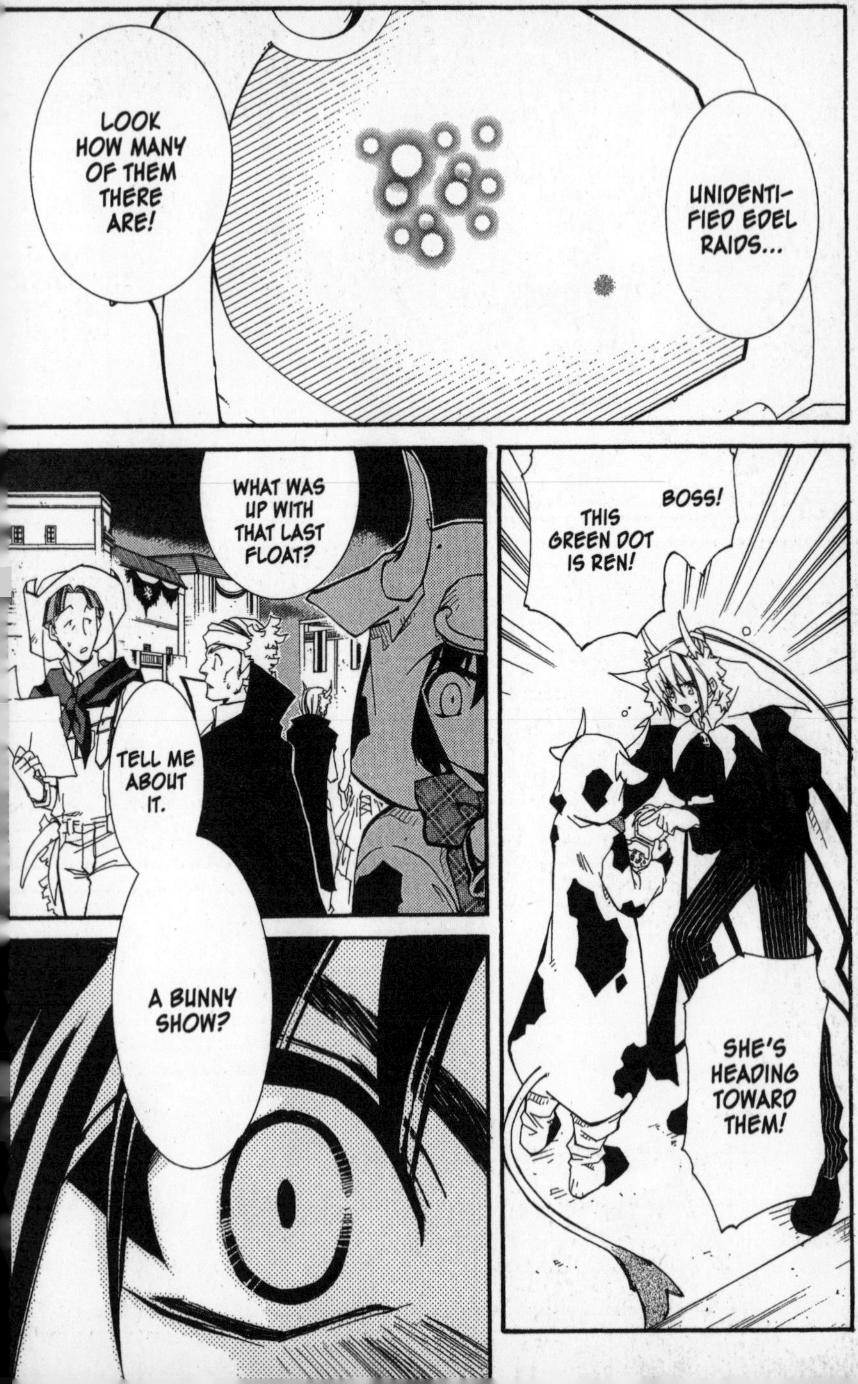
UNIDENTI-FIED EDEL RAIDS...
LOOK HOW MANY OF THEM THERE ARE!
BOSS!
THIS GREEN DOT IS REN!
SHE'S HEADING TOWARD THEM!
WHAT WAS UP WITH THAT LAST FLOAT?
TELL ME ABOUT IT.
A BUNNY SHOW?

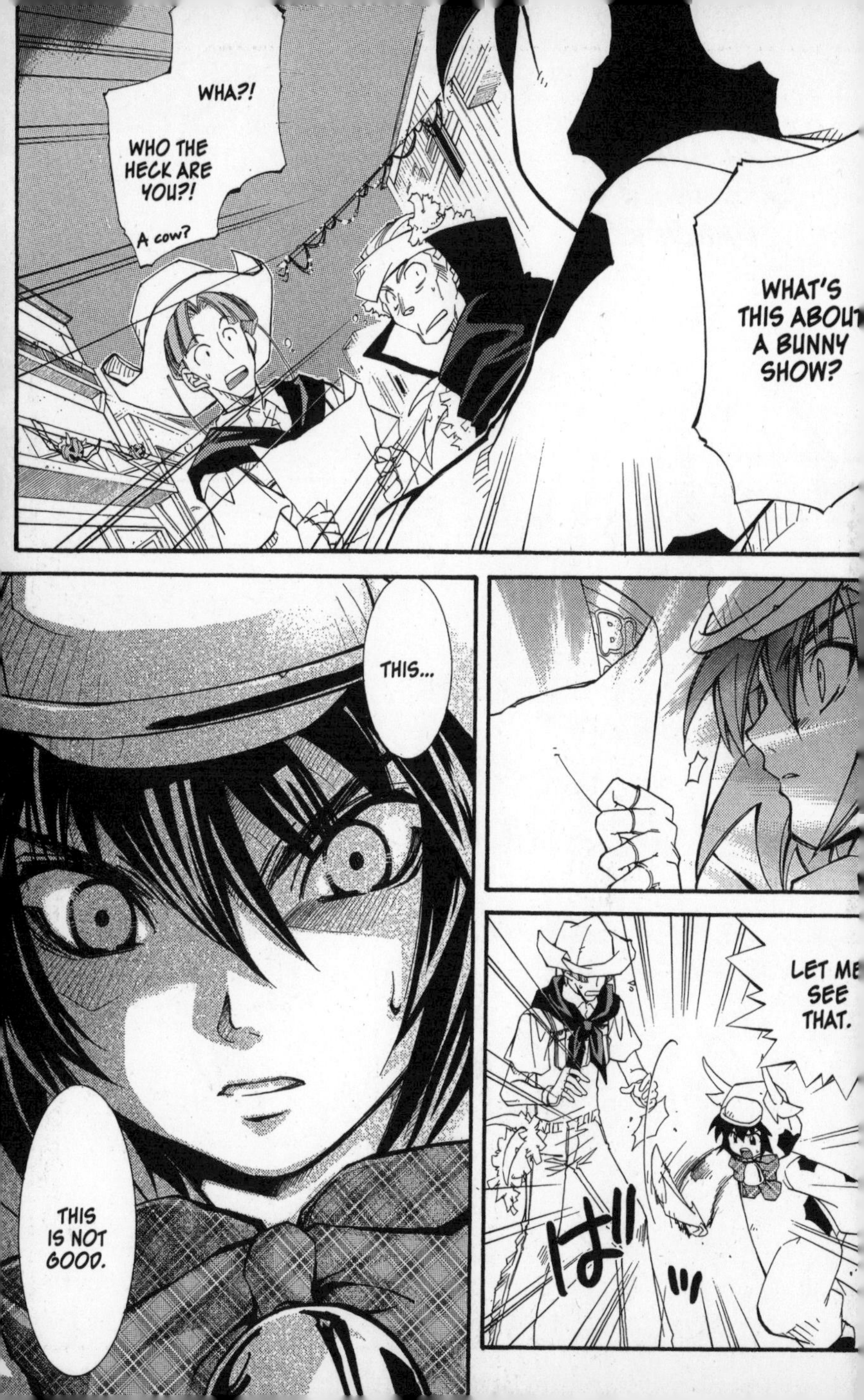
WHAT'S THIS ABOUT A BUNNY SHOW?
WHA?!
WHO THE HECK ARE YOU?!
A cow?
LET ME SEE THAT.
はッ
THIS...
THIS IS NOT GOOD.

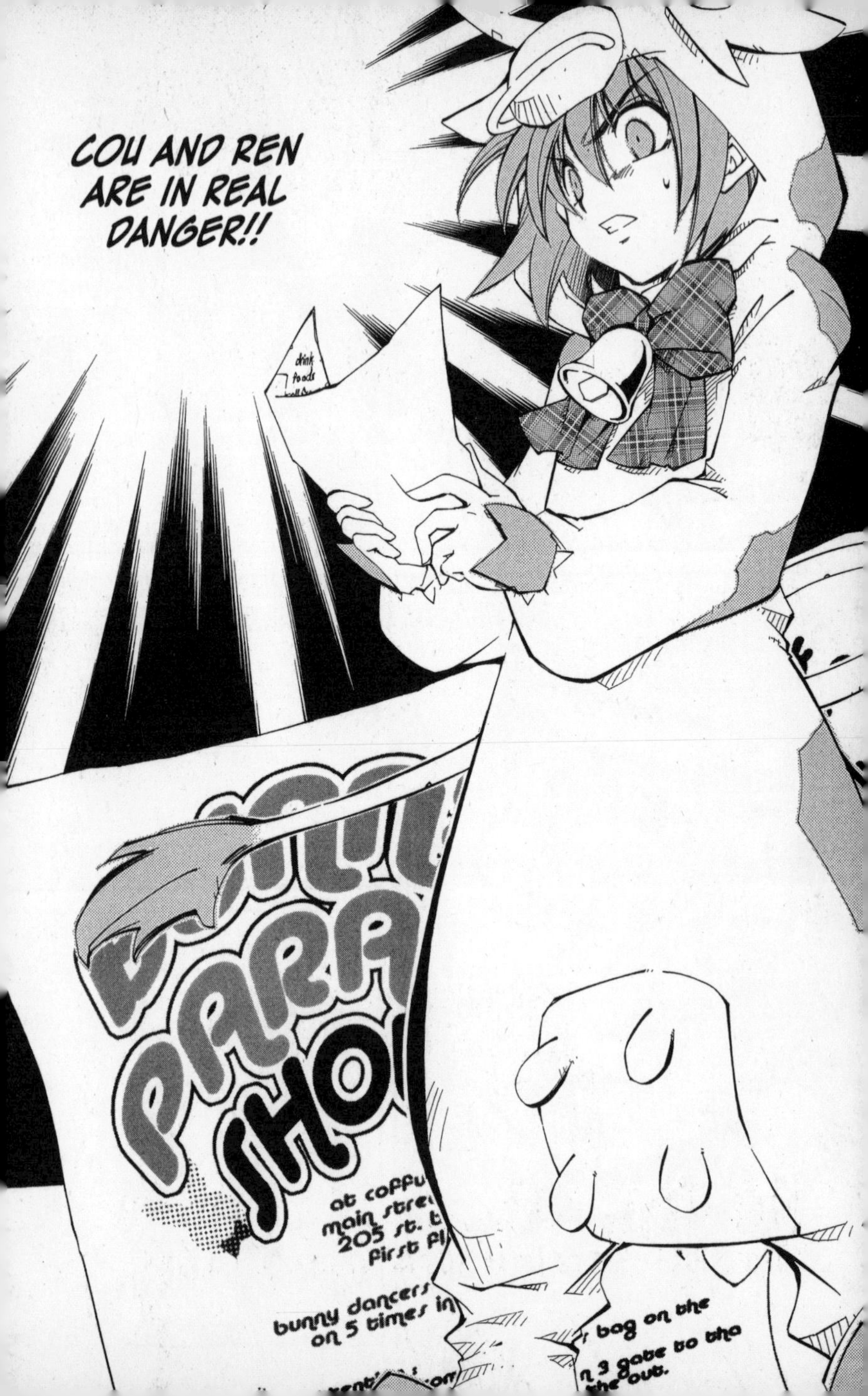
COU AND REN
ARE IN REAL
DANGER!!
drink
foods
at coffu
main stre
205 st.
first Pl
bunny dancers
on 5 times in
bog on the

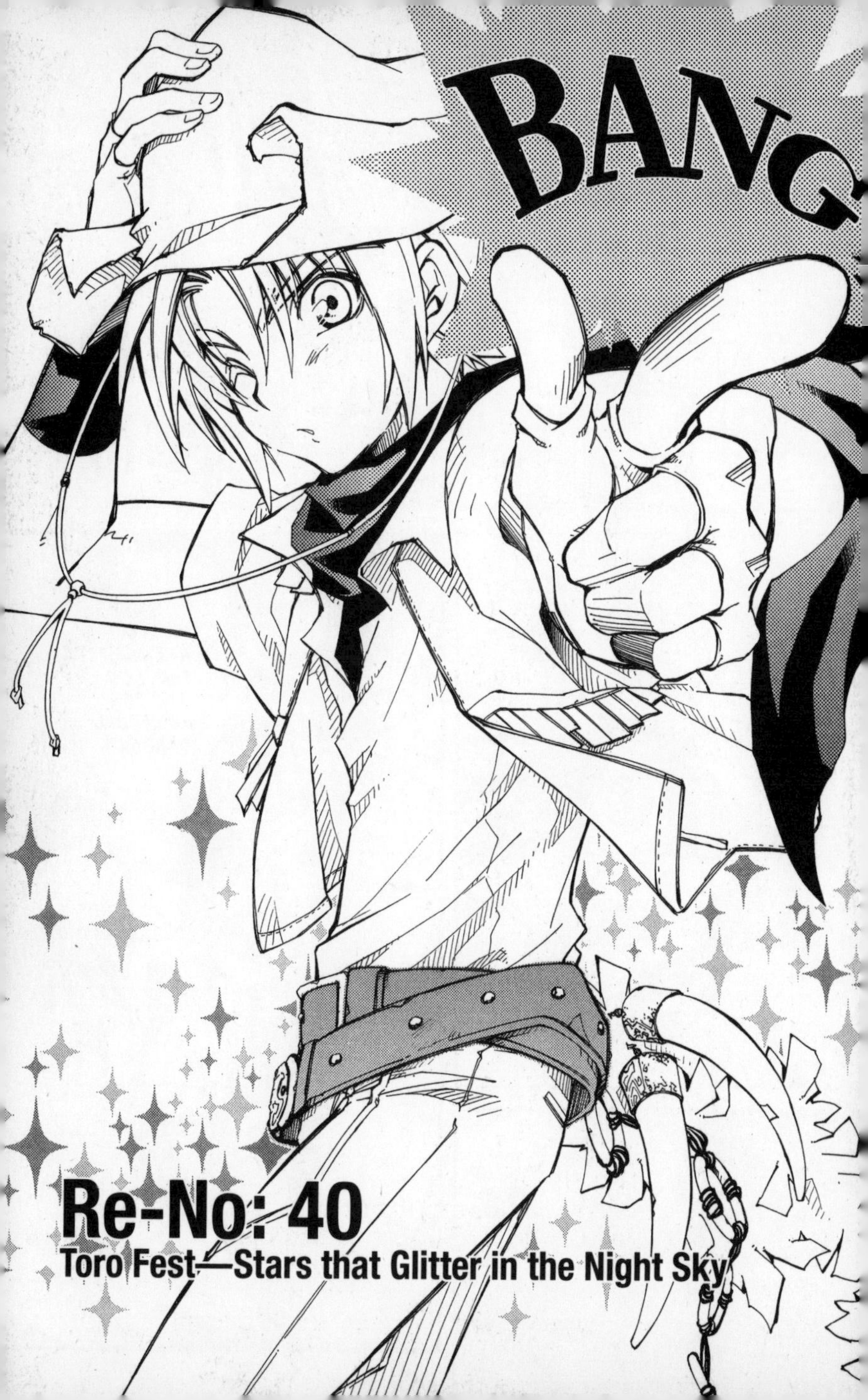
BANG

Re-No: 40

Toro Fest—Stars that Glitter in the Night Sky

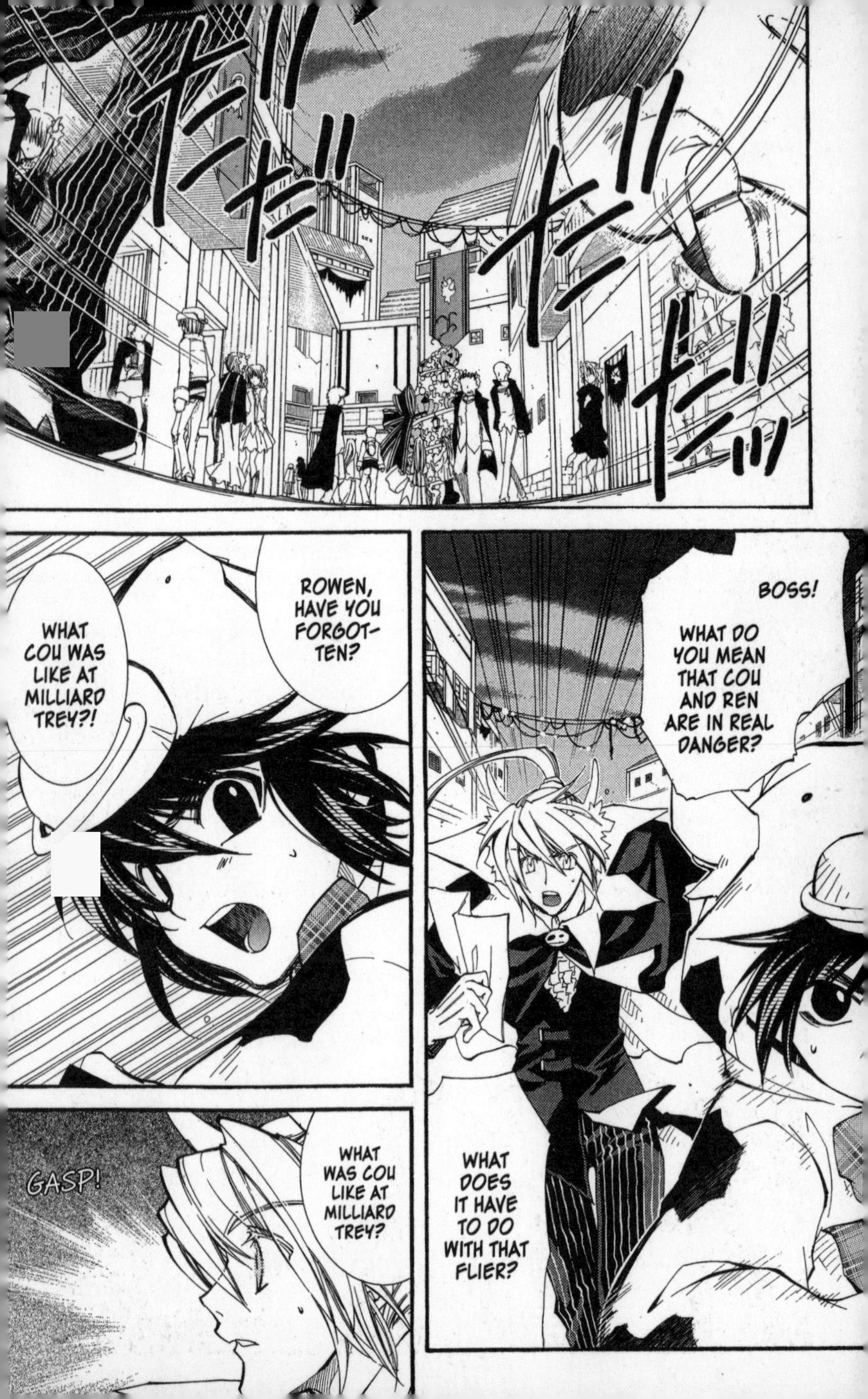
BOSS!
WHAT DO YOU MEAN THAT COU AND REN ARE IN REAL DANGER?
WHAT DOES IT HAVE TO DO WITH THAT FLIER?
ROWEN, HAVE YOU FORGOT-TEN?
WHAT COU WAS LIKE AT MILLIARD TREY?!
WHAT WAS COU LIKE AT MILLIARD TREY?
GASP!

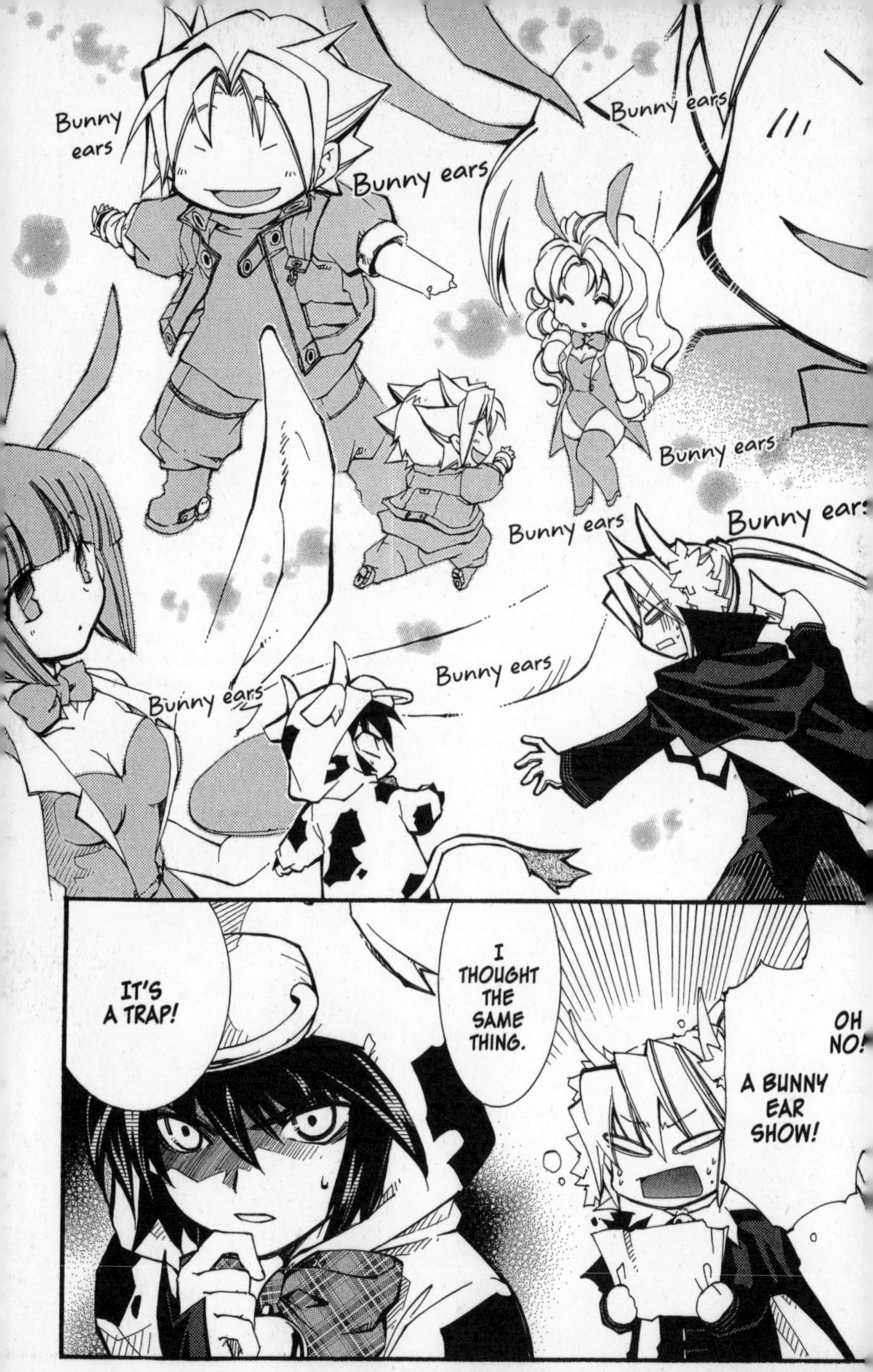

Bunny ears
Bunny ears
Bunny ears
Bunny ear
Bunny ears
Bunny ears
Bunny ears
Bunny ears
OH NO!
A BUNNY EAR SHOW!
I THOUGHT THE SAME THING.
IT'S A TRAP!

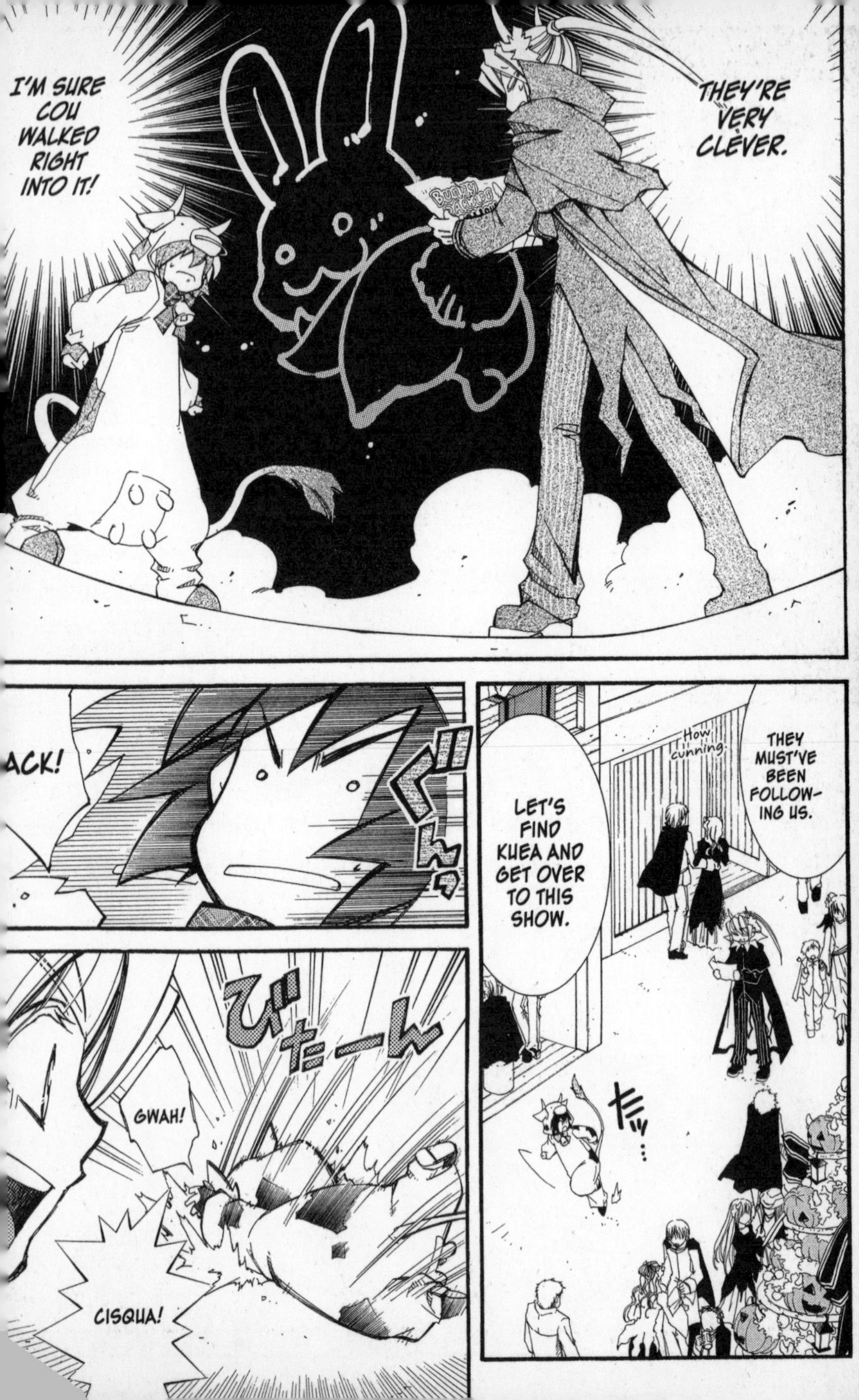
THEY'RE VERY CLEVER.
I'M SURE COU WALKED RIGHT INTO IT!
THEY MUST'VE BEEN FOLLOWING US.
How cunning.
LET'S FIND KUEA AND GET OVER TO THIS SHOW.
ACK!
びたーん
GWAH!
CISQUA!

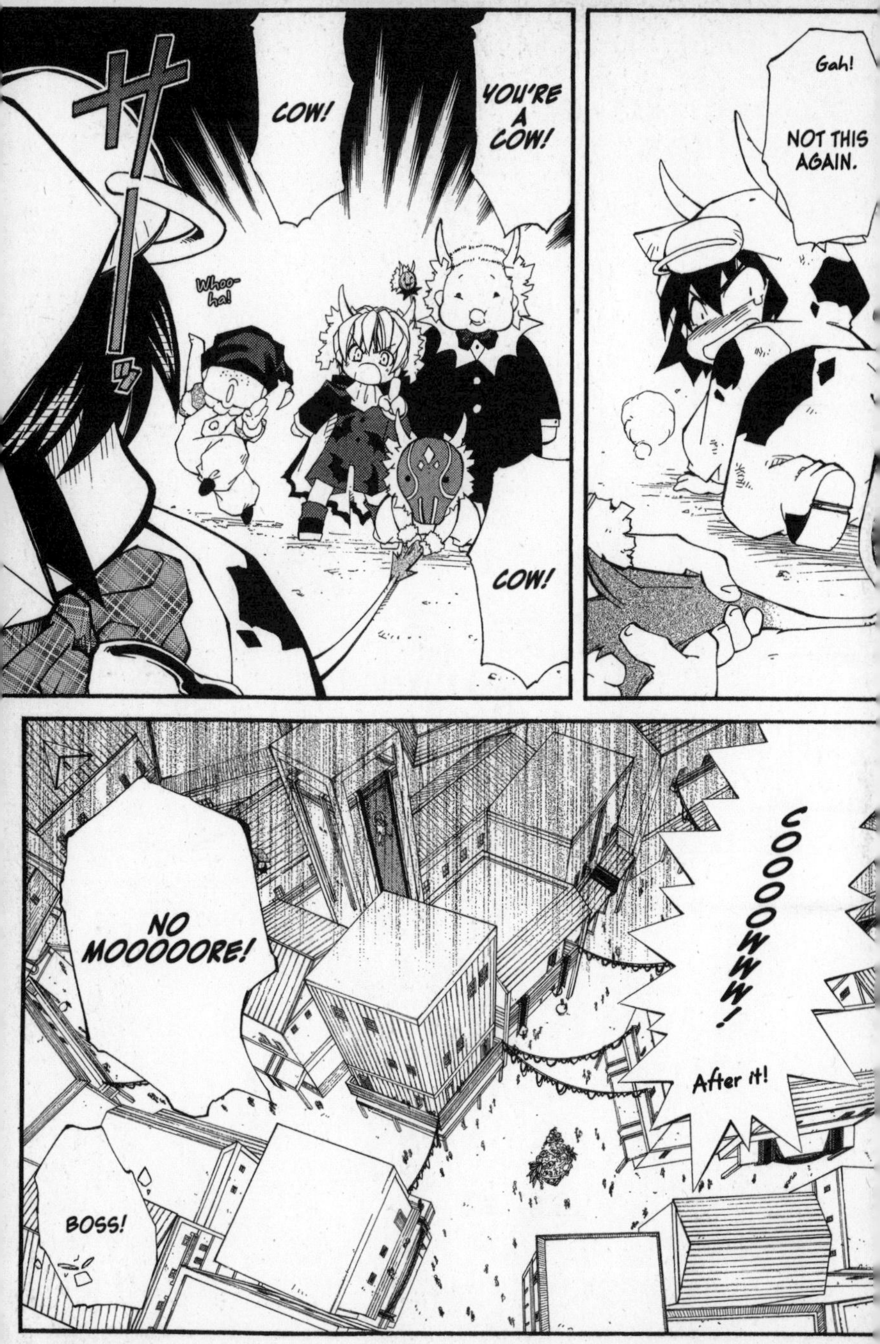
Gah!
NOT THIS AGAIN.
YOU'RE A COW!
COW!
Whoo-ha!
COW!
COOOOOWWW!
After it!
NO MOOOOORE!
BOSS!

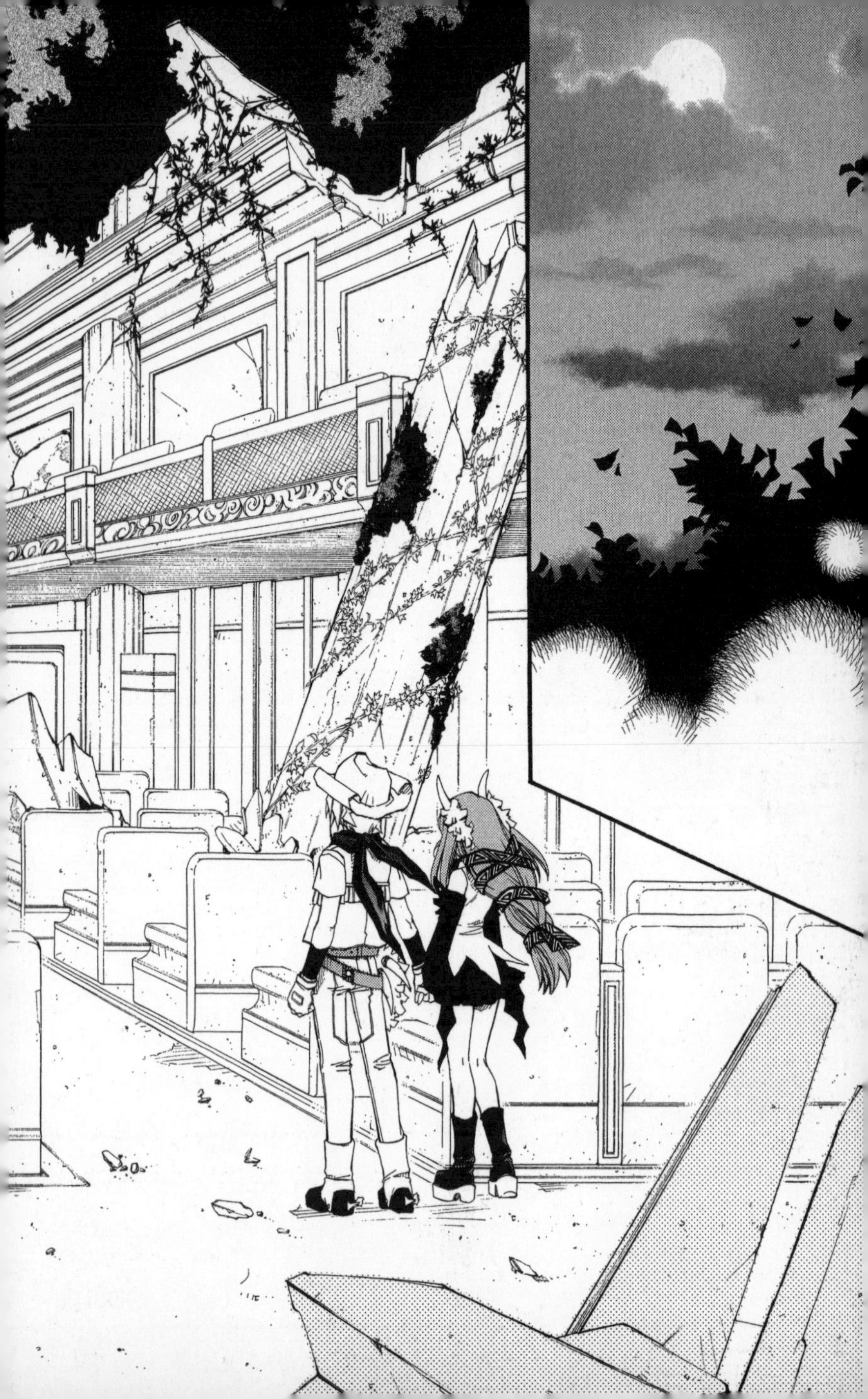

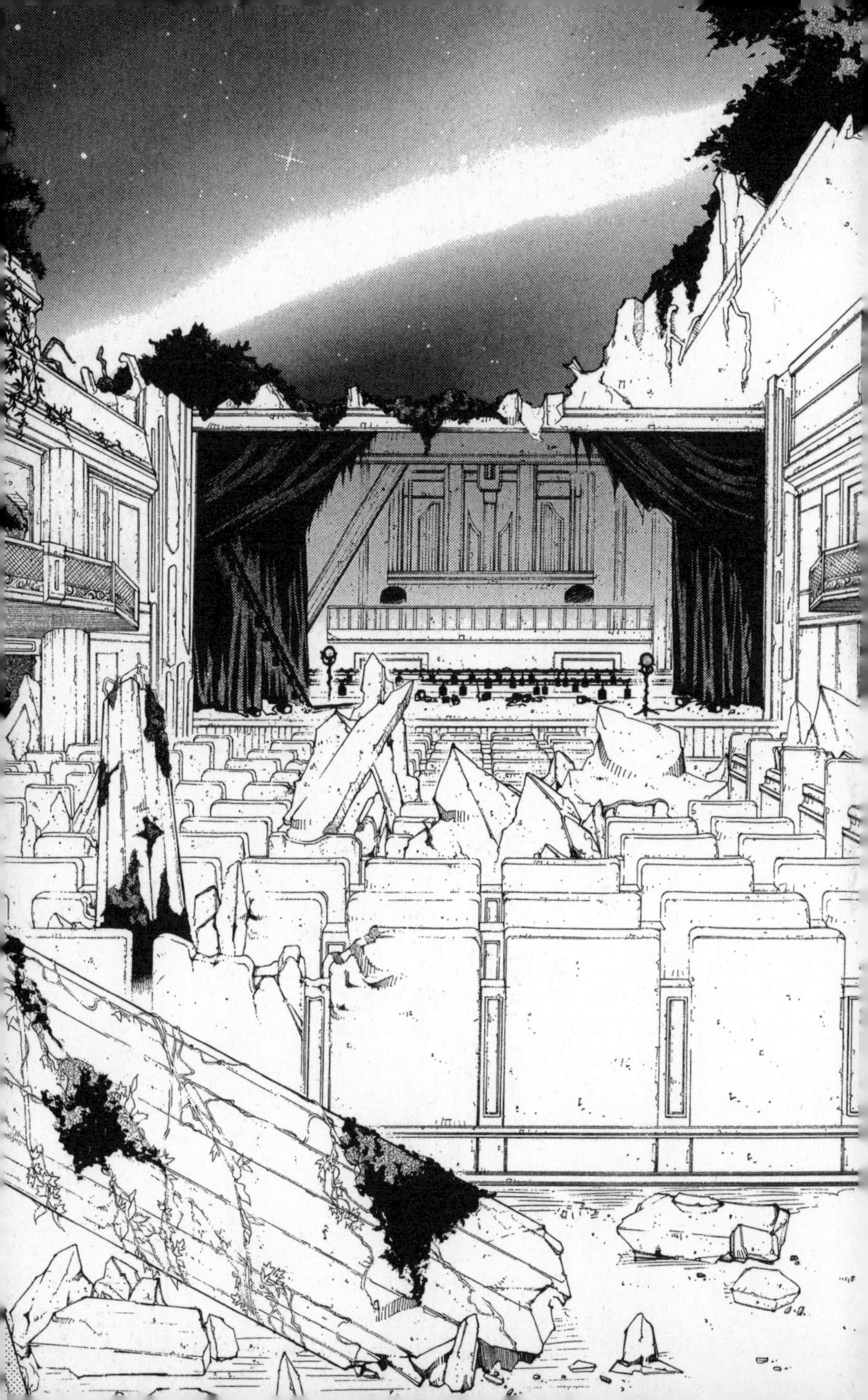

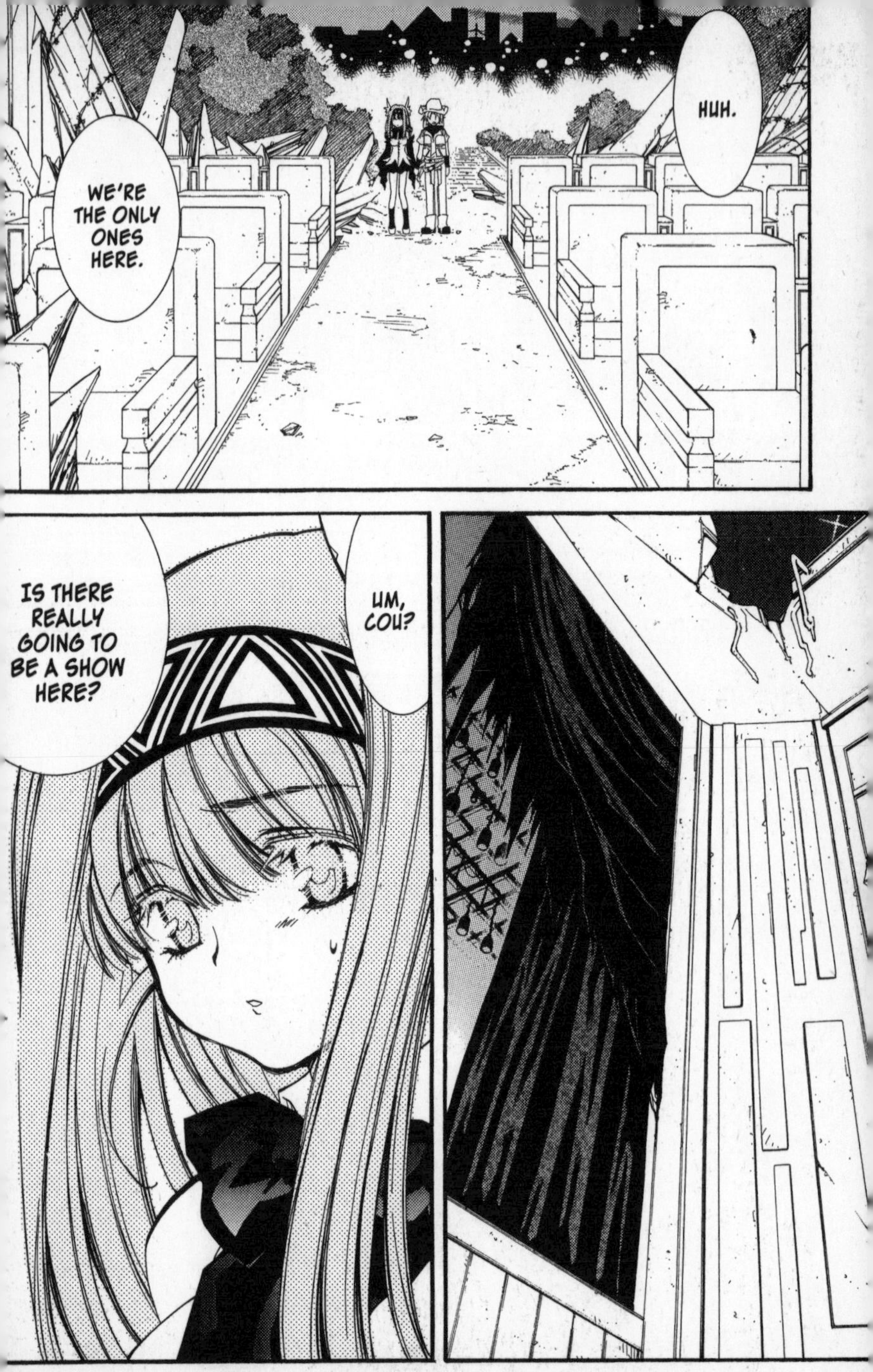
HUH.
WE'RE THE ONLY ONES HERE.
UM, COU?
IS THERE REALLY GOING TO BE A SHOW HERE?

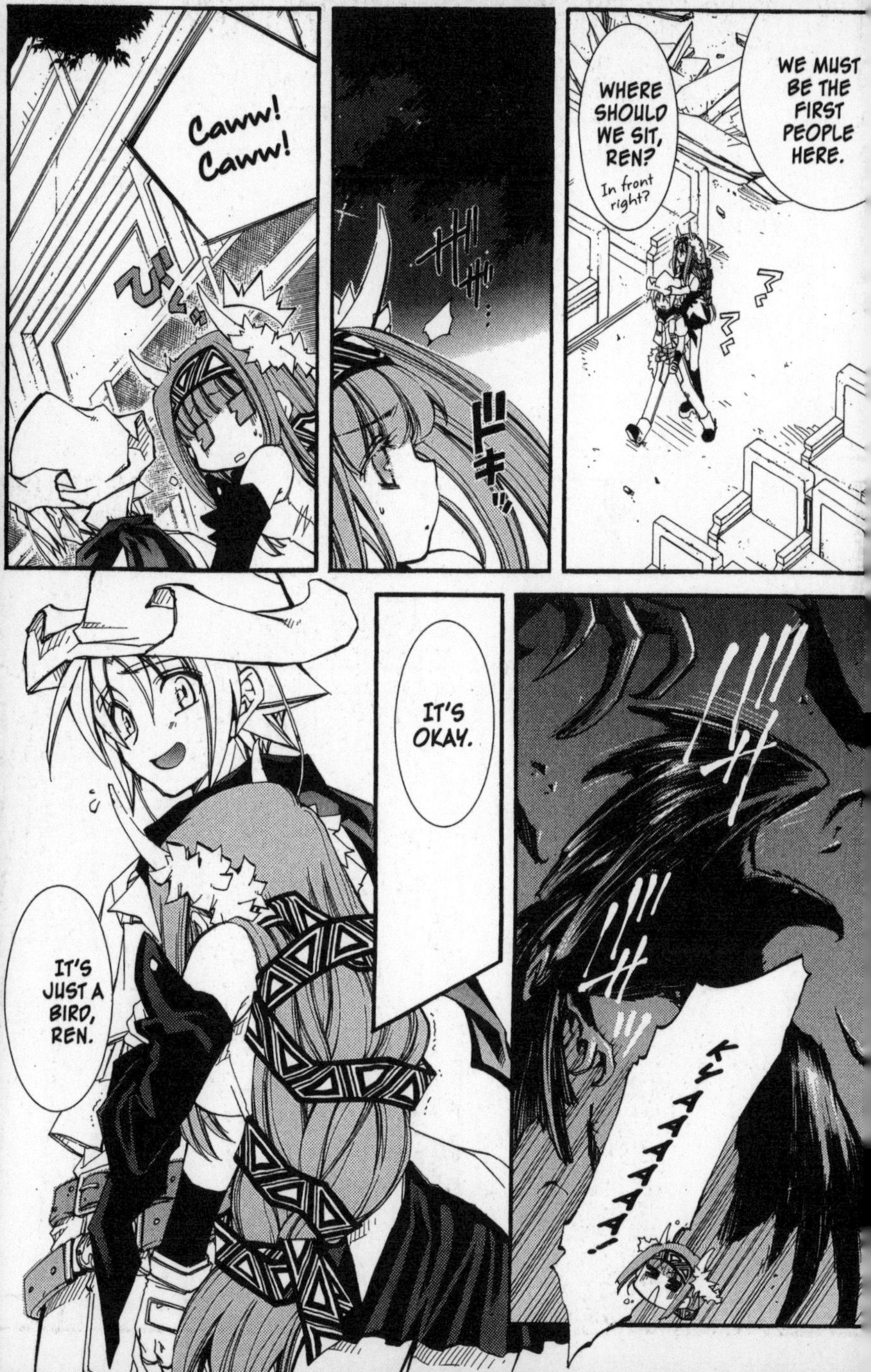
WE MUST BE THE FIRST PEOPLE HERE.
WHERE SHOULD WE SIT, REN?
In front right?
ドキッ
Caww! Caww!
KYAAAAAAA!
IT'S OKAY.
IT'S JUST A BIRD, REN.

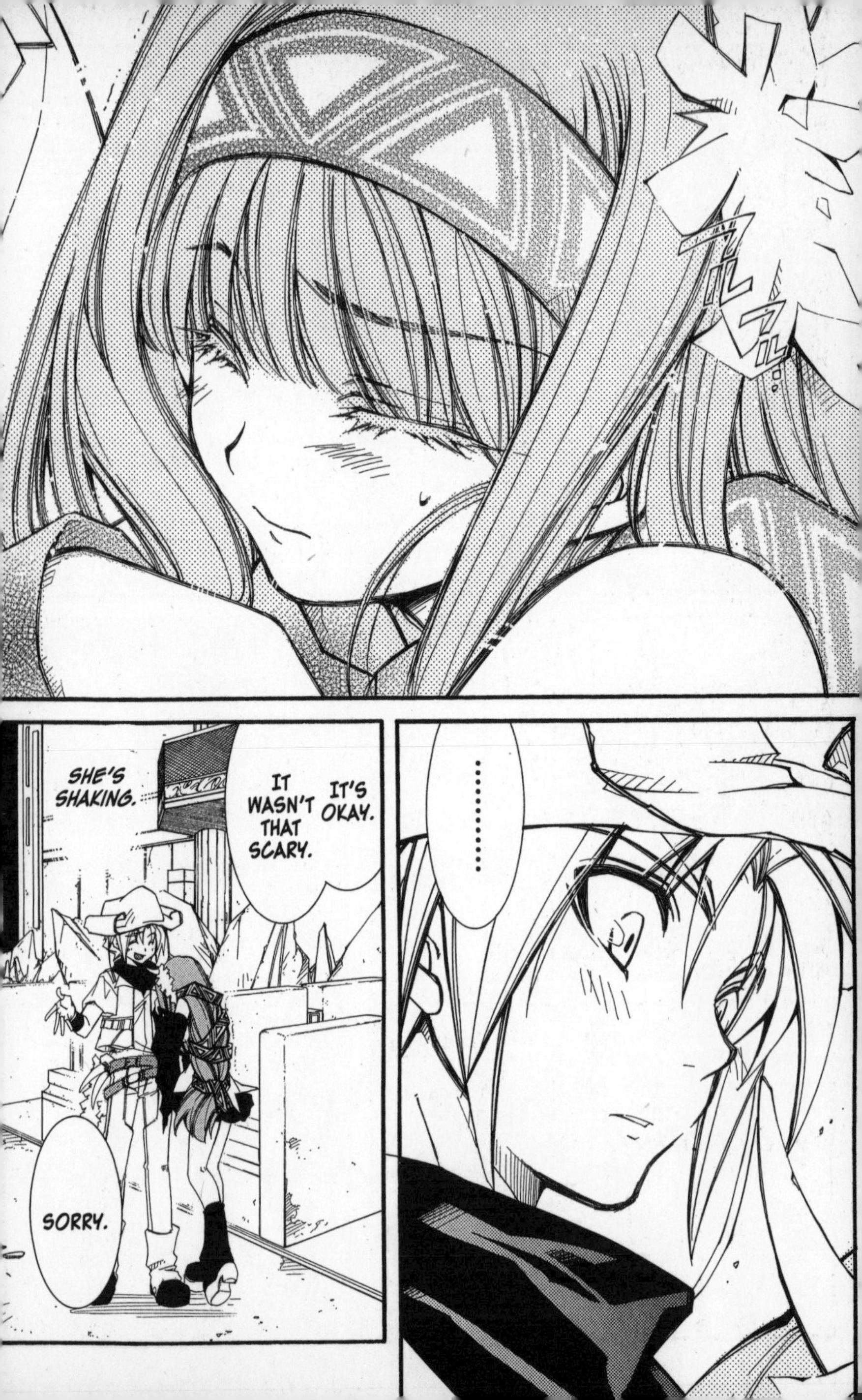
....
IT'S OKAY.
IT WASN'T THAT SCARY.
SHE'S SHAKING.
SORRY.

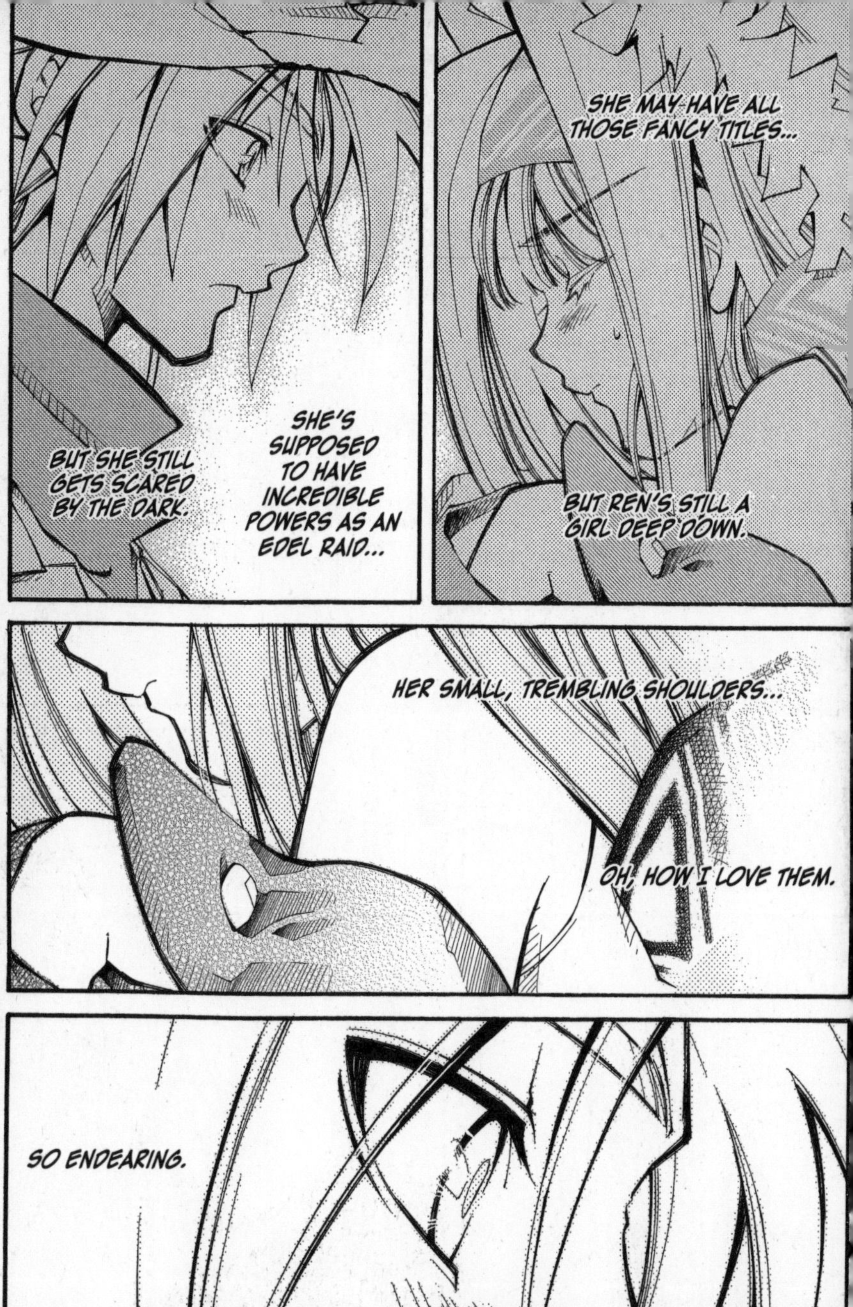
SHE MAY HAVE ALL THOSE FANCY TITLES...
BUT REN'S STILL A GIRL DEEP DOWN.
SHE'S SUPPOSED TO HAVE INCREDIBLE POWERS AS AN EDEL RAID...
BUT SHE STILL GETS SCARED BY THE DARK.
HER SMALL, TREMBLING SHOULDERS...
OH, HOW I LOVE THEM.
SO ENDEARING.

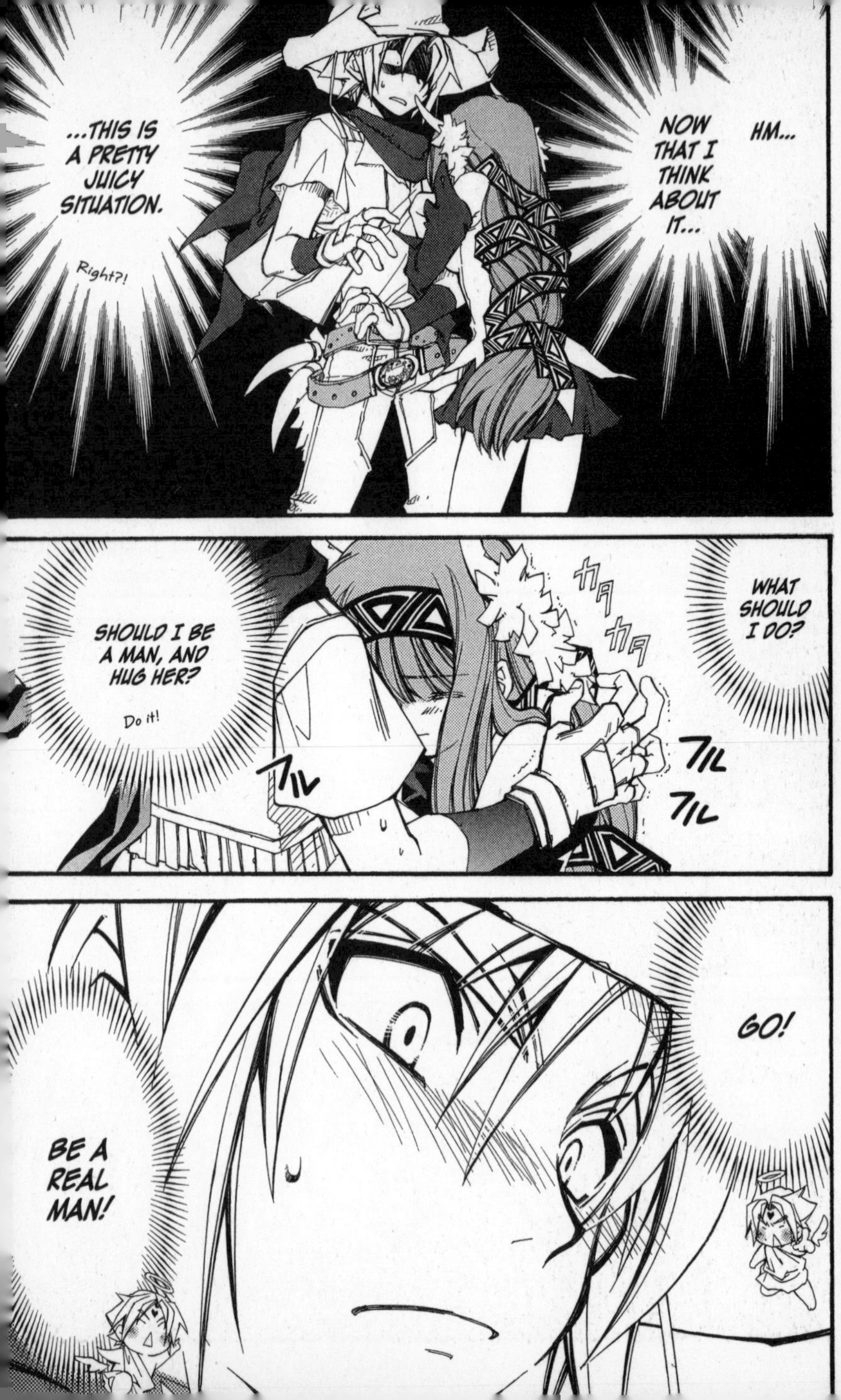
HM...
NOW THAT I THINK ABOUT IT...
...THIS IS A PRETTY JUICY SITUATION.
Right?!
WHAT SHOULD I DO?
カタ カタ
フル
フル
SHOULD I BE A MAN, AND HUG HER?
Do it!
フル
GO!
BE A REAL MAN!

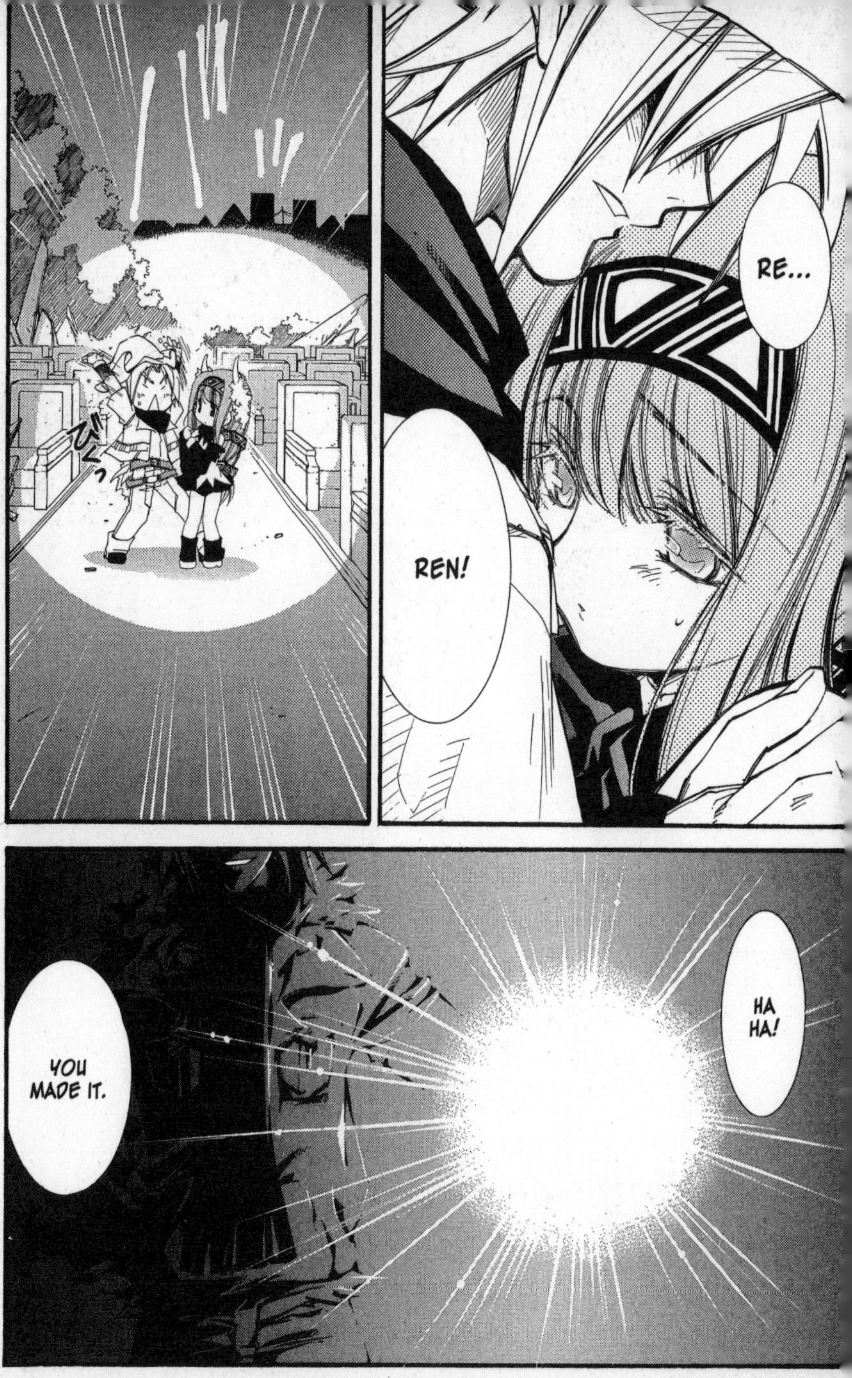
RE...
REN!
びくっ
HA HA!
YOU MADE IT.

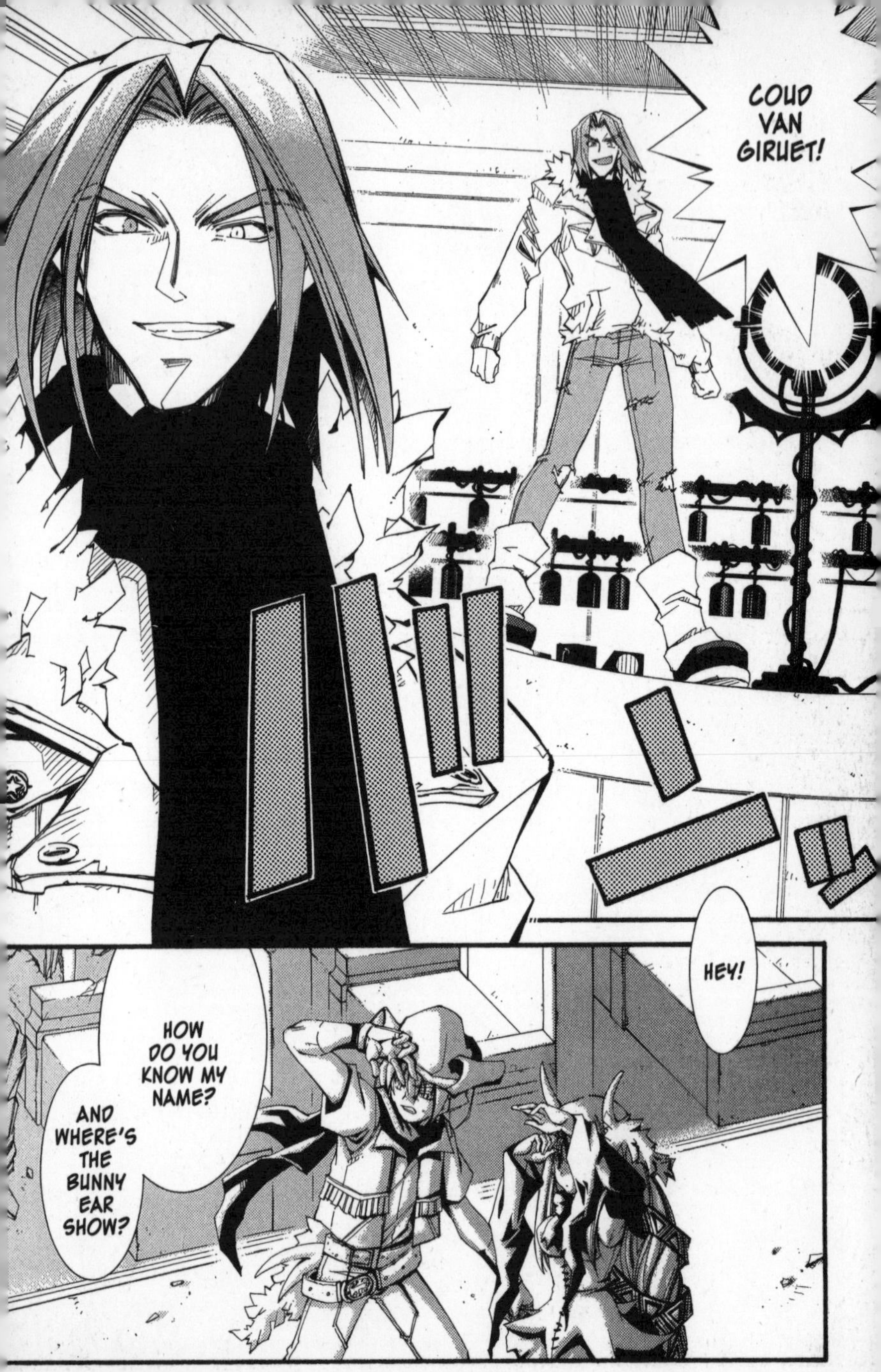
COUD VAN GIRUET!
HEY!
HOW DO YOU KNOW MY NAME?
AND WHERE'S THE BUNNY EAR SHOW?

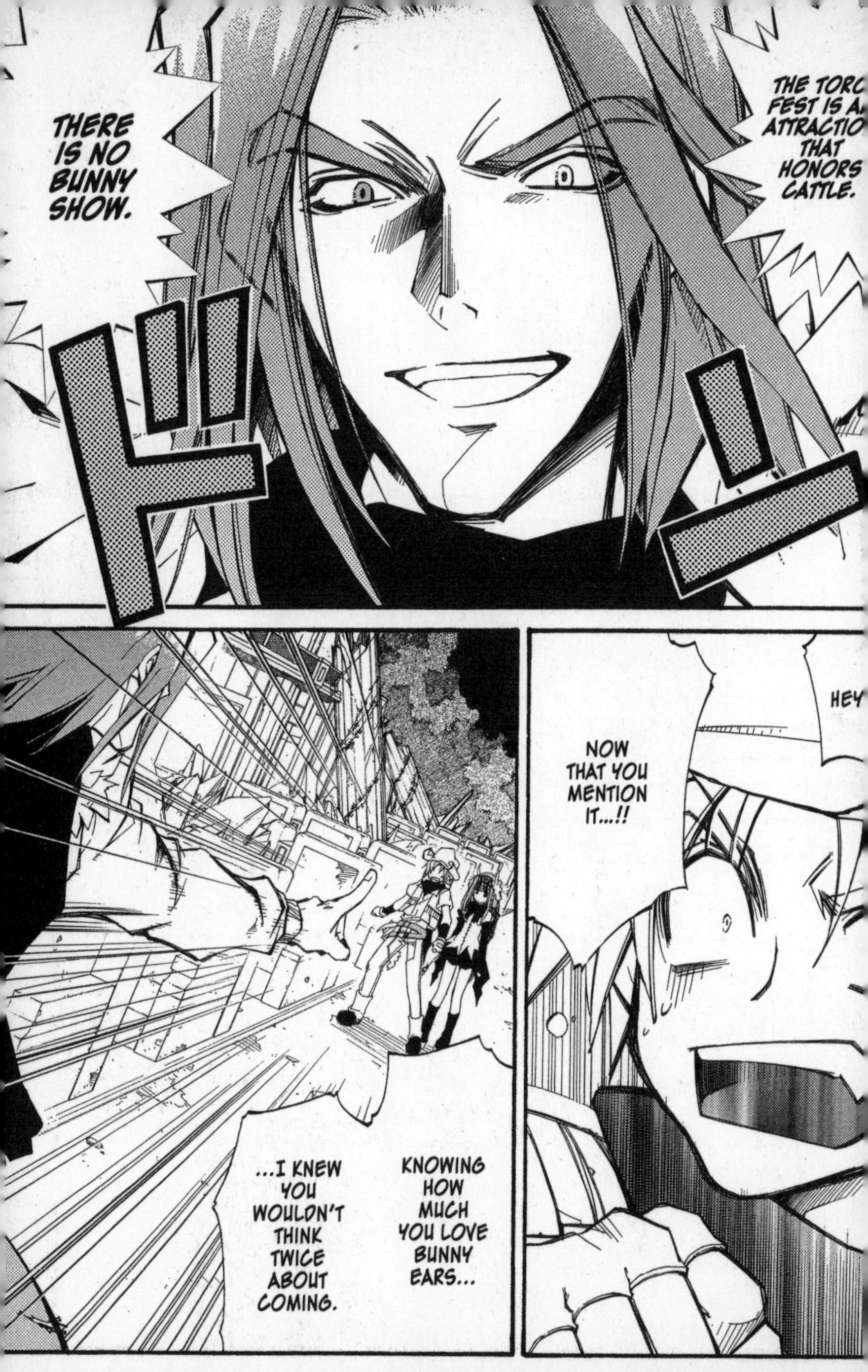
THE TORC FEST IS A ATTRACTIO THAT HONORS CATTLE.
THERE IS NO BUNNY SHOW.
HEY
NOW THAT YOU MENTION IT...!!
KNOWING HOW MUCH YOU LOVE BUNNY EARS...
...I KNEW YOU WOULDN'T THINK TWICE ABOUT COMING.

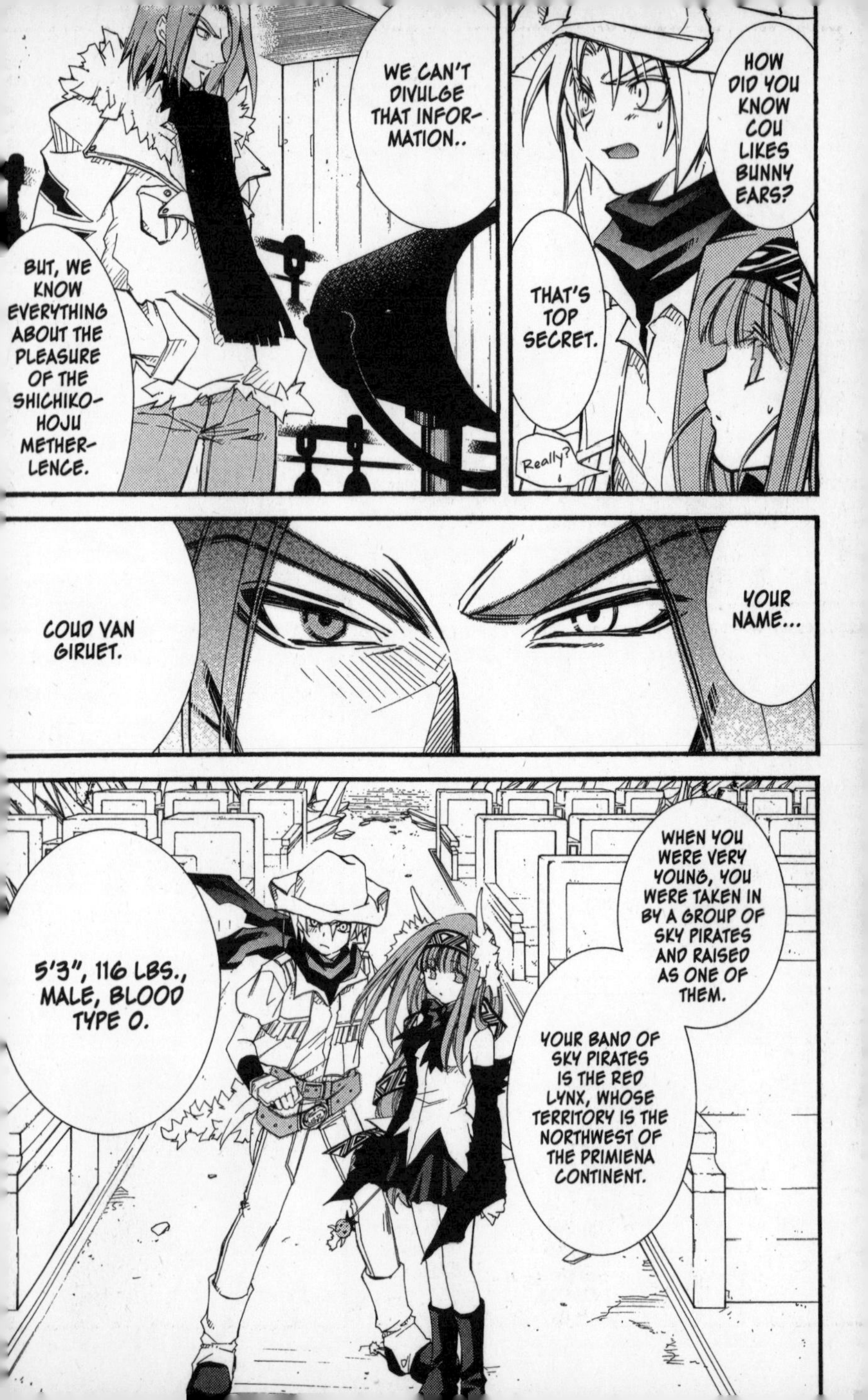
HOW DID YOU KNOW COU LIKES BUNNY EARS?
THAT'S TOP SECRET.
Really?
WE CAN'T DIVULGE THAT INFORMATION..
BUT, WE KNOW EVERYTHING ABOUT THE PLEASURE OF THE SHICHIKO-HOJU METHER-LENCE.
YOUR NAME...
COUD VAN GIRUET.
WHEN YOU WERE VERY YOUNG, YOU WERE TAKEN IN BY A GROUP OF SKY PIRATES AND RAISED AS ONE OF THEM.
YOUR BAND OF SKY PIRATES IS THE RED LYNX, WHOSE TERRITORY IS THE NORTHWEST OF THE PRIMIENA CONTINENT.
5'3", 116 LBS., MALE, BLOOD TYPE O.

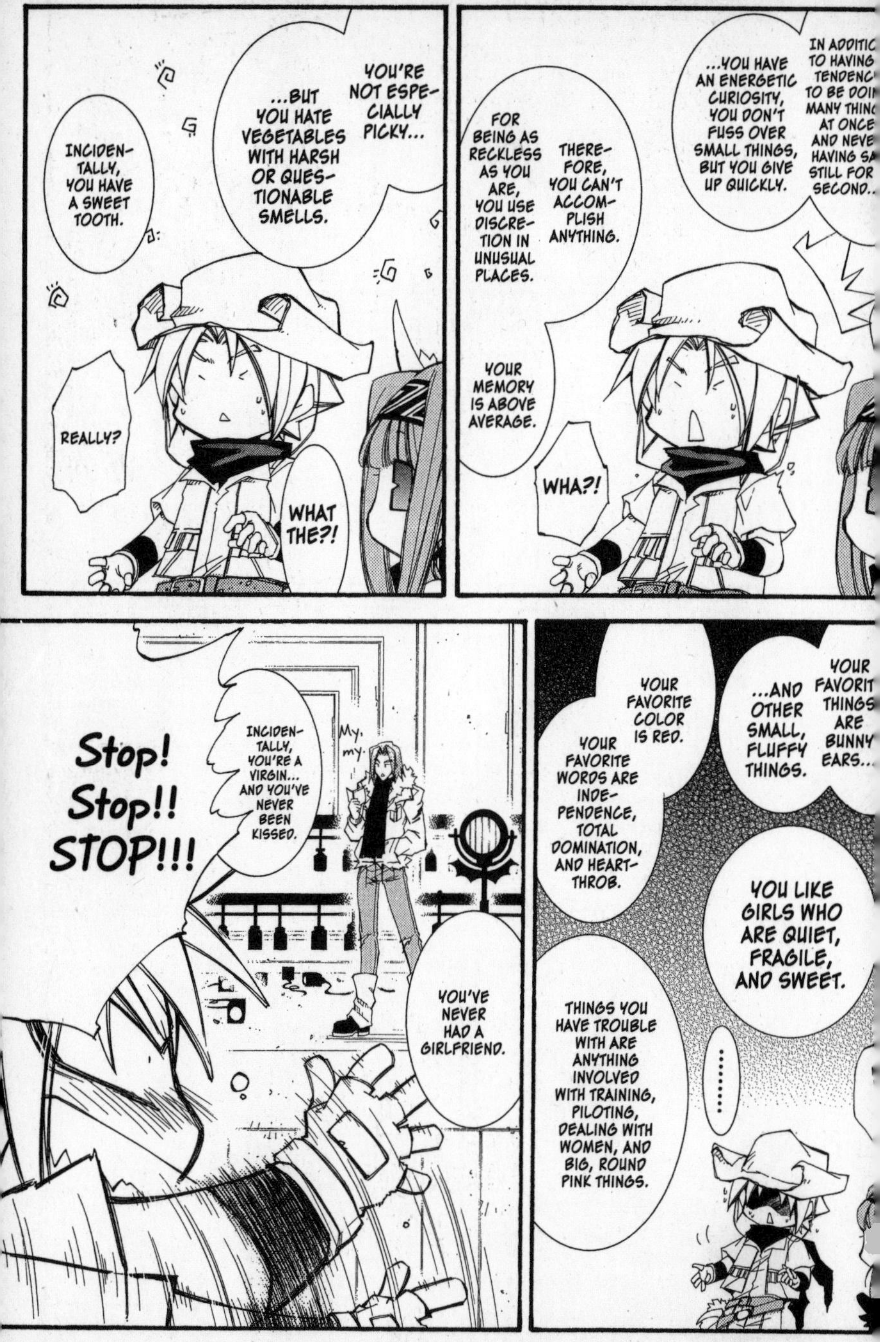
IN ADDITIC TO HAVING TENDENC TO BE DOII MANY THINC AT ONCE AND NEVE HAVING SA STILL FOR SECOND...
...YOU HAVE AN ENERGETIC CURIOSITY, YOU DON'T FUSS OVER SMALL THINGS, BUT YOU GIVE UP QUICKLY.
THERE-FORE, YOU CAN'T ACCOM-PLISH ANYTHING.
FOR BEING AS RECKLESS AS YOU ARE, YOU USE DISCRE-TION IN UNUSUAL PLACES.
YOUR MEMORY IS ABOVE AVERAGE.
WHA?!
YOU'RE NOT ESPE-CIALLY PICKY...
...BUT YOU HATE VEGETABLES WITH HARSH OR QUES-TIONABLE SMELLS.
INCIDEN-TALLY, YOU HAVE A SWEET TOOTH.
WHAT THE?!
REALLY?
YOUR FAVORIT THINGS ARE BUNNY EARS...
...AND OTHER SMALL, FLUFFY THINGS.
YOUR FAVORITE COLOR IS RED.
YOUR FAVORITE WORDS ARE INDE-PENDENCE, TOTAL DOMINATION, AND HEART-THROB.
YOU LIKE GIRLS WHO ARE QUIET, FRAGILE, AND SWEET.
......
THINGS YOU HAVE TROUBLE WITH ARE ANYTHING INVOLVED WITH TRAINING, PILOTING, DEALING WITH WOMEN, AND BIG, ROUND PINK THINGS.
INCIDEN-TALLY, YOU'RE A VIRGIN... AND YOU'VE NEVER BEEN KISSED.
My, my.
Stop! Stop!! STOP!!!
YOU'VE NEVER HAD A GIRLFRIEND.

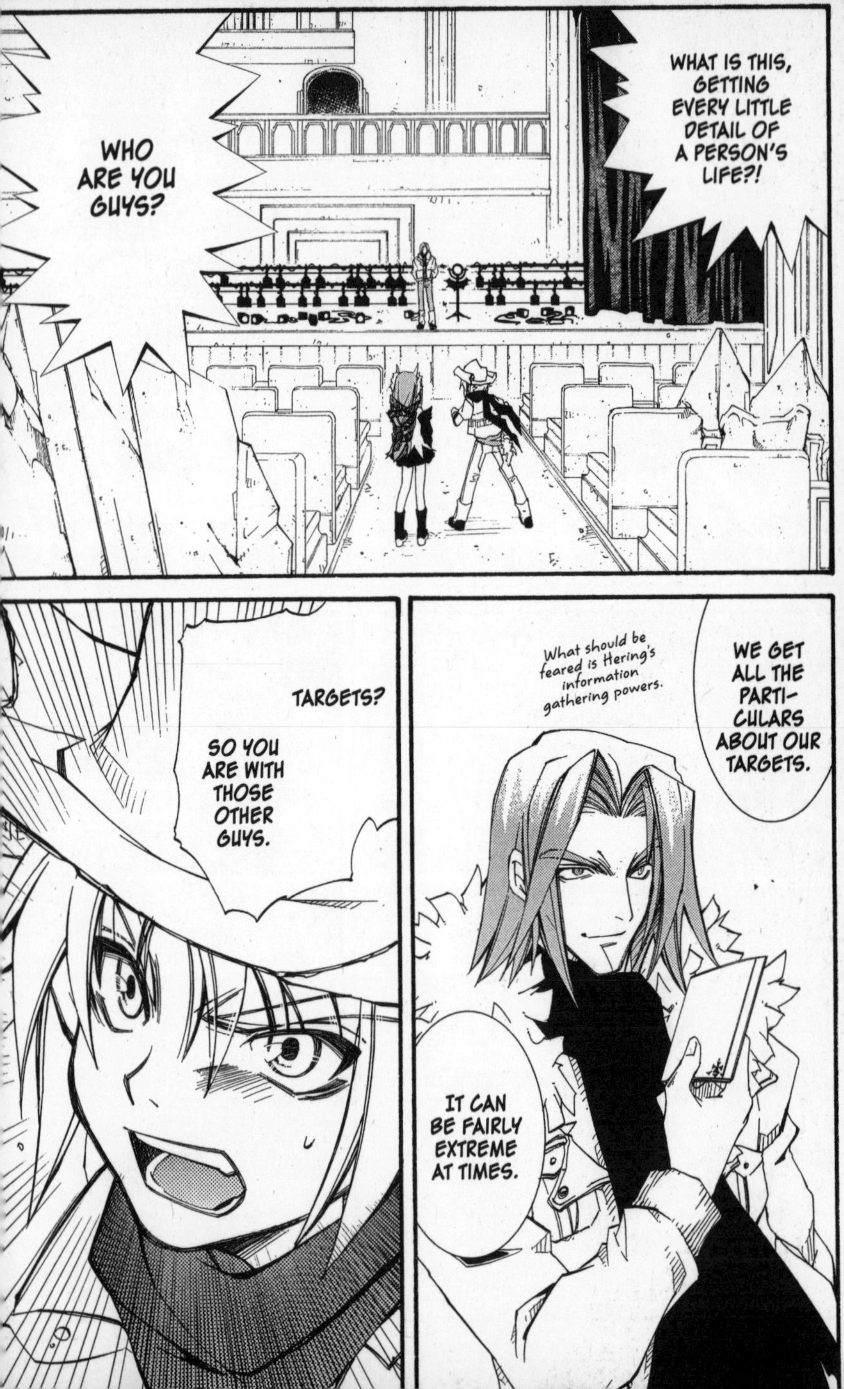
WHAT IS THIS, GETTING EVERY LITTLE DETAIL OF A PERSON'S LIFE?!
WHO ARE YOU GUYS?
WE GET ALL THE PARTI-CULARS ABOUT OUR TARGETS.
What should be feared is Hering's information gathering powers.
IT CAN BE FAIRLY EXTREME AT TIMES.
TARGETS?
SO YOU ARE WITH THOSE OTHER GUYS.

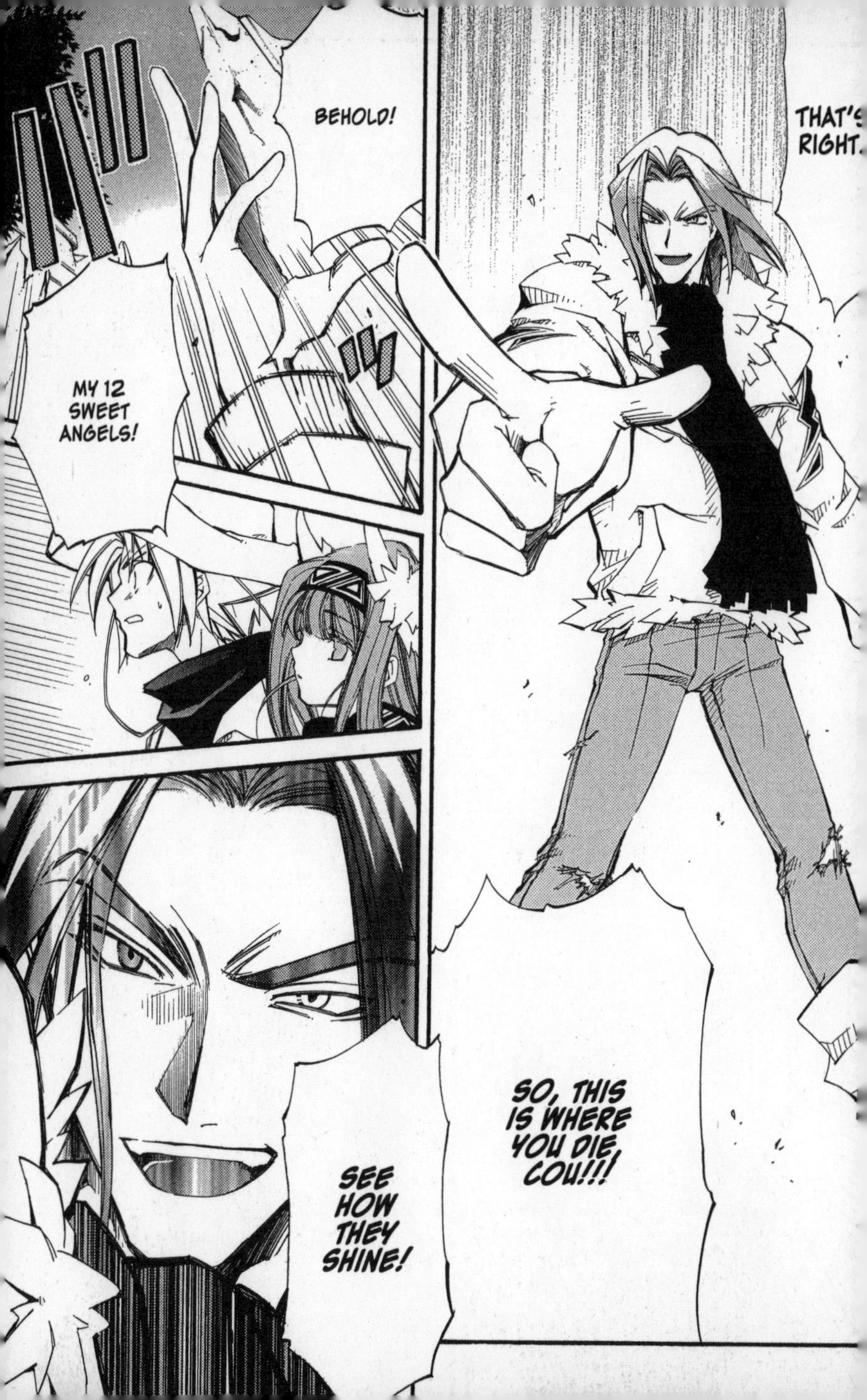
THAT'S RIGHT.
SO, THIS IS WHERE YOU DIE, COU!!!
BEHOLD!
MY 12 SWEET ANGELS!
SEE HOW THEY SHINE!

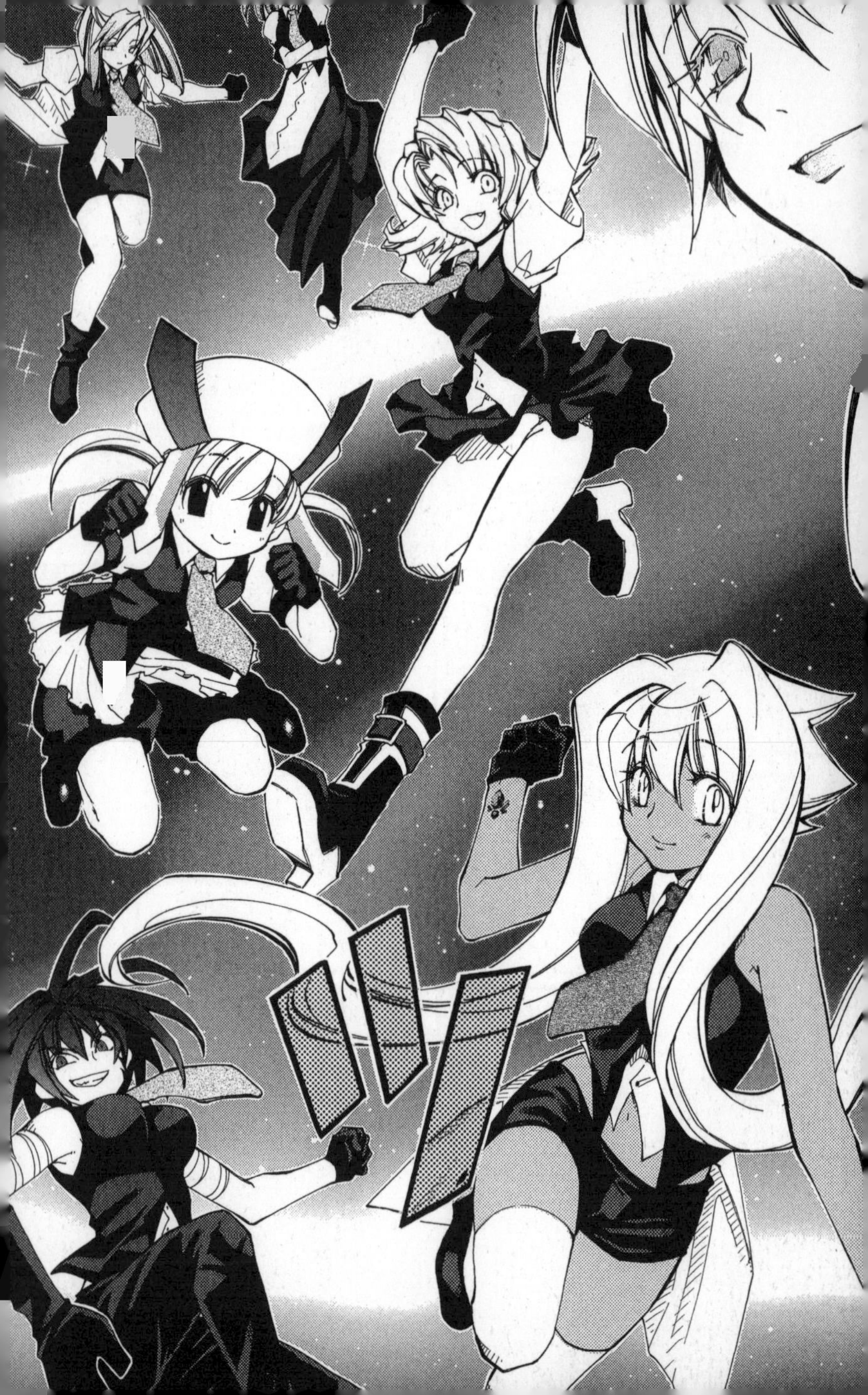

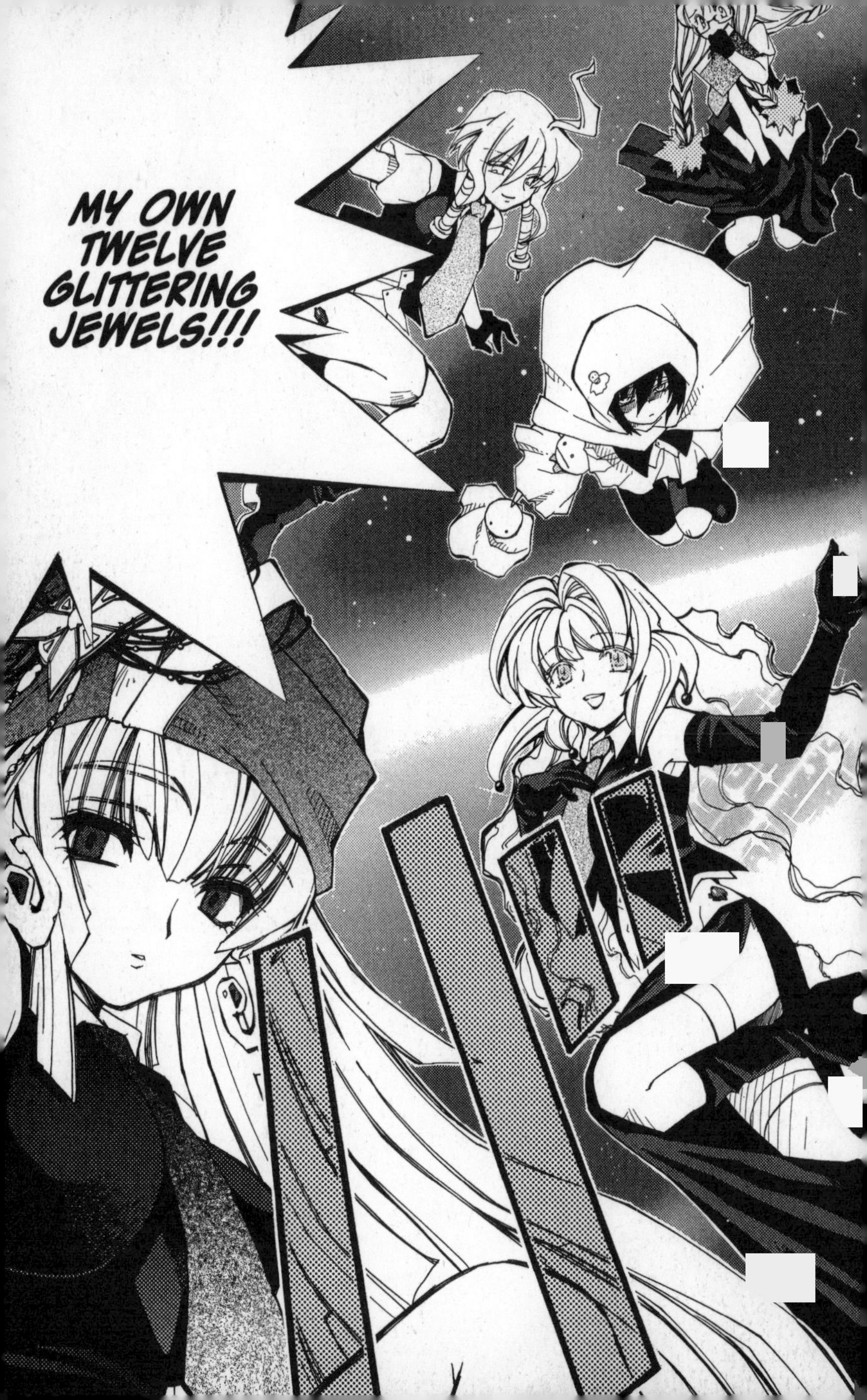
MY OWN TWELVE GLITTERING JEWELS!!!

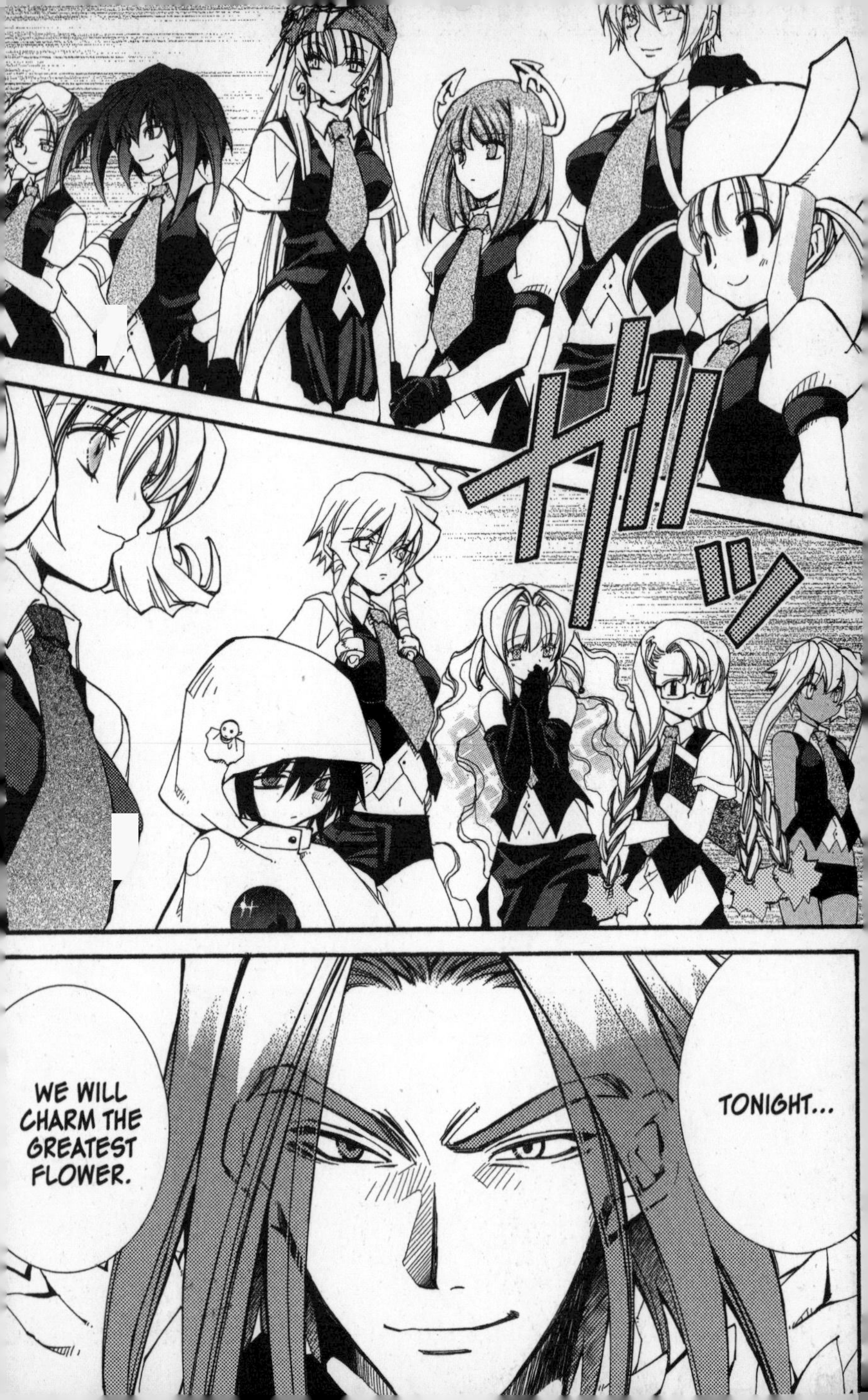
ザッ
TONIGHT...
WE WILL CHARM THE GREATEST FLOWER.

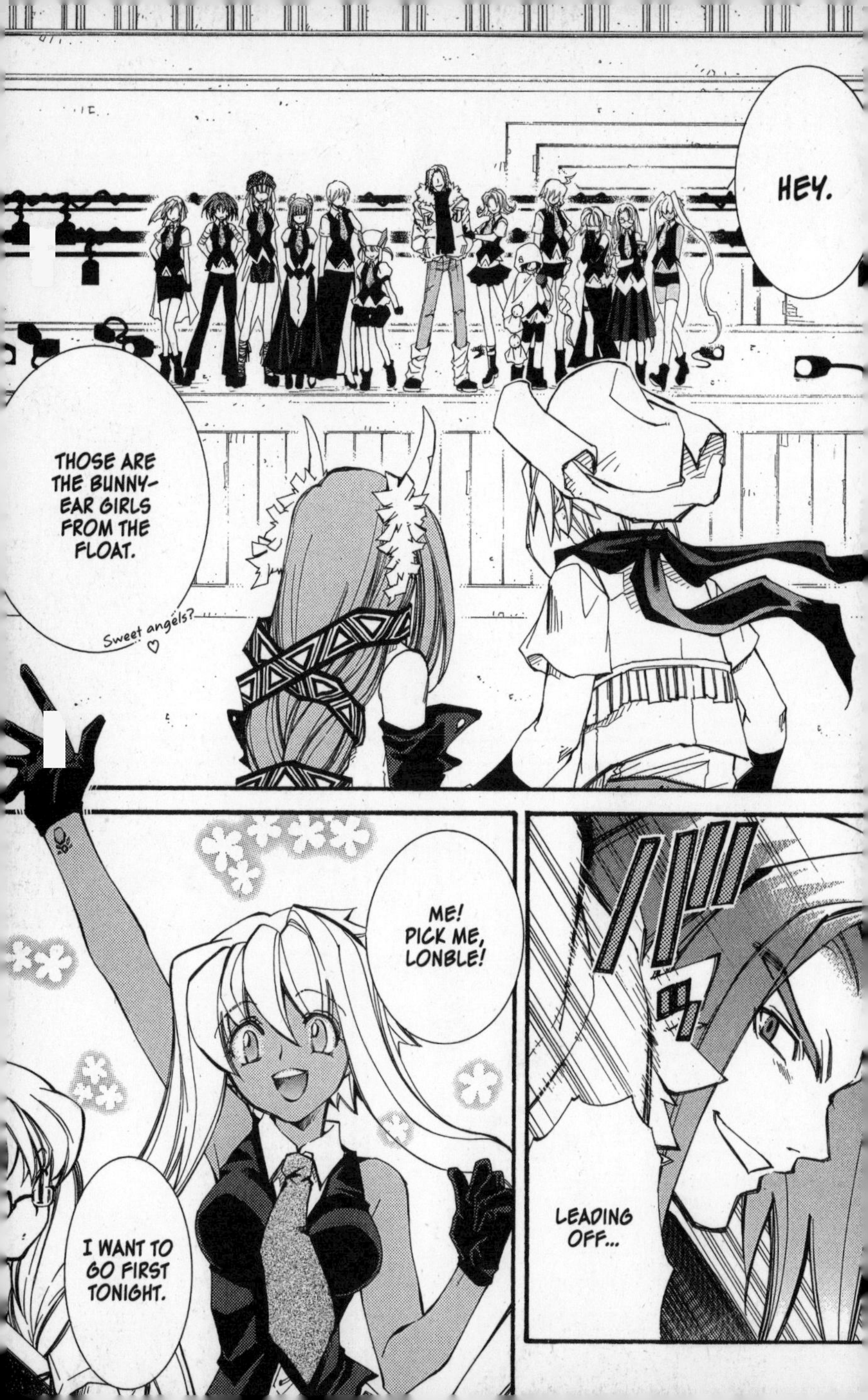
HEY.
THOSE ARE THE BUNNY-EAR GIRLS FROM THE FLOAT.
Sweet angels? ♡
LEADING OFF...
ME! PICK ME, LONBLE!
I WANT TO GO FIRST TONIGHT.

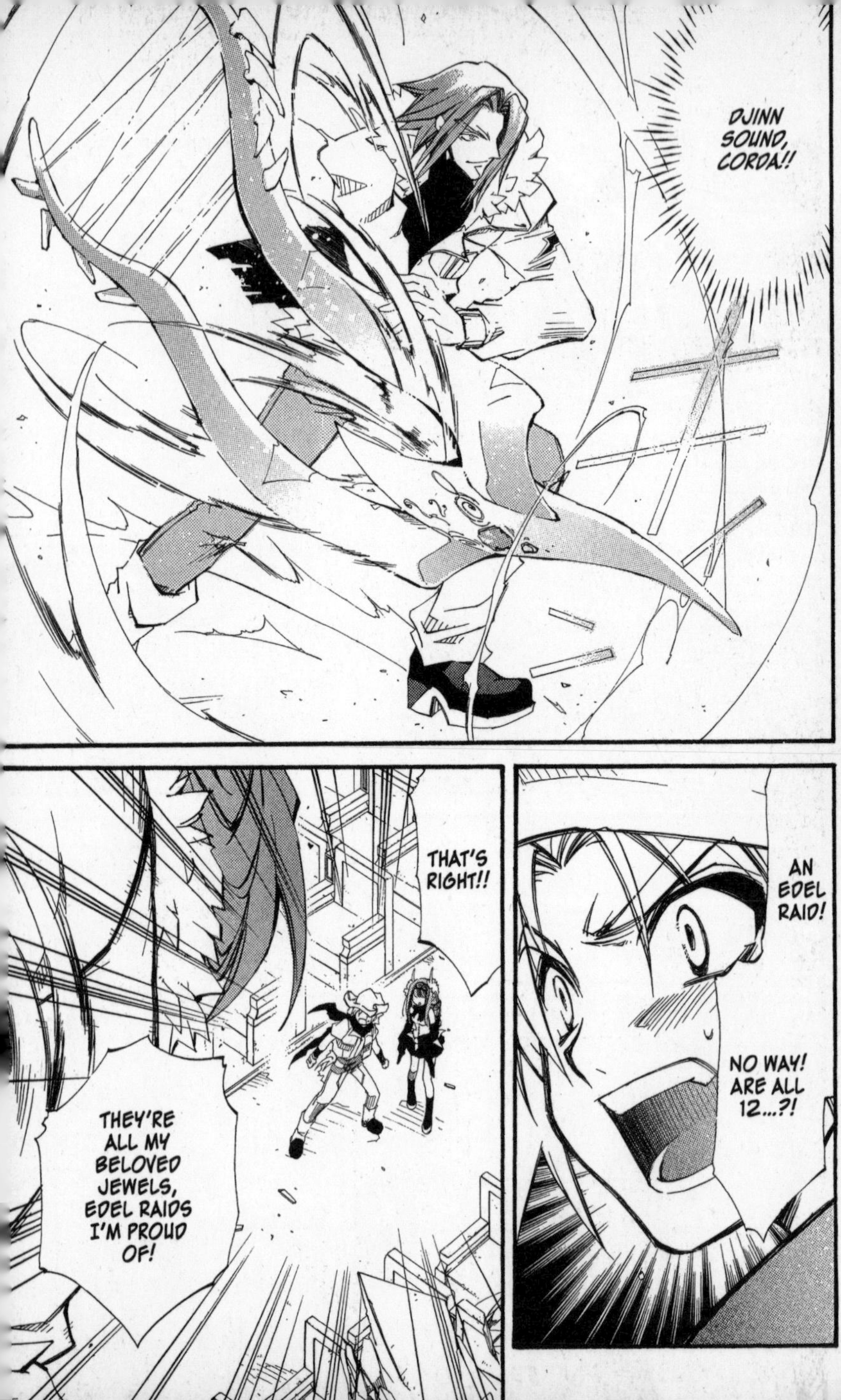
DJINN SOUND, CORDA!!
AN EDEL RAID!
NO WAY! ARE ALL 12...?!
THAT'S RIGHT!!
THEY'RE ALL MY BELOVED JEWELS, EDEL RAIDS I'M PROUD OF!

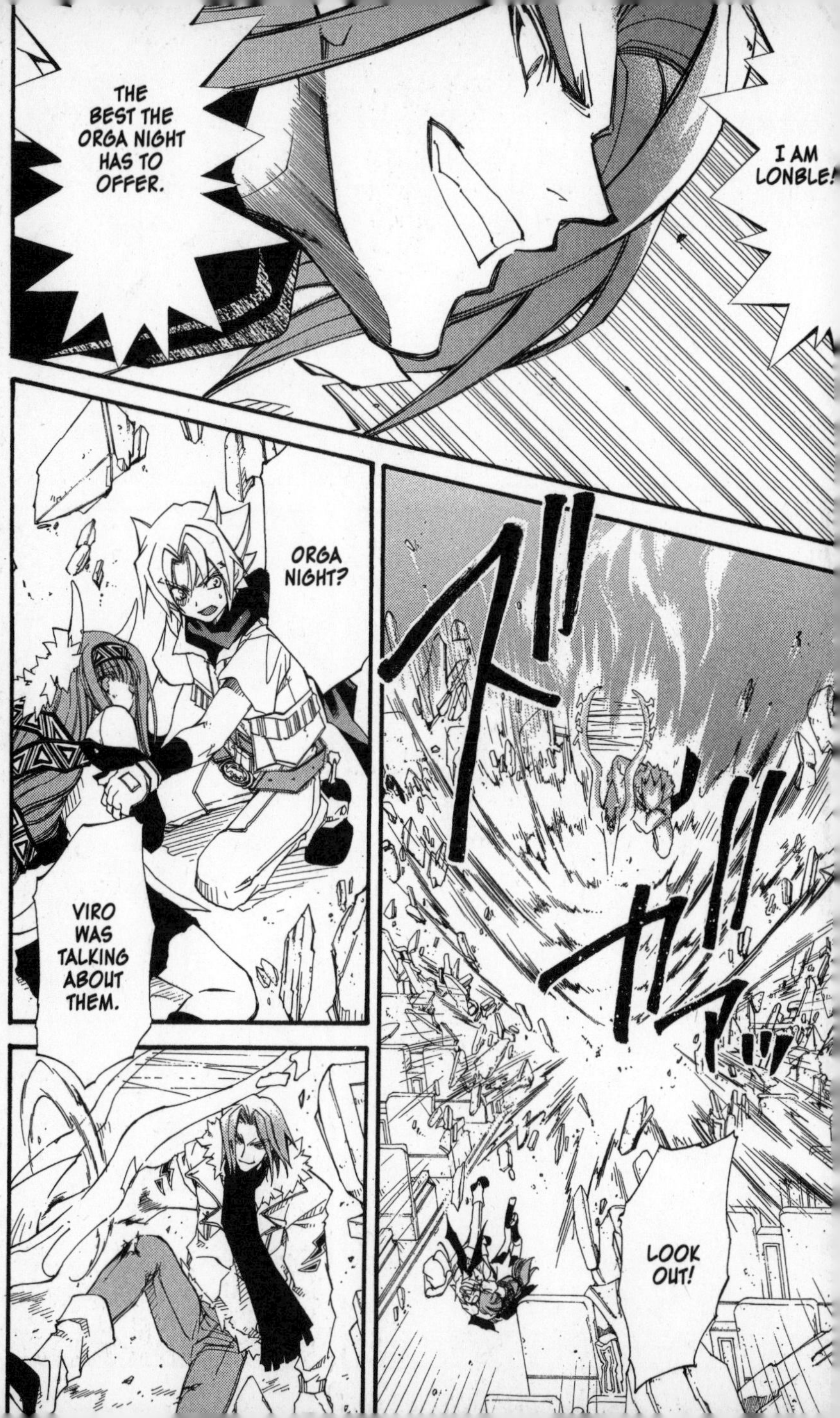
I AM LONBLE!
THE BEST THE ORGA NIGHT HAS TO OFFER.
LOOK OUT!
ORGA NIGHT?
VIRO WAS TALKING ABOUT THEM.

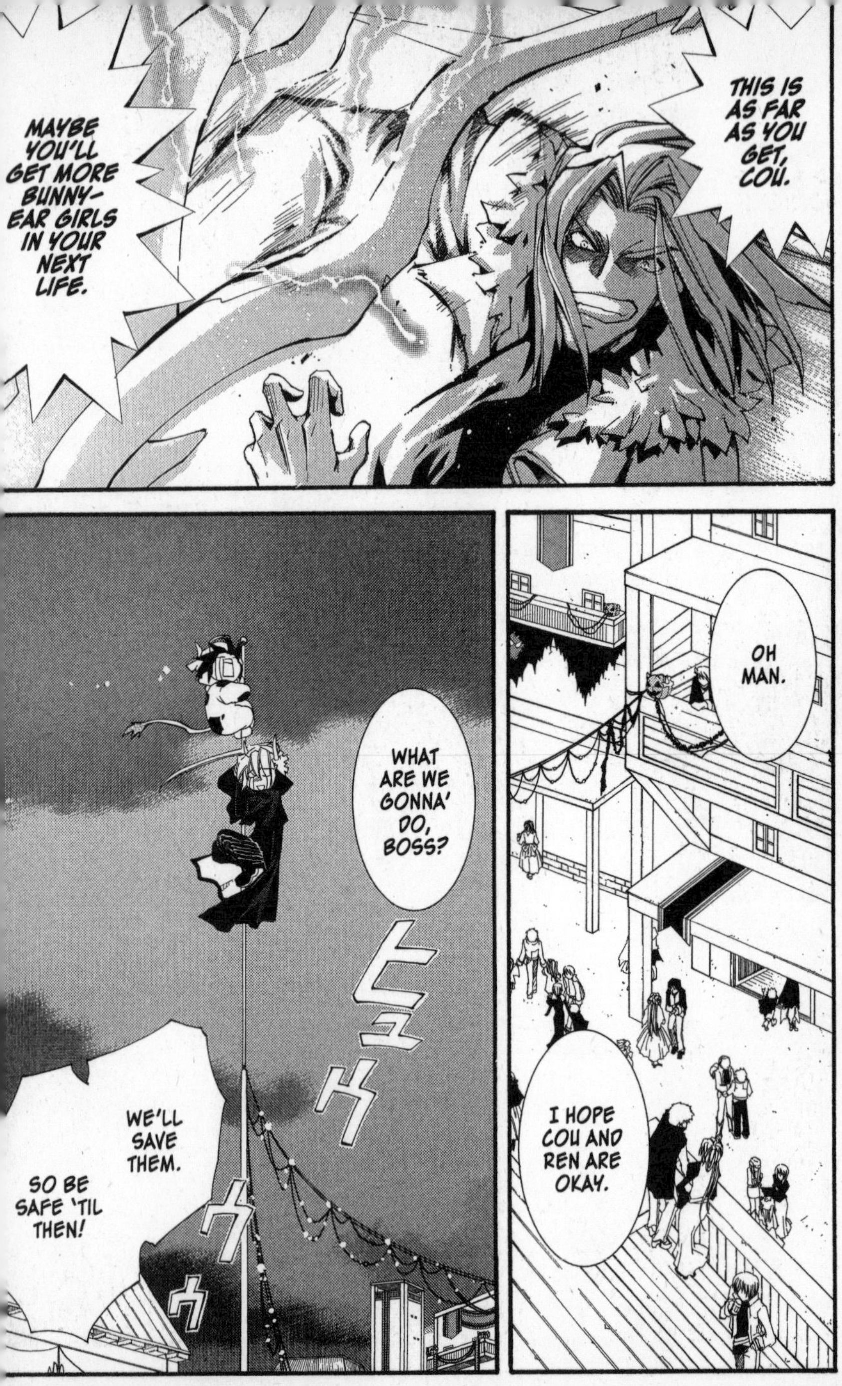

THIS IS AS FAR AS YOU GET, COU.
MAYBE YOU'LL GET MORE BUNNY-EAR GIRLS IN YOUR NEXT LIFE.
OH MAN.
I HOPE COU AND REN ARE OKAY.
WHAT ARE WE GONNA' DO, BOSS?
ヒュウゥ
WE'LL SAVE THEM.
SO BE SAFE 'TIL THEN!

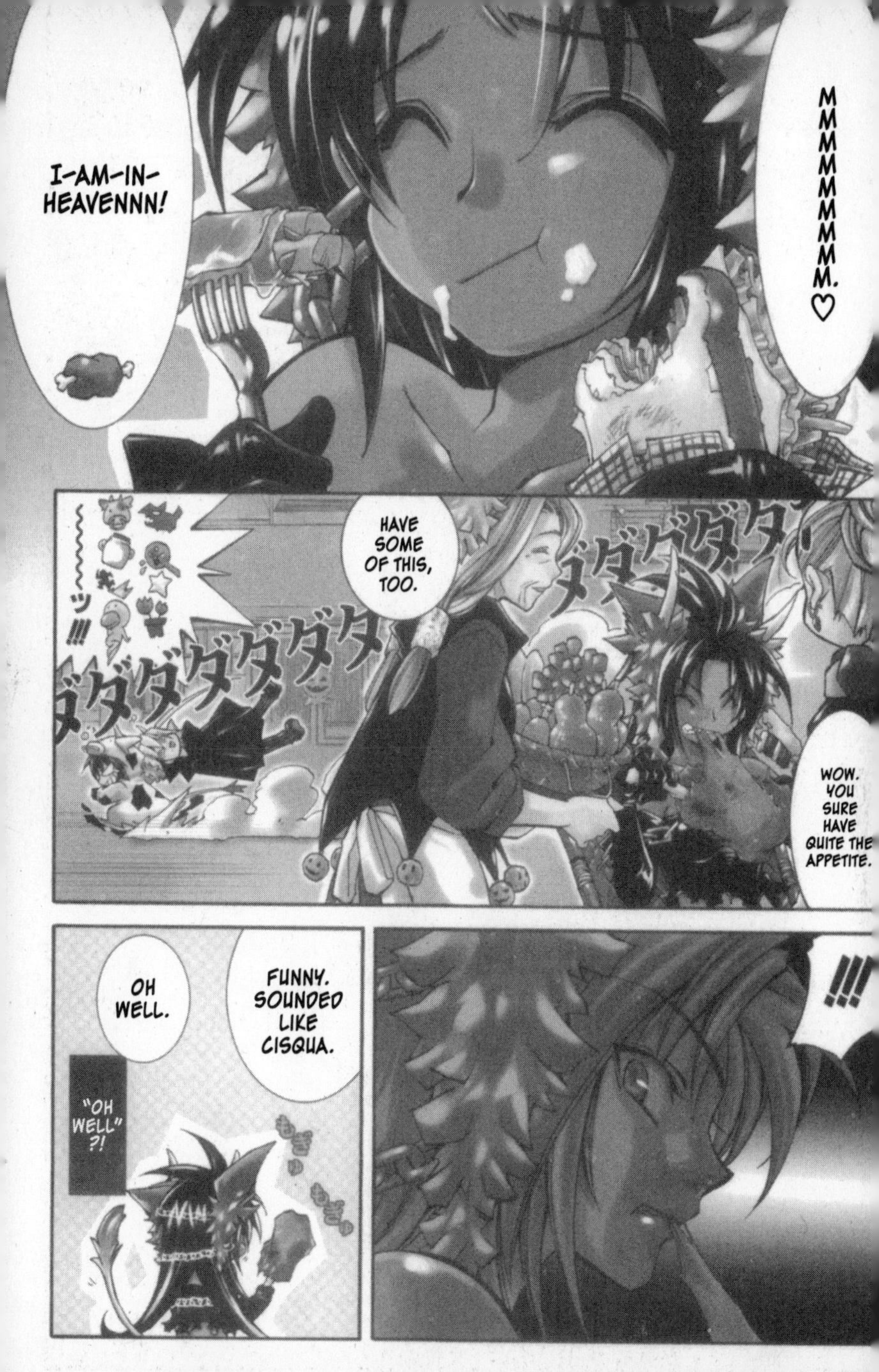
MMMMMMMMMM.♡
I-AM-IN-HEAVENNN!
WOW. YOU SURE HAVE QUITE THE APPETITE.
HAVE SOME OF THIS, TOO.
!!!
FUNNY. SOUNDED LIKE CISQUA.
OH WELL.
"OH WELL"?!

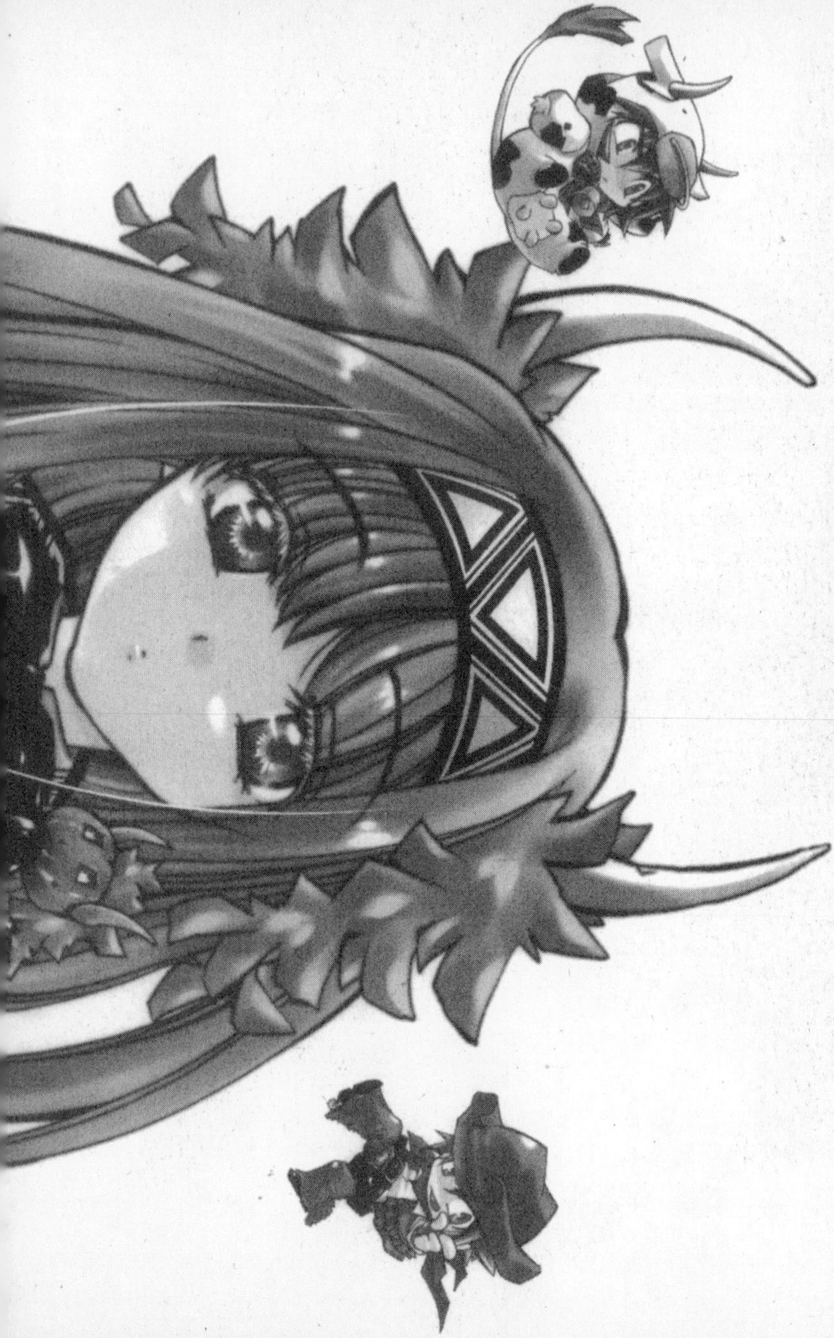

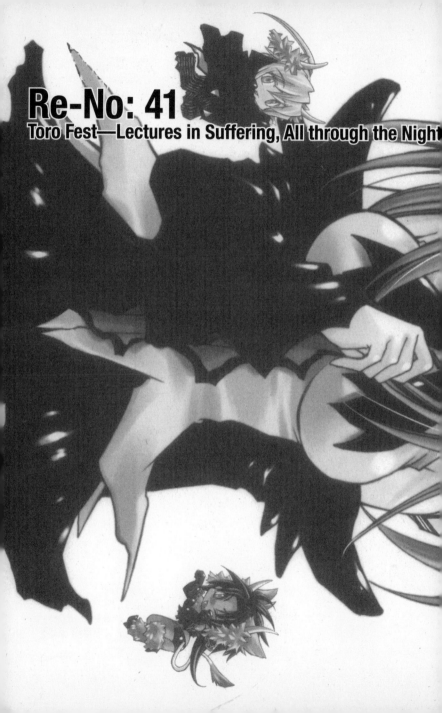

Re-No: 41
Toro Fest—Lectures in Suffering, All through the Night

ELEMENTAL GELADE

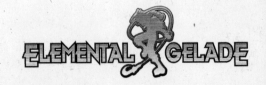

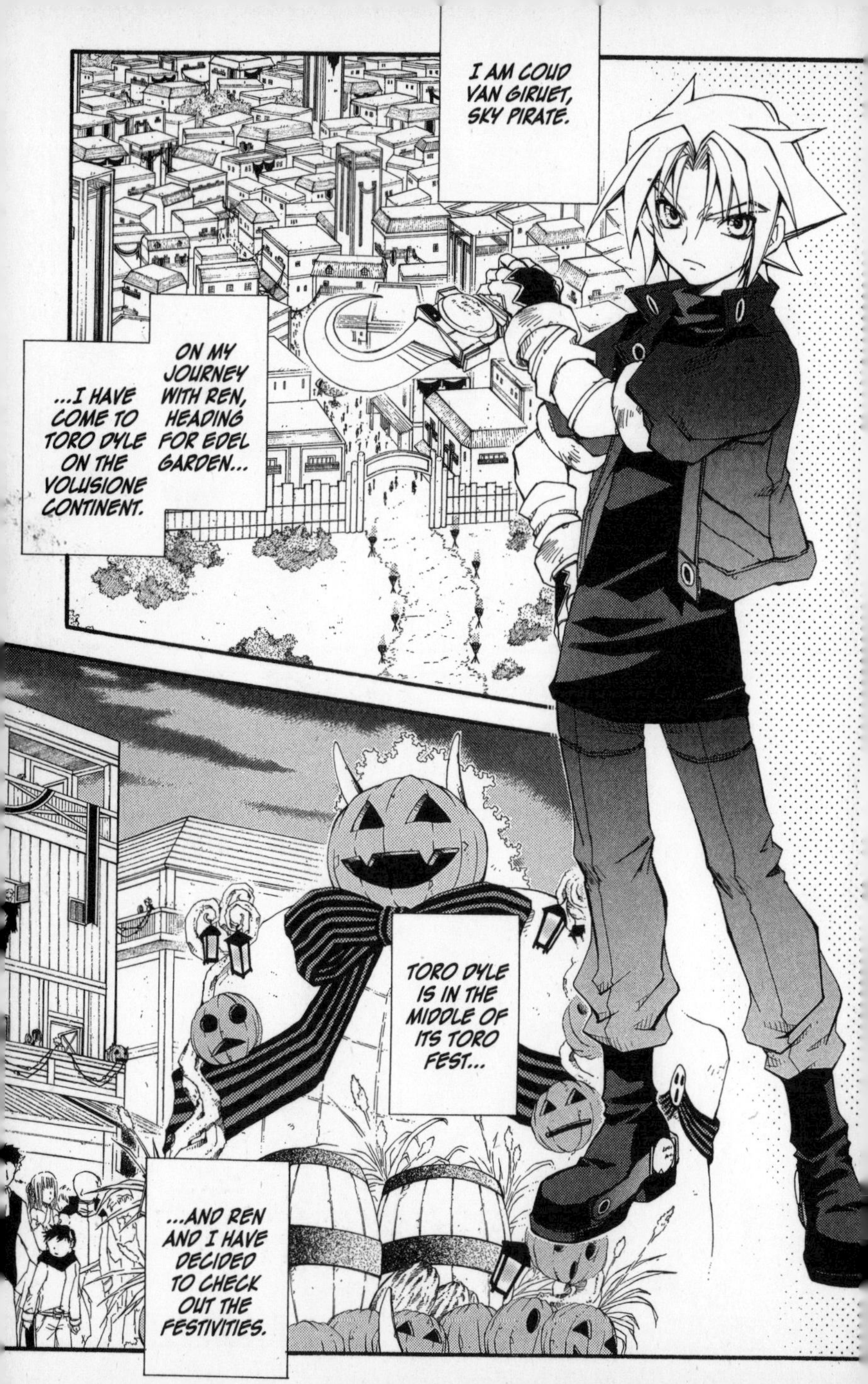
I AM COUD VAN GIRUET, SKY PIRATE.
ON MY JOURNEY WITH REN, HEADING FOR EDEL GARDEN...
...I HAVE COME TO TORO DYLE ON THE VOLUSIONE CONTINENT.
TORO DYLE IS IN THE MIDDLE OF ITS TORO FEST...
...AND REN AND I HAVE DECIDED TO CHECK OUT THE FESTIVITIES.

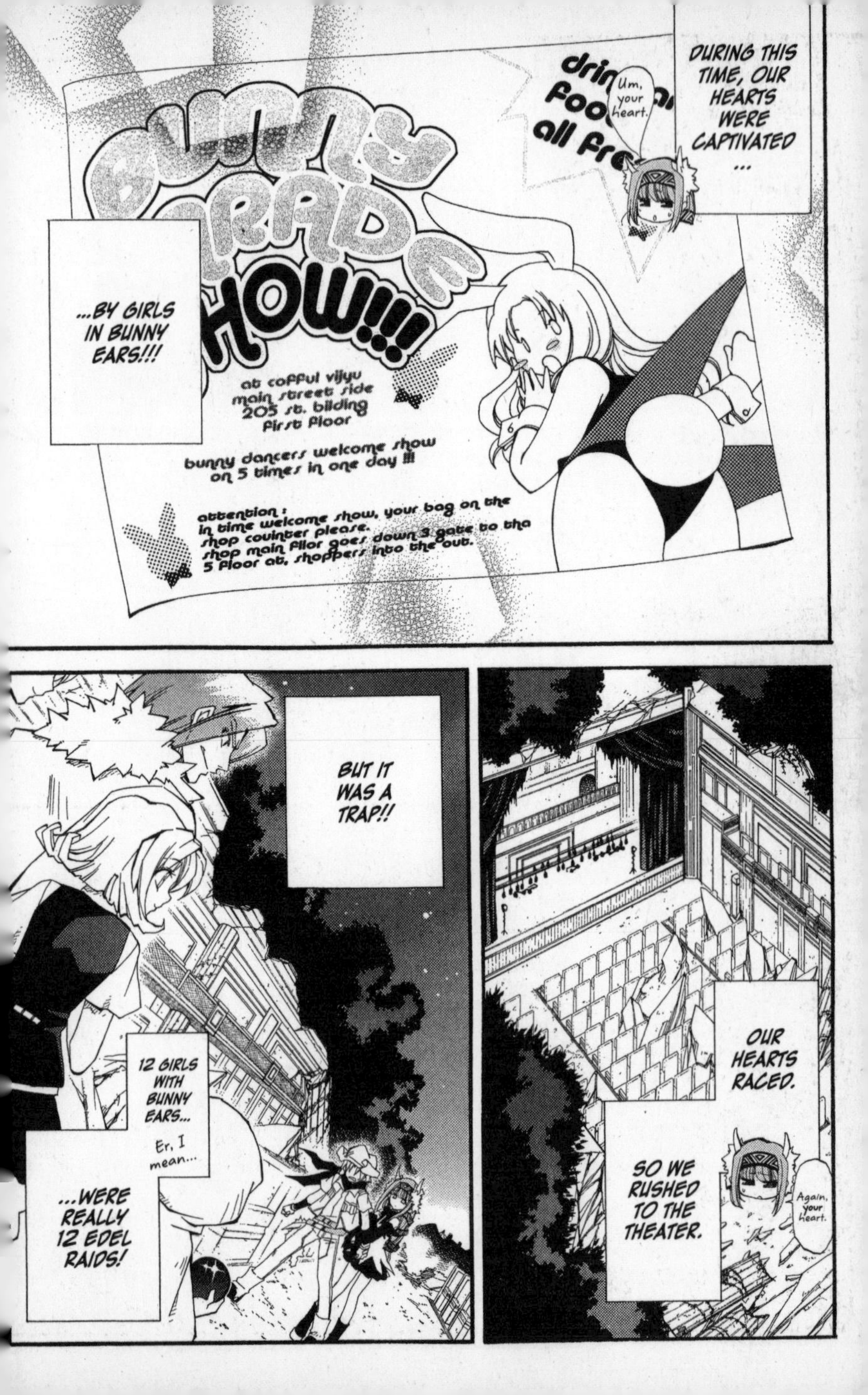
DURING THIS TIME, OUR HEARTS WERE CAPTIVATED ...
Um, your heart.
at cofful vijyu main street side 205 st. bilding first floor
bunny dancers welcome show on 5 times in one day !!!
attention : in time welcome show, your bag on the shop counter please. shop main fllor goes down 3 gate to tha 5 floor at, shoppers into the out.
...BY GIRLS IN BUNNY EARS!!!
OUR HEARTS RACED.
SO WE RUSHED TO THE THEATER.
Again, your heart.
BUT IT WAS A TRAP!!
12 GIRLS WITH BUNNY EARS...
Er, I mean...
...WERE REALLY 12 EDEL RAIDS!

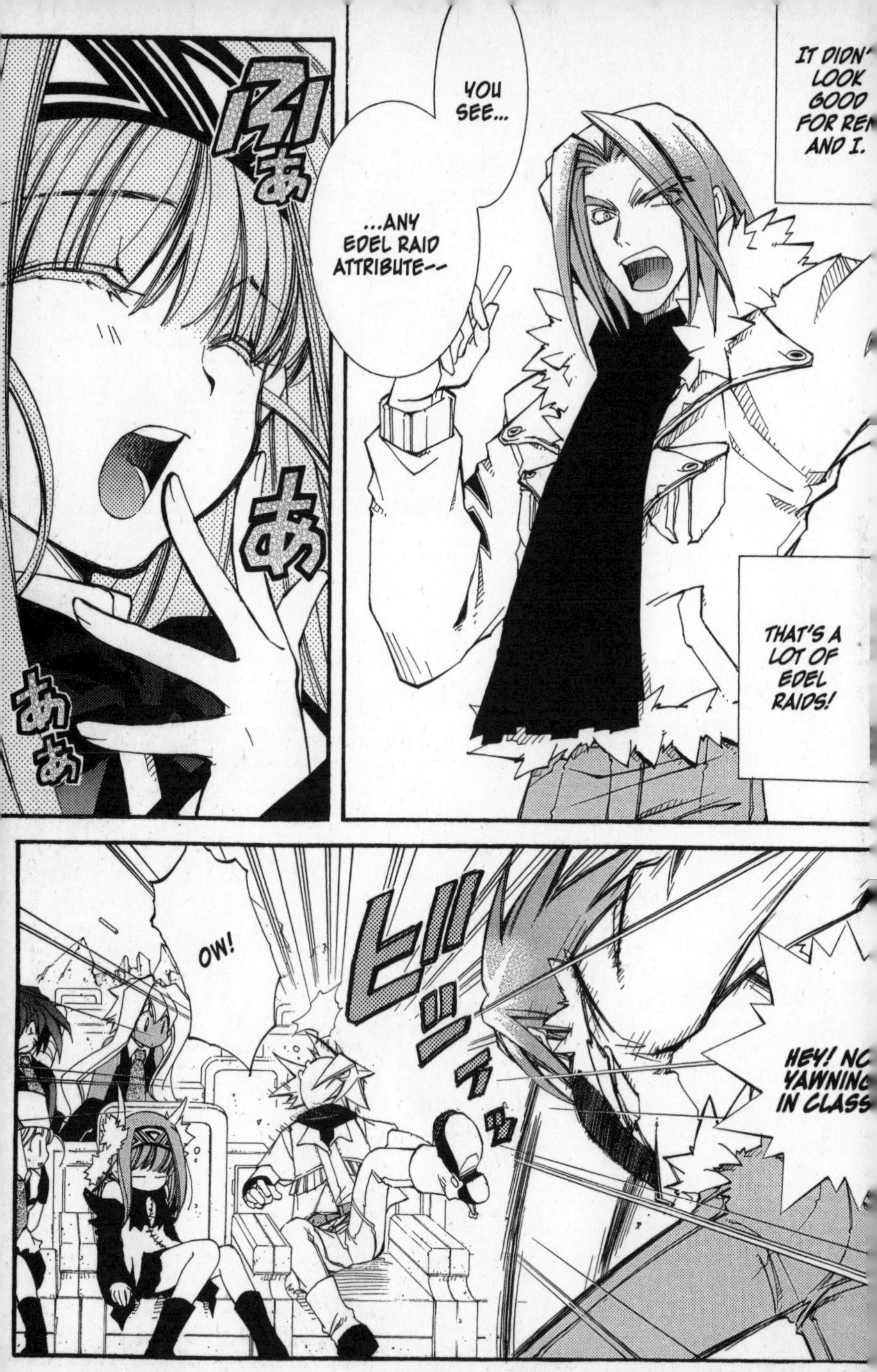
IT DIDN' LOOK GOOD FOR REN AND I.
YOU SEE...
...ANY EDEL RAID ATTRIBUTE--
THAT'S A LOT OF EDEL RAIDS!
ふあ
あ
ああ
HEY! NO YAWNING IN CLASS
ビッ
OW!

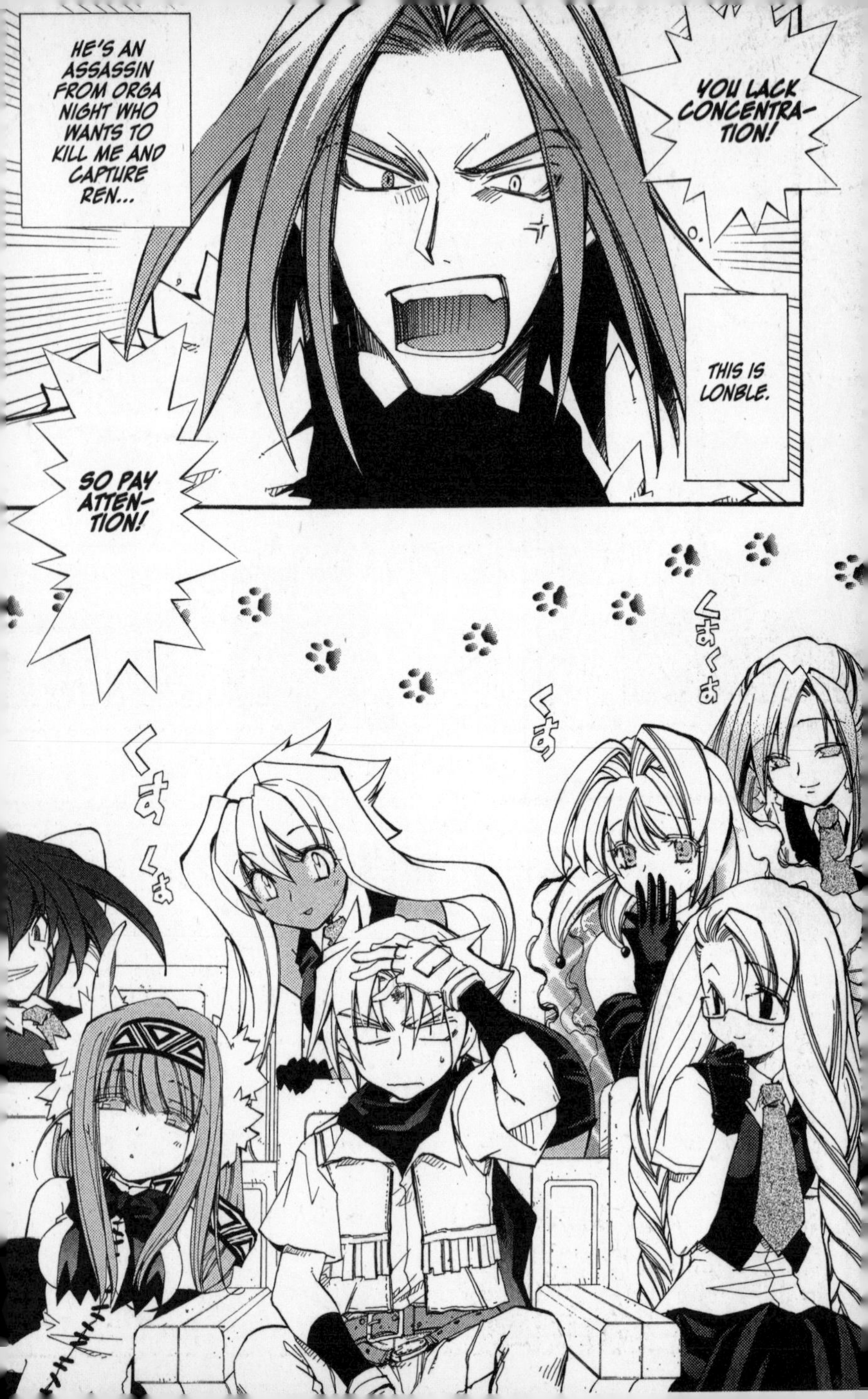

YOU LACK CONCENTRATION!
HE'S AN ASSASSIN FROM ORGA NIGHT WHO WANTS TO KILL ME AND CAPTURE REN...
THIS IS LONBLE.
SO PAY ATTENTION!
くぉくぉ
くぉ
くぉくぉ

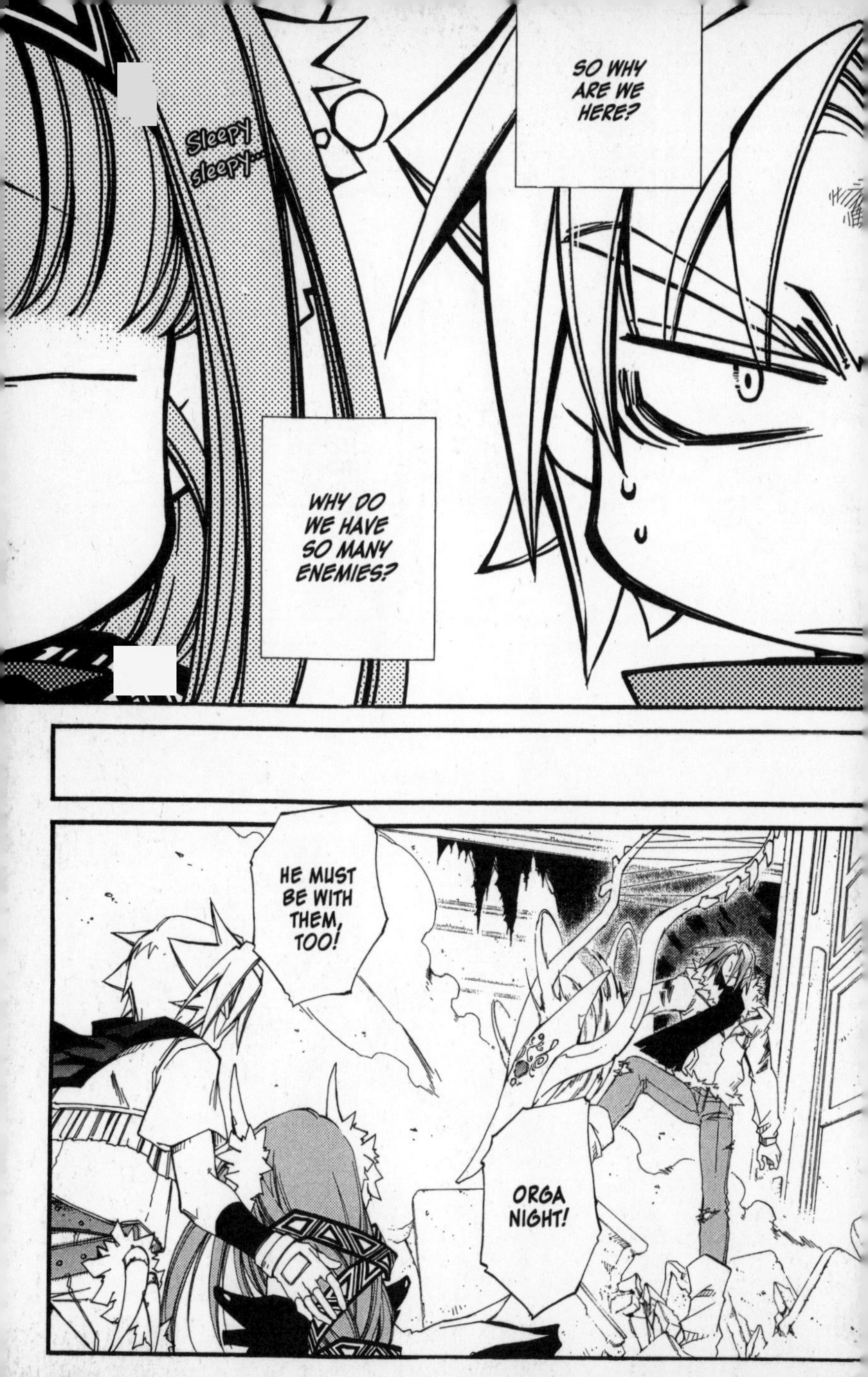
SO WHY ARE WE HERE?
WHY DO WE HAVE SO MANY ENEMIES?
Sleepy sleepy...
HE MUST BE WITH THEM, TOO!
ORGA NIGHT!

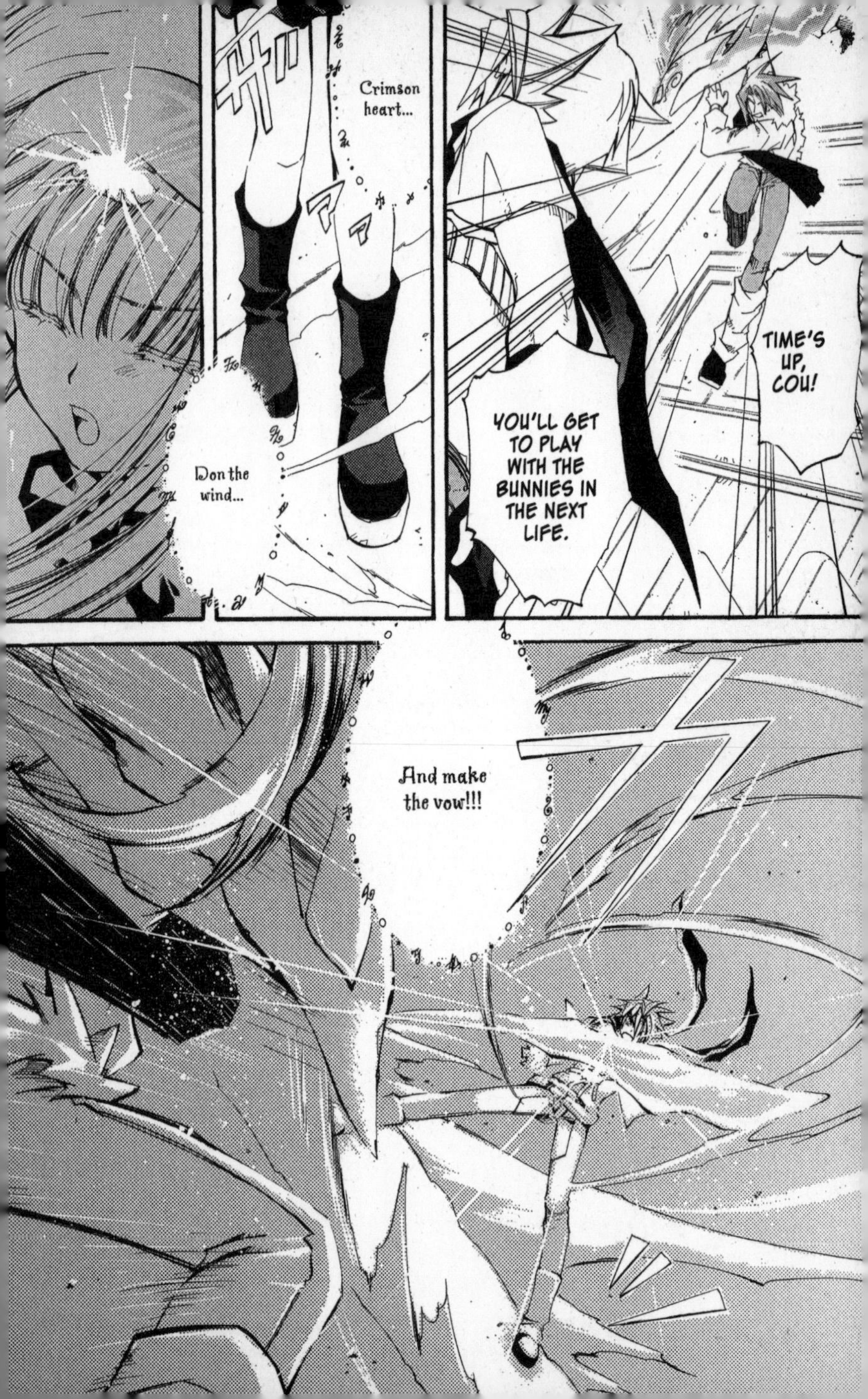
TIME'S UP, COU!
YOU'LL GET TO PLAY WITH THE BUNNIES IN THE NEXT LIFE.
Crimson heart...
Don the wind...
And make the vow!!!

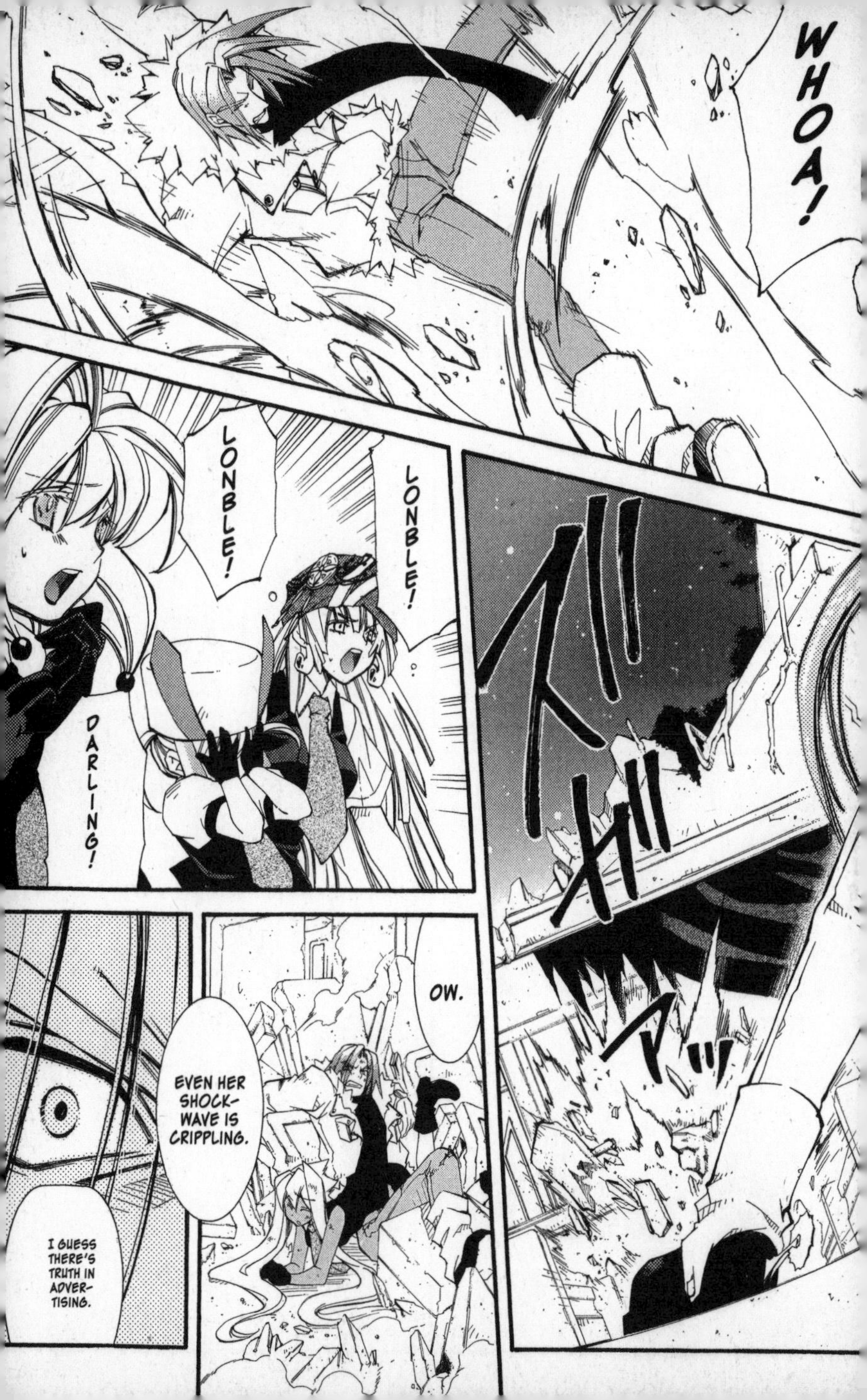
WHOA!
LONBLE!
LONBLE!
DARLING!
OW.
EVEN HER SHOCK-WAVE IS CRIPPLING.
I GUESS THERE'S TRUTH IN ADVER-TISING.

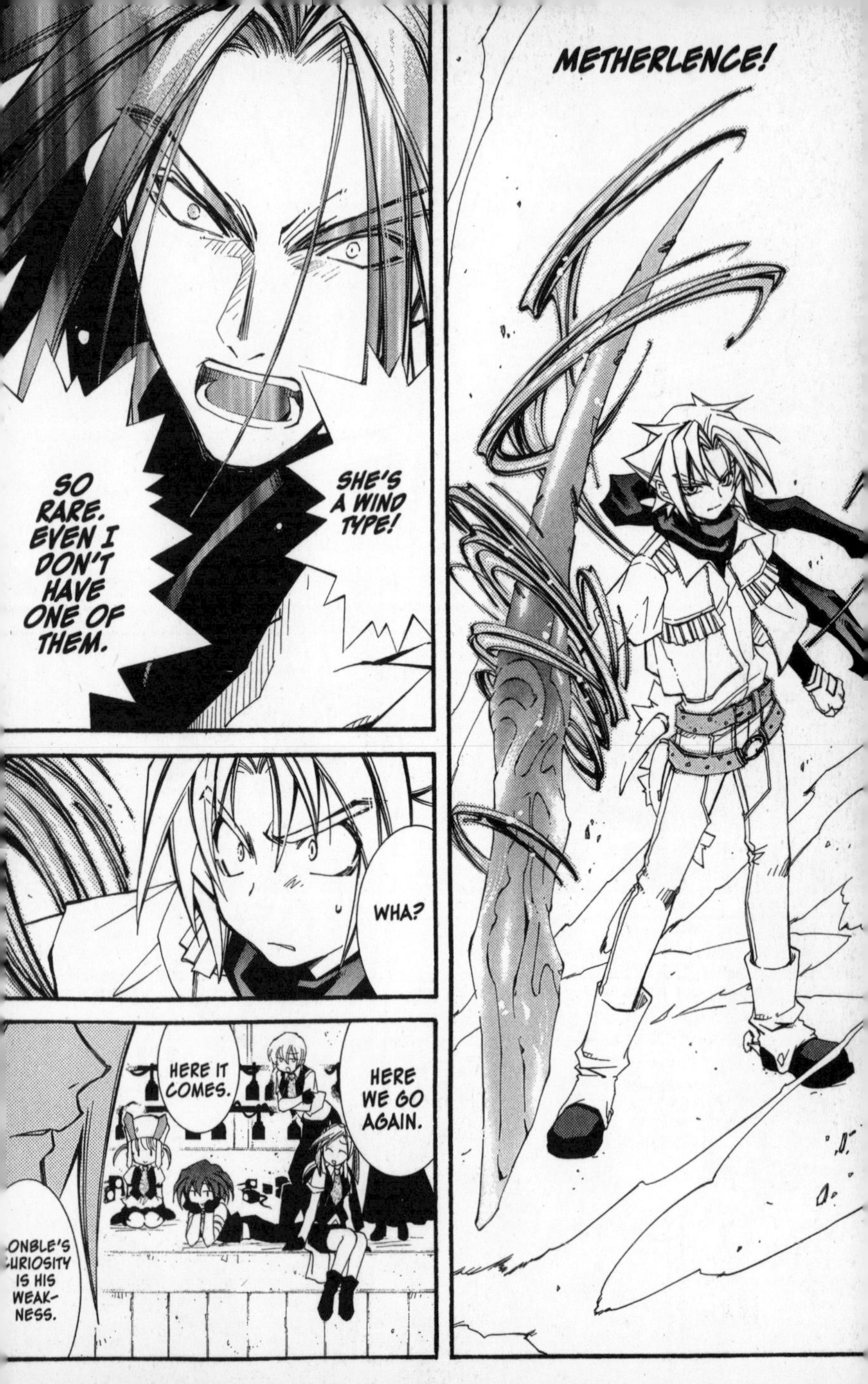
METHERLENCE!
SHE'S A WIND TYPE!
SO RARE. EVEN I DON'T HAVE ONE OF THEM.
WHA?
HERE WE GO AGAIN.
HERE IT COMES.
ONBLE'S CURIOSITY IS HIS WEAK-NESS.

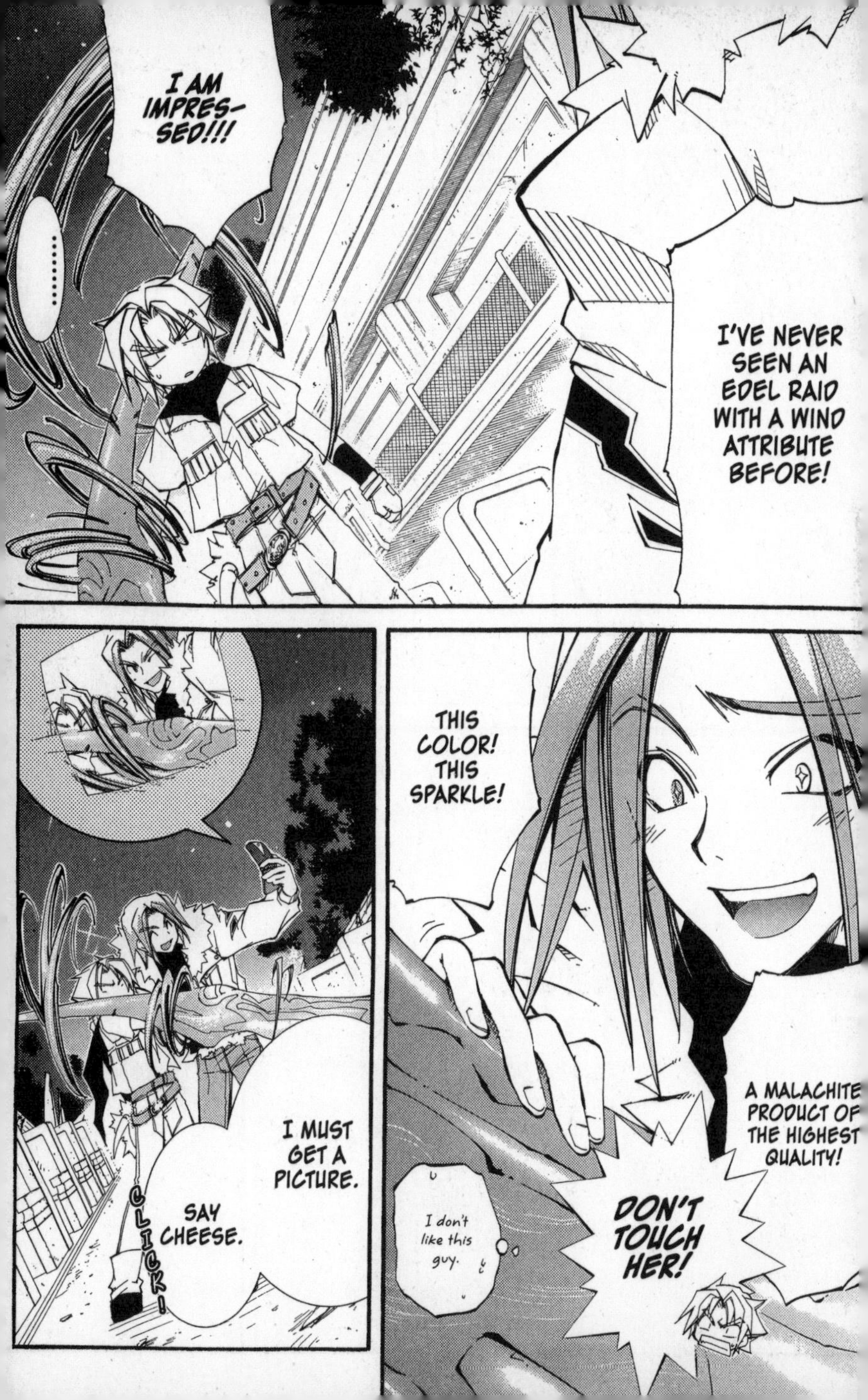
I'VE NEVER SEEN AN EDEL RAID WITH A WIND ATTRIBUTE BEFORE!
I AM IMPRES-SED!!!
......
THIS COLOR! THIS SPARKLE!
A MALACHITE PRODUCT OF THE HIGHEST QUALITY!
DON'T TOUCH HER!
I don't like this guy.
I MUST GET A PICTURE.
SAY CHEESE.
CLICK!

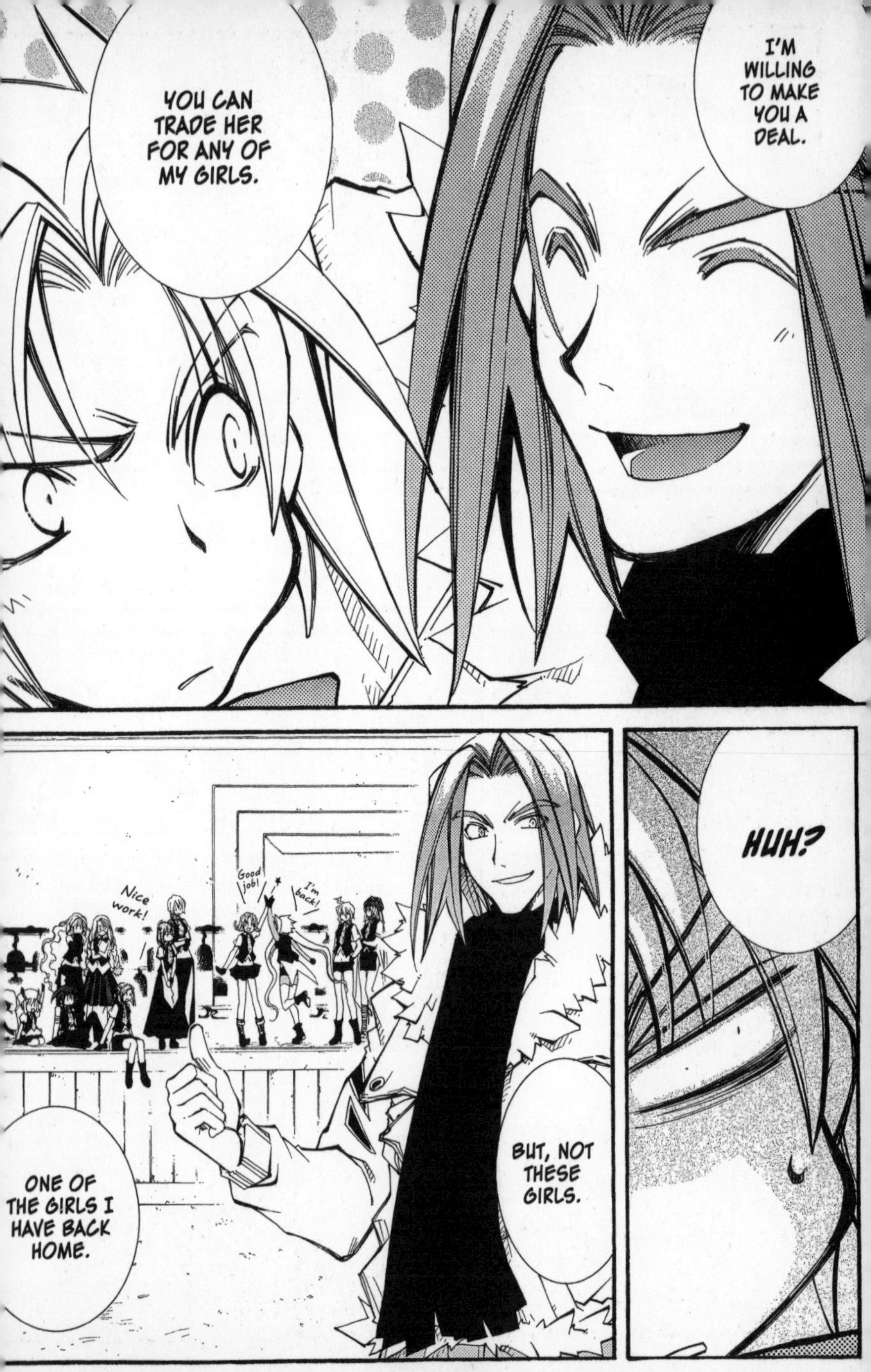
I'M WILLING TO MAKE YOU A DEAL.
YOU CAN TRADE HER FOR ANY OF MY GIRLS.
HUH?
BUT, NOT THESE GIRLS.
I'm back!
Good job!
Nice work!
ONE OF THE GIRLS I HAVE BACK HOME.

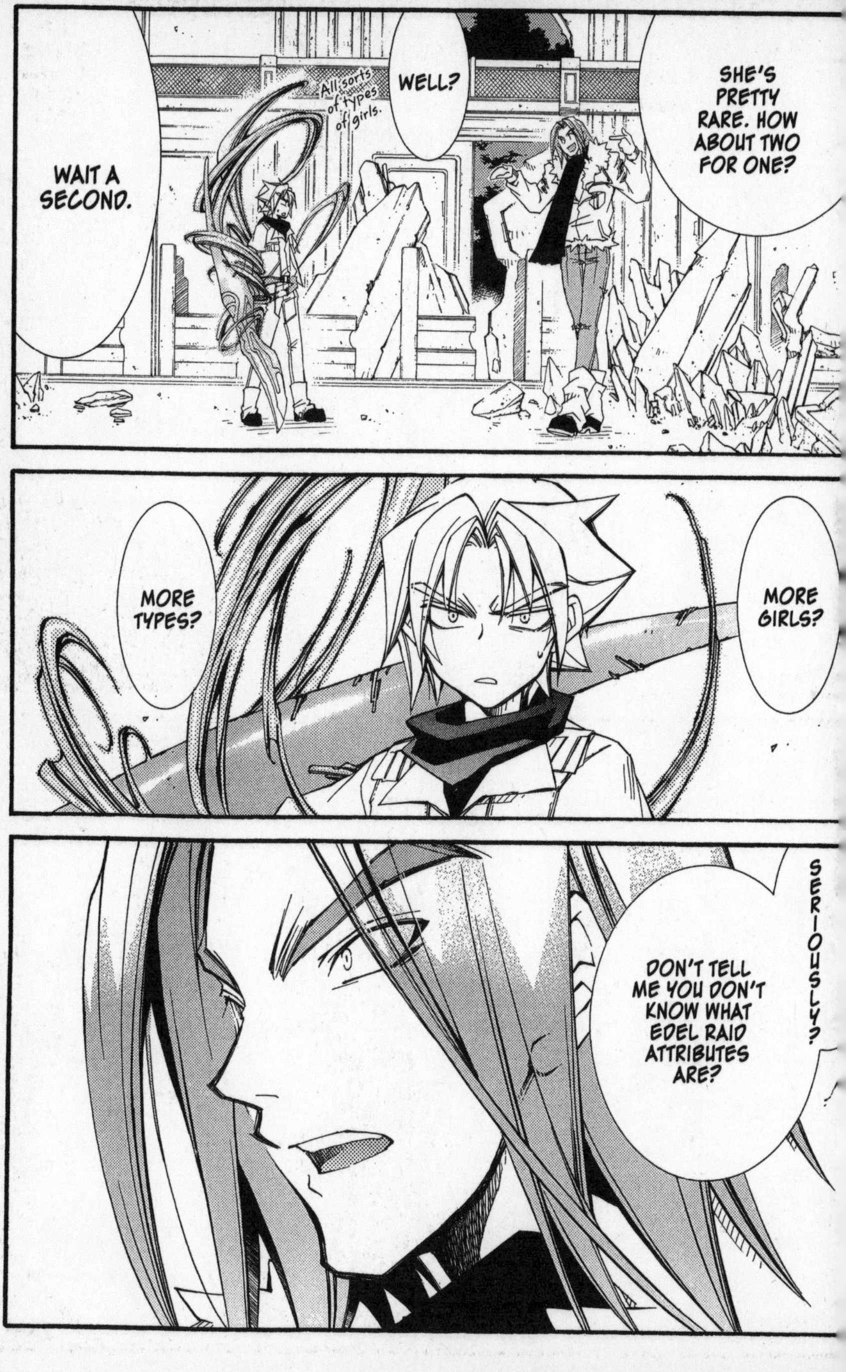
SHE'S PRETTY RARE. HOW ABOUT TWO FOR ONE?
WELL?
All sorts of types of girls.
WAIT A SECOND.
MORE GIRLS?
MORE TYPES?
SERIOUSLY?
DON'T TELL ME YOU DON'T KNOW WHAT EDEL RAID ATTRIBUTES ARE?

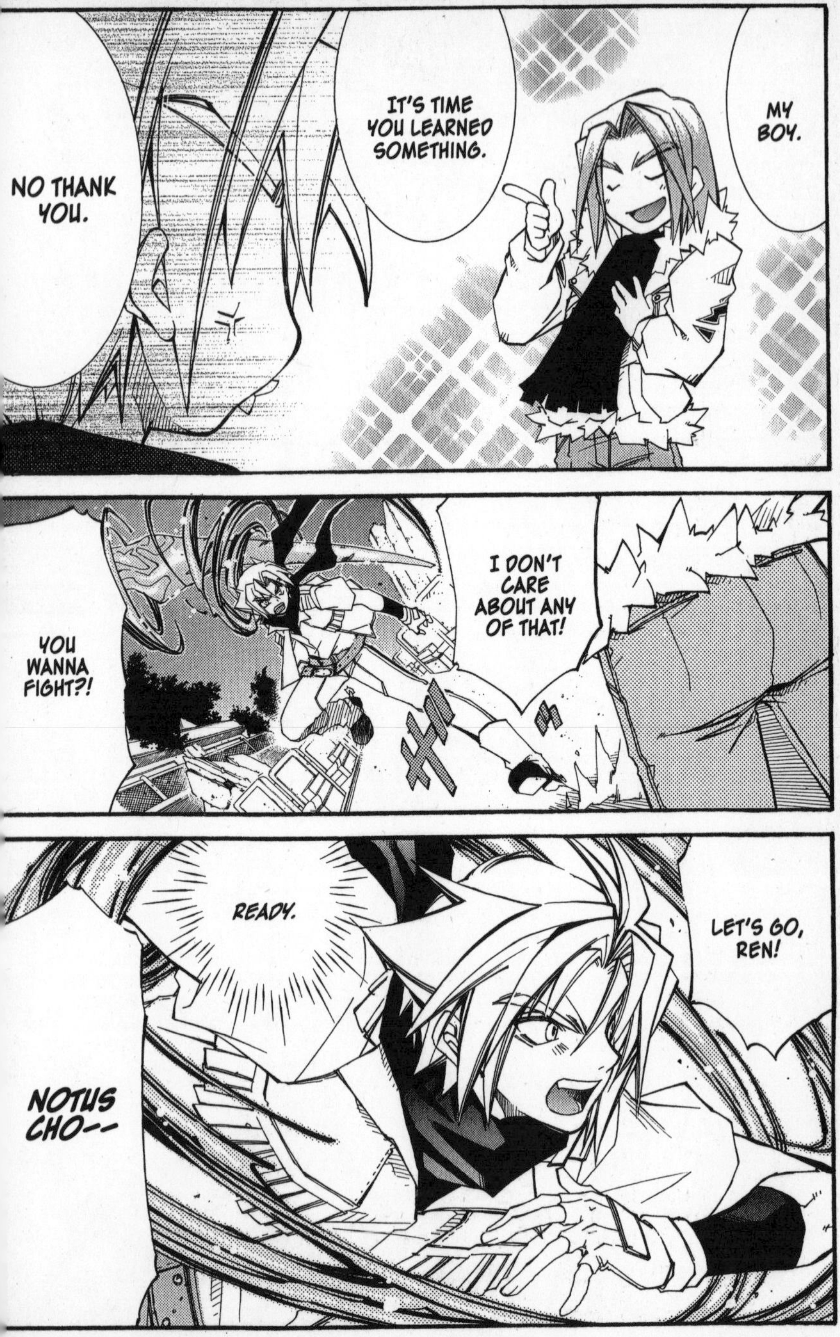
MY BOY.
IT'S TIME YOU LEARNED SOMETHING.
NO THANK YOU.
I DON'T CARE ABOUT ANY OF THAT!
YOU WANNA FIGHT?!
LET'S GO, REN!
READY.
NOTUS CHO--

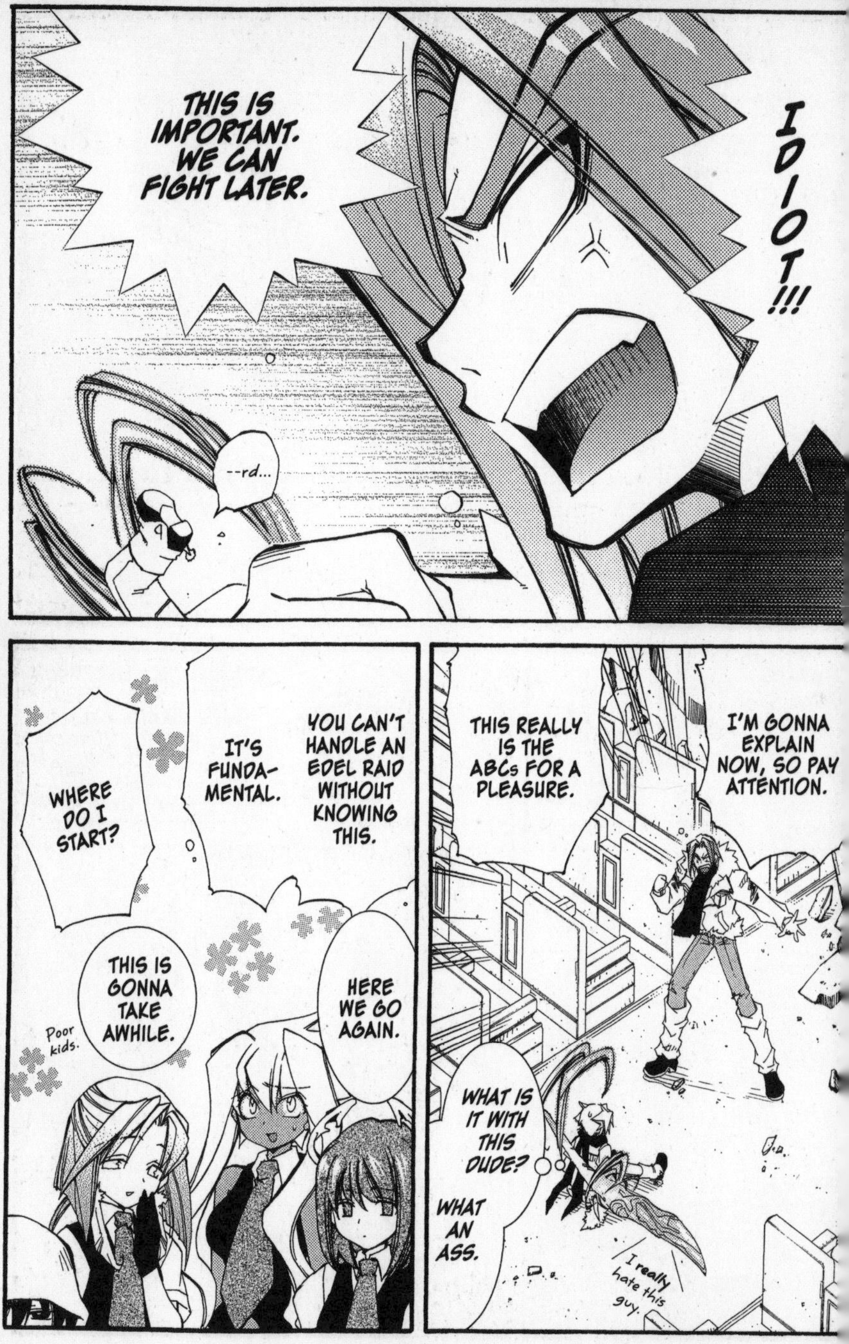
IDIOT!!!
THIS IS IMPORTANT. WE CAN FIGHT LATER.
--rd...
I'M GONNA EXPLAIN NOW, SO PAY ATTENTION.
THIS REALLY IS THE ABCs FOR A PLEASURE.
WHAT IS IT WITH THIS DUDE?
WHAT AN ASS.
I really hate this guy.
YOU CAN'T HANDLE AN EDEL RAID WITHOUT KNOWING THIS.
IT'S FUNDA-MENTAL.
WHERE DO I START?
HERE WE GO AGAIN.
THIS IS GONNA TAKE AWHILE.
Poor kids.

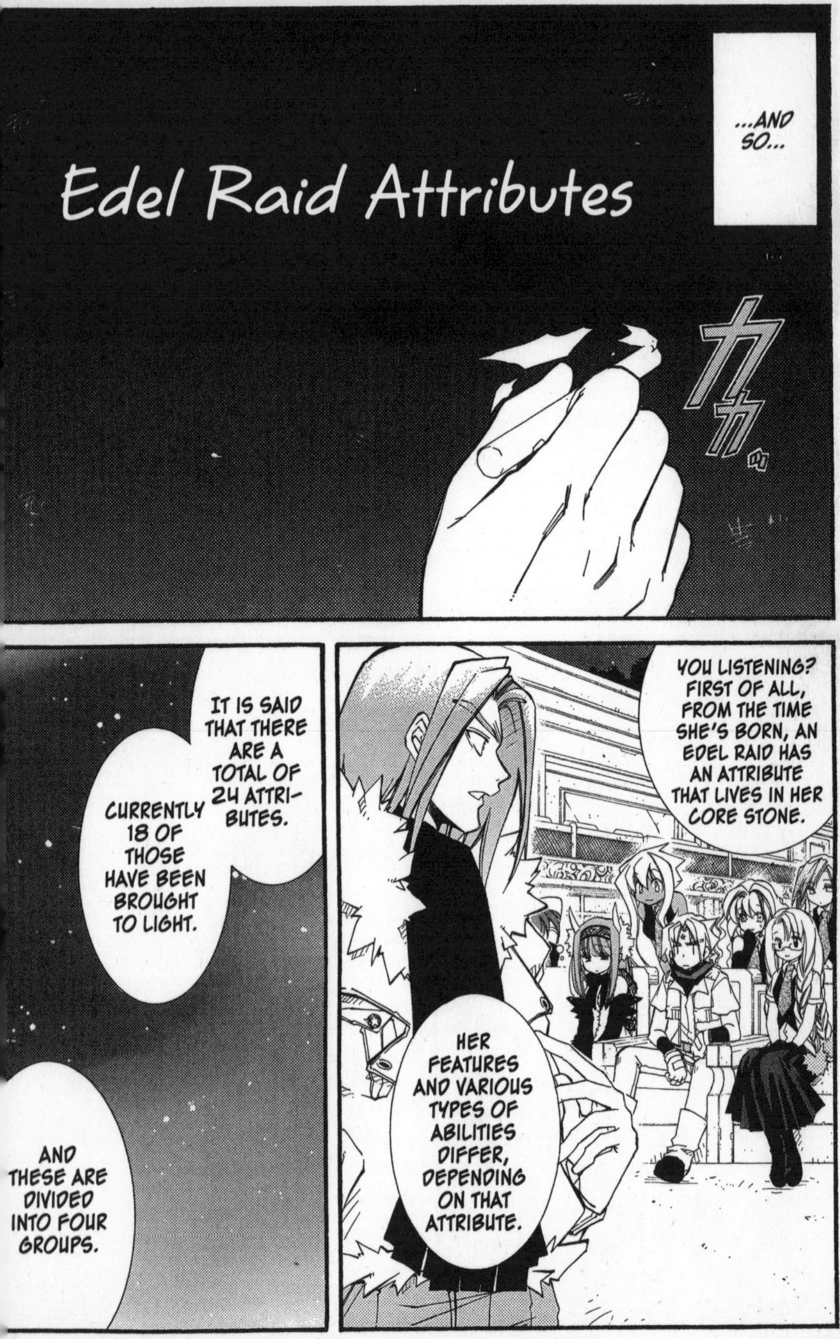
...AND SO...
Edel Raid Attributes
カカ
YOU LISTENING? FIRST OF ALL, FROM THE TIME SHE'S BORN, AN EDEL RAID HAS AN ATTRIBUTE THAT LIVES IN HER CORE STONE.
HER FEATURES AND VARIOUS TYPES OF ABILITIES DIFFER, DEPENDING ON THAT ATTRIBUTE.
IT IS SAID THAT THERE ARE A TOTAL OF 24 ATTRIBUTES.
CURRENTLY 18 OF THOSE HAVE BEEN BROUGHT TO LIGHT.
AND THESE ARE DIVIDED INTO FOUR GROUPS.

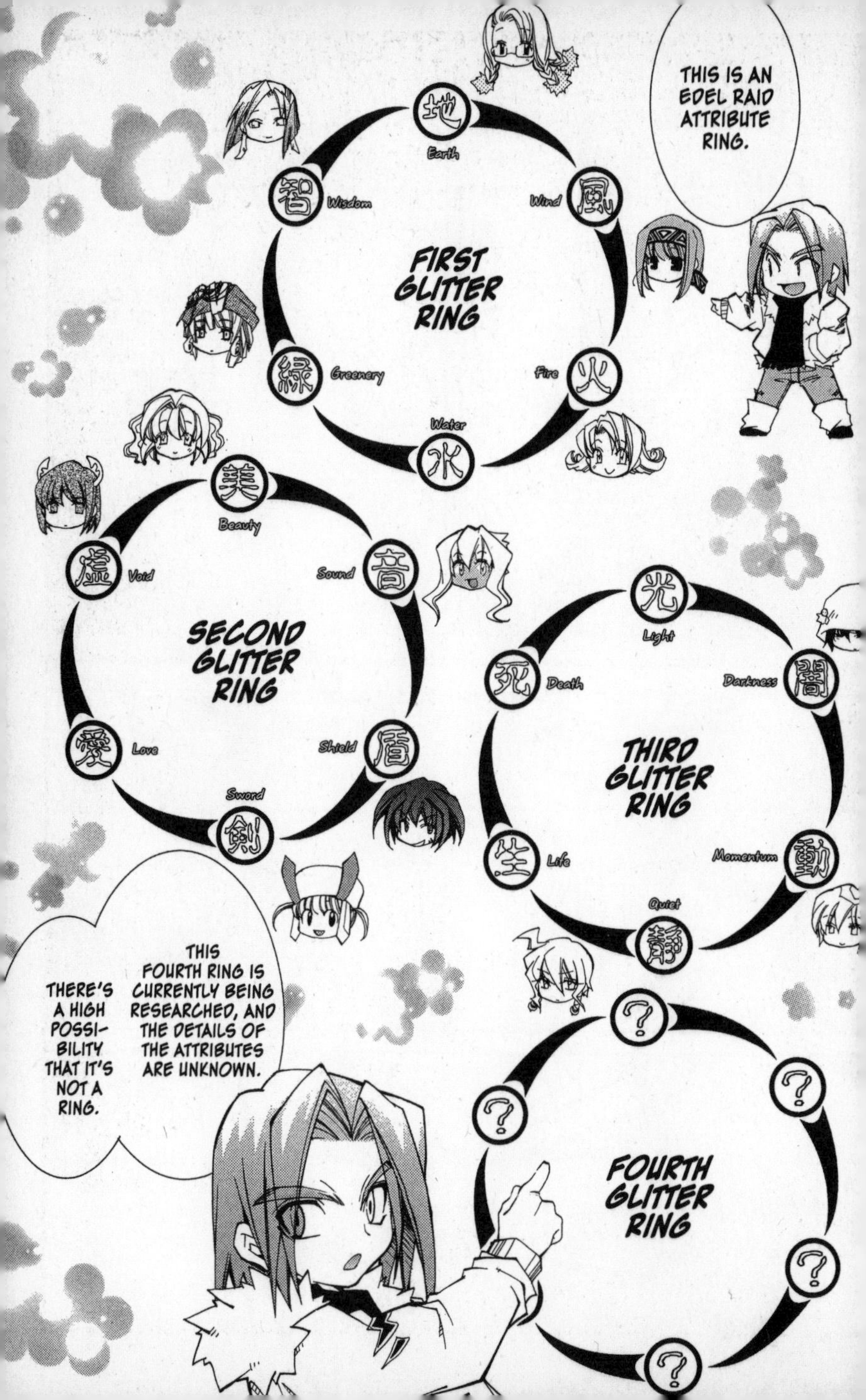
THIS IS AN EDEL RAID ATTRIBUTE RING.
FIRST GLITTER RING
地 Earth
風 Wind
火 Fire
水 Water
緑 Greenery
智 Wisdom
SECOND GLITTER RING
美 Beauty
音 Sound
盾 Shield
剣 Sword
愛 Love
虚 Void
THIRD GLITTER RING
光 Light
闇 Darkness
動 Momentum
静 Quiet
生 Life
死 Death
FOURTH GLITTER RING
?
?
?
?
?
THIS FOURTH RING IS CURRENTLY BEING RESEARCHED, AND THE DETAILS OF THE ATTRIBUTES ARE UNKNOWN.
THERE'S A HIGH POSSI-BILITY THAT IT'S NOT A RING.

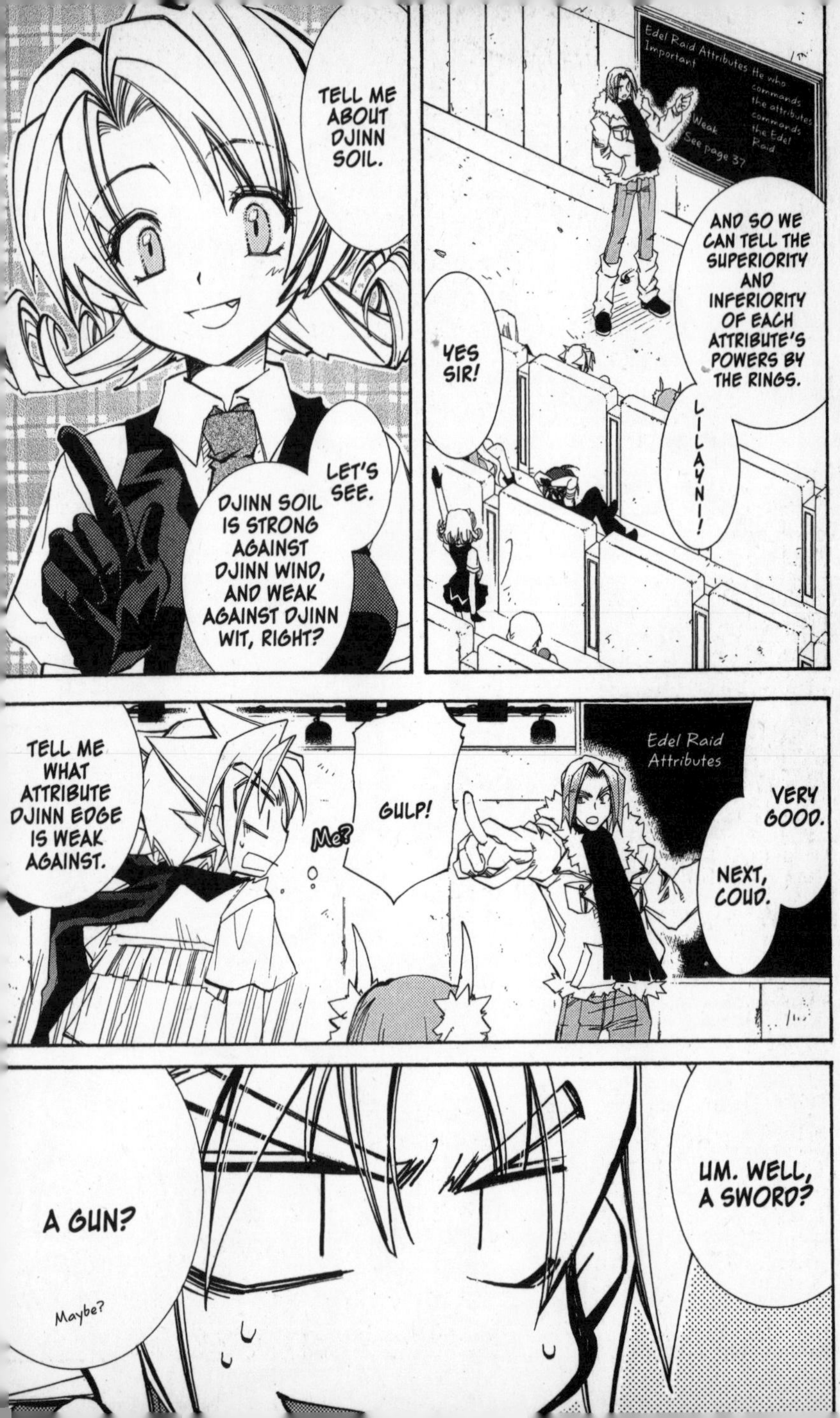
Edel Raid Attributes
Important
He who commands the attributes commands the Edel Raid
Weak
See page 37
AND SO WE CAN TELL THE SUPERIORITY AND INFERIORITY OF EACH ATTRIBUTE'S POWERS BY THE RINGS.
LILAYN!!
YES SIR!
TELL ME ABOUT DJINN SOIL.
LET'S SEE.
DJINN SOIL IS STRONG AGAINST DJINN WIND, AND WEAK AGAINST DJINN WIT, RIGHT?
Edel Raid Attributes
VERY GOOD.
NEXT, COUD.
GULP!
Me?
TELL ME WHAT ATTRIBUTE DJINN EDGE IS WEAK AGAINST.
UM. WELL, A SWORD?
A GUN?
Maybe?

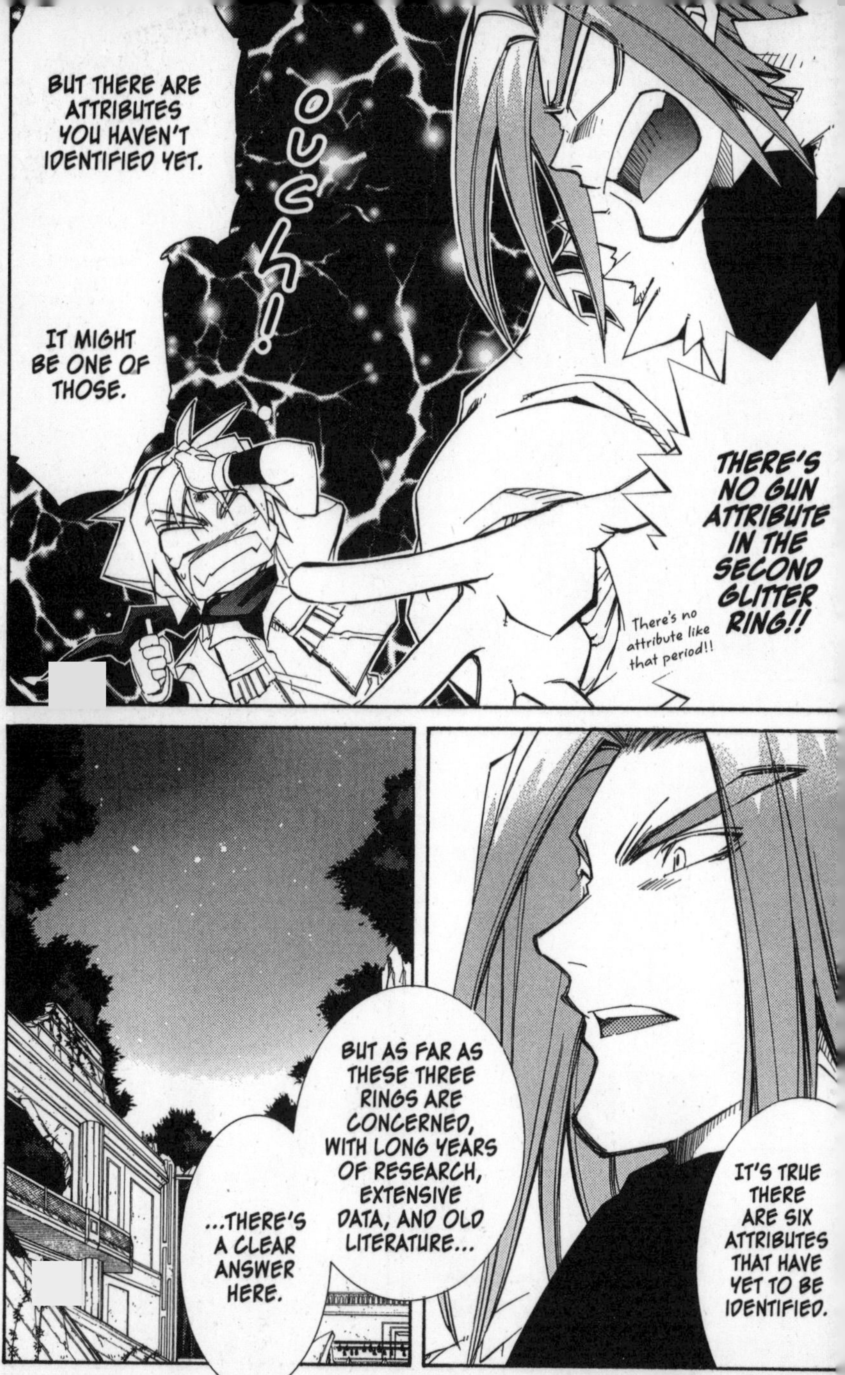
BUT THERE ARE ATTRIBUTES YOU HAVEN'T IDENTIFIED YET.
IT MIGHT BE ONE OF THOSE.
OUCH!
THERE'S NO GUN ATTRIBUTE IN THE SECOND GLITTER RING!!
There's no attribute like that period!!
IT'S TRUE THERE ARE SIX ATTRIBUTES THAT HAVE YET TO BE IDENTIFIED.
BUT AS FAR AS THESE THREE RINGS ARE CONCERNED, WITH LONG YEARS OF RESEARCH, EXTENSIVE DATA, AND OLD LITERATURE...
...THERE'S A CLEAR ANSWER HERE.

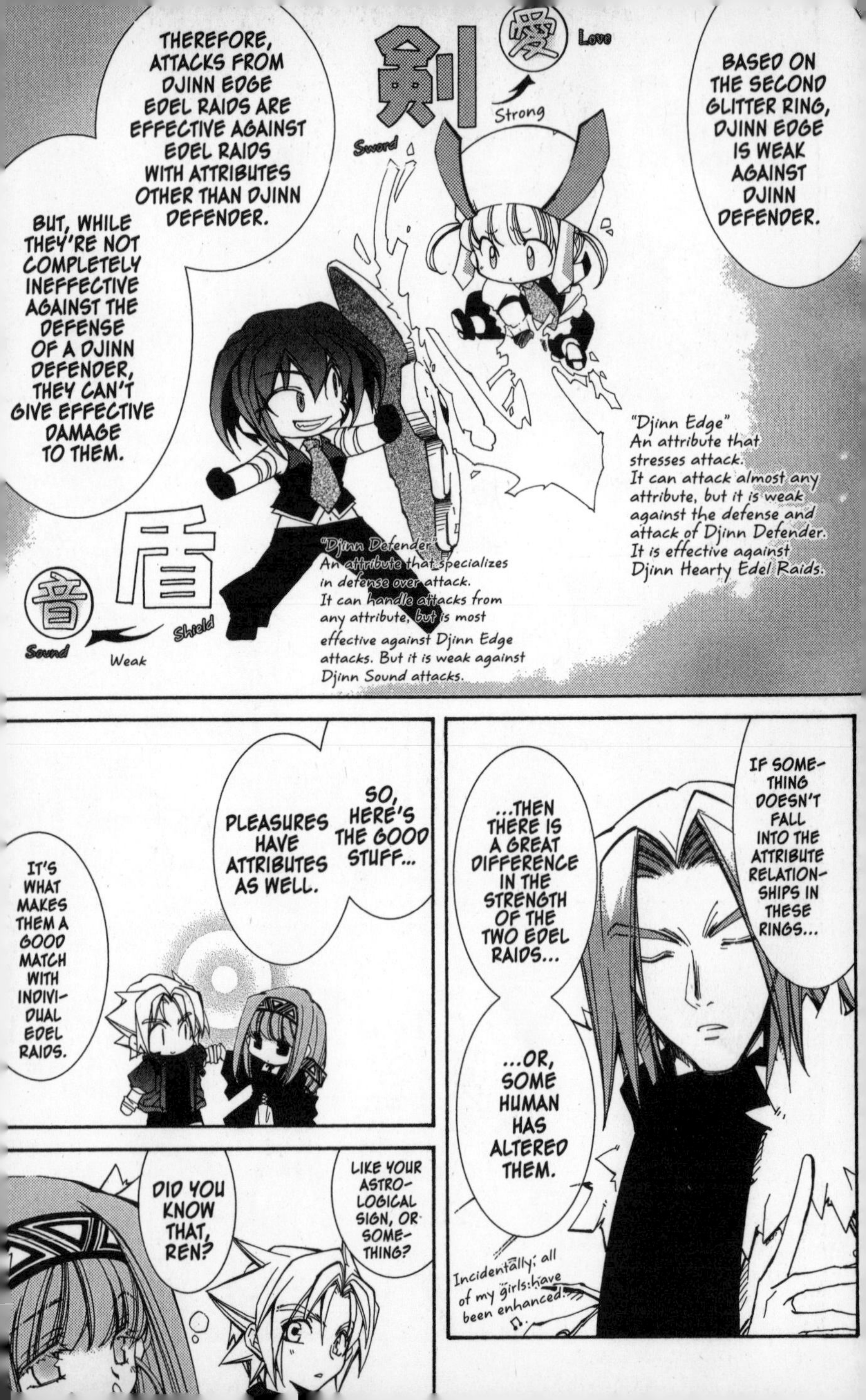
BASED ON THE SECOND GLITTER RING, DJINN EDGE IS WEAK AGAINST DJINN DEFENDER.
THEREFORE, ATTACKS FROM DJINN EDGE EDEL RAIDS ARE EFFECTIVE AGAINST EDEL RAIDS WITH ATTRIBUTES OTHER THAN DJINN DEFENDER.
BUT, WHILE THEY'RE NOT COMPLETELY INEFFECTIVE AGAINST THE DEFENSE OF A DJINN DEFENDER, THEY CAN'T GIVE EFFECTIVE DAMAGE TO THEM.
愛 Love
剣 Sword
Strong
"Djinn Edge" An attribute that stresses attack. It can attack almost any attribute, but it is weak against the defense and attack of Djinn Defender. It is effective against Djinn Hearty Edel Raids.
"Djinn Defender" An attribute that specializes in defense over attack. It can handle attacks from any attribute, but is most effective against Djinn Edge attacks. But it is weak against Djinn Sound attacks.
盾 Shield
音 Sound
Weak
IF SOMETHING DOESN'T FALL INTO THE ATTRIBUTE RELATIONSHIPS IN THESE RINGS...
...THEN THERE IS A GREAT DIFFERENCE IN THE STRENGTH OF THE TWO EDEL RAIDS...
...OR, SOME HUMAN HAS ALTERED THEM.
Incidentally, all of my girls have been enhanced ♪
SO, HERE'S THE GOOD STUFF...
PLEASURES HAVE ATTRIBUTES AS WELL.
IT'S WHAT MAKES THEM A GOOD MATCH WITH INDIVIDUAL EDEL RAIDS.
LIKE YOUR ASTROLOGICAL SIGN, OR SOMETHING?
DID YOU KNOW THAT, REN?

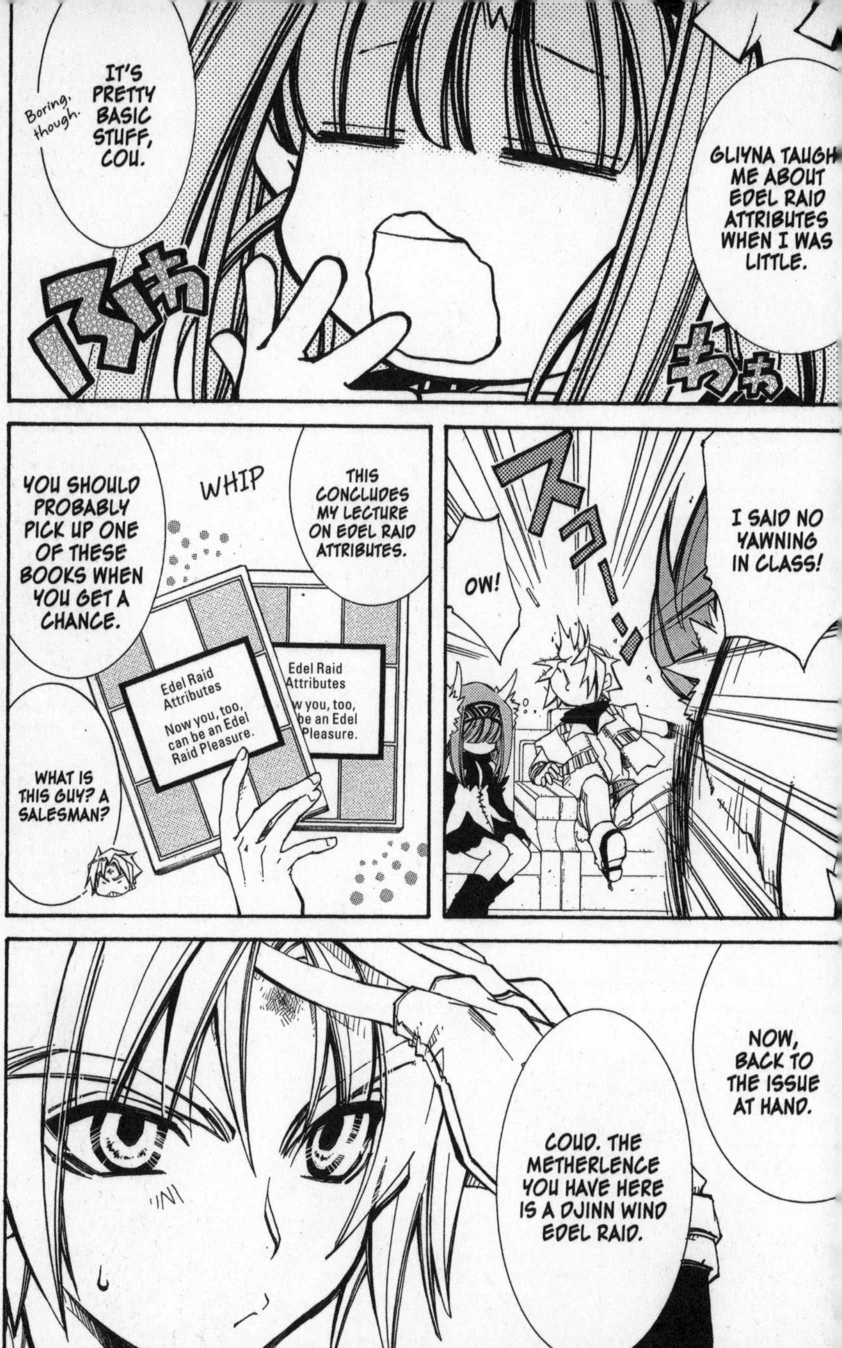
GLIYNA TAUGH ME ABOUT EDEL RAID ATTRIBUTES WHEN I WAS LITTLE.
IT'S PRETTY BASIC STUFF, COU.
Boring, though.
I SAID NO YAWNING IN CLASS!
OW!
THIS CONCLUDES MY LECTURE ON EDEL RAID ATTRIBUTES.
WHIP
YOU SHOULD PROBABLY PICK UP ONE OF THESE BOOKS WHEN YOU GET A CHANCE.
Edel Raid Attributes
Now you, too, can be an Edel Raid Pleasure.
WHAT IS THIS GUY? A SALESMAN?
NOW, BACK TO THE ISSUE AT HAND.
COUD. THE METHERLENCE YOU HAVE HERE IS A DJINN WIND EDEL RAID.

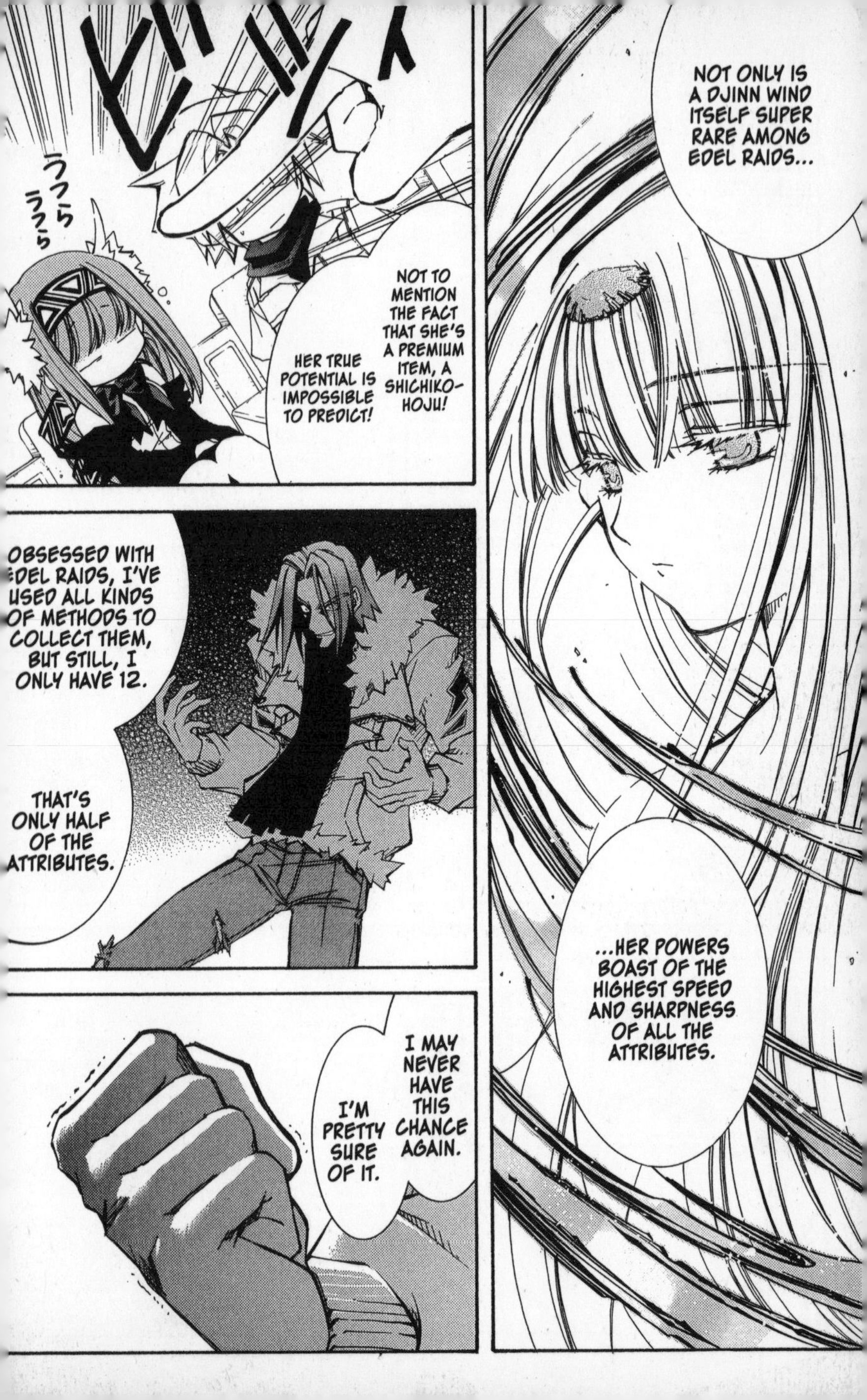
NOT ONLY IS A DJINN WIND ITSELF SUPER RARE AMONG EDEL RAIDS...
...HER POWERS BOAST OF THE HIGHEST SPEED AND SHARPNESS OF ALL THE ATTRIBUTES.
NOT TO MENTION THE FACT THAT SHE'S A PREMIUM ITEM, A SHICHIKO-HOJU!
HER TRUE POTENTIAL IS IMPOSSIBLE TO PREDICT!
OBSESSED WITH EDEL RAIDS, I'VE USED ALL KINDS OF METHODS TO COLLECT THEM, BUT STILL, I ONLY HAVE 12.
THAT'S ONLY HALF OF THE ATTRIBUTES.
I MAY NEVER HAVE THIS CHANCE AGAIN.
I'M PRETTY SURE OF IT.

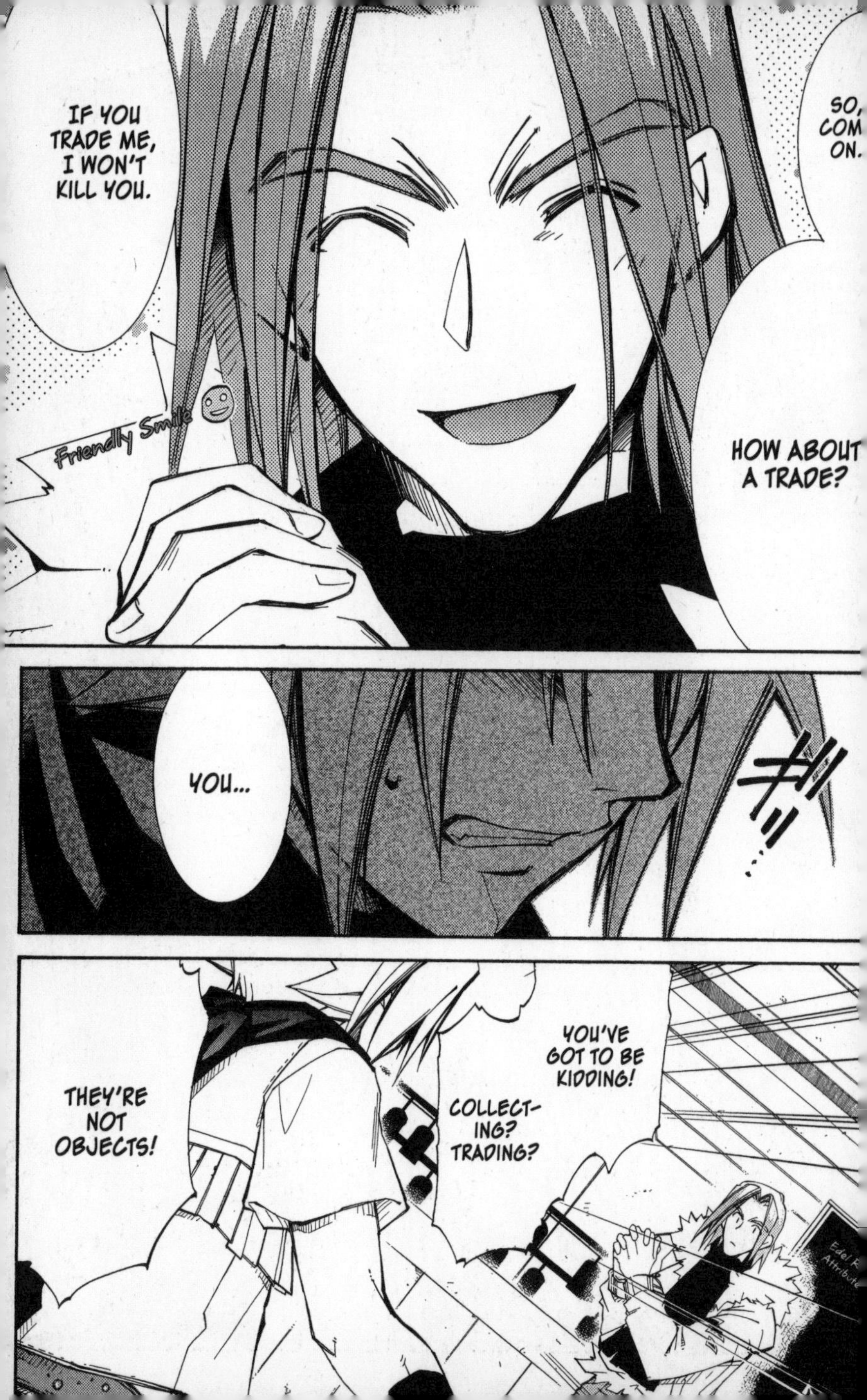
SO, COM ON.
HOW ABOUT A TRADE?
IF YOU TRADE ME, I WON'T KILL YOU.
Friendly Smile
YOU...
YOU'VE GOT TO BE KIDDING!
COLLECT-ING? TRADING?
THEY'RE NOT OBJECTS!

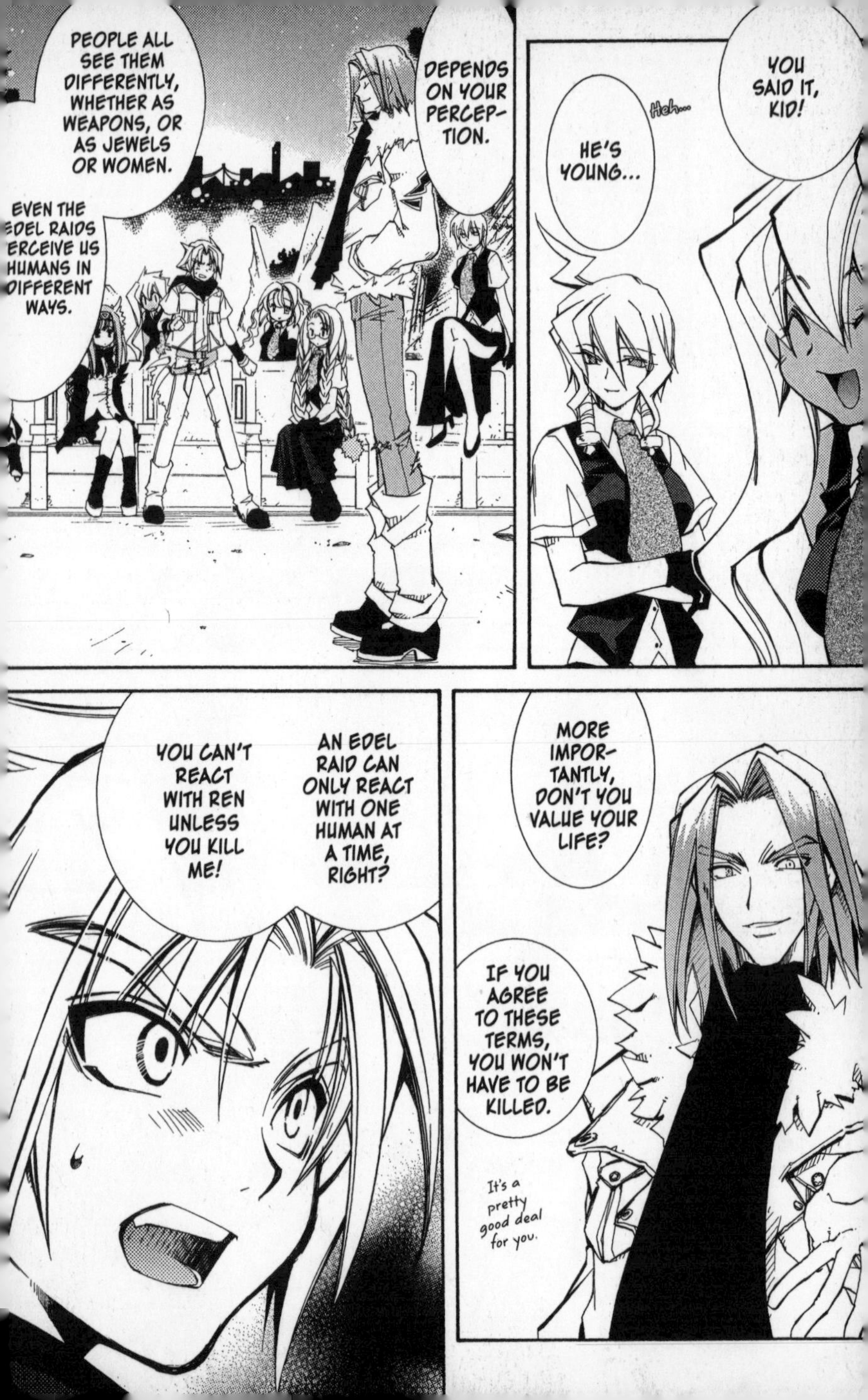
YOU SAID IT, KID!
Heh...
HE'S YOUNG...
DEPENDS ON YOUR PERCEPTION.
PEOPLE ALL SEE THEM DIFFERENTLY, WHETHER AS WEAPONS, OR AS JEWELS OR WOMEN.
EVEN THE EDEL RAIDS ERCEIVE US HUMANS IN DIFFERENT WAYS.
MORE IMPORTANTLY, DON'T YOU VALUE YOUR LIFE?
IF YOU AGREE TO THESE TERMS, YOU WON'T HAVE TO BE KILLED.
It's a pretty good deal for you.
AN EDEL RAID CAN ONLY REACT WITH ONE HUMAN AT A TIME, RIGHT?
YOU CAN'T REACT WITH REN UNLESS YOU KILL ME!

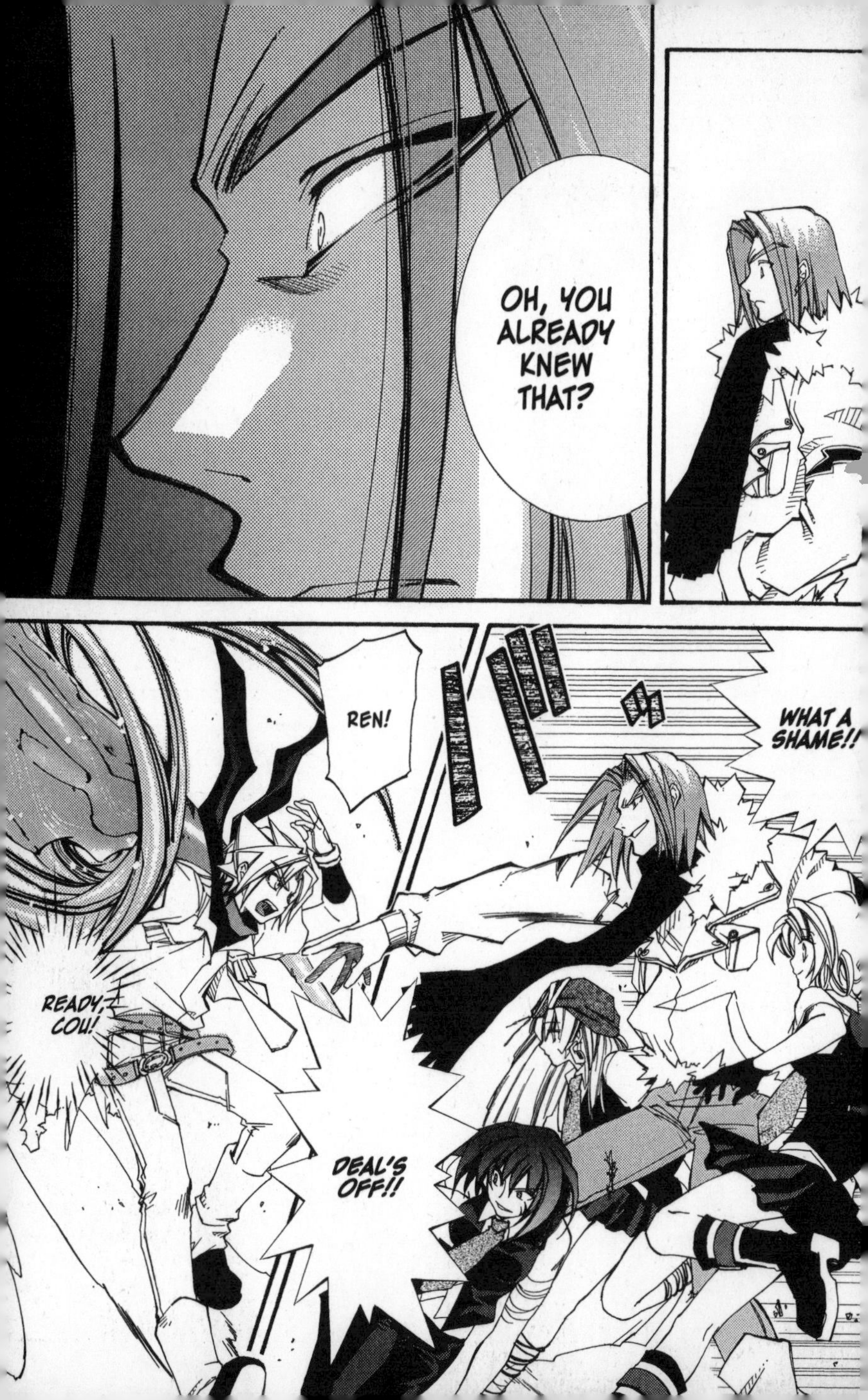
OH, YOU ALREADY KNEW THAT?
WHAT A SHAME!!
REN!
READY, COU!
DEAL'S OFF!!

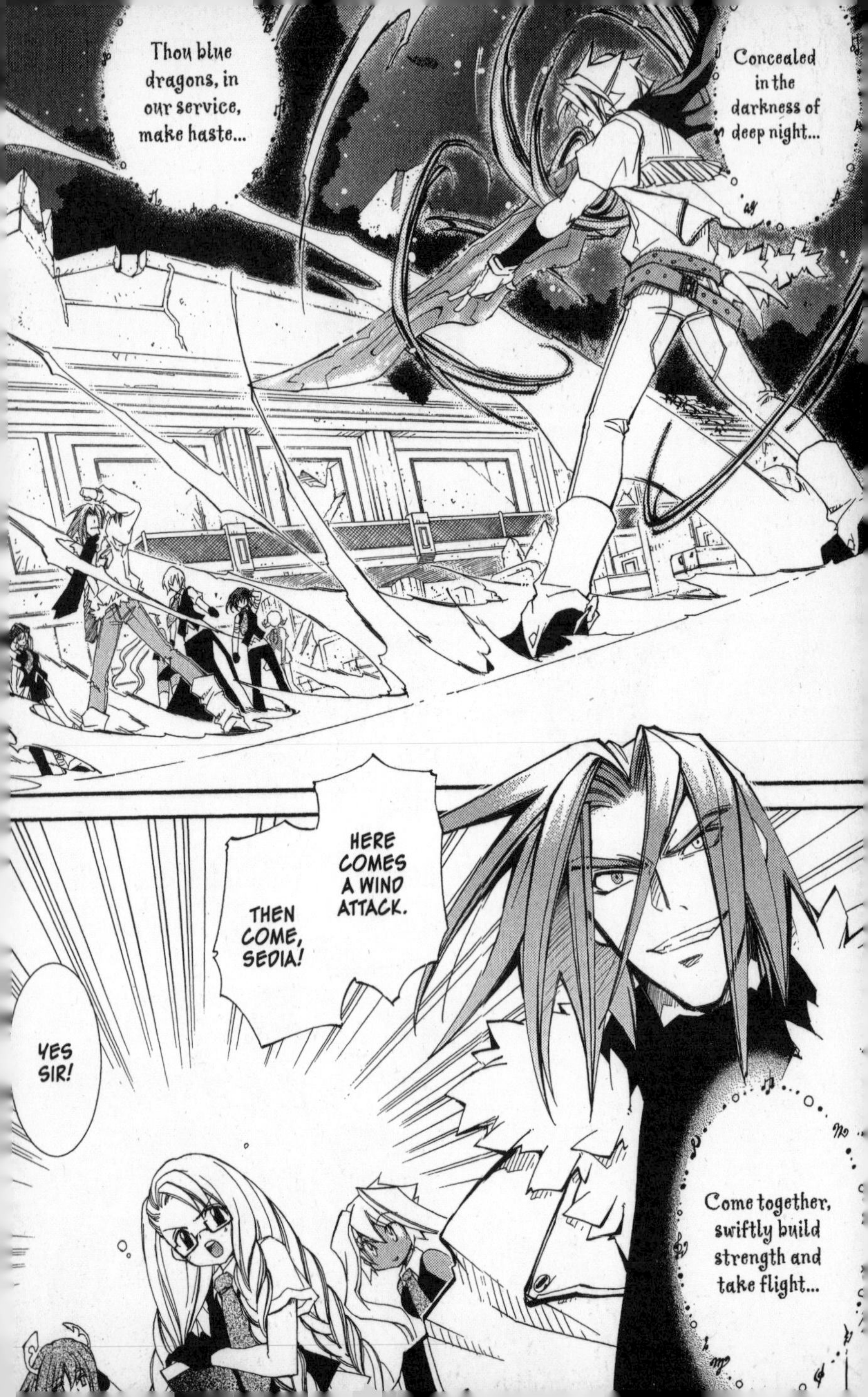
Concealed in the darkness of deep night...
Thou blue dragons, in our service, make haste...
HERE COMES A WIND ATTACK.
THEN COME, SEDIA!
YES SIR!
Come together, swiftly build strength and take flight...

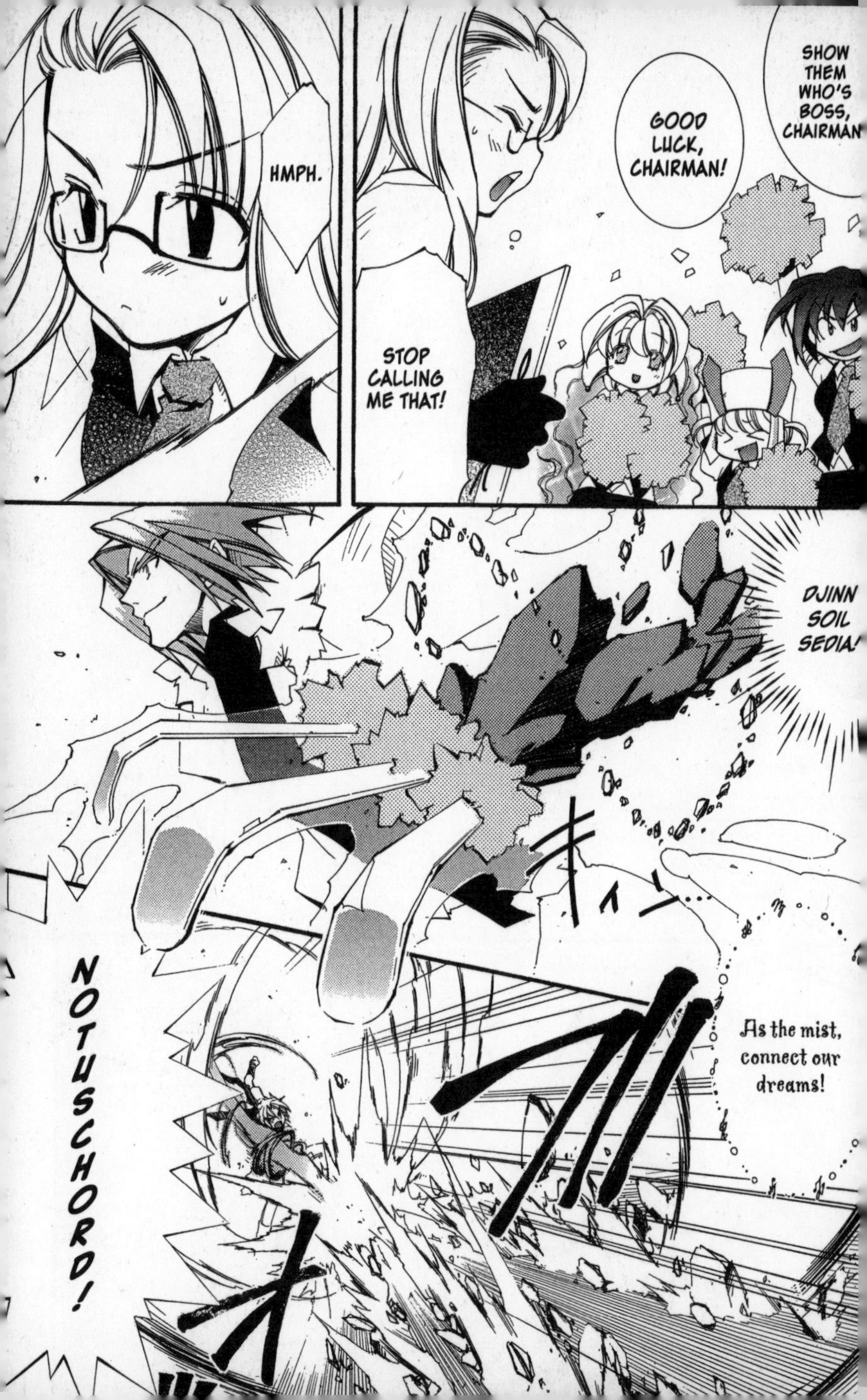
SHOW THEM WHO'S BOSS, CHAIRMAN
GOOD LUCK, CHAIRMAN!
STOP CALLING ME THAT!
HMPH.
DJINN SOIL SEDIA!
As the mist, connect our dreams!
NOTUSCHORD!

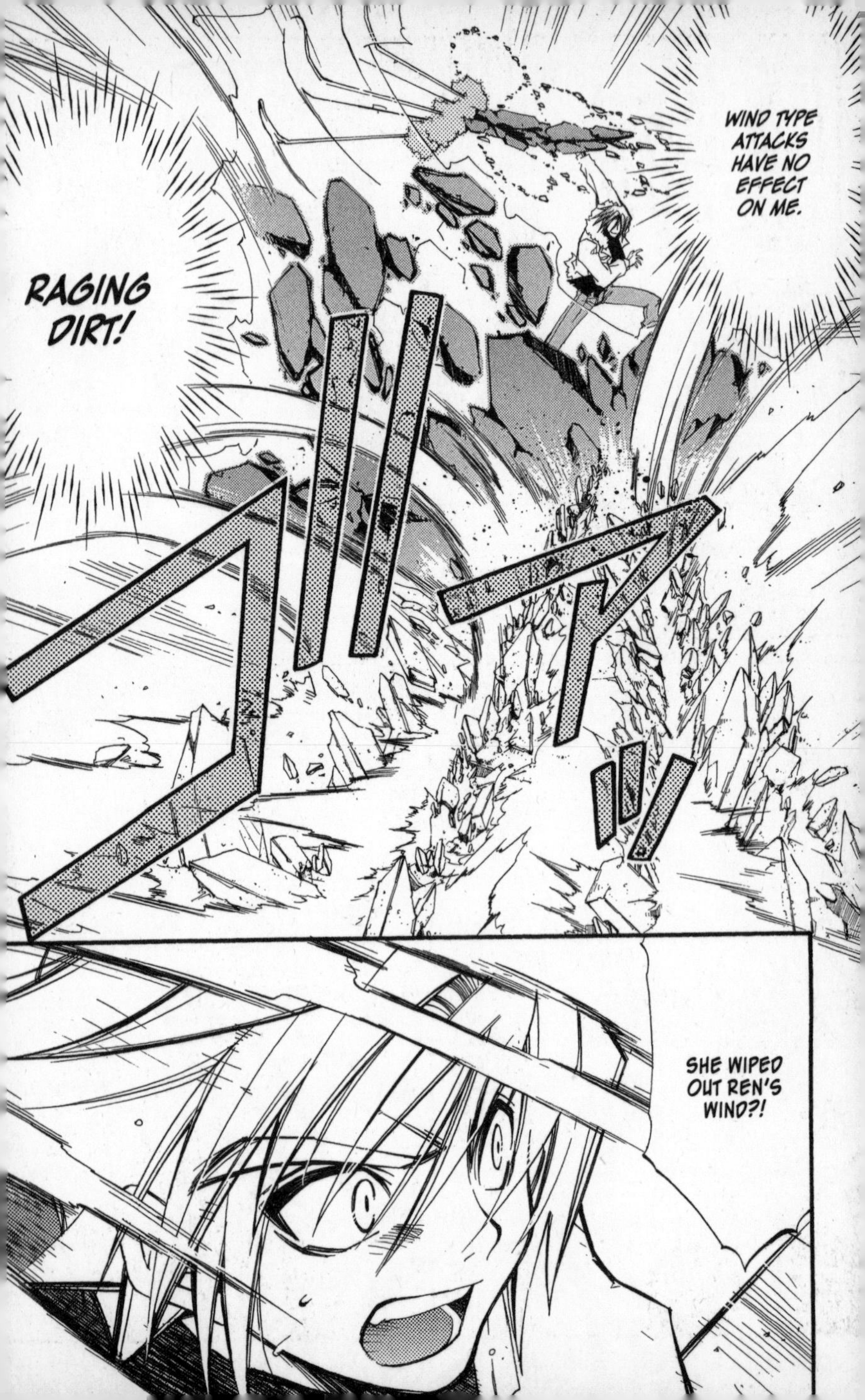
WIND TYPE ATTACKS HAVE NO EFFECT ON ME.
RAGING DIRT!
SHE WIPED OUT REN'S WIND?!

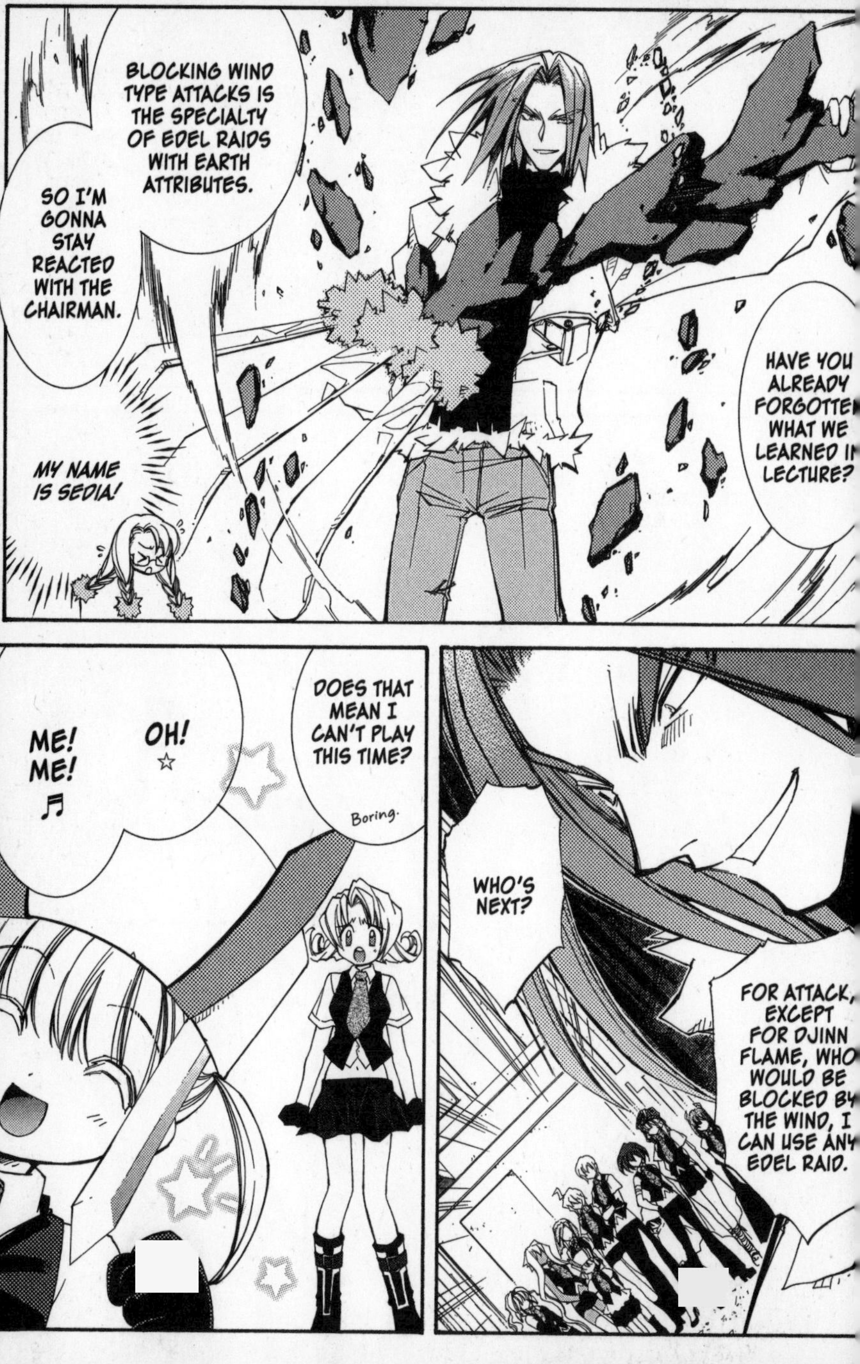
HAVE YOU ALREADY FORGOTTE WHAT WE LEARNED I LECTURE?
BLOCKING WIND TYPE ATTACKS IS THE SPECIALTY OF EDEL RAIDS WITH EARTH ATTRIBUTES.
SO I'M GONNA STAY REACTED WITH THE CHAIRMAN.
MY NAME IS SEDIA!
WHO'S NEXT?
FOR ATTACK, EXCEPT FOR DJINN FLAME, WHO WOULD BE BLOCKED BY THE WIND, I CAN USE ANY EDEL RAID.
DOES THAT MEAN I CAN'T PLAY THIS TIME?
Boring.
OH! ☆
ME! ME! ♬

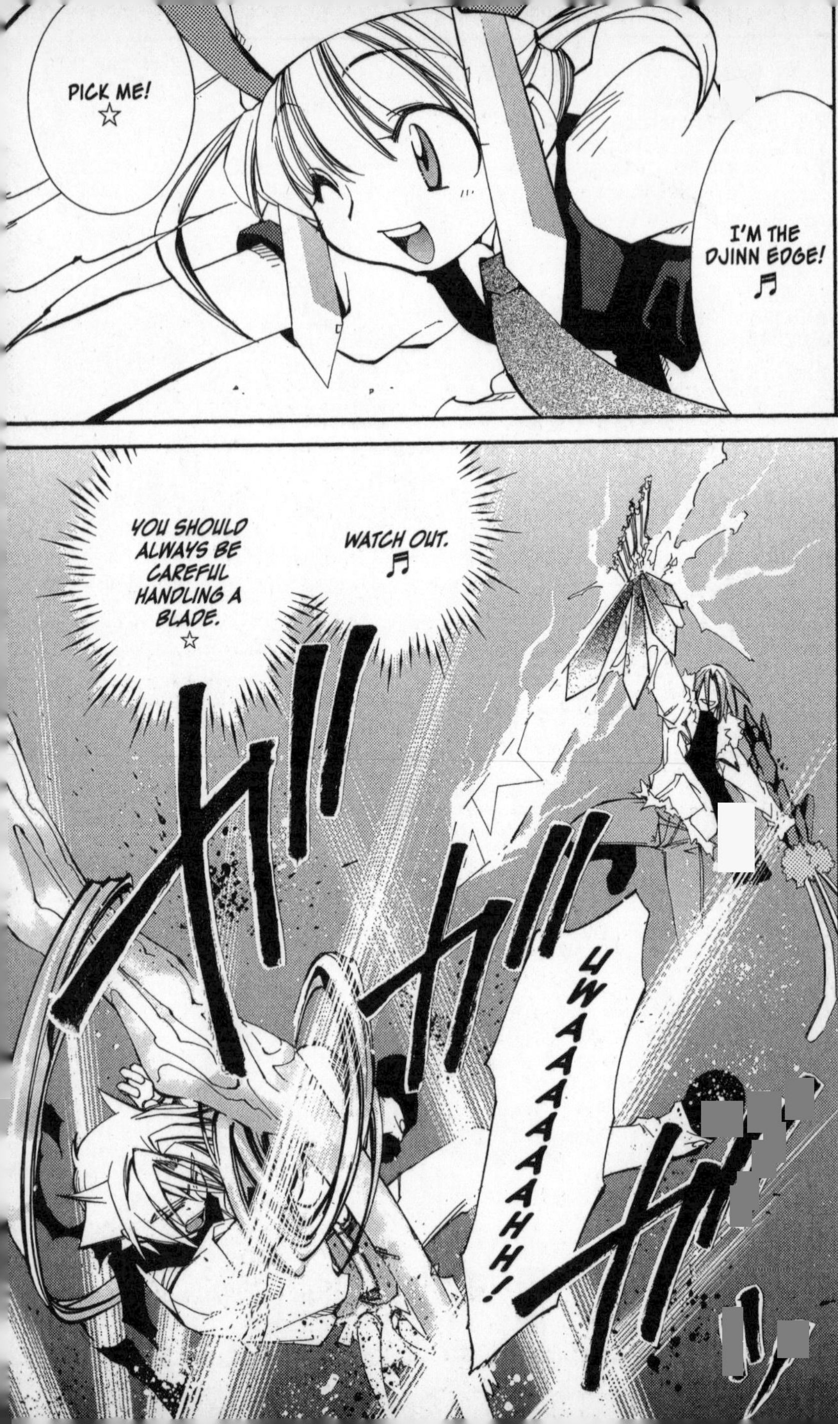
I'M THE DJINN EDGE! ♬
PICK ME! ☆
WATCH OUT. ♬
YOU SHOULD ALWAYS BE CAREFUL HANDLING A BLADE. ☆
UWAAAAAAAAAH!

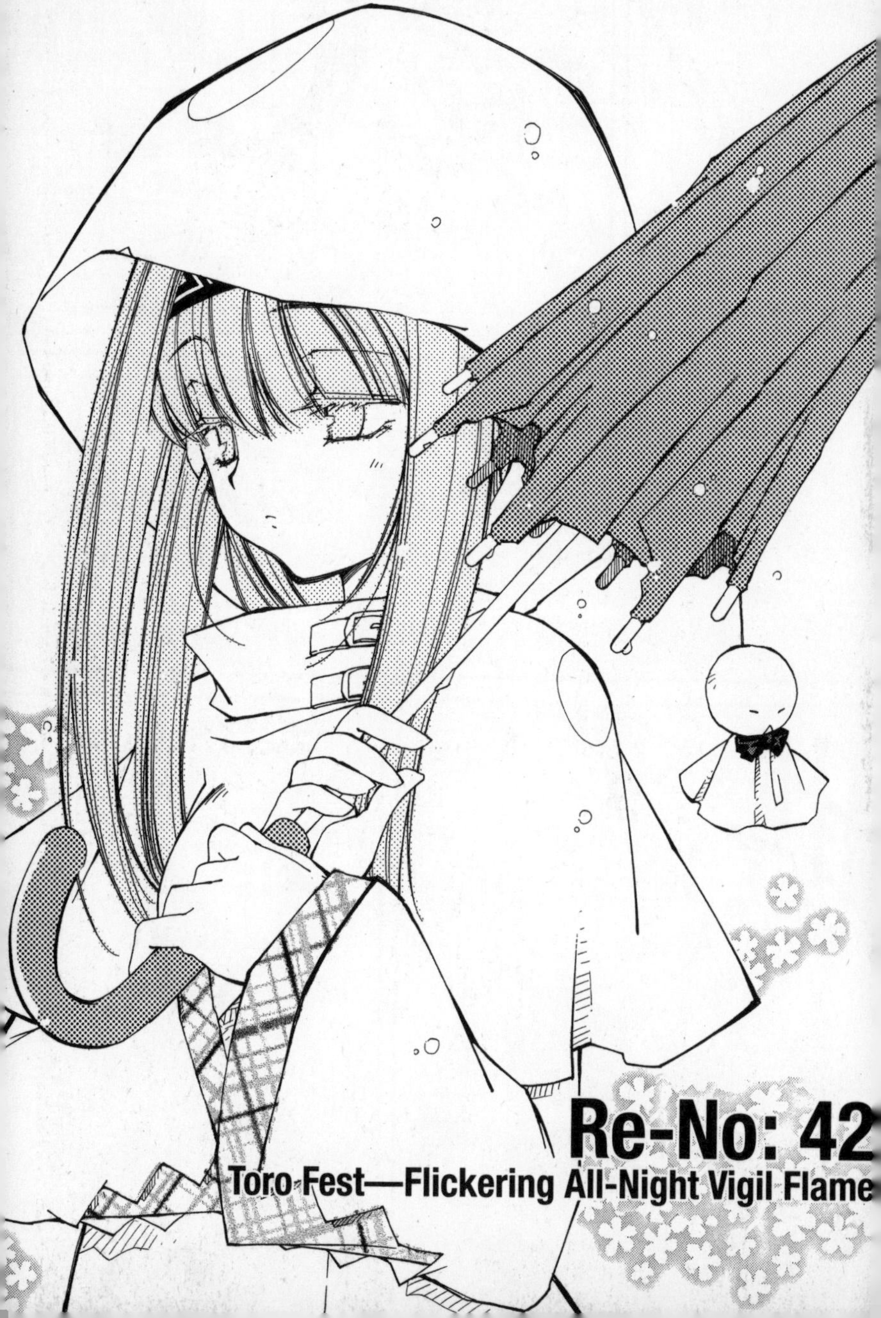

Re-No: 42

Toro Fest—Flickering All-Night Vigil Flame

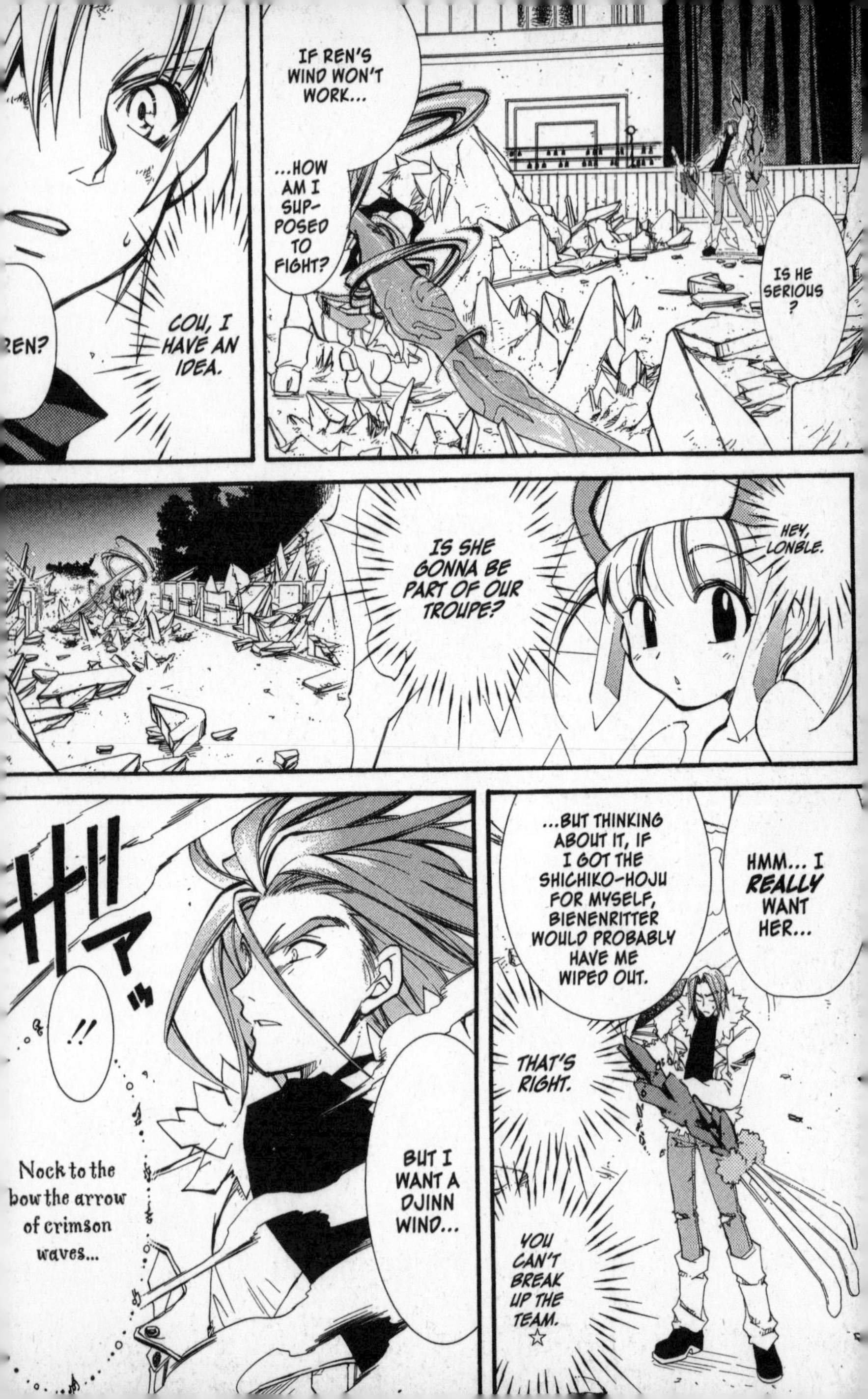
IS HE SERIOUS?
IF REN'S WIND WON'T WORK...
...HOW AM I SUP-POSED TO FIGHT?
COU, I HAVE AN IDEA.
REN?
HEY, LONBLE.
IS SHE GONNA BE PART OF OUR TROUPE?
HMM... I **REALLY** WANT HER...
...BUT THINKING ABOUT IT, IF I GOT THE SHICHIKO-HOJU FOR MYSELF, BIENENRITTER WOULD PROBABLY HAVE ME WIPED OUT.
THAT'S RIGHT.
YOU CAN'T BREAK UP THE TEAM. ☆
BUT I WANT A DJINN WIND...
!!
Nock to the bow the arrow of crimson waves...

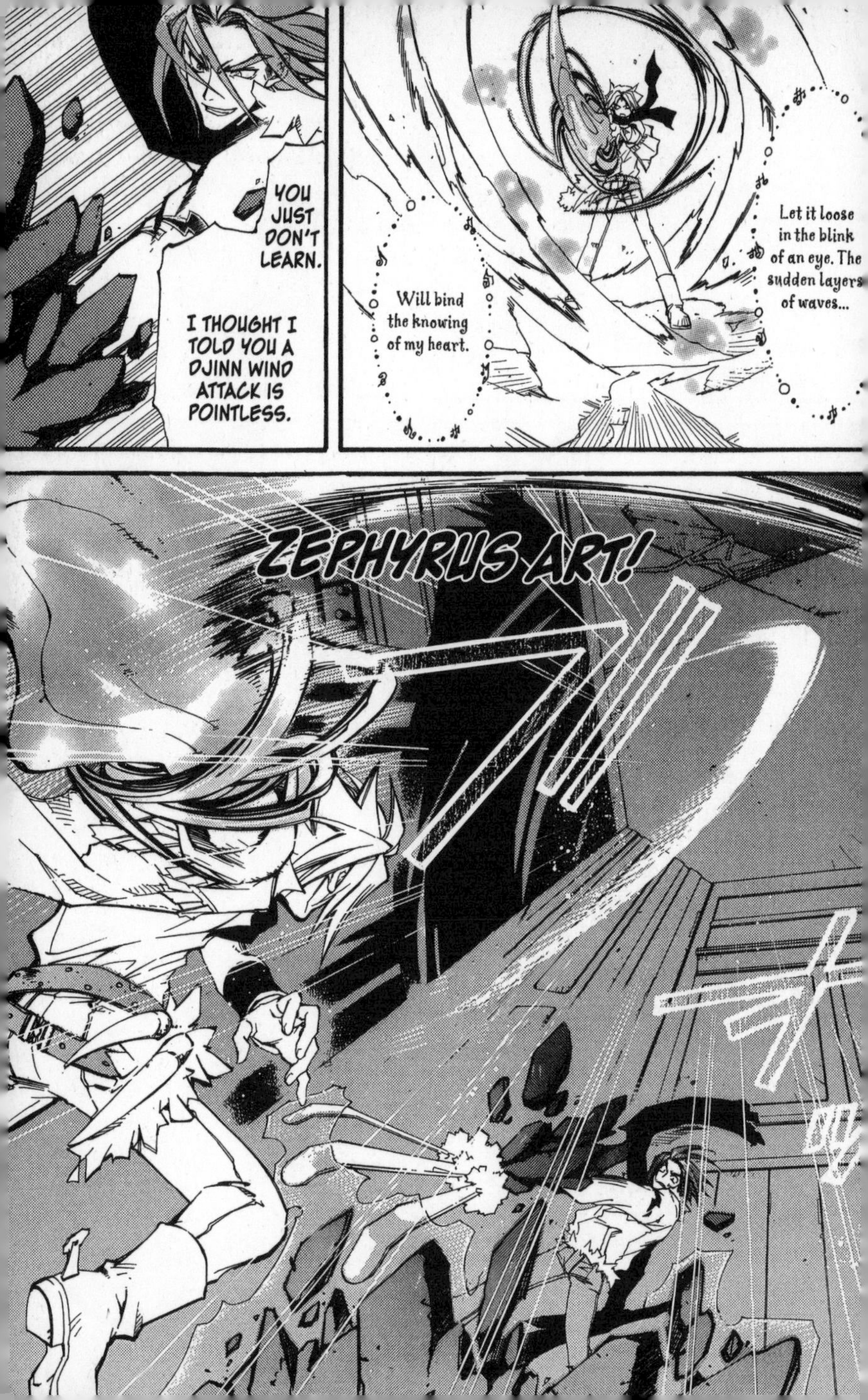
Let it loose in the blink of an eye. The sudden layers of waves...
Will bind the knowing of my heart.
YOU JUST DON'T LEARN.
I THOUGHT I TOLD YOU A DJINN WIND ATTACK IS POINTLESS.
ZEPHYRUS ART!

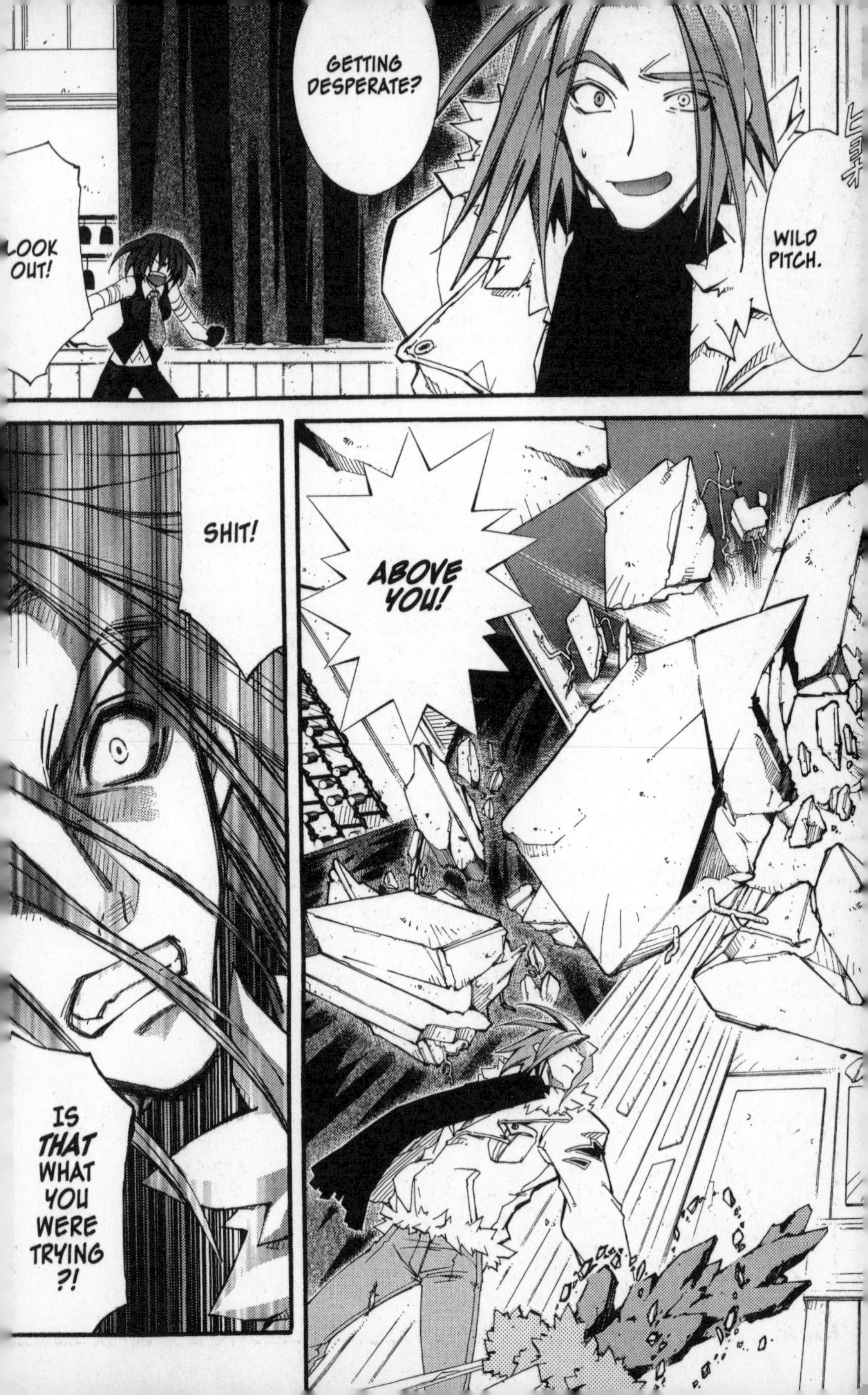
GETTING DESPERATE?
WILD PITCH.
LOOK OUT!
ABOVE YOU!
SHIT!
IS THAT WHAT YOU WERE TRYING ?!

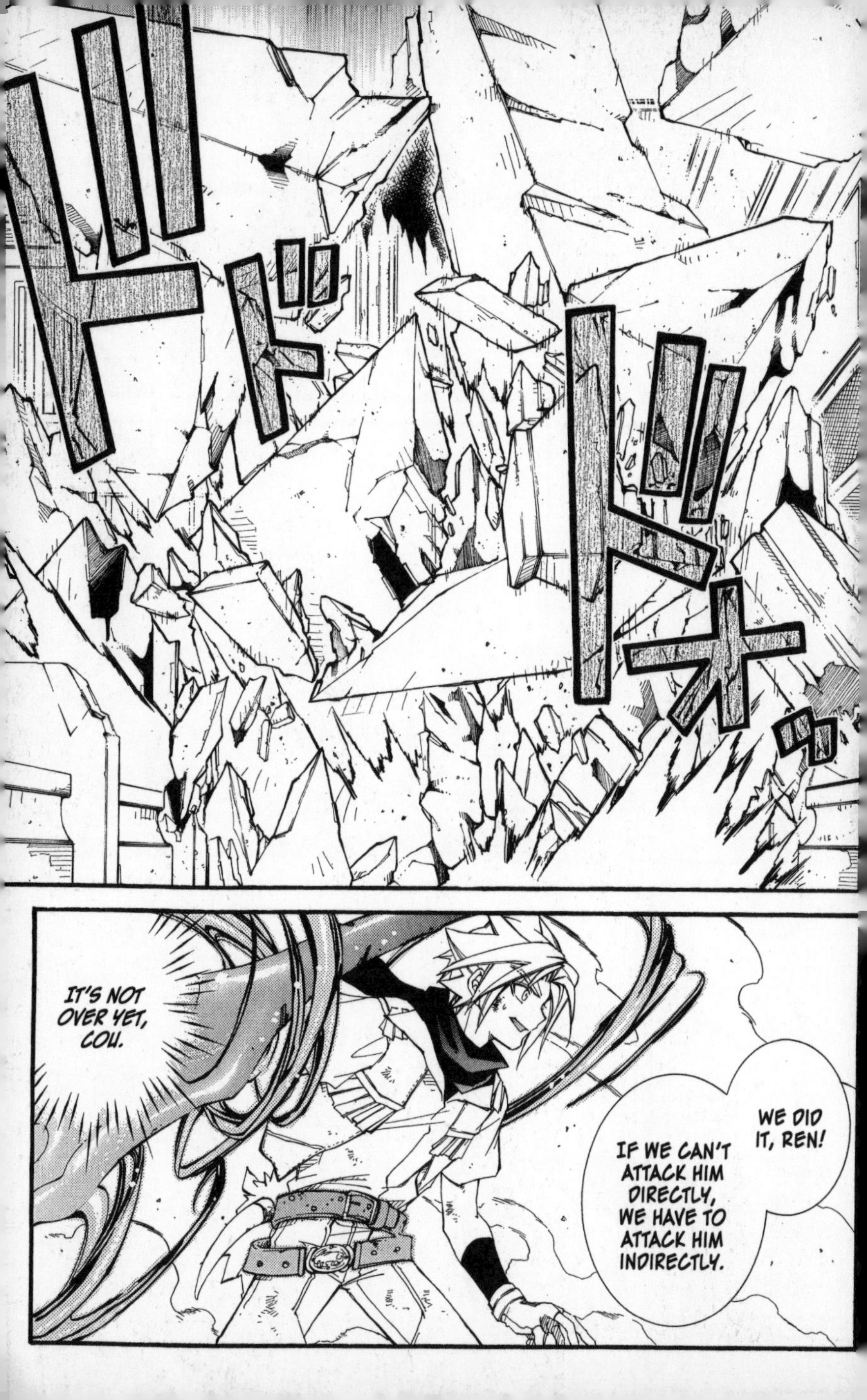
WE DID IT, REN!
IF WE CAN'T ATTACK HIM DIRECTLY, WE HAVE TO ATTACK HIM INDIRECTLY.
IT'S NOT OVER YET, COU.

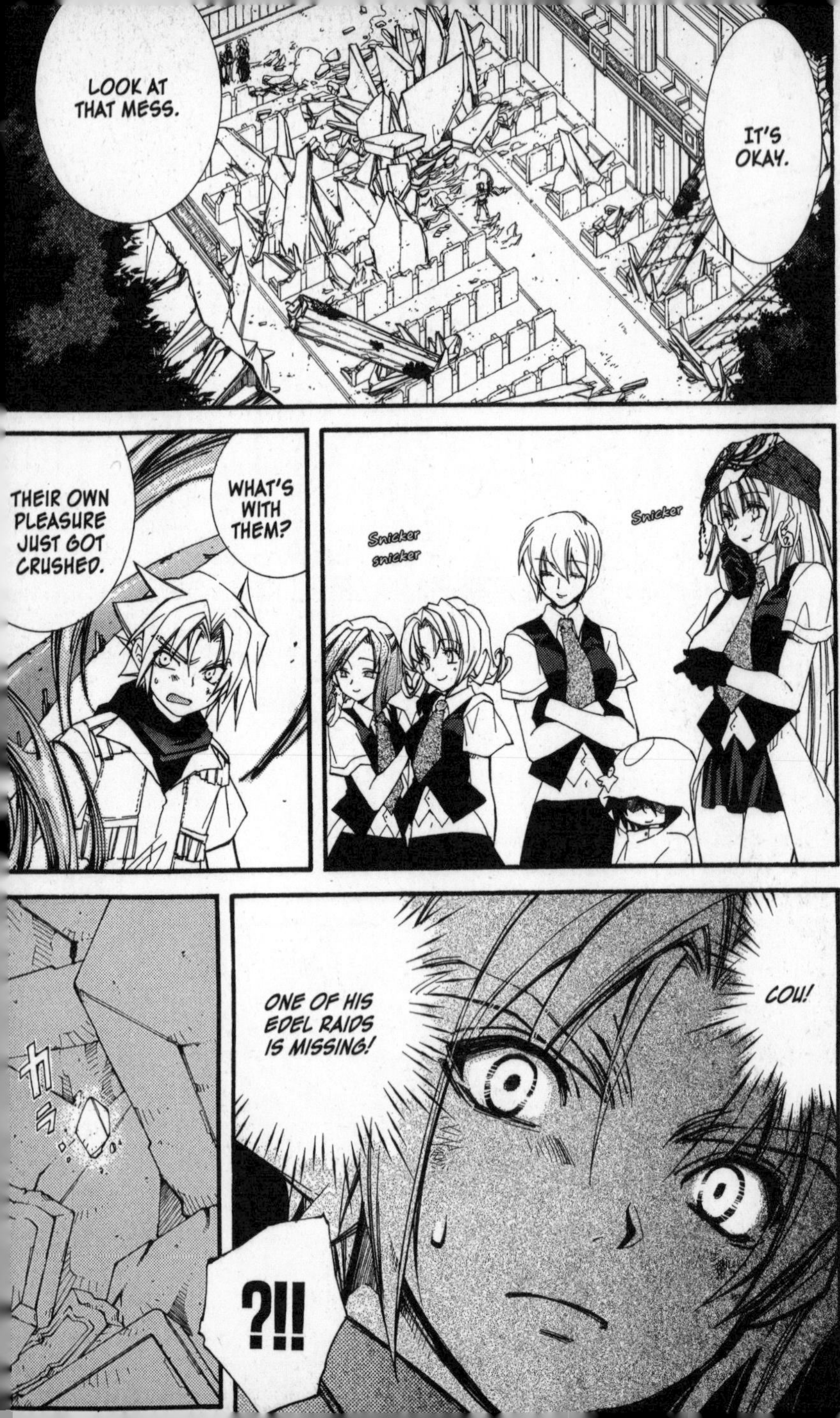
IT'S OKAY.
LOOK AT THAT MESS.
Snicker
Snicker snicker
WHAT'S WITH THEM?
THEIR OWN PLEASURE JUST GOT CRUSHED.
COU!
ONE OF HIS EDEL RAIDS IS MISSING!
?!!
カラ

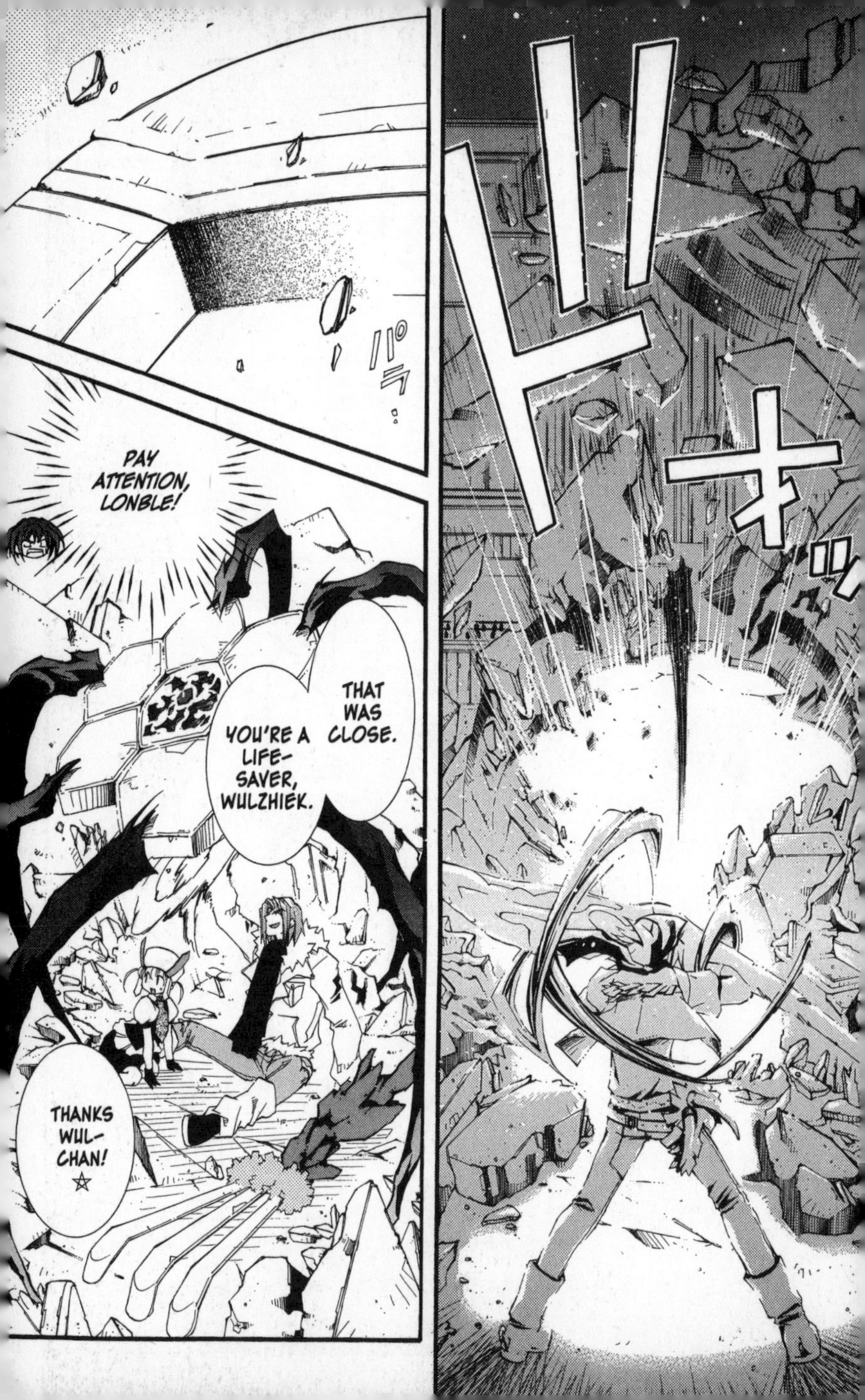
ドオッ
パラ
PAY ATTENTION, LONBLE!
THAT WAS CLOSE.
YOU'RE A LIFE-SAVER, WULZHIEK.
THANKS WUL-CHAN! ☆

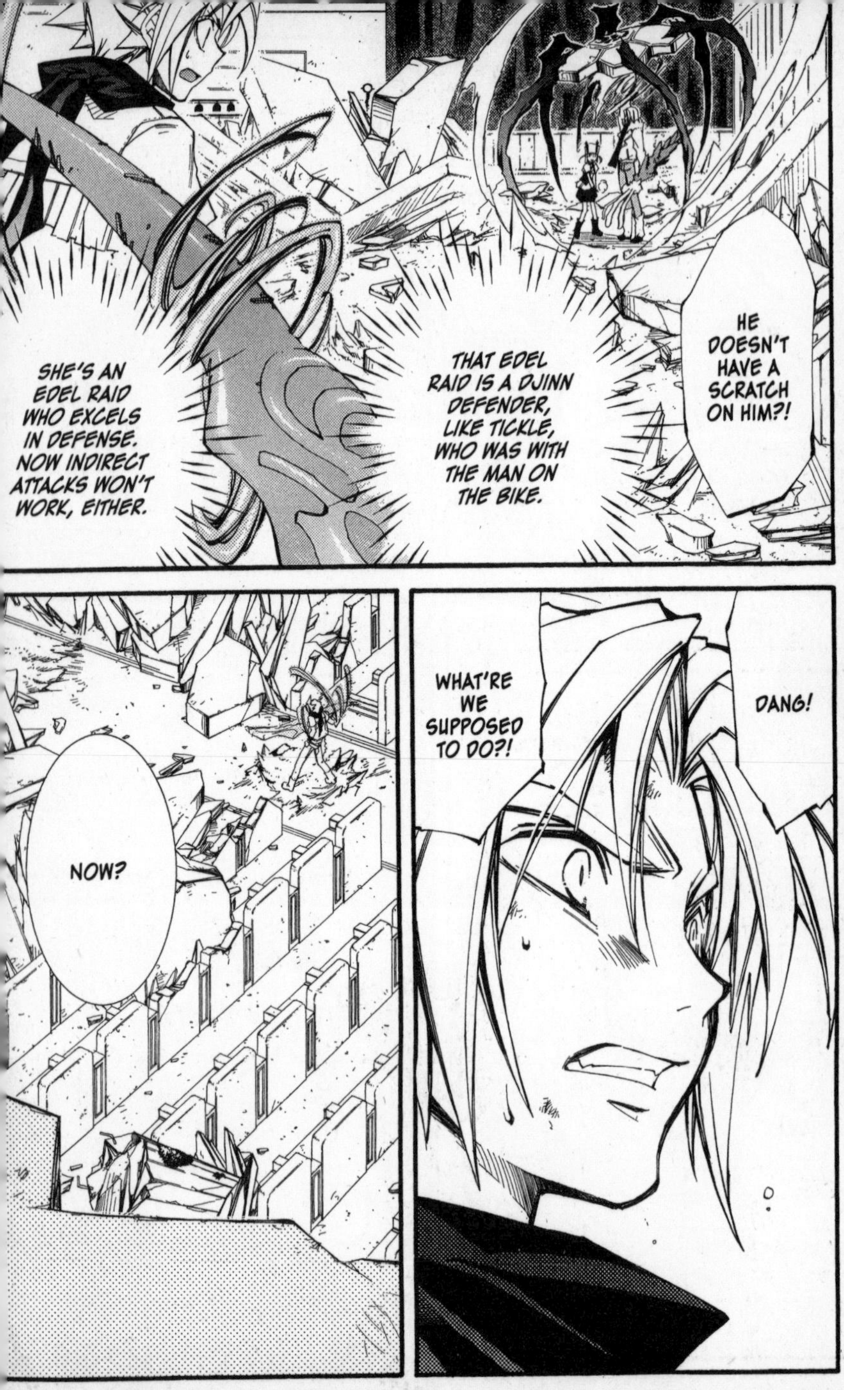
HE DOESN'T HAVE A SCRATCH ON HIM?!
THAT EDEL RAID IS A DJINN DEFENDER, LIKE TICKLE, WHO WAS WITH THE MAN ON THE BIKE.
SHE'S AN EDEL RAID WHO EXCELS IN DEFENSE. NOW INDIRECT ATTACKS WON'T WORK, EITHER.
DANG!
WHAT'RE WE SUPPOSED TO DO?!
NOW?

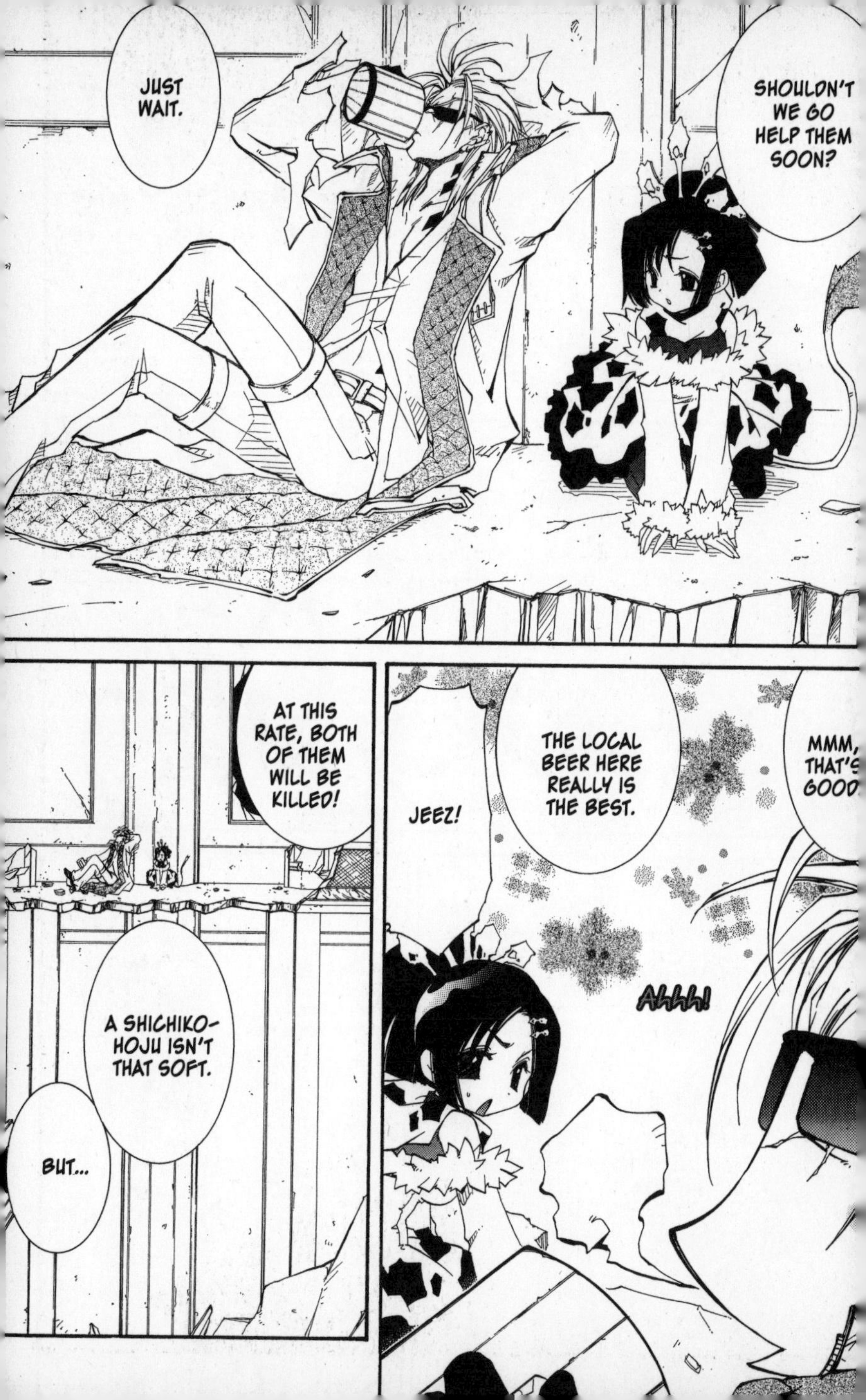
SHOULDN'T WE GO HELP THEM SOON?
JUST WAIT.
MMM, THAT'S GOOD
THE LOCAL BEER HERE REALLY IS THE BEST.
JEEZ!
Ahhh!
AT THIS RATE, BOTH OF THEM WILL BE KILLED!
A SHICHIKO-HOJU ISN'T THAT SOFT.
BUT...

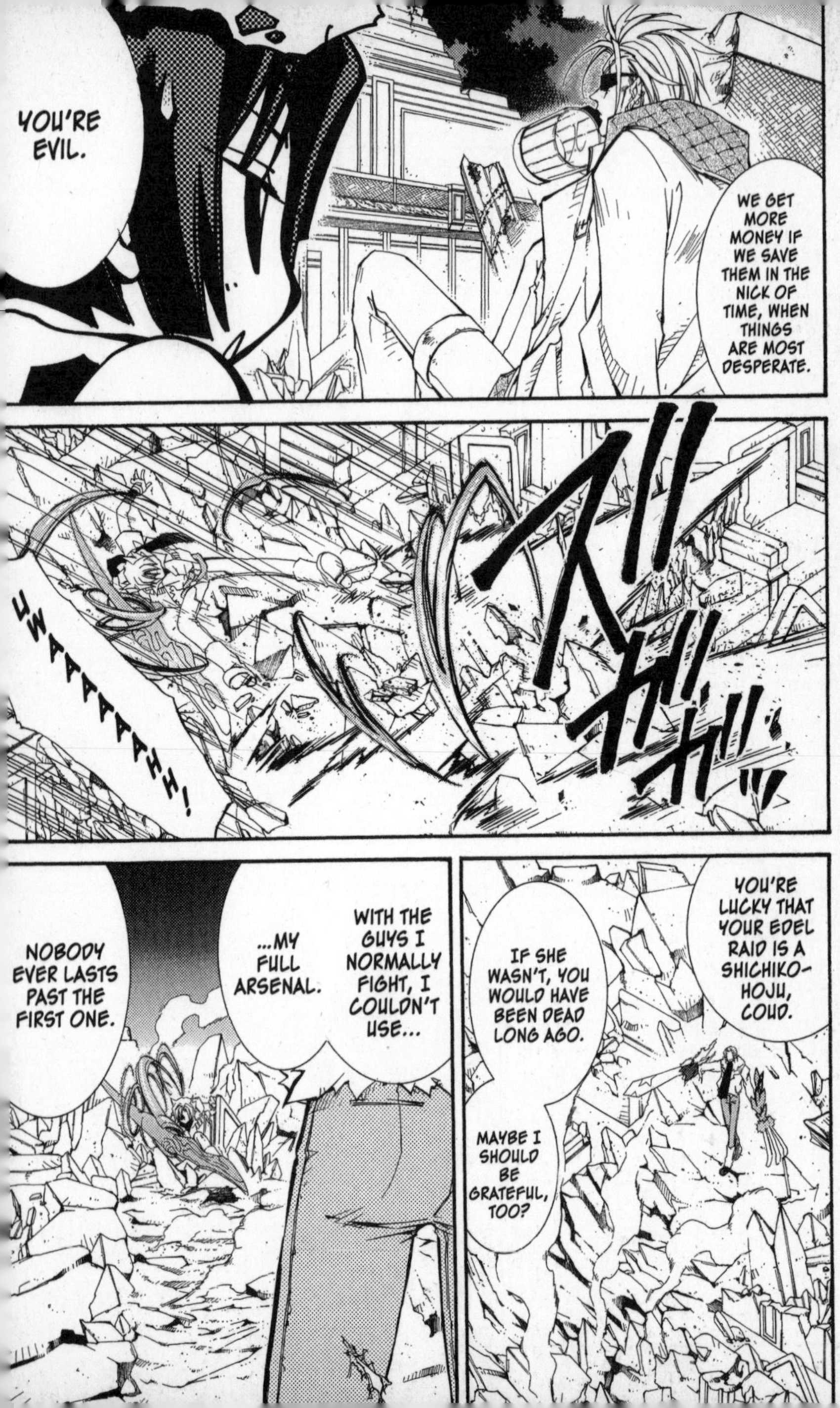
WE GET MORE MONEY IF WE SAVE THEM IN THE NICK OF TIME, WHEN THINGS ARE MOST DESPERATE.
YOU'RE EVIL.
UWAAAAAAHH!
YOU'RE LUCKY THAT YOUR EDEL RAID IS A SHICHIKO-HOJU, COUD.
IF SHE WASN'T, YOU WOULD HAVE BEEN DEAD LONG AGO.
MAYBE I SHOULD BE GRATEFUL, TOO?
WITH THE GUYS I NORMALLY FIGHT, I COULDN'T USE...
...MY FULL ARSENAL.
NOBODY EVER LASTS PAST THE FIRST ONE.

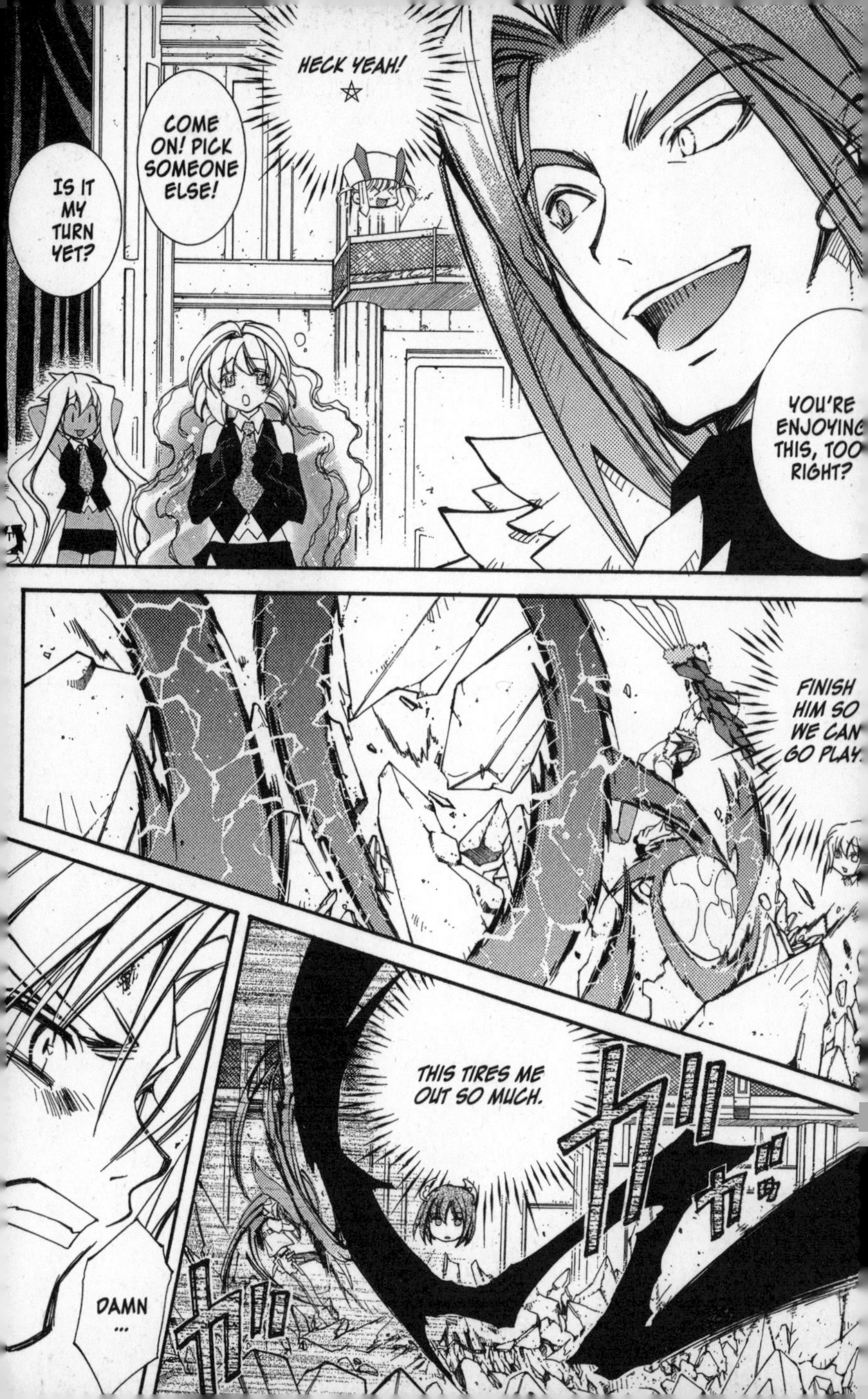
YOU'RE ENJOYING THIS, TOO RIGHT?
HECK YEAH! ☆
COME ON! PICK SOMEONE ELSE!
IS IT MY TURN YET?
FINISH HIM SO WE CAN GO PLAY.
THIS TIRES ME OUT SO MUCH.
DAMN ...

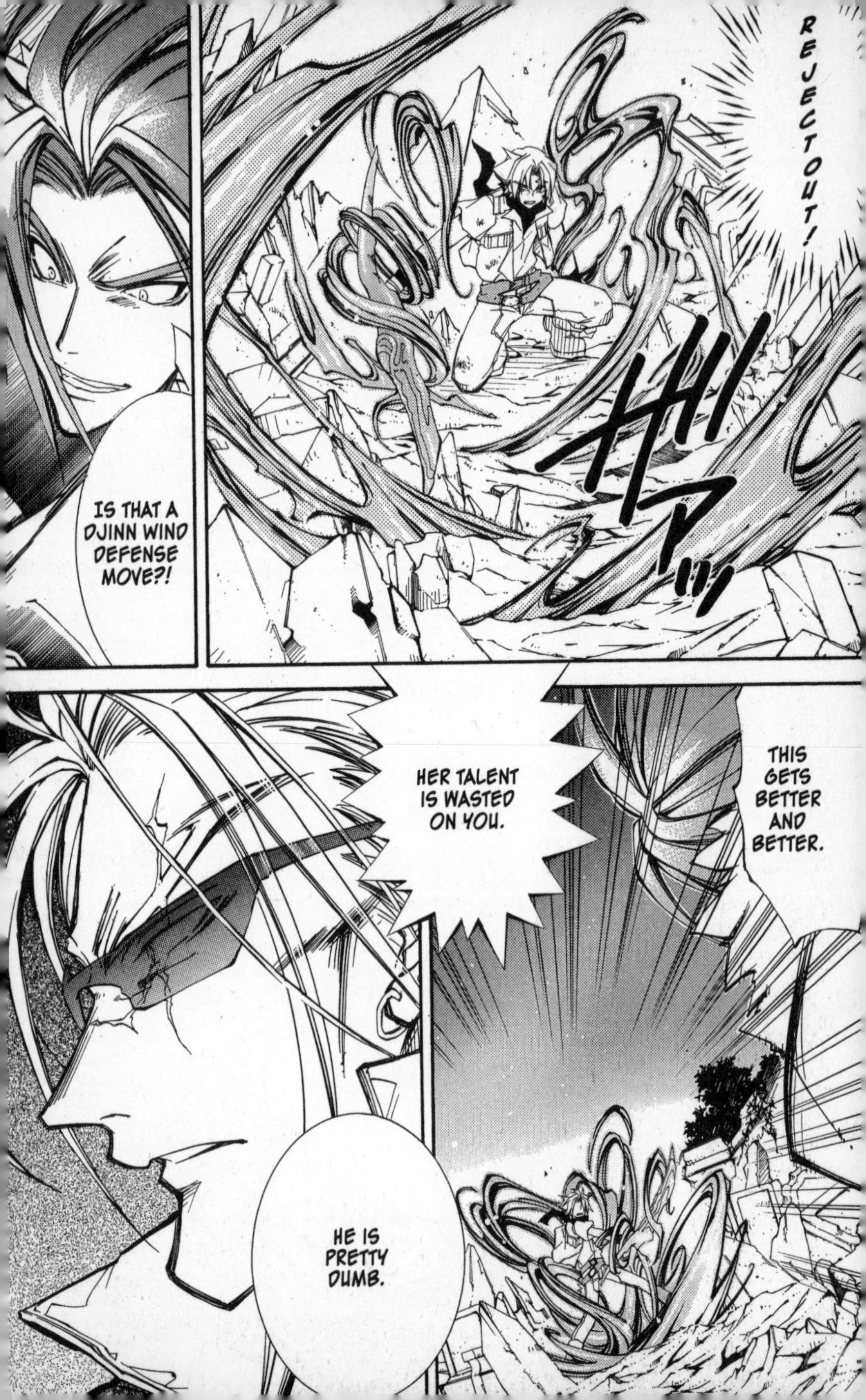
REJECTOUT!
IS THAT A DJINN WIND DEFENSE MOVE?!
THIS GETS BETTER AND BETTER.
HER TALENT IS WASTED ON YOU.
HE IS PRETTY DUMB.

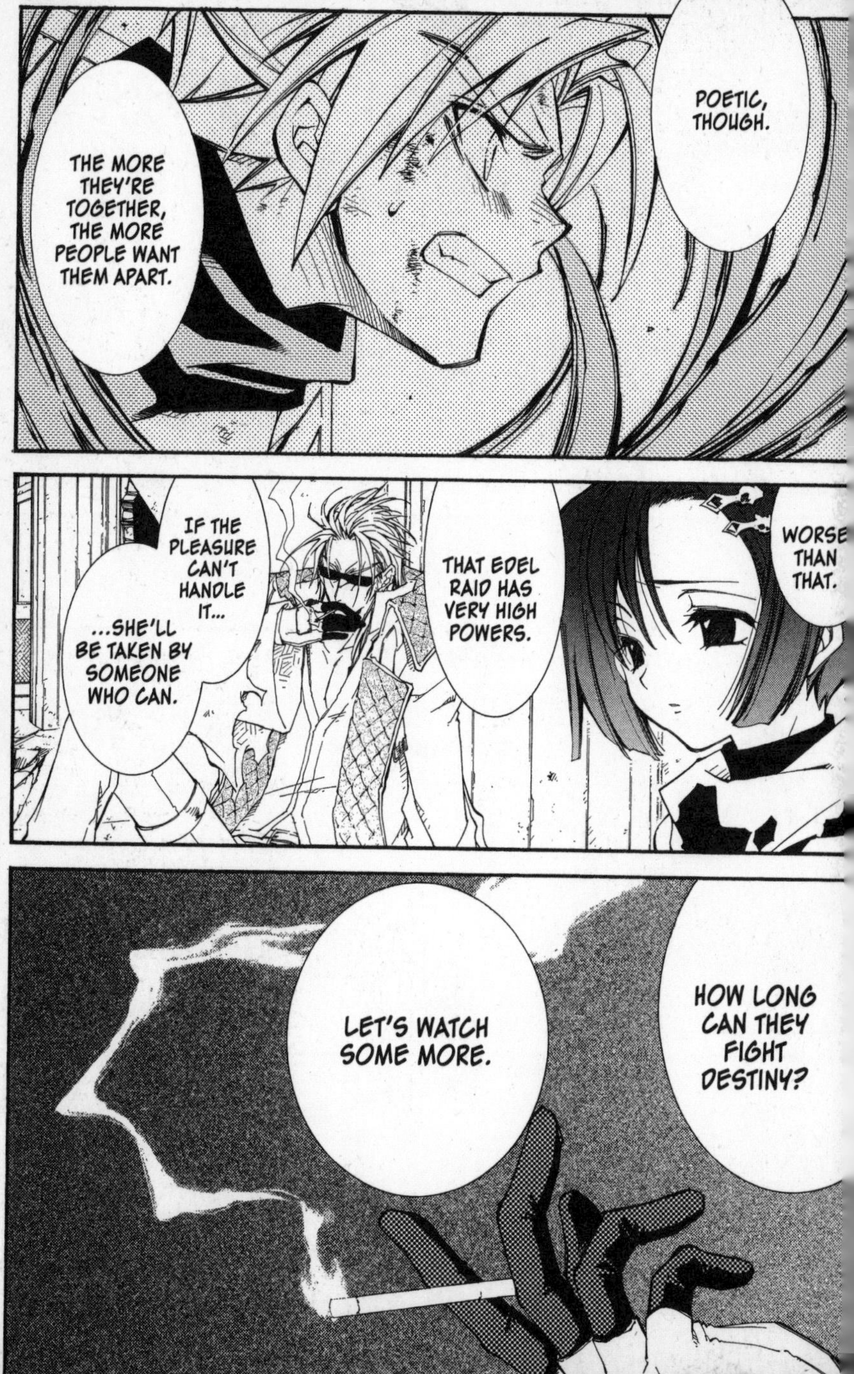
POETIC, THOUGH.
THE MORE THEY'RE TOGETHER, THE MORE PEOPLE WANT THEM APART.
WORSE THAN THAT.
THAT EDEL RAID HAS VERY HIGH POWERS.
IF THE PLEASURE CAN'T HANDLE IT...
...SHE'LL BE TAKEN BY SOMEONE WHO CAN.
HOW LONG CAN THEY FIGHT DESTINY?
LET'S WATCH SOME MORE.

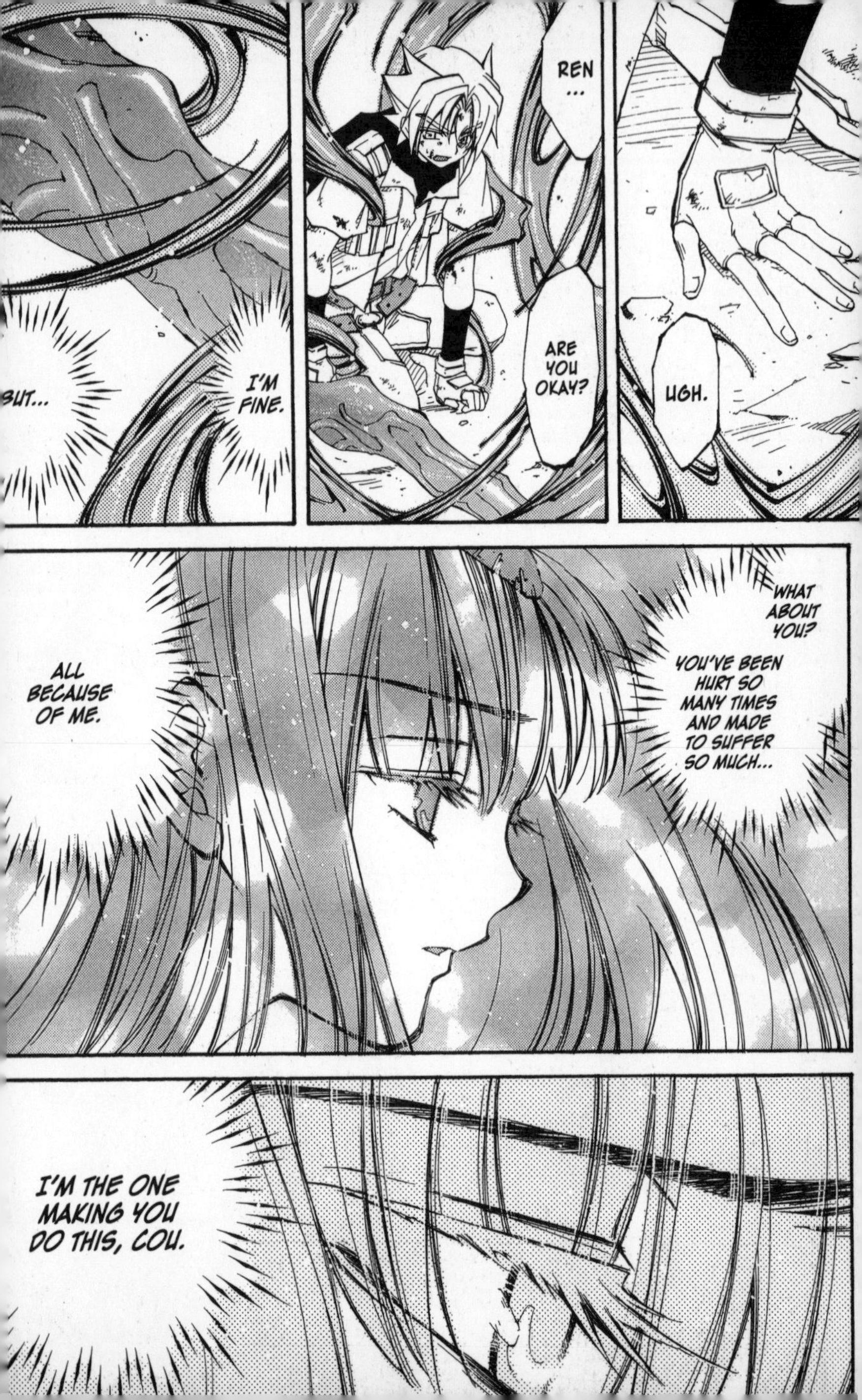
UGH.
REN...
ARE YOU OKAY?
I'M FINE.
BUT...
WHAT ABOUT YOU?
YOU'VE BEEN HURT SO MANY TIMES AND MADE TO SUFFER SO MUCH...
ALL BECAUSE OF ME.
I'M THE ONE MAKING YOU DO THIS, COU.

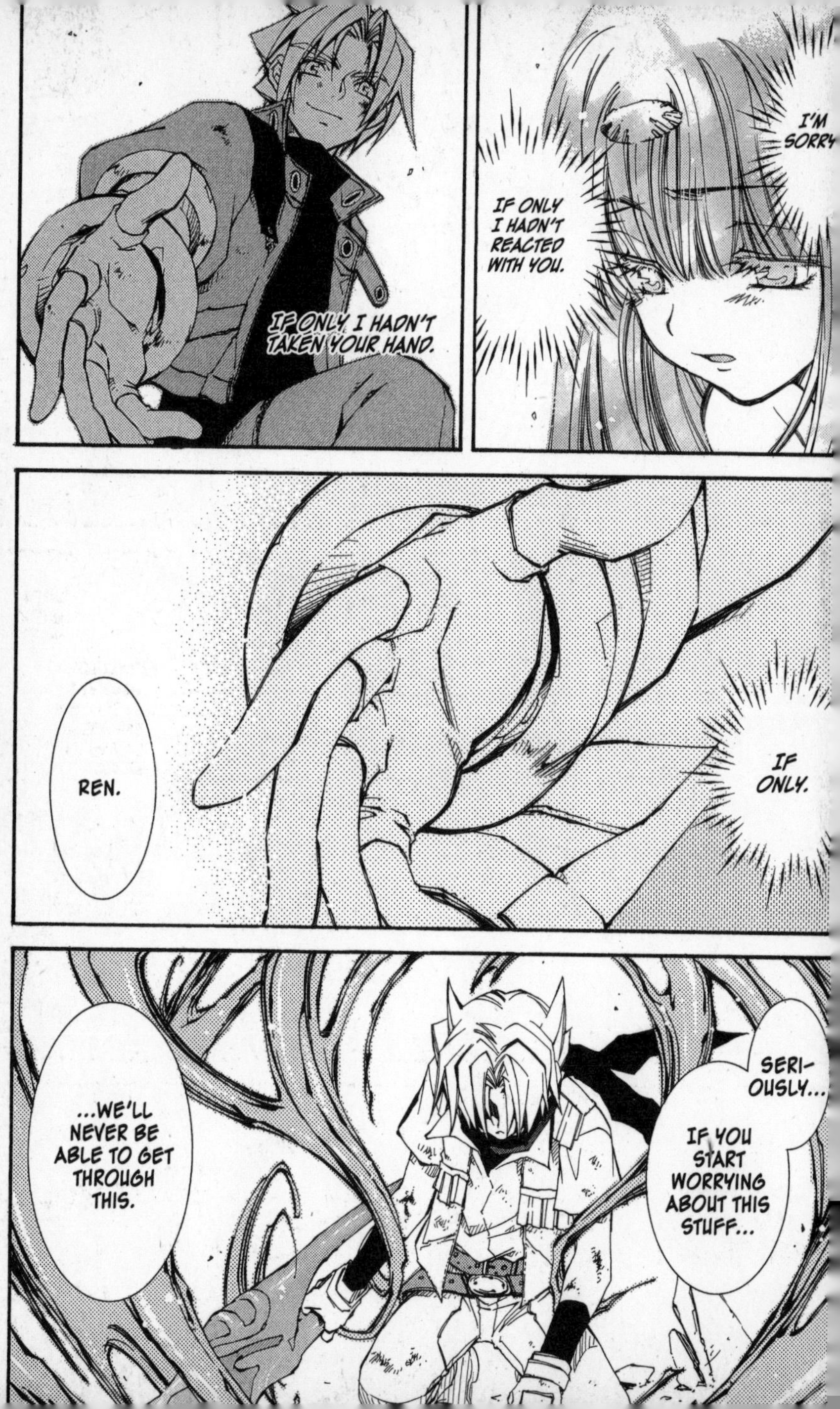
I'M SORRY
IF ONLY I HADN'T REACTED WITH YOU.
IF ONLY I HADN'T TAKEN YOUR HAND.
IF ONLY.
REN.
SERI-OUSLY...
IF YOU START WORRYING ABOUT THIS STUFF...
...WE'LL NEVER BE ABLE TO GET THROUGH THIS.

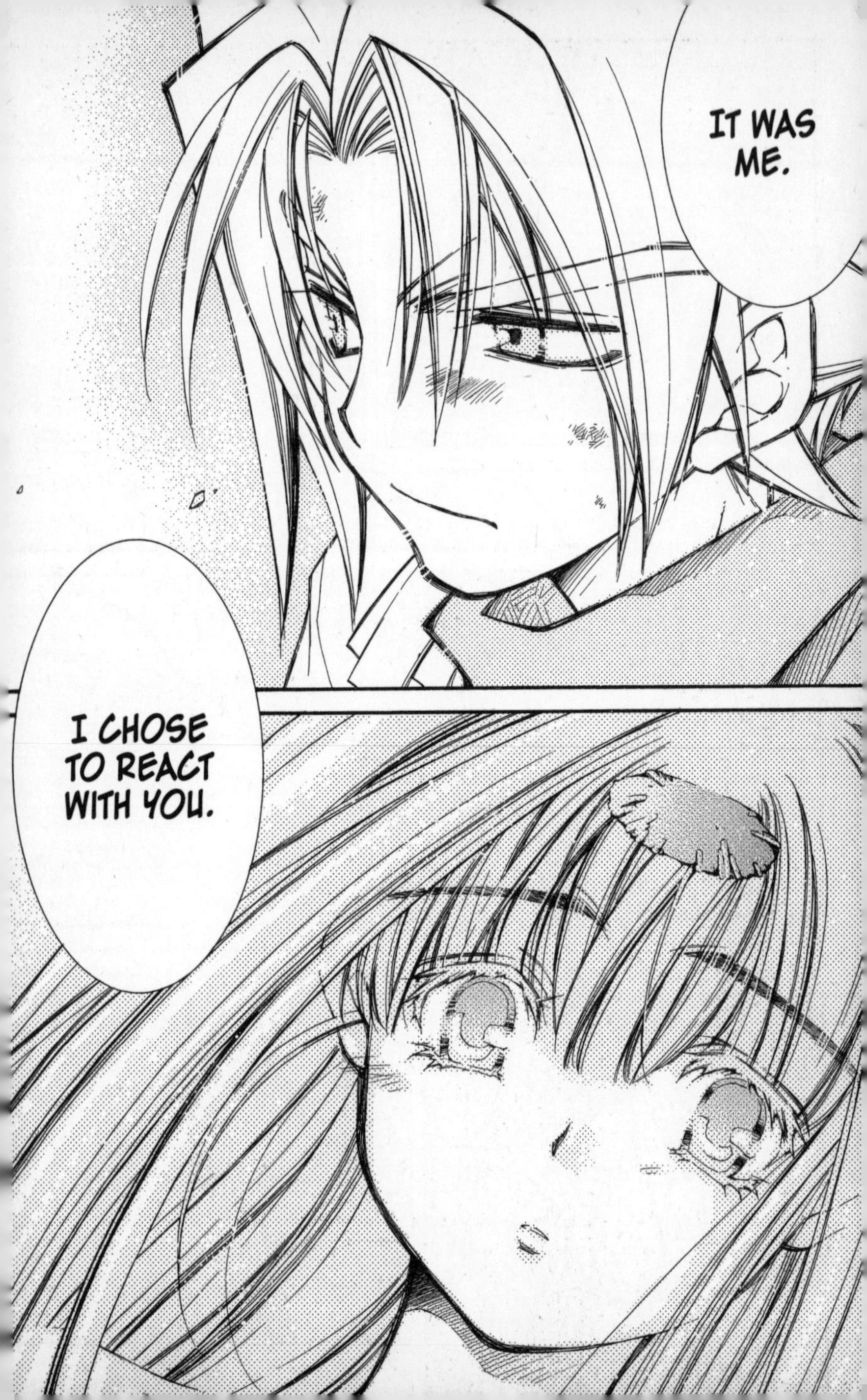
IT WAS ME.
I CHOSE TO REACT WITH YOU.

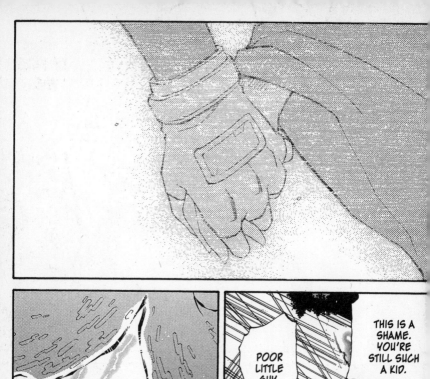

THIS IS A SHAME. YOU'RE STILL SUCH A KID.

POOR LITTLE GUY.

IF YOU HADN'T HAD TO GO AND STICK YOUR HAND IN A SHICHIKO-HOJU...

...YOU COULD'VE LIVED A LOT LONGER.

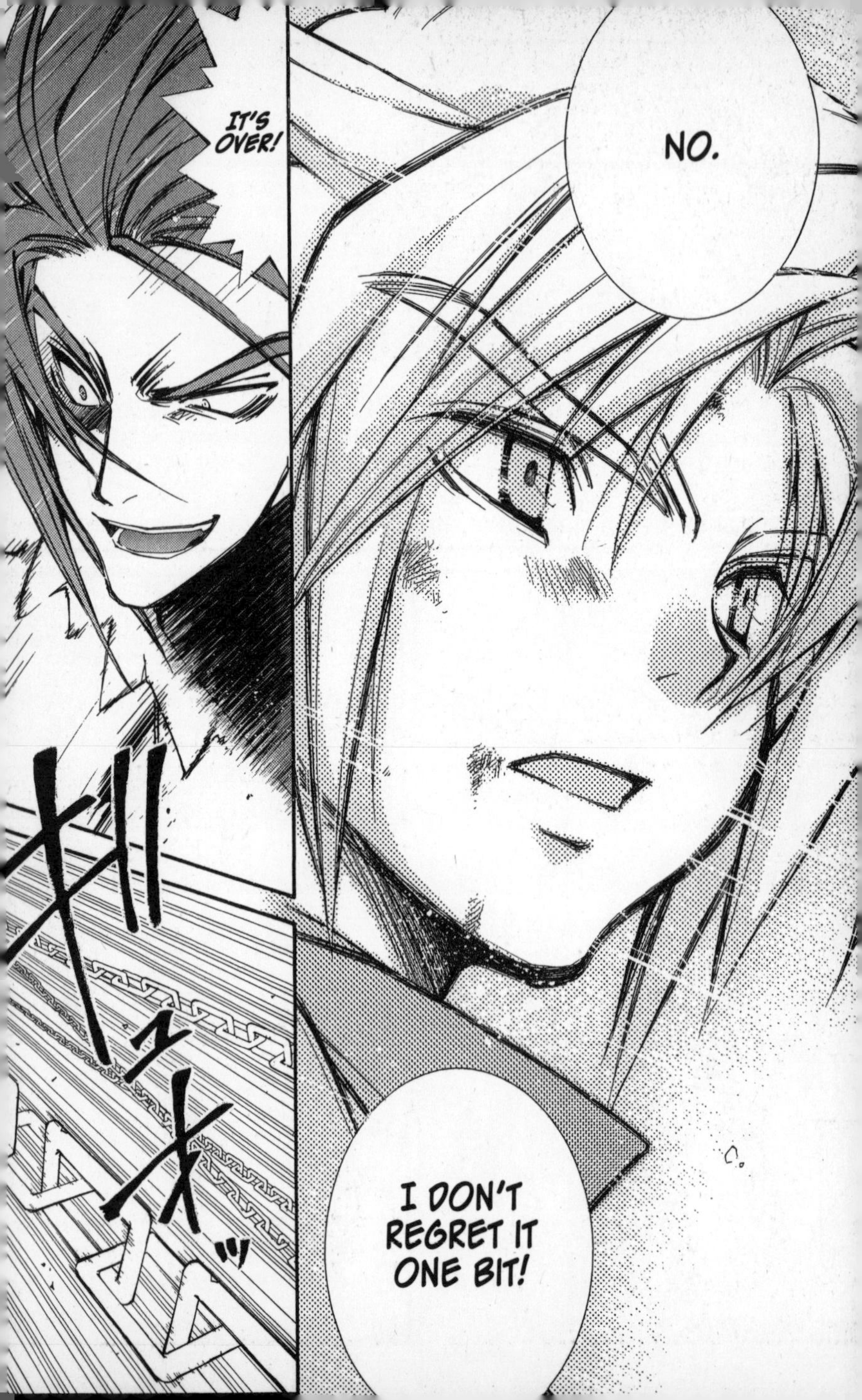
NO.
I DON'T REGRET IT ONE BIT!
IT'S OVER!

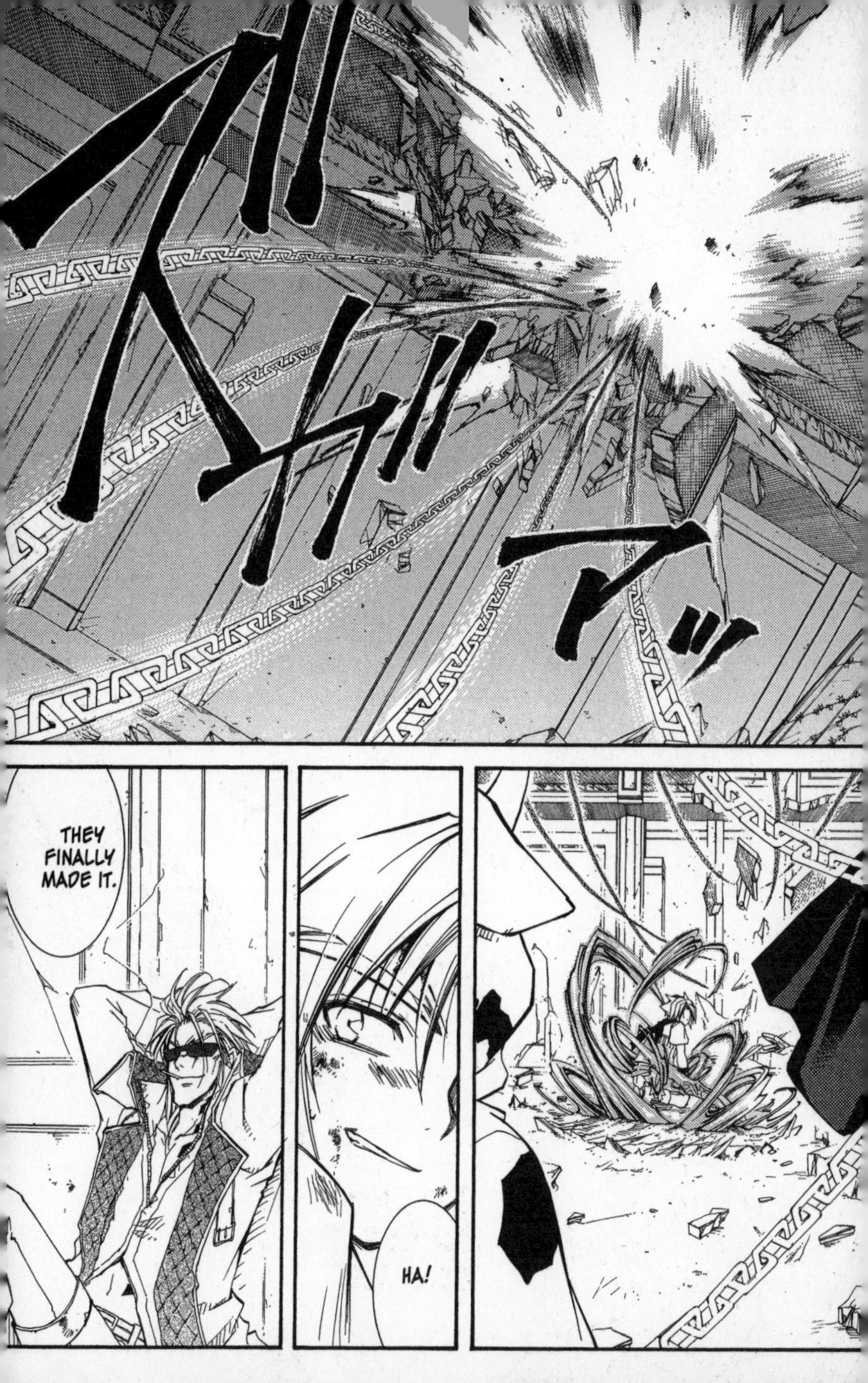
ズガァッ
HA!
THEY FINALLY MADE IT.

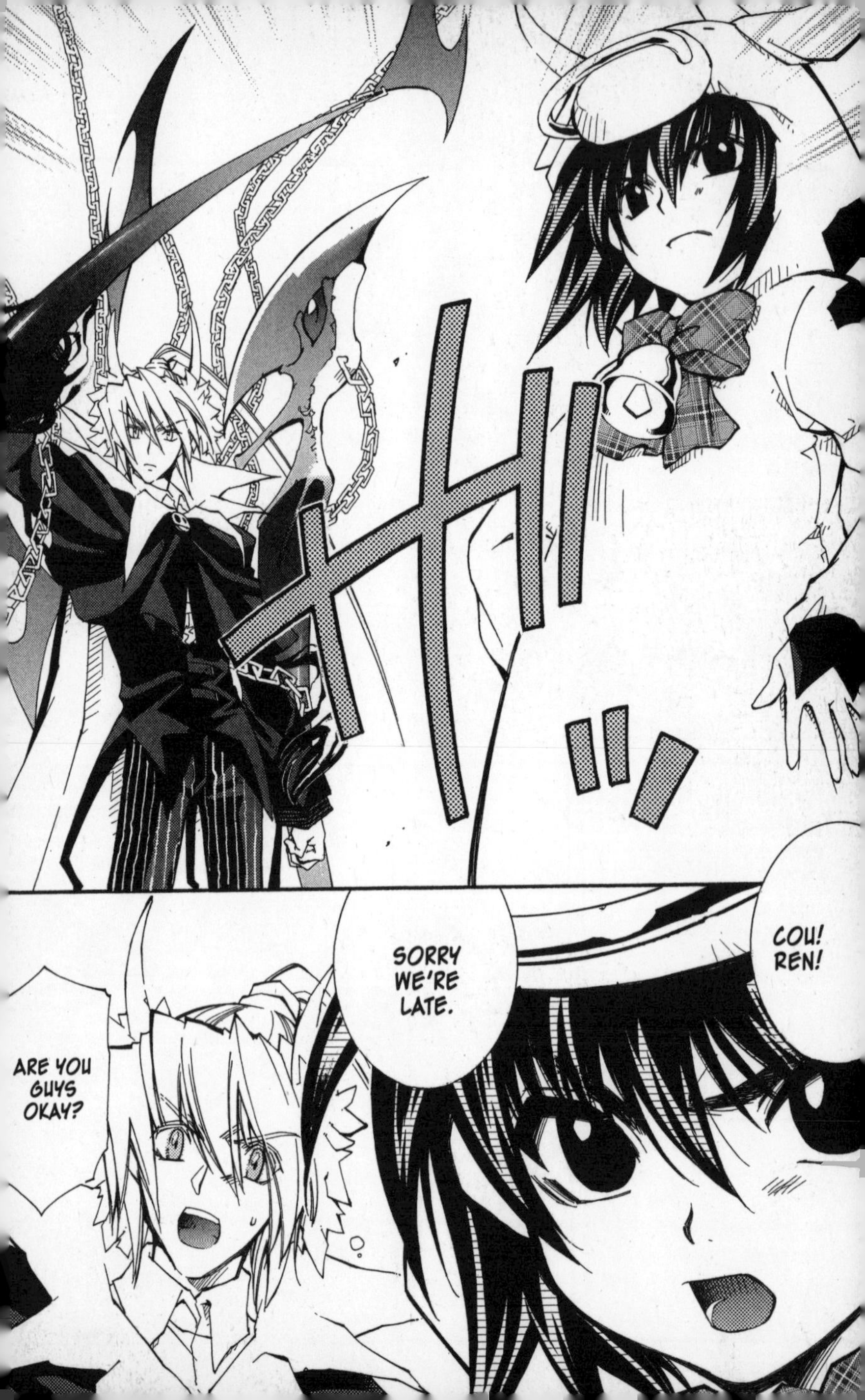
COU! REN!
SORRY WE'RE LATE.
ARE YOU GUYS OKAY?

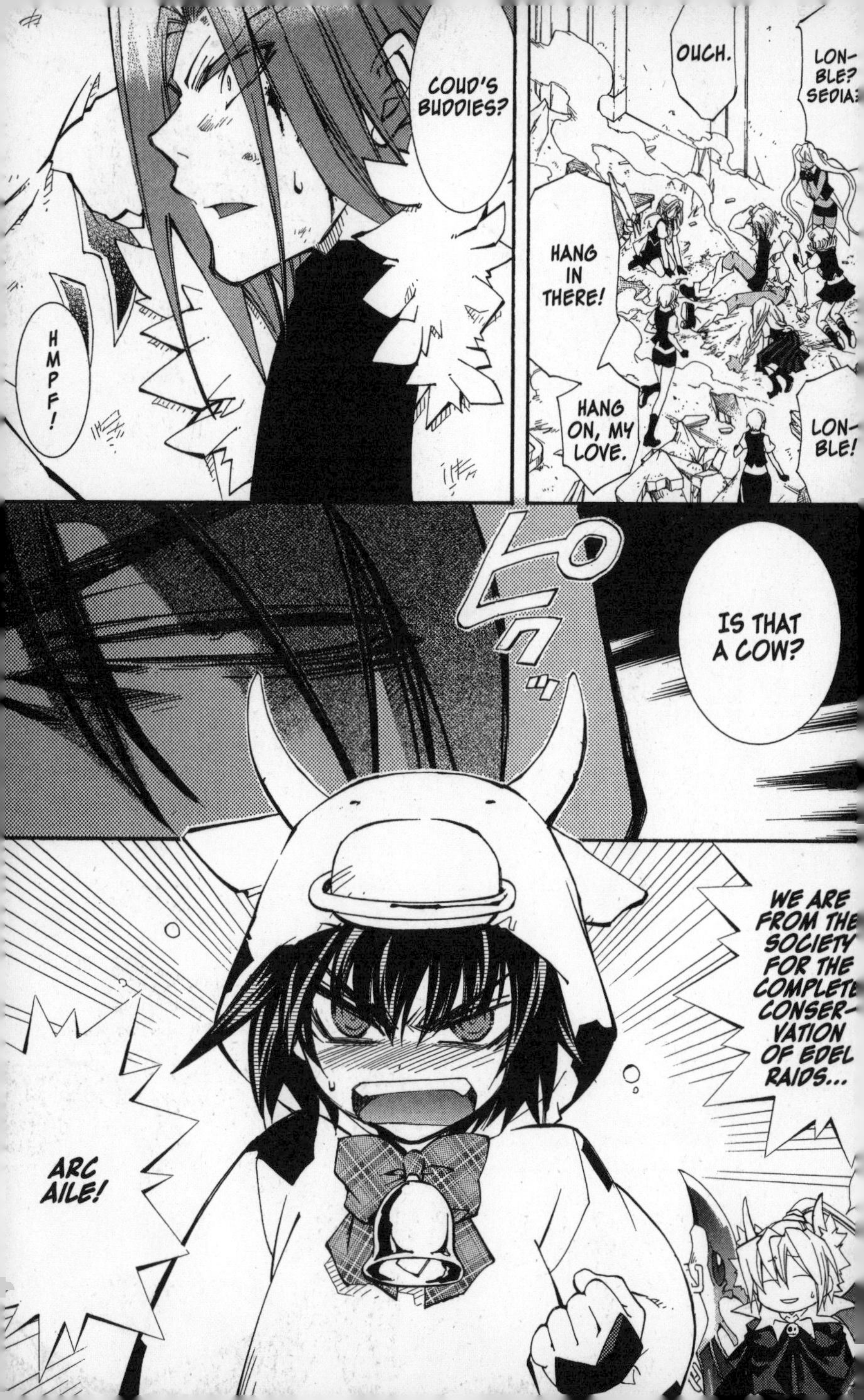
LON-BLE? SEDIA?
OUCH.
HANG IN THERE!
LON-BLE!
HANG ON, MY LOVE.
COUD'S BUDDIES?
HMPF!
IS THAT A COW?
ピクッ
WE ARE FROM THE SOCIETY FOR THE COMPLETE CONSERVATION OF EDEL RAIDS...
ARC AILE!

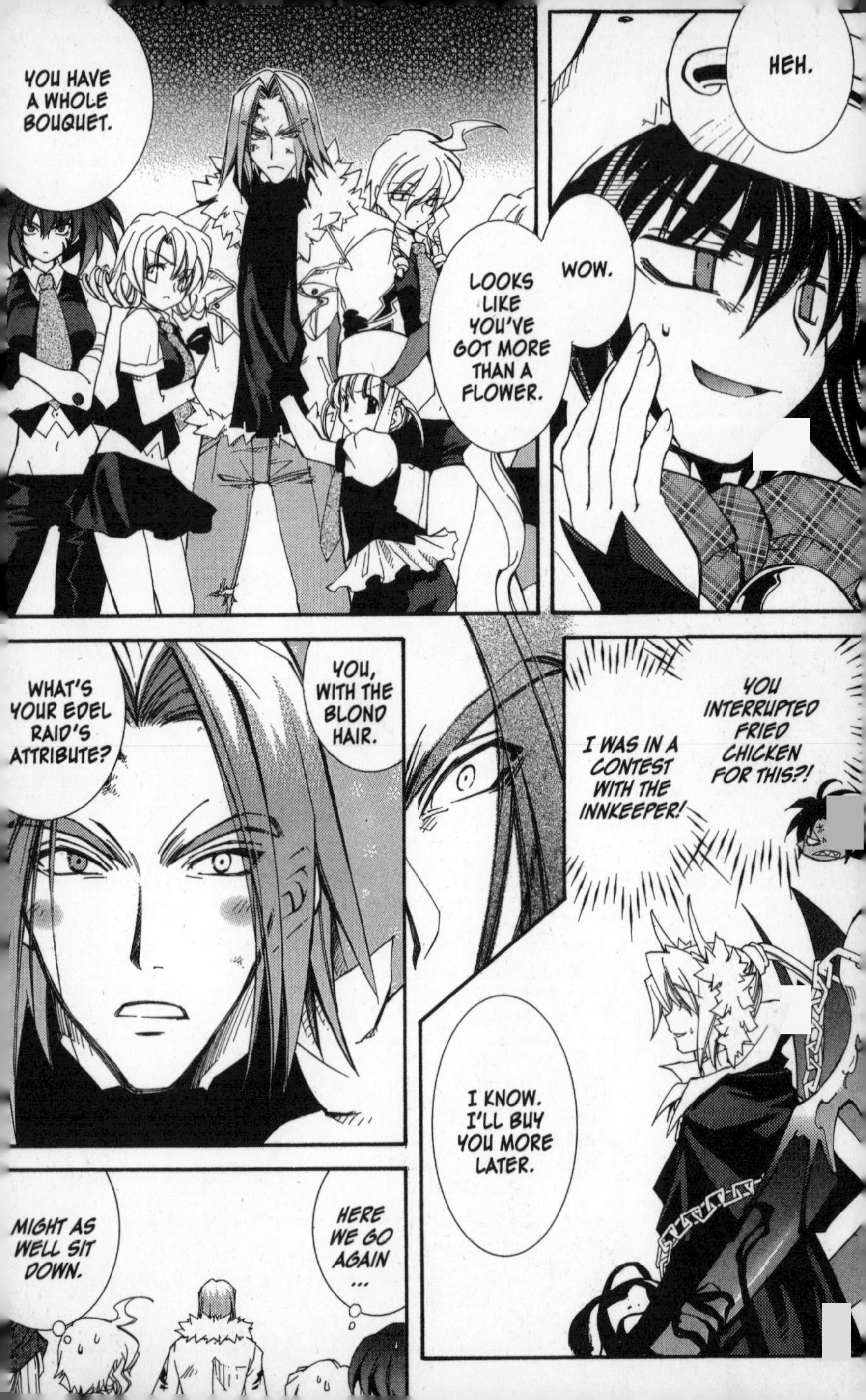
HEH.
WOW.
LOOKS LIKE YOU'VE GOT MORE THAN A FLOWER.
YOU HAVE A WHOLE BOUQUET.
YOU INTERRUPTED FRIED CHICKEN FOR THIS?!
I WAS IN A CONTEST WITH THE INNKEEPER!
I KNOW. I'LL BUY YOU MORE LATER.
YOU, WITH THE BLOND HAIR.
WHAT'S YOUR EDEL RAID'S ATTRIBUTE?
HERE WE GO AGAIN...
MIGHT AS WELL SIT DOWN.

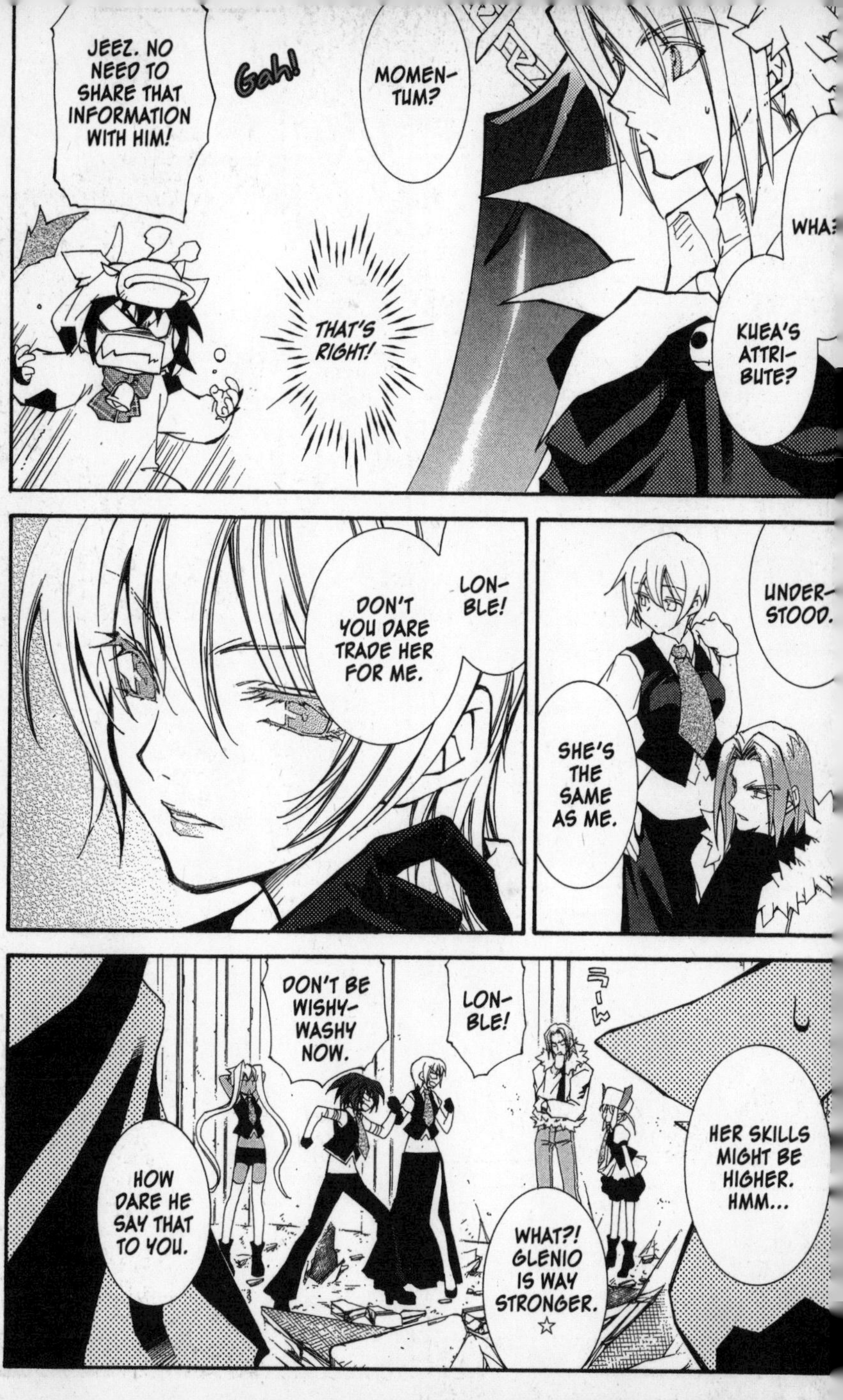
WHA?
KUEA'S ATTRIBUTE?
MOMENTUM?
THAT'S RIGHT!
Gah!
JEEZ. NO NEED TO SHARE THAT INFORMATION WITH HIM!
UNDERSTOOD.
SHE'S THE SAME AS ME.
LONBLE!
DON'T YOU DARE TRADE HER FOR ME.
HER SKILLS MIGHT BE HIGHER. HMM...
WHAT?! GLENIO IS WAY STRONGER. ☆
LONBLE!
DON'T BE WISHY-WASHY NOW.
HOW DARE HE SAY THAT TO YOU.

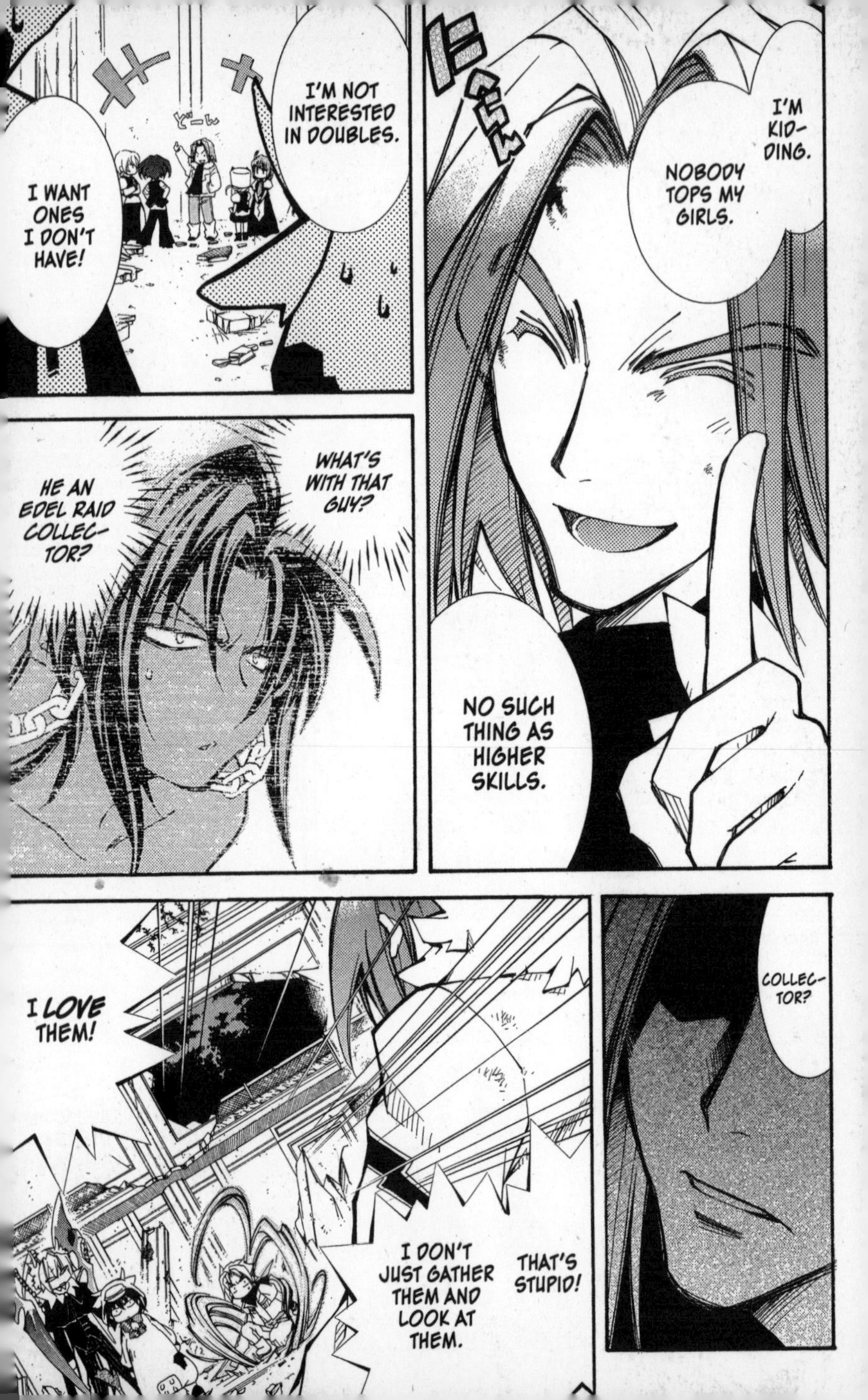
I'M KID-DING.
NOBODY TOPS MY GIRLS.
NO SUCH THING AS HIGHER SKILLS.
I'M NOT INTERESTED IN DOUBLES.
I WANT ONES I DON'T HAVE!
WHAT'S WITH THAT GUY?
HE AN EDEL RAID COLLEC-TOR?
COLLEC-TOR?
THAT'S STUPID!
I DON'T JUST GATHER THEM AND LOOK AT THEM.
I LOVE THEM!

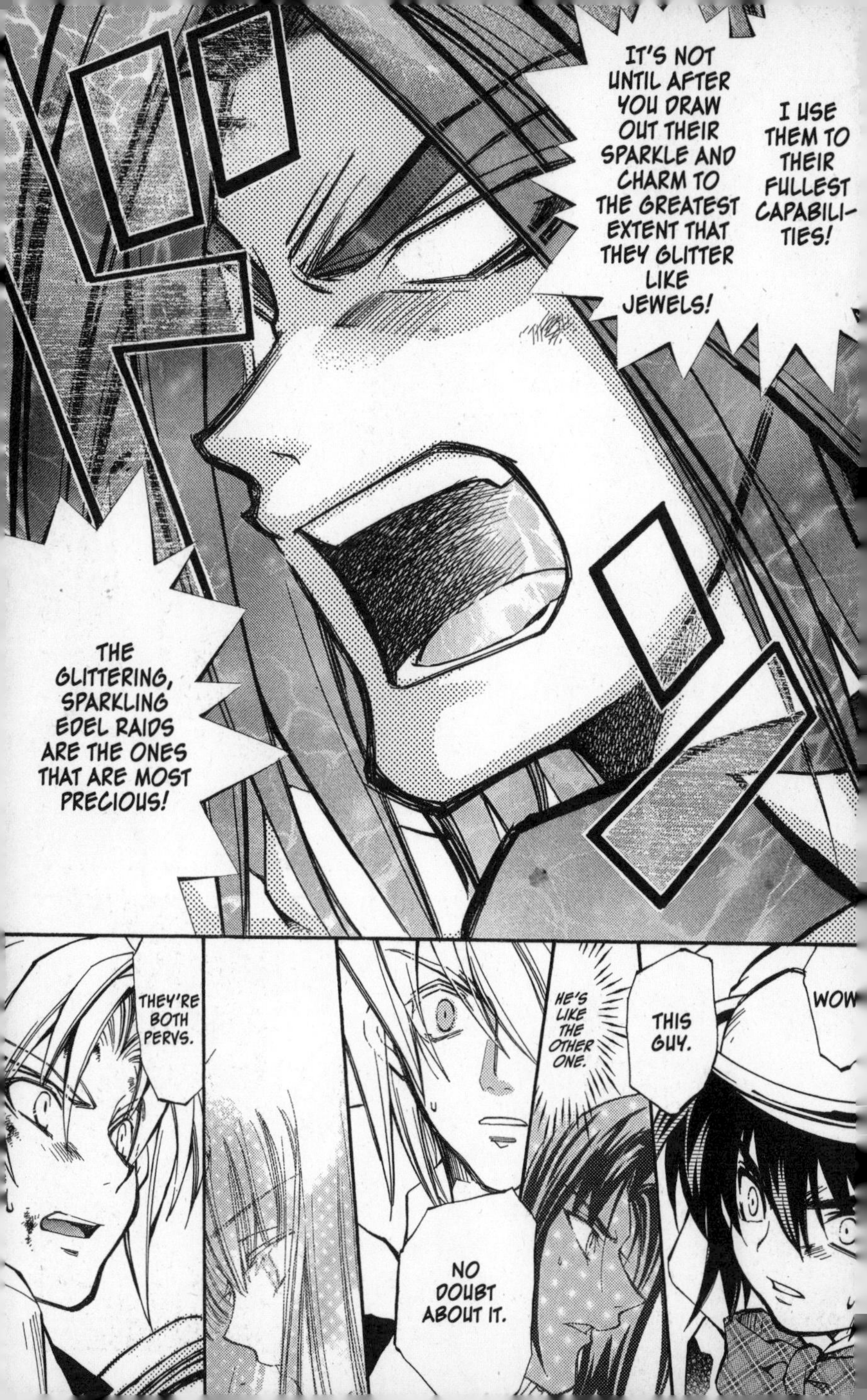
I USE THEM TO THEIR FULLEST CAPABILI-TIES!
IT'S NOT UNTIL AFTER YOU DRAW OUT THEIR SPARKLE AND CHARM TO THE GREATEST EXTENT THAT THEY GLITTER LIKE JEWELS!
THE GLITTERING, SPARKLING EDEL RAIDS ARE THE ONES THAT ARE MOST PRECIOUS!
WOW
THIS GUY.
HE'S LIKE THE OTHER ONE.
NO DOUBT ABOUT IT.
THEY'RE BOTH PERVS.

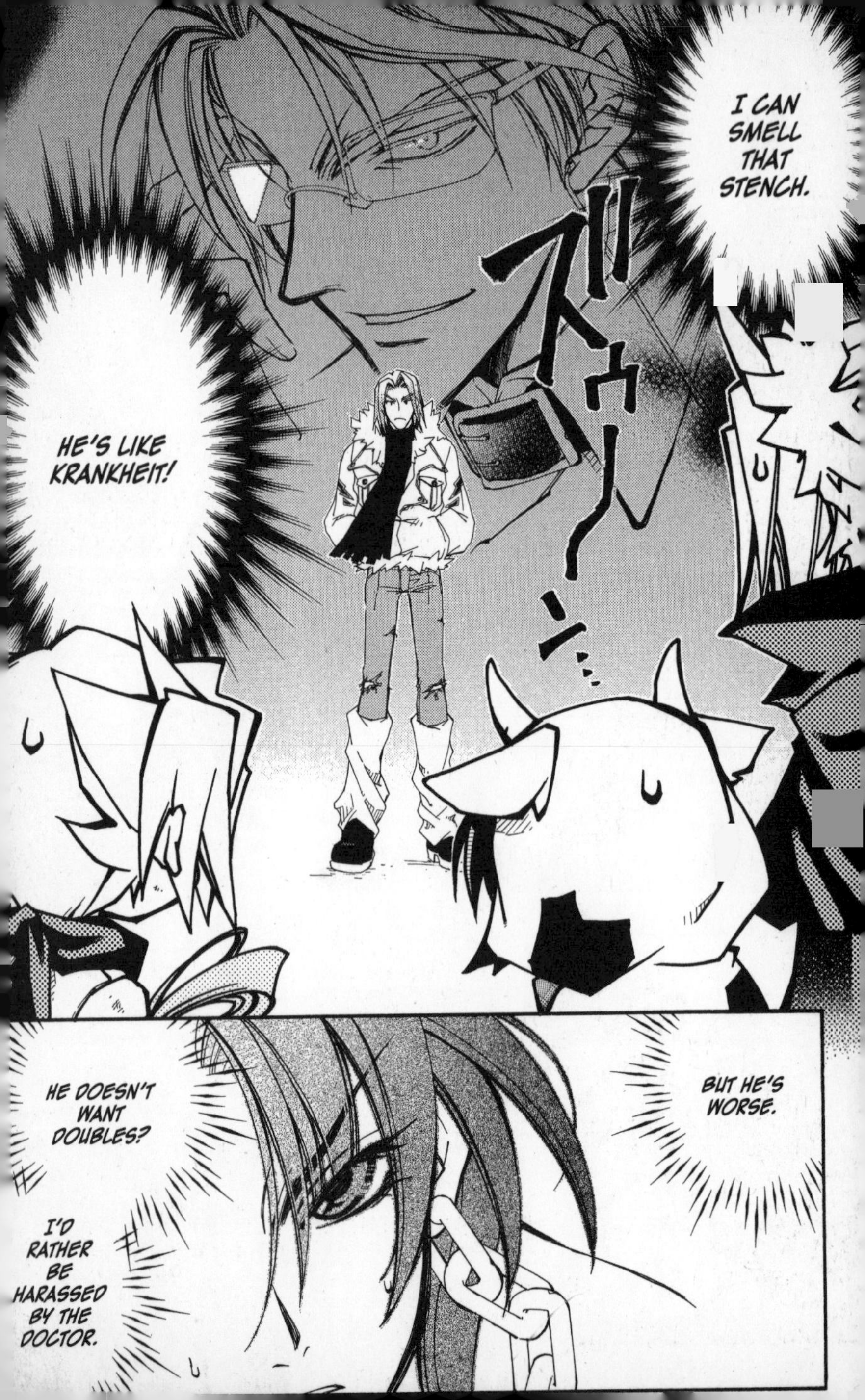
I CAN SMELL THAT STENCH.
HE'S LIKE KRANKHEIT!
BUT HE'S WORSE.
HE DOESN'T WANT DOUBLES?
I'D RATHER BE HARASSED BY THE DOCTOR.

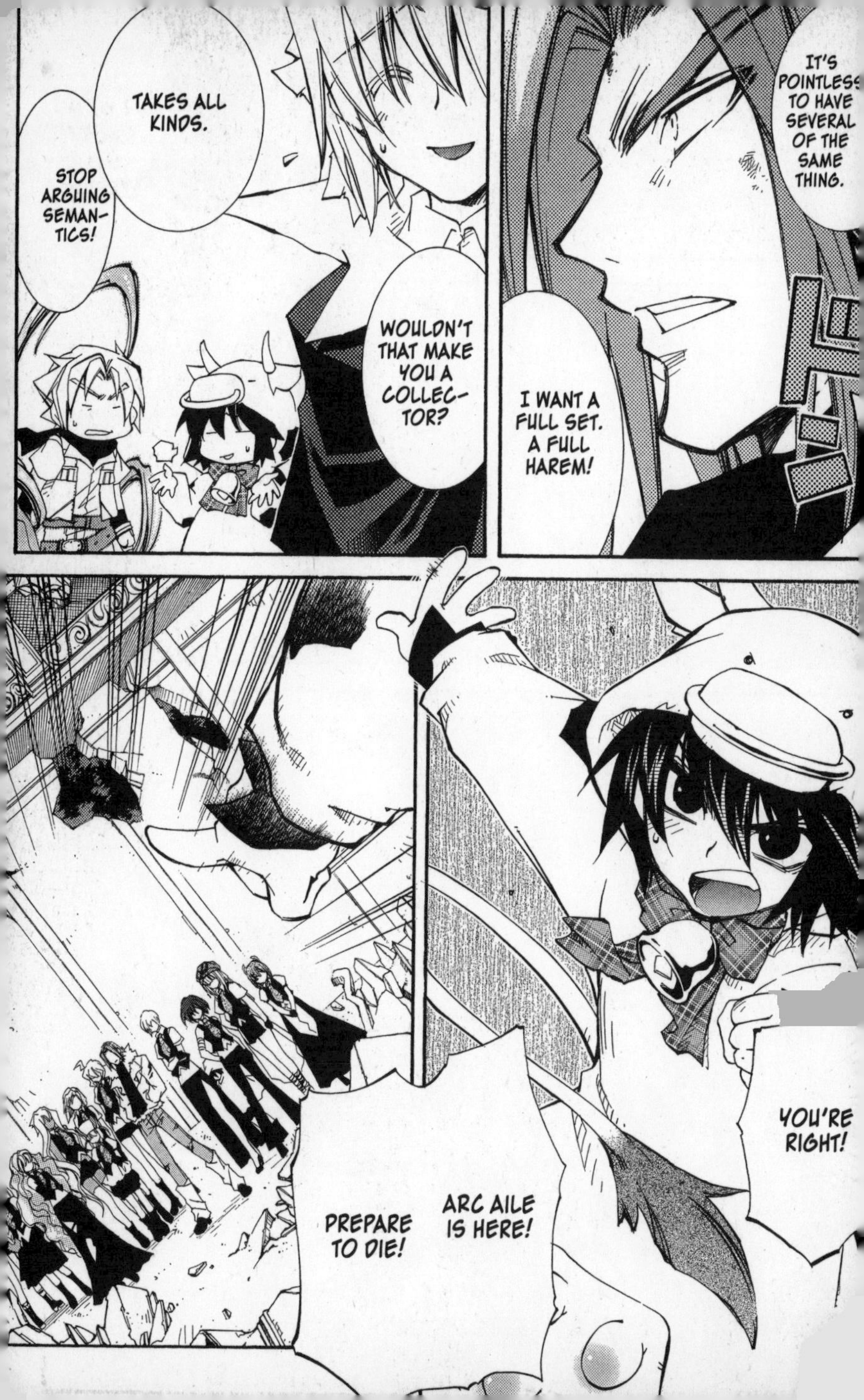
IT'S POINTLESS TO HAVE SEVERAL OF THE SAME THING.
I WANT A FULL SET. A FULL HAREM!
WOULDN'T THAT MAKE YOU A COLLECTOR?
TAKES ALL KINDS.
STOP ARGUING SEMANTICS!
YOU'RE RIGHT!
ARC AILE IS HERE!
PREPARE TO DIE!

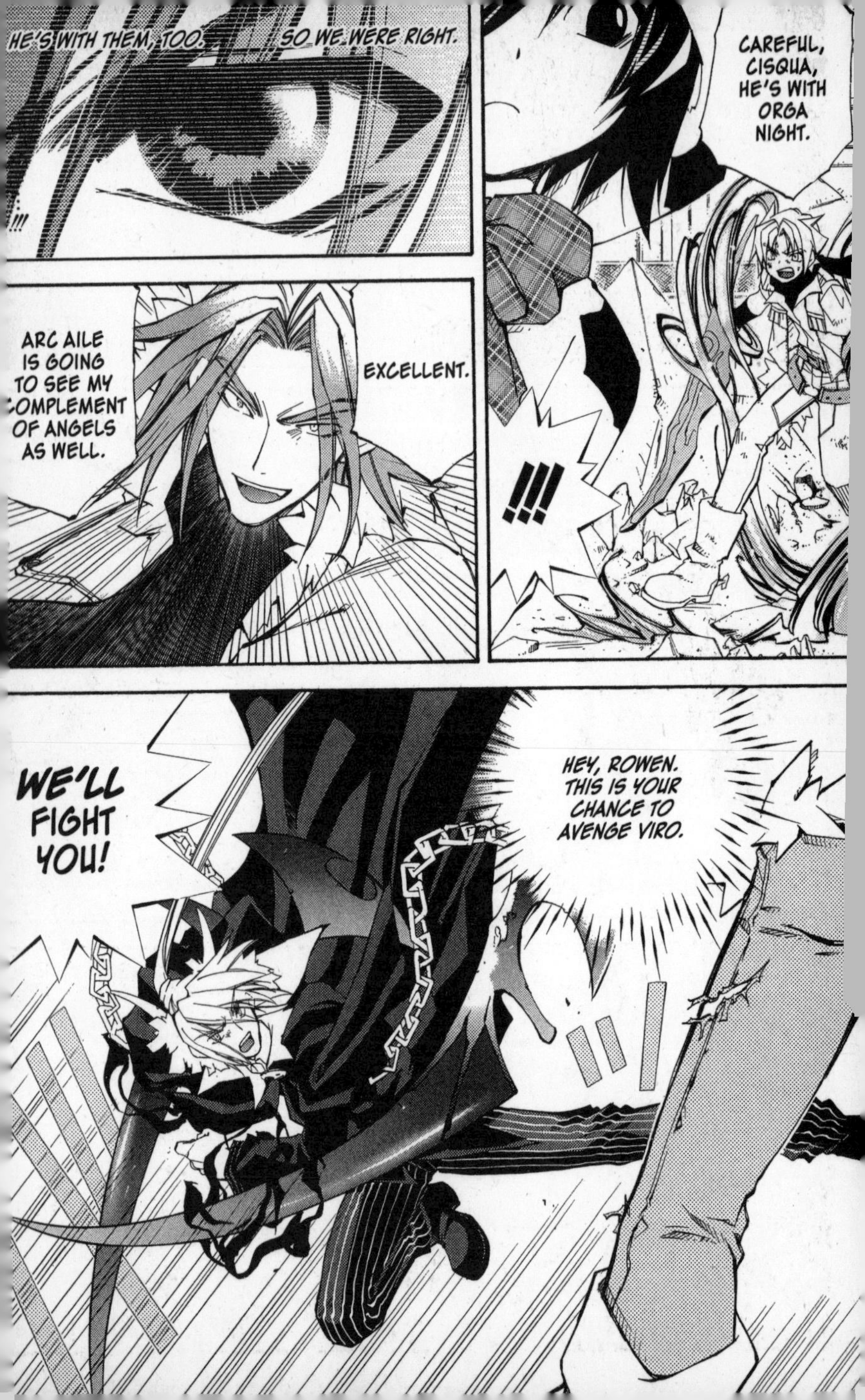
CAREFUL, CISQUA, HE'S WITH ORGA NIGHT.
!!!
SO WE WERE RIGHT.
HE'S WITH THEM, TOO.
!!!
EXCELLENT.
ARC AILE IS GOING TO SEE MY COMPLEMENT OF ANGELS AS WELL.
HEY, ROWEN. THIS IS YOUR CHANCE TO AVENGE VIRO.
WE'LL FIGHT YOU!

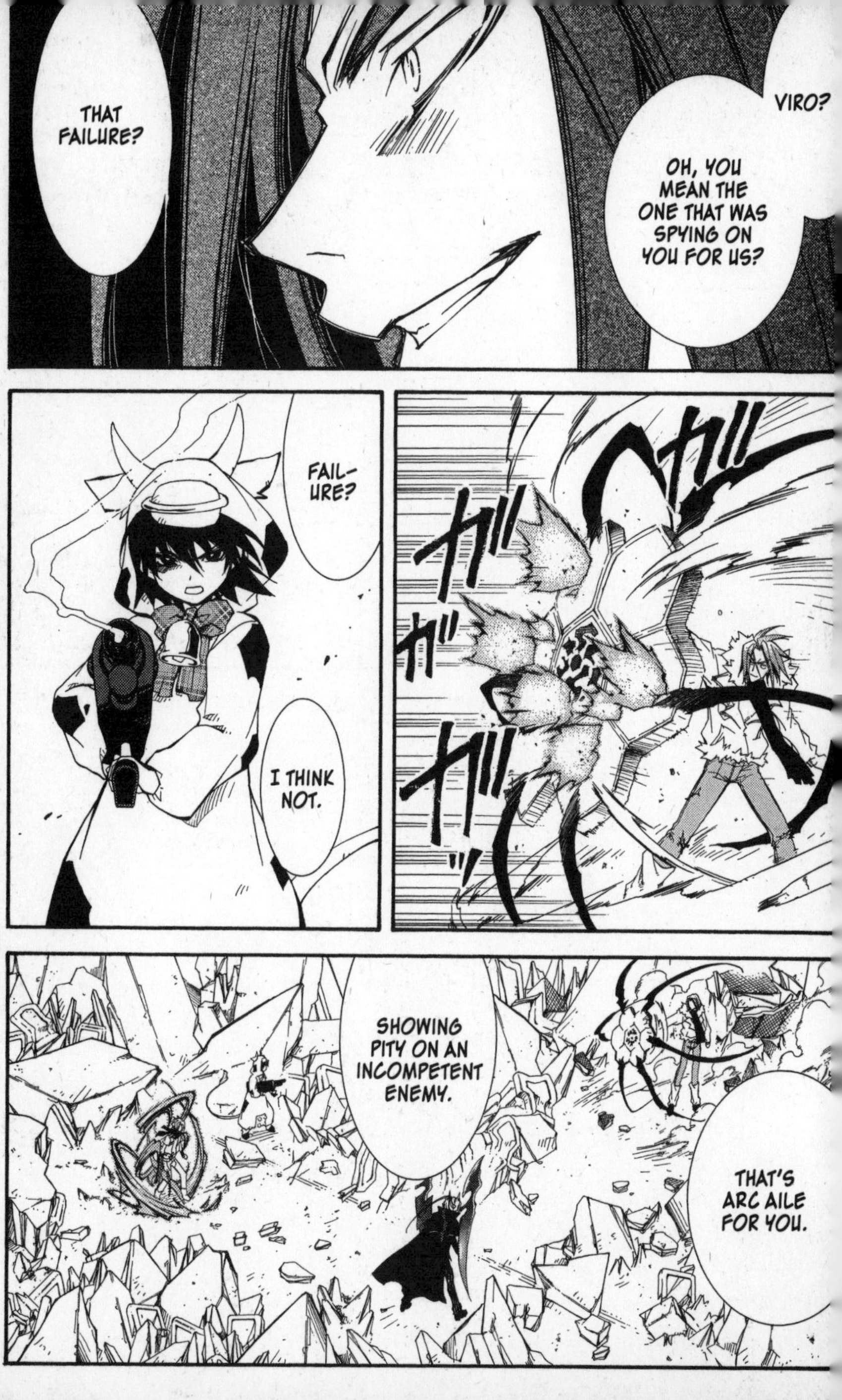
VIRO?
OH, YOU MEAN THE ONE THAT WAS SPYING ON YOU FOR US?
THAT FAILURE?
FAIL-URE?
I THINK NOT.
THAT'S ARC AILE FOR YOU.
SHOWING PITY ON AN INCOMPETENT ENEMY.

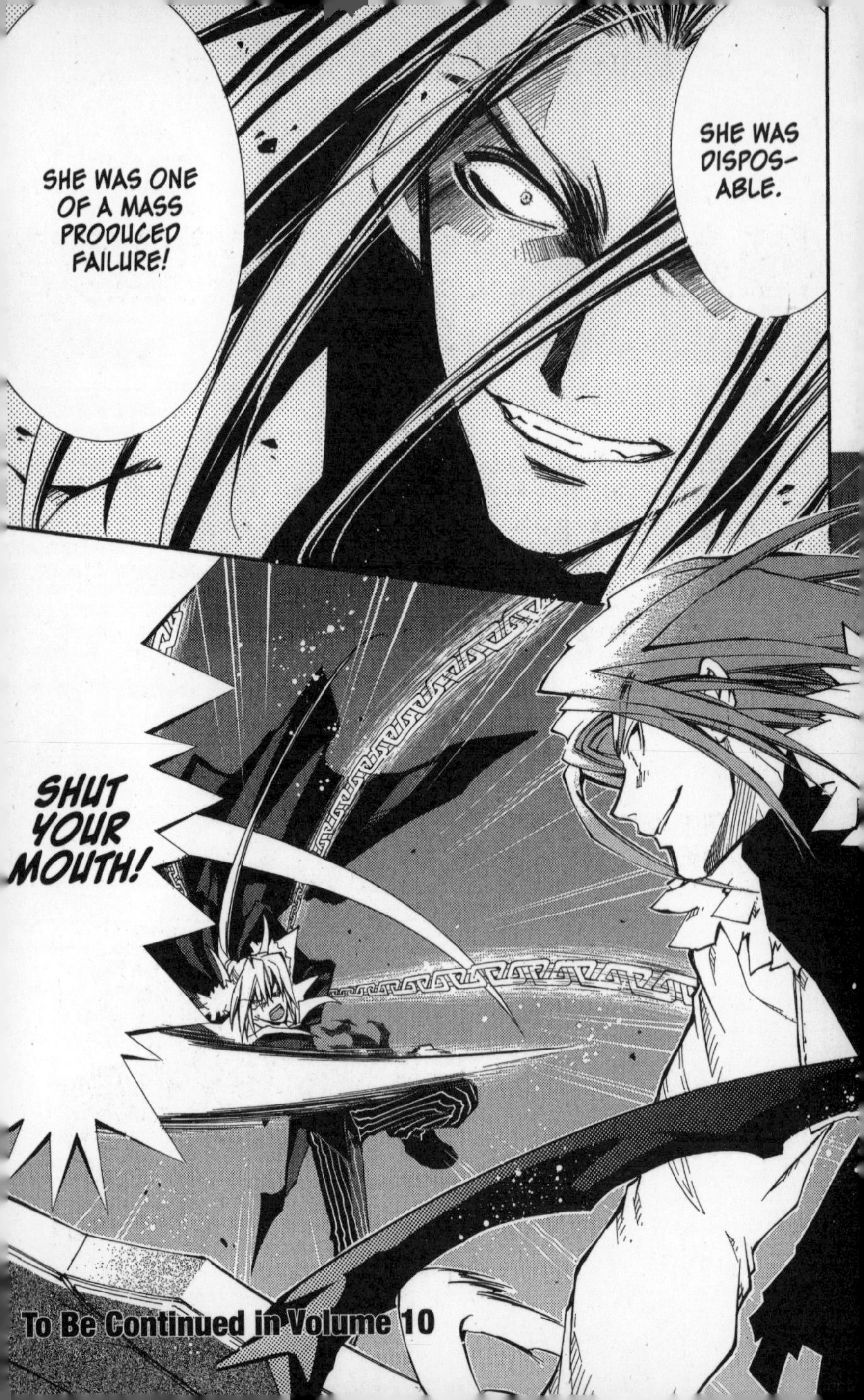
SHE WAS DISPOS-ABLE.
SHE WAS ONE OF A MASS PRODUCED FAILURE!
SHUT YOUR MOUTH!
To Be Continued in Volume 10

In The Next Volume of

ELEMENTAL GELADE

WITH ROWEN AND CISQUA SHOWING UP TO RESCUE COUD AND REN, THE TABLES MAY HAVE TURNED IN THE BATTLE AGAINST LONBLE. BUT WITH AN ARSENAL OF TWELVE EDEL RAIDS AT HIS DISPOSAL, LONBLE ISN'T GOING TO BE TAKEN DOWN EASILY. WILL IT BE UP TO COW-CISQUA TO SAVE THE DAY?!

FIND OUT IN THE NEXT THRILLING VOLUME!

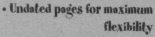

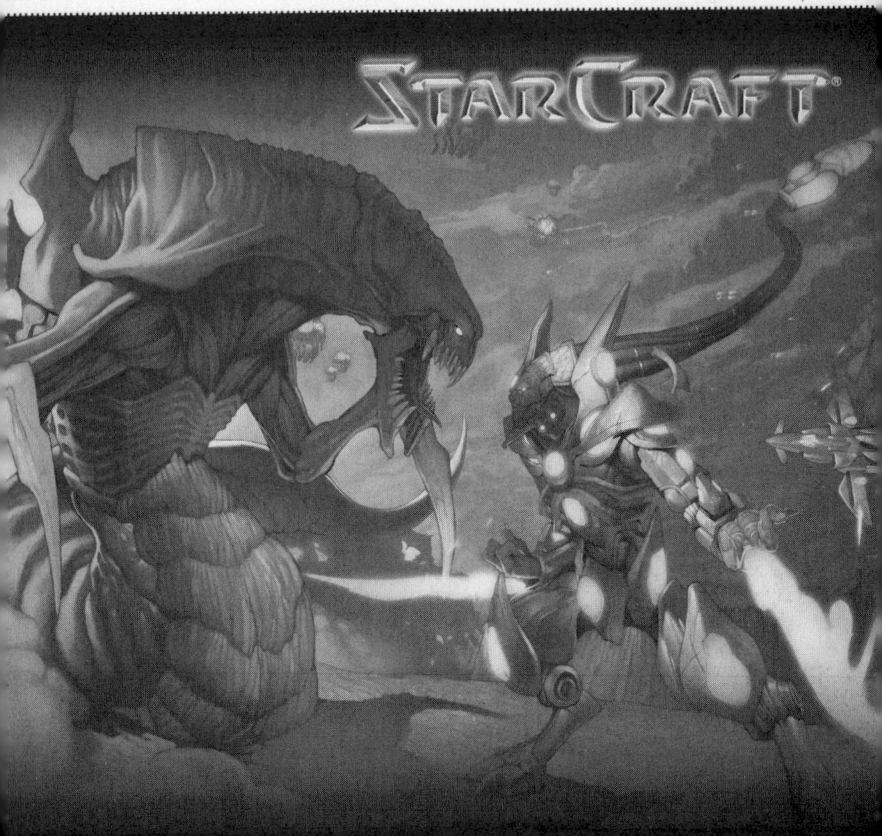
STARCRAFT

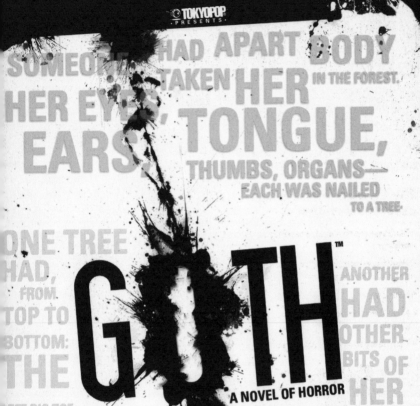

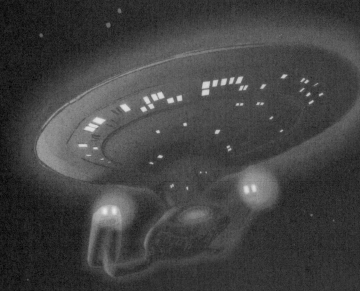

STOP!

This is the back of the book.
You wouldn't want to spoil a great ending!

This book is printed "manga-style," in the authentic Japanese right-to-left format. Since none of the artwork has been flipped or altered, readers get to experience the story just as the creator intended. You've been asking for it, so TOKYOPOP® delivered: authentic, hot-off-the-press, and far more fun!

DIRECTIONS

1
2
3
4
5
6
7
8
9
10

If this is your first time reading manga-style, here's a quick guide to help you understand how it works.

It's easy... just start in the top right panel and follow the numbers. Have fun, and look for more 100% authentic manga from TOKYOPOP®!

THE MANGA REVOLUTION · LEADING · 漫画革命

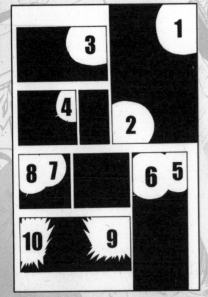